# A Maritime History of East Asia

# A Maritime History of East Asia

Edited by

Masashi HANEDA

and

Mihoko OKA

Kyoto University Press

First published in Japanese in 2013 as *Umi kara mita rekishi* by University of Tokyo Press.

This English edition published in 2019 jointly by:

Kyoto University Press
69 Yoshida Konoe-cho
Sakyo-ku, Kyoto 606-8315
Japan
Telephone: +81-75-761-6182
Fax: +81-75-761-6190
Email: sales@kyoto-up.or.jp
Web: http://www.kyoto-up.or.jp

Trans Pacific Press
PO Box 164, Balwyn North, Melbourne
Victoria 3104, Australia
Telephone: +61-3-9859-1112
Fax: +61-3-8611-7989
Email: tpp.mail@gmail.com
Web: http://www.transpacificpress.com

© Masashi Haneda and Mihoko Oka 2019.

Edited by Miriam Riley.

Designed and set by Sarah Tuke, Melbourne, Australia.

Printed by Asia Printing Office Corporation, Nagano, Japan.

**Distributors**

**Australia and New Zealand**
James Bennett Pty Ltd
Locked Bag 537
Frenchs Forest NSW 2086
Australia
Telephone: +61-(0)2-8988-5000
Fax: +61-(0)2-8988-5031
Email: info@bennett.com.au
Web: www.bennett.com.au

**USA and Canada**
Independent Publishers Group (IPG)
814 N. Franklin Street
Chicago, IL 60610
USA
Telephone inquiries: +1-312-337-0747
Order placement: 800-888-4741 (domestic only)
Fax: +1-312-337-5985
Email: frontdesk@ipgbook.com
Web: http://www.ipgbook.com

**Asia and the Pacific (except Japan)**
Kinokuniya Company Ltd.
*Head office*:
3-7-10 Shimomeguro
Meguro-ku
Tokyo 153-8504
Japan
Telephone: +81-(0)3-6910-0531
Fax: +81-(0)3-6420-1362
Email: bkimp@kinokuniya.co.jp
Web: www.kinokuniya.co.jp
*Asia-Pacific office*:
Kinokuniya Book Stores of Singapore Pte., Ltd.
391B Orchard Road #13-06/07/08
Ngee Ann City Tower B
Singapore 238874
Telephone: +65-6276-5558
Fax: +65-6276-5570
Email: SSO@kinokuniya.co.jp

The publication of this book was supported by a Grant-in-Aid for Publication of Scientific Research Results (Grant Number 18HP5258), provided by the Japan Society for the Promotion of Science, to which we express our sincere appreciation.

All rights reserved. No reproduction of any part of this book may take place without the written permission of Kyoto University Press or Trans Pacific Press.

ISBN    978–1–925608–93–9

# Contents

| | |
|---|---|
| Figures | vii |
| Tables | ix |
| Photographs | ix |
| Editors' Biographies | x |
| Contributors to the English version | x |
| Acknowledgements | xi |
| Preface to the English Edition | xiii |
| | |
| Prologue | 1 |
| | |
| **Part 1: The Open Sea, from 1250 to 1350** | |
| | |
| 1.1 General Overview | 47 |
| 1.2 The Background to Maritime Interaction and Its Agents | 61 |
| 1.3 Increased Openness: Maritime Merchants Expand Maritime Interactions | 71 |
| 1.4 What Conflicts with the Mongols Wrought: Isolationism Within Openness | 89 |
| 1.5 Traffic in Goods and Technology: Expanding the Field of Interaction and Mutual Exchange | 107 |
| | |
| **Part 2: Competing for the Sea, from 1500 to 1600** | |
| | |
| 2.1 General Overview | 123 |
| 2.2 The Age of the Wokou: Transformations in the Structure of East Asian Trade | 139 |
| 2.3 The Age of Maritime Merchants | 163 |
| 2.4 Development of Diverse and Hybrid Cultures | 185 |

Part 3: The Compartmentalized Sea, from 1700 to 1800

| | |
|---|---:|
| 3.1 General Overview | 213 |
| 3.2 Maritime Merchants and "Compartmentalization" Among Early Modern States | 231 |
| 3.3 Compression and Concentration of Interactions and Residences | 263 |
| 3.4 Trans-Oceanic Movements of Goods and Information | 299 |
| Bibliography | 331 |
| Historical Geography Index | 353 |
| Name Index | 357 |
| Subject Index | 359 |

# Figures

| | | |
|---|---|---|
| 1 | Nanjing ship | 37 |
| 2 | Map of maritime East Asia, 1250–1350 | 46 |
| 3 | Reconstruction of Hakata | 79 |
| 4 | Map of great canals and sea-lanes of the Yuan Era | 87 |
| 5 | Ningbo Buddhist painting | 117 |
| 6 | Map of maritime East Asia 1500–1600 | 122 |
| 7 | Circumnavigation of Francesco Carletti | 125 |
| 8 | Portuguese carracks, galleon, square-rigged caravel and galleys | 149 |
| 9 | Port city and its hinterlands | 173 |
| 10 | Macao in the seventeenth century | 175 |
| 11 | Circulation of silver in the world circa 1600 | 179 |
| 12 | Japanese soldiers in the Philippines | 181 |
| 13 | Southern barbarian ship at shore | 197 |
| 14 | *Folangji-pao* | 201 |
| 15 | *Teikan zusetsu* (Ch. *Dijian tushuo*) | 205 |
| 16 | Map of maritime East Asia, 1700–1800 | 212 |
| 17 | Diplomacy and passage control by "early modern states" | 235 |
| 18 | Trading houses in Guangzhou | 237 |
| 19 | *Shinkō-sen* ships of Ryukyu | 243 |
| 20 | *Kitamae-bune* (north-bound ships) congested in Matsumae | 251 |
| 21 | *Shinpai* licence dated April 13, 1734 | 265 |
| 22 | The Japanese envoy from Tsushima making a bow at a monument in a hall likened to the Korean King in Choryang, Busan | 273 |
| 23 | Dutch ship at shore in Nagasaki Bay | 279 |

24 Ryukyuan house in Fuzhou 285
25 Dejima, Nagasaki 287
26 Tōjin-yashiki (Chinese compound) 289
27 The landscape of Choryang Waegwan (Japan House)
   in Busan 291
28 An Ainu chief, Ikotoi 309
29 Foreigners' images in pre-modern Japan 323

# Tables

1  Tributary system in the first half of the fifteenth century    129
2  Spatial structure of the 1570 system    169

# Photographs

1  Stone carving of ancient Arabic writing in Quanzhou    55
2  Remaining defensive stone walls in Hakata Bay    103
3  Yuan silver ingot    109
4  Jingdezhen's blue-and-white ware    113

# Editors' Biographies

Masashi Haneda is a professor at the Institute for Advanced Studies on Asia and vice-president in charge of global engagement of the University of Tokyo. He specializes in the field of world/global history and has published a number of academic works not only in Japanese, but also in English, French and Chinese, including *Toward the Creation of a New World History* (Japan Publishing Industry Foundation for Culture, 2018), and *Gurobaru hisutorii-to higashi-ajia-shi* (Global History and the History of East Asia) (University of Tokyo Press, 2016).

Mihoko Oka is an associate professor of the Historiographical Institute, the University of Tokyo. Her interests are broadly in the area of the maritime and economic history of East Asia in relation to European countries during the sixteenth to seventeenth centuries. She won the "17th Tçuzu Rodrigues Prize" (Prémio Literário "Rodrigues, o Intérprete") for her monograph *The Namban Trade: Merchants and Missionaries* (University of Tokyo Press, 2010, in Japanese), and has also published numerous academic articles on Kirishitan history in Japan.

# Contributors to the English version

*Akiyoshi Fujita (Prologue)*
Professor, Faculty of International Studies, Tenri University

*Masahiko Morihira (Part 1)*
Professor, Faculty of Humanities, Kyushu University

*Gakusho Nakajima (Part 2)*
Associate Professor, Faculty of Humanities, Kyushu University

*Yu Hashimoto (Part 2)*
Associate Professor, Graduate School of Letters, Hokkaido University

*Kiyohiko Sugiyama (Part 3)*
Associate Professor, Graduate School of Arts and Sciences, the University of Tokyo

*Miki Watanabe (Part 3)*
Associate Professor, Graduate School of Arts and Sciences, the University of Tokyo

# Acknowledgements

Cooperation and support were given by a great number of people in the process of bringing this book to publication. Financial support was also received from several organizations for the translation, proofreading and publication of this volume. We list below, with our sincere gratitude, those people and organizations that provided cooperation and support, summarized according to their roles. In the end, however, the structure and contents of the book are the sole responsibility of the editors, Haneda Masashi and Oka Mihoko.

## Participants in preparing the English edition

*Editorial cooperation*: Fujita Akiyoshi, Hashimoto Yū, Morihira Masahiko, Nakajima Gakushō, Sugiyama Kiyohiko and Watanabe Miki.

*Editorial support*: Itō Kōji, Mukai Masaki, Nagamori Mitsunobu, Yamazaki Takeshi and Yokkaichi Yasuhiro.

*English proofreading*: Claire Cooper and Peter Shapinsky.

*English editing and proofreading assistance*: Ōhashi Akiko, Takaku Mitsuru and Birgit Tremml-Werner.

*Preparation of the initial English draft*: Lingua Guild, Inc.

*Financial support for English translation, proofreading and publication*: MEXT Grant-in-Aid for Scientific Research on Innovative Areas (Representative: Kojima Tsuyoshi); Institute for Advanced Studies on Asia, the University of Tokyo; the Kajima Foundation; Japan Society for the Promotion of Science (Grant-in-Aid for Publication of Scientific Research Results).

## Participants in editing the original Japanese edition

*General editor*: Haneda Masashi.

*Prologue*: author-editors Haneda Masashi (chief editor) and Fujita Akiyoshi.

*Contributors*: Morihira Masahiko, Oka Motoshi and Yoshio Hiroshi.

*Part 1*: author-editors Morihira Masahiko (chief editor), Enomoto Wataru, Mukai Masaki, Oka Motoshi, Saeki Kōji, Yamauchi Shinji and Yokkaichi Yasuhiro.

*Contributors*: Obata Hiroki and Takahashi Tadahiko.

*Part 2*: author-editors Nakajima Gakushō (chief editor), Itō Kōji, Hashimoto Yū, Oka Mihoko and Yamazaki Takeshi.

*Contributors*: Fujita Akiyoshi, Kage Toshio, Kuba Takashi, Noda Asami, Takatsu Takashi, Yokkaichi Yasuhiro and Yonetani Hitoshi.

*Part 3*: author-editors Sugiyama Kiyohiko (chief editor), Fujita Akiyoshi and Watanabe Miki.

*Contributors*: Haneda Masashi, Hasuda Takashi, Iwai Shigeki, Nagamori Mitsunobu and Okamoto Hiromichi.

*Proofreading the original Japanese edition*: Fukasawa Katsumi, Inoue Tomotaka, Kojima Tsuyoshi, Murai Shōsuke and Watanabe Junsei.

The University of Tokyo Press and editor Yamamoto Tōru provided great assistance at the time of publication of the original Japanese edition. For the publication of this book, Suzuki Tetsuya and Nakamura Reiko of Kyoto University Press, who have extensive experience in the publication of English books, carried out thorough editorial work in an efficient and meticulous manner. Thanks are also due to Miriam Riley, structural editor for Trans Pacific Press, for her scrupulous and competent editorial work in bringing the project to its final stage. We would like to take this opportunity to express our deep gratitude to Mr. Suzuki and Ms. Riley for their assistance in the publication of this book.

# Preface to the English Edition

This book is the English translation of the Japanese *Umi kara mita rekishi*, published in 2013. As six years have passed since the publication of the Japanese edition, we can no longer claim that the contents incorporate the latest research findings. Nevertheless, we believe that this book has unique characteristics that make reading it very worthwhile, especially for readers in the English-speaking world. I would, therefore, first like to introduce two particularly important qualities of the book.

The original Japanese edition (referred to hereafter as "the Japanese edition"), which forms the basis of this book, discusses the history of "maritime East Asia" (this term itself is a new spatial concept in Japanese) that Japanese historians, aware of the context of debates in Japanese academic associations, compiled mainly on the basis of research findings published in the Japanese language. Readers were primarily assumed to be intellectuals and students able to read Japanese. Knowing that readers would not be limited to experts in the field, we did not apply the purely academic style of annotating all reference materials, but simply included a list of works at the end of the book. In doing so, we sought to convey the latest academic findings in a manner as easily readable as possible to persons with a certain degree of prior knowledge and a broad interest in the subject matter. The themes dealt with in the Japanese edition possibly differ from those normally found in the English-speaking world, but are compelling even to non-specialists, at least in Japan. The Japanese edition, therefore, is not an elite academic book, and neither can it be said to be a popular book attracting a wide readership. Rather, it is a general academic book aimed at a non-specialist level. This type of publication is common in Japan but may be unusual among books published in the English-speaking world. This is the first important characteristic of this book. The structure and contents of the English edition remain unchanged from those of the Japanese edition.

As you will understand from the reference list, the Japanese edition provides a comprehensive listing of Japanese-language research, especially books, published up to the date of publication. This is the minimal condition that must be adhered to for academic works published in Japanese. In contrast, we only list those works in related research fields originally published in Chinese, Korean or Western languages such as English that were directly referred to during the writing of the book. For this reason, there may be doubts about the academic worth or level of the Japanese edition due to the insufficient citation of English-language research literature. However, since large numbers of research papers and books that have utilized non-Japanese research sources are among the Japanese works referred to, the Japanese edition in fact incorporated far more non-Japanese research outcomes than indicated by the books and papers listed in the bibliography. On the other hand, many books published in English do not have a sufficient list of Japanese-language reference materials in related fields because they are "hard to access", "have a dissimilar research context" or, above all, "are hard to read". This English edition, a translation of the Japanese edition that discussed the history of maritime East Asia and referred to all the latest Japanese-language research – relatively unknown in the English-speaking world – embodies the positive significance of filling intellectual lacunae in the English-speaking world.

We sincerely hope that you, the reader, will not cast this book aside because it is a translation and will take the time to look through it from cover to cover. We believe that if you do so, you will certainly make truly interesting discoveries. You may encounter unfamiliar themes and perspectives that have been overlooked in the English-speaking world. Regarding particular themes, you may see differences in the way issues are introduced or approached, in the emphases or in the interpretation or understanding of events. Many of these are due to differences in the authors' positionalities. It is not a matter of which is right or wrong; there are dissimilarities in Japanese-language works and those written in the English-speaking world regarding the positionality of authors and their target audience. We really hope readers will enjoy these differences. Thus far, a great number of publications in English and other Western languages have been translated into Japanese, but very few in the opposite direction. People who only read English are sometimes surprisingly uninformed about the structure of knowledge, common sense, ways of thinking and discursive styles of the non-English-speaking world. We very much hope that this book will contribute, if only in a very small way, to the rectification of this intellectual asymmetry.

The second characteristic of this book is that, while it is an outcome of collaborative research involving many researchers, its nature is quite distinct from what one would generally associate with the term "co-authored". Collaborative research in the humanities and social sciences usually takes the form of several workshops or symposia on a common theme, after which individual researchers write their own papers while making use of the discussions and information exchanged at the meetings. Editors then compile the researchers' papers into a book for publication. The differences in approach and understanding among the papers included in the resulting book are accepted and framed positively as expressions of the researchers' unique and diverse views. What is stressed, above all, is each individual's research and its achievements.

When planning the Japanese edition, we deliberately adopted a methodology that diverges from this common humanities and social science research practice. Instead, we held frequent research meetings and engaged in comprehensive discussions until a consensus was reached among all participants. Having thus attained common ground on basic concepts, historical facts and the methods behind historical descriptions, the participants interpreted and portrayed the history of "maritime East Asia" in a truly collective fashion. In preparing draft manuscripts, the content did not inevitably rely on the unique perspective of the author assigned to a particular section, but rather on the understanding shared by all research group participants. The intention here was to produce a truly co-authored work, where specific specialist achievements regarding individual and relatively minor themes would combine to create an integrated and coherent narrative that ran throughout the whole book. We believed that this method would allow us to present the outcomes of a large-scale collaborative research project at a level and breadth unachievable through independent research carried out by individual researchers. We thus attempted to break new ground in the presentation of collaborative research outcomes in the humanities and social sciences.

I would like to mention here the publication process for the Japanese edition. The "Maritime East Asia History Research Group", involving the participation of about thirty researchers, sparked the publication of the Japanese edition. This research group was established as one part of the large-scale collaborative research project titled "Maritime Cross-Cultural Exchange in East Asia and the Formation of Japanese Traditional Culture" (research representative Professor Kojima Tsuyoshi of the University of Tokyo) conducted through the use of a grant-in-aid from Japan's Ministry of Education, Culture, Sports, Science and Technology from 2005 to 2010.

Lively research activities were carried out in the three years from April 2007 to March 2010. Including the research meetings of each of the three groups formed according to the research period in question, conferences involving all research group participants, meetings of the leaders of the three groups and various other meetings, gatherings related to the Maritime East Asia History Research Group were held almost every month to deepen discussions on building the consensus mentioned above.

Dynamic exchanges of views and information also took place via the online mailing list. Over the three years, 1,676 messages were exchanged between group members. A report on the work in progress was given at the general meeting of the large-scale collaborative research project in November 2008, at which we received generous criticism and advice from people outside our research group. Furthermore, through the support of Professor Ge Zhaoguang, a symposium titled "Maritime East Asia in World History" was held at Fudan University's National Institute for Advanced Humanistic Studies in China in June 2009, at which a frank exchange of views took place with Chinese researchers. A record of the symposium was published by the National Institute for Advanced Humanistic Studies[1].

As it is perfectly natural for there to be differences in the approach and views of individual researchers working on the same theme, the discussions at each of the research group meetings were very animated, and sometimes heated. Unfortunately, as a result, a consensus was not reached among all participants on each of the points. However, the fact that the Japanese edition was published as the fruit of the research group's labor indicates that our attempt was successful in that we achieved what we set out to do.

Consolidating perspectives and writing the text was conducted in the following manner.

1. Author-editors in charge of the writing and editing of the Prologue and the three parts of the book were determined (see Acknowledgements for details). These researchers collaborated in the preparation of drafts, which were then submitted to each section of the research group or the group as a whole. The author-editors then rewrote or revised the drafts on the basis of the comments and information provided by the research group participants.

---

1 Fudan University National Institute for Advanced Humanistic Studies (ed.), 世界史中的東亜海域 (Maritime East Asia in World History), Shanghai: Zhonghua Shuju, 2011.

2. A chief editor for each part was established. These editors read through the Prologue and all three parts and assumed responsibility for organizing the manuscripts for each part. They then crosschecked the contents to eliminate repetition and contradictions, and defined the meanings of technical terms. The chief editors and their areas of responsibility are as follows. Prologue: Haneda Masashi; Part 1: Morihira Masahiko; Part 2: Nakajima Gakushō; Part 3: Sugiyama Kiyohiko. In addition, Haneda Masashi took on the role of managing stylistic and terminological consistency for the entire book.
3. Five researchers, whose names are also mentioned in the Acknowledgements, were requested to read through the drafts, providing us with a large number of comments that were reflected in the final version as far as possible.
4. The chief editors of the Prologue and three parts polished the final manuscripts, which were then submitted to the publisher, the University of Tokyo Press, and subsequently cooperated with the various editorial tasks (proofreading, footnote preparation, illustration selection) up to the date of publication.

Responsibility for the content of the Japanese version lies with five persons: the chief editors mentioned above as well as Fujita Akiyoshi, who was involved in the editing of the Prologue and Parts 2 and 3. It should be noted, however, that the Japanese edition was published as Volume I of a six-part series titled *Higashi ajia kai-iki ni kogidasu* (Rowing to Maritime East Asia), and in accordance with the policy of the overall series that there should be only one editor for each volume, Haneda Masashi was selected as the editor for Volume I. Thus, final responsibility for the content of the Japanese version lies with Haneda Masashi.

At some point prior to the publication of the Japanese edition, we felt we would also like to bring the contents of the book to the awareness of researchers overseas. As mentioned above, this was because, in addition to Japanese-language research being relatively unknown overseas, the Japanese edition is firstly a high-quality work representing the full abilities of researchers in their respective fields in Japan. Secondly, maritime history is a field of research that is currently attracting the attention of historians around the world, especially those researching global history, and the Japanese edition comprises content capable of sufficiently responding to the interests of such historians and researchers. For this reason, even prior to the publication of the Japanese edition, work was begun on translating the manuscript into English. Nevertheless, this was not a simple task. I will not go into details here, suffice to say that the translation work that began from around the end of 2010 went through many twists and turns until the final manuscript was submitted to Kyoto University Press in the early summer of 2018. Although there was a period when we almost despaired of having the English translation published due to the immense complexity involved, we were very fortunate in gaining the understanding and cooperation of a large number of people and organizations, and through the concerted effort of Oka Mihoko were finally able to push forward to a position where publication of this English edition came within reach. Without the camaraderie, trust and teamwork among the key players involved in the book, nurtured through the Maritime East Asia History Research Group, and the down-to-earth work ethic and leadership of the effective editor, Oka Mihoko, completion of this book would not have been possible. We sincerely hope that this book, involving a surprisingly large number of people who have expended enormous amounts of time and effort to achieve its completion, will be a significant work that will attract the attention of readers in the English-speaking world.

To ensure that the translation conveyed the authors' intentions as accurately as possible, the English in the book was checked by not only the chief editor of each part of the Japanese edition, but was also reviewed several times by many of the author-editors. The most significant problem here was how to translate into English the vocabulary and expressions used in the languages of the different areas of maritime East Asia in the pre-modern era. In the Japanese edition, unless there were appropriate expressions in modern Japanese for the concepts and vocabulary in Chinese, Japanese and Korean, we decided to use the original languages to express these terms because we thought that, rather than resulting in misunderstandings through translation into modern Japanese, readers would probably find it easier to understand these terms if presented in their original languages.

In the case of Japanese text, Japanese people are generally able to comprehend the intended meaning without feeling that anything is particularly strange when Chinese characters are used to indicate pre-modern Japanese, Chinese or Korean terms in their original languages. With English, however, things are not so simple. If the original language were used, involving the insertion of incomprehensible words into the text, the book would become very difficult to read. Also, English words that corresponded to concepts and terms of the relevant era that no longer exist in modern Japanese could not be found, and neither was it a simple task to insert brief explanations into the text. We considered various solutions to this problem, but in the end, since there was no other suitable method, we decided to insert quite a large number of Japanese, Chinese and Korean terms into the text in their original form. We would like to apologize here for the fact that this makes it difficult to read through the text smoothly. As far as possible we have endeavored to provide English explanations at the first instance of each of the terms in each chapter. We very much hope that readers will understand that this measure was unavoidable in attempting to express in modern English matters concerning pre-modern maritime East Asia, the two contexts being separated by so much time and space.

There is one further point regarding words and expressions used in this book that we would like to ask readers to bear in mind. This concerns the words "China", "Korea" and "Japan". In the Japanese edition, we employed these words simply as terms to indicate places. As this book discusses the pre-modern era, however, we considered it necessary to be extremely careful about using words that refer to present-day sovereign nation-states and their peoples. In the Japanese edition, therefore, we referred to the people of the Chinese continent as "Ka-jin" (華人), distinguishing this from the term "Chūgoku-jin" (中国人, people of China) used to describe the people of present-day China. We did this because we felt that the people of a country could only be represented as a collective in the context of the existence of a sovereign nation-state. In the same way, "Kōrai-jin" (高麗人, people of Goryeo), "Chōsen-jin" (朝鮮人, people of Joseon) and so on are used to refer to the people of the Korean Peninsula.

In contrast, there is no suitable name other than "Nihon-jin" (日本人, people of Japan) in the Japanese language to indicate the people who inhabited the pre-modern Japanese Archipelago. Thus, in the Japanese edition, we endeavored to use a variety of expressive means to, as far as possible, avoid using the word "Japanese". Even so, when referring to the whole population of the Japanese Archipelago it was at times necessary to use the word "Japanese".

In English, meanwhile, the words "China"/"Chinese", "Japan"/"Japanese" and "Korea"/"Korean" are used diachronically, across succeeding eras, to refer not only to geographical areas, but also to indicate political entities and the people governed by them. "Ming China", "people of Ming China" and so on appear from time to time in works on the pre-modern era to express the existence of dynasties and political administrations, but, at the same time, words such as "China" are also used. It is probably true to say that the natures of the English and Japanese languages have significant fundamental differences in their understanding and awareness of states, peoples and their histories. Whatever the case may be, the means used to distinguish between the names of human groups in the pre-modern and modern eras in the Japanese edition have not been sufficiently developed in this English edition for reasons outlined above.

In relation to this point, it appears that the expression "Japanese pirates" is frequently used in English to refer to people who engaged in smuggling and certain acts of piracy in maritime East Asia in the latter half of the fourteenth and in the sixteenth century. In Chinese, these people were known as "*wokou*" (倭寇), and that term has been translated literally into English ("*wo*" was the ancient name for the Japanese used by the Chinese and Koreans). For further details, see the explanation in Part 2 of this book, however, at least in the sixteenth century, it is the common perception amongst Japanese academic associations that the group known as "*wokou*" was not comprised solely of "Japanese people". For this reason, please understand that this English edition uses the original language term "*wokou*" as is.

We are fortunate in that the Japanese edition has been well-received and has been favorably introduced to the public in reviews in Japanese newspapers and other media. The book has attracted interest not only in Japan but also overseas, where a translation in traditional-character Chinese has been published in Taiwan[2] and a Korean version in Seoul[3]. A translation in simplified Chinese characters is in preparation. The publication of this English translation is a source of great pleasure for all our colleagues who participated in discussions in the Maritime East Asia History Research Group. We sincerely hope that this book will contribute to the vibrancy of academic exchanges between Japanese and overseas researchers in related fields, and that it will also act as a catalyst for a great number of readers in the English-speaking world to develop an interest in the past events of maritime East Asia and encourage them to take a new look at world history.

Masashi HANEDA

---

2 *Cong haiyang kan lishi*, translated by Zhang Yating, Taipei: Guangchang Chuban, 2017.
3 *Bada-eseo Bon Yeoksa: Gaebang, Gyeonghap, Gongsaeng-Dongasia 700 Nyeon-ui Munmyeong Gyoryusa*, translated by Cho Younghun and Chong Soonli, Seoul: Mineumsa, 2018.

# Prologue

## An Invitation to East Asian History from a Maritime Perspective

## Charting a maritime history

### What is "history from a maritime perspective"?

*Chinese potatoes and Japanese potatoes*
What kind of a history is one "from a maritime perspective"? How would it differ from familiar historiography, and why should we look at history through a new lens? Let us begin answering these questions by referring to several familiar matters.

From the late sixteenth to the early seventeenth century, several new farm crops native to Latin America came to be cultivated nearly simultaneously in many parts of East Asia. Chili pepper (*capsicum annuum*) was one such crop. In the Japanese Archipelago, it was called "*to-garashi*" (Tang pepper) or "*namban-kosho*" ("southern barbarian" pepper), ostensibly because the crop had been brought by people of Tang (唐) (Chinese) descent or by "*namban*" (南蛮), a term used to refer to Portuguese or Spanish traders meaning "southern barbarians". In ancient China, it was also often called "*fanjiao*" (番椒) (pepper from barbarian countries). On the Korean Peninsula, however, the crop was reportedly called "*wae-kyoja*" (Japanese pepper) immediately after its introduction. On the other hand, the variety of chili pepper widely grown in the Ryukyu Islands is known as "*kōrēgusu*", with "*kōrē*" thought to have derived from the Goryeo Dynasty on the Korean Peninsula. Although chili pepper was brought to East Asia on European merchant ships, information on the crop's place of origin and transmission route differed significantly from one place to the next. Given the fact that the crop was introduced into various parts of East Asia almost simultaneously, one cannot but wonder why the same crop came to be perceived so differently in different places.

Let us next turn to sweet potato, another crop native to Latin America. The common name of the crop on Japan's main and northern islands is "*satsuma-imo*", meaning "potato that originated from Satsuma" (薩摩芋). In northern Kyushu, the sweet potato is sometimes called "*Ryukyu-imo*" (Ryukyu potato, 琉球芋), while in southern Kyushu, including Satsuma, it is commonly referred to as "*kara-imo*" (唐芋) (potato from China). On the Korean Peninsula, it is known as "*goguma*", a term thought to derive from the crop's name on Tsushima Island, "*kōkō-imo*" (孝行芋), meaning "dutiful potato". In Okinawa, too, it is often called "*kara-imo*" today; although until the eighteenth century it was also known as "*bansu*". Ryukyuan historical documents reporting on the introduction of the potato in the period from the late sixteenth to the early seventeenth century described it as "*bansho*" (番薯), a name that was in wide use in China at the time. On the question of how the potato was introduced into China, however, views differ radically from one region to the next. In Guangdong, for example, it is believed that the potato was introduced in 1580 by residents of Dongguan Prefecture along the Guangzhou Bay from Annam; on the other hand, a common legend in Fujian has it that residents of Changle Prefecture at the mouth of the Min River brought the potato back from Luzon in 1593.

Even within China, a completely different story about the origin of the potato circulated in the vicinity of the Zhoushan Islands in Zhejiang. One of the islands, a renowned pilgrimage site for the worship of Guanyin (the Goddess of Mercy), is called "Putuo Shan" (Mount Putuo). In 1607, a group of local *shidafu* (scholar-officials)[1] in the Zhedong area in the eastern part of Zhejiang Province compiled a local gazetteer titled *Putuo Shan Zhi* (A Gazetteer of Mount Putuo). In a passage describing the island's products, the gazetteer mentions "*fanshu*" (番薯) (barbarian potato), with an attached explanation stating that the potato "tastes very sweet [...] was originally from Japan". Here, the "*fan*" (番) in the potato's name refers to Japan. The same "*fanshu*" that was called "*kara-imo*" in Ryukyu and Satsuma was regarded as a potato from Japan. This view ascribing the origin of the potato to Japan was reproduced in its entirety

---

1 "*Shidafu*" in traditional China signified "scholar-officials" or "scholar-gentlemen", who, well versed in Confucian classics and equipped with profound scholarly knowledge, constituted the ruling stratum of elite intellectuals. During and after the Song Dynasty, it was also used as a general term connoting those involved in the imperial examination system or the bureaucratic system.

in *Nanhai Putuo Shan Zhi* (A Gazetteer of Mount Putuo in the South Sea) compiled one hundred years later. Though far less convincing than the legendary narratives in Guangdong and Fujian, which claim that the potato was brought in by maritime merchants from Southeast Asia, when judged by present-day standards, the assertion in *Putuo Shan Zhi* that the potato originated from Japan seems to have had something to do with the fact that Mount Putuo was one of the hubs of maritime trade with Japan.

These examples suggest a dynamic divergence of folklore about the processes by which chili peppers and sweet potatoes were introduced into East Asia, including some stories that are at first glance outlandish. Even recent years have seen the publication of studies that attempt to explain this folklore rationally using various sources or by pursuing various lines of reasoning. Some of these studies are noteworthy, including those that pay attention to the differences in crop varieties, but most are so intent on determining the authenticity of a certain myth that they either end up failing to pay due attention to numerous historical records and other folklore, or falling into the trap of pursuing the nationalistic question of "which people were the first to introduce a particular crop?" On the whole, the ongoing discussion about the introduction of new crops has been carried out in a rather unproductive manner. One effective way to escape from this deadlock would seem to be a bold change in our way of thinking.

Existing studies and discussions on the question start from the basic premise that a certain item is transmitted or introduced from Country A to Country B. Our proposal is that we should question this very premise, and instead assume that when the people of Satsuma said "Tang" and the people of Zhedong said "Japan" they were actually referring to the same "place". In other words, the people of "Dongguan", "Changle" and "Japan", who were respectively believed to have introduced sweet potatoes to Guangdong, Fujian and Zhejiang, and even Namban-jin (南蛮人) (southern barbarians or Iberian traders), were active on the same "stage", even if they were not collaborating.

Where, then, was this "place" or "stage" located? The answer is "the sea". In other words, rather than thinking that sweet potatoes and chili peppers came from one country or another, we should instead view them as coming from the "sea"; this maritime world was regarded as "Tang" by residents of one area, as "Wae" (倭) or "Japan" by those of another and even as "Ryukyu" or "Kōrē" by people living elsewhere.

Many readers may be appalled by the preceding paragraph and find it absurdly outlandish, but it does encapsulate the way of thinking that runs throughout this volume that claims to present East Asian history from a maritime perspective. Let us elaborate on this perspective by looking at it from a slightly different angle.

### *The maritime world and the "nationality" of land*

Merchants or traders who were active on the stage of the sea are called "maritime merchants" or "maritime traders". The same maritime merchants were sometimes recorded in different places as if they had come from different countries of origin. For example, Jin Zhen was the captain of the ship on which ninth century Japanese Buddhist monk En'nin[2] returned to Japan after studying in Tang China. While in China, Jin Zhen was regarded as a "native of Silla", but upon reaching Japan, he was identified as a "native of Tang" by the Dazaifu, the Japanese regional government in Kyushu. Similarly, Qin Lianghui, a contemporary of Jin Zhen, was regarded as a "native of Silla" while in Tang, but during his stay in Japan was called a "merchant from the Great Kingdom of Tang" when he helped the Buddhist monk Enchin[3], a rival of En'nin, leave the country to study in China. Furthermore, Li Yanshiao, another ally of Enchin, was regarded in Japan as a "merchant from the Great Tang" as well as a "merchant of the Home Country (Japan)", but in Chinese ports he was described as a "*bohaiguo shangzhu*" – a "master trader from Bohai".

Similar examples are found among maritime merchants who served as official state envoys. Zhou Liangshi (Jp. Shu Ryoshi), who visited Ningbo in China from Japan in 1026 in the capacity of *Dazaifu shinpōshi* (Cn. *taizaifu jinfengshi*; tribute-offering envoy of the Dazaifu), was called a "*daisoukoku-shoukaku*" (a merchant from the Great Song) while in Japan. Xu Derong, who came and went between the Song Dynasty and the Goryeo Dynasty[4] carrying diplomatic documents of each country during the 1160s,

---

2 En'nin (794–864), also known posthumously as Jikaku Daishi, was a priest of Tendai Buddhism. He authored *Nittō Guhō Junrei Kōki*, which was translated into English by Edwin O. Reischauer under the title *Ennin's Diary: The Record of a Pilgrimage to China in Search of the Law*.

3 Enchin (814–891), also known posthumously as Chisho Daishi, was a priest of Tendai Buddhism.

4 The Goryeo Dynasty, founded on the Korean Peninsula by Wang Kon, existed from 918 to 1392.

had his title recorded in the Song as a *Gaoli gangshou* (captain of the Goryeo Dynasty) when dispatched there from Korea, but was called a "Song *dougang*" (captain from the Song Dynasty) while in Goryeo; both titles – *gangshou* and *dougang* – were alternative names for "*haishang*" (maritime merchant). Similarly, Pu Jiaxin, who in 1004 and 1019 traveled by sea to the Song as a tribute envoy of Dashi in West Asia, appeared in the Song court as a tribute envoy of Wuxun (the city of Sohar in Oman), and again in 1015 as a tribute envoy of Zhulian (the Chola Dynasty in South India). Meanwhile, the tribute envoy Goeku Utsuchi, who was dispatched to the Ming Dynasty by the Chuzan Kingdom of Ryukyu in 1391 and 1396, visited the Ming in 1404 as an envoy representing the San-nan (Nanzan) Kingdom of Ryukyu. These examples show that the same maritime merchants were identified using the names of different countries depending on the context. What should their legitimate national identities be?

These apparent states of confusion seem to have derived from the fact that the land-based political powers at the time were not particularly interested in maritime merchants' birthplaces or ethnic origins, but rather in their point of departure and which governments dispatched them as envoys. People and political powers on the receiving end of ships and merchants coming from the maritime world were content so long as the visiting ships and merchants could be identified with the name of a land-based country they had heard of.

In fact, among those living in the maritime world were some who did not pay much attention to their own ethnic origins or birthplaces. Take, for instance, a stone monument in Ningbo inscribed with the names of three individuals, Zhang Gongyi, Ding Yuan and Zhang Ning, who in 1167 donated the money to pave a temple's entrance path with cobblestones. Judging from their names, the three men were clearly of Chinese descent, but they respectively identified themselves as a native of Pucheng Prefecture in Jiangzhou Province, now residing temporarily in Japan, a resident of Hakata Port, the Dazaifu, Japan and a resident of the Dazaifu, Japan. In contrast to Zhang Gongyi, who self-identified as a native of Pucheng Prefecture, Jiangzhou Province (present-day Pucheng District, Jiangyang City, Fujian Province), the two other men simply self-identified as sojourners temporarily staying in Japan, without specifying their ethnic or geographical origins.

This was also the case for ships that sailed in the East Asian maritime world. In 1323 or thereabouts, a trading ship on its way from Ningbo to Hakata sank off the coast of Sinan in the present-day Republic of Korea. The sunken ship was discovered in 1976, and, judging from its construction and the materials used, it was undeniably a junk ship built in China; however, written on wooden shipping tags attached to the cargo were the names of Buddhist temples and Shinto shrines in Japan, including Tōfukuji Temple[5] and Hakozakigū Shrine[6]. A range of Japanese and Chinese utensils were also salvaged, including Chinese-style *zalian* pans[7], spoons and Japanese lacquered wooden bowls, as well as *geta* (Japanese wooden clogs). The ship's crew likely consisted of both Japanese and Chinese sailors. It is questionable whether such a ship can be regarded as a "Japanese vessel" or a "Yuan (Chinese) vessel"[8].

When sweet potatoes and chili peppers were introduced into East Asia, the varied nature of the sea world was far more pronounced than in the previous period. In the early seventeenth century, vessels called "*shuinsen*" (red-seal ships) visited various Southeast Asian ports. These trading ships carried *shuinjō* (red-seal patents), or permits to travel abroad, issued by the Tokugawa Shogunate or other authorities, and were usually called "Japanese vessels". The red-seal ships were once regarded as a symbol of the southward advance of the Japanese. In actuality, approximately thirty percent of the permits were issued to "foreigners", including Chinese and Europeans. Moreover, many of the ships licensed and operated by Japanese *daimyōs* (domainal lords) and Japanese traders were actually under the command of Chinese or European captains. Conversely, there were also cases where Japanese captains were in service aboard ships operated by Chinese or Europeans as licensees. In 1626, a *Suminokura-sen*, a red-seal ship operated by a wealthy merchant based in Kyoto called

---

5 Tōfukuji was founded in Kyoto in 1236 by the imperial chancellor Kujō Michiie with the monk En'ni as founding priest. It was later designated as the fourth of the five Zen temples constituting the Kyoto Five Mountains System (Kyoto Gozan).
6 Hakozakigū is a Hachimangū (a Shrine of the God of War) located in Hakozaki, Higashi-ku, Fukuoka City. One of the major Engishiki-naisha (shrines listed in Engishiki laws), it was ranked as Chikuzenkoku Icihinomiya (the First Shrine of Chikuzen Province). In olden times, the shrine had close connections with the Dazaifu, and was involved in Japan-Song trade.
7 Pans with a large number of small holes at the bottom used for draining hot water and oil.
8 The remains of a sunken ship were discovered off the coast of Sinan, Jeollanam-do, in the Republic of Korea. In addition to the ship's body, a large volume of the load, including bone china and porcelain and wooden shipping tags, was salvaged. An intensive investigation of the remains ascertained that the ship was a Chinese junk engaged in Japan-China trade in the early half of the fourteenth century.

Suminokura Ryōi, was formally placed under the care of a Japanese captain, but recruited Spanish, Portuguese, Dutch or other experienced seafarers in Nagasaki to serve as its navigator, helmsman and other officers. This suggests that when officers are taken into account, the ethnic diversity of the crews of red-seal ships increases by a certain extent. Much the same is true for cargo consigners and investors who financed the voyages.

By turning our attention to the crew members of the red-seal ships, we can see, for example, that a red-seal ship dispatched by the British factory in Hirado was a Chinese-style junk ship. A red-seal ship owned by a Japanese trader, captured in *ema* (votive picture tablet) form, was also a junk ship, but of a hybrid variety in the sense that its bow and other parts were refurbished into the European style. In 1630, employees of the Dutch factory witnessed two European-style galleons in Nagasaki, one owned by a Chinese trader and the other by a Japanese trader. The latter ship had been borrowed by a Chinese trader and was preparing to set sail; furthermore, its navigator was a Dutch seafarer who, after having been aboard Spanish ships on the trans-Pacific route for many years, settled down in Nagasaki, married a Japanese woman and was engaged in the trade business. Is it at all possible to unequivocally determine the countries to which these ships belonged? It is possible to argue, for example, that the British factory's red-seal ship belonged to Japan, based on the fact that it was licensed by a Japanese authority. It is also possible to claim that it was a British ship because of its business operator, or that it was a Chinese ship due to its design. These examples suggest that attempts to look at pre-modern phenomena in the sea world from a perspective predicated on the modern perception that human beings and ships have nationalities can often result in confusion.

### *What is a "maritime region"?*
Throughout this volume, spaces in the sea world that cannot be analyzed using "country" as a unit of demarcation are called "maritime regions". "Maritime region" does not connote a certain bounded expanse of ocean in the natural geographic sense; instead, it signifies the sea as a space in which humans live as well as an arena in which humans, goods and information move around and come into contact with each other. The word "region" is often used, not in the sense of a demarcated portion of land surface area, but rather in the sense of various expanses of arenas of living and activities. A "maritime region" may well be regarded as an "area" centering on sea waters. However, for those accustomed to looking

at history from the perspective of a certain country or looking at human activities by giving priority to those on land, it is very difficult to perceive, and often impossible to comprehend, what a "maritime region" is. This has remained unchanged since olden times and explains why people and things that have come to a certain area from a maritime region have often been called by terms affiliated with places or countries deemed symbolic of the overseas world, such as "Tang" and "Kōrē".

From a land-centered view, a maritime region may appear as a space reminiscent of a black box about which we can perceive nothing aside from points of entry and exit, or as a world of outlaws rife with pirates and smugglers. However, it can also be characterized as an arena where residents of islands and coastal areas live by catching fish and making salt, and where traders and seafarers make a living by transporting people and goods aboard their ships. It can even be characterized as an historical space in which sea-going ships made long-distance voyages, carrying diplomatic envoys traveling to and from foreign lands according to the orders of those in power, as well as eager Buddhist monks departing for or returning from studying abroad, and in which warships fully laden with soldiers were occasionally active. It is the history of this vision of "maritime region" that we are attempting to portray in this volume.

We do not claim that history begins from the sea, nor are we trying to depict a history of maritime regions by isolating them from the land. We hope our readers will not misunderstand this point. All we are trying to do is to describe a history of maritime regions from the perspectives of people who lived in a historical space created in the sea through the interactions among people, goods and information.

Let us elaborate by citing one example. In pre-modern East Asia, a policy very peculiar to the region called "*haijin*" was implemented, designed to preclude private operators from going to sea or engaging in maritime trade. The Yongle Emperor of the Ming Dynasty[9], who resolutely pursued this policy, issued the following order immediately after his enthronement:

---

9 The Yongle Emperor (1360–1424) was the third emperor of the Ming Dynasty (reigning from 1402 to 1424). He was originally assigned to Beiping (present-day Beijing) in the capacity of the Prince of Yan, but he staged an internal fight, overthrowing his nephew the Jianwen Emperor, and ascended to the throne. The Yongle Emperor moved the capital to Beijing and pursued active diplomatic policies by launching South-Sea expeditions and personally leading campaigns against the Mongols.

> According to reports from envoys, many barbarians living in seclusion on ocean islands are secretly in league with outlaws among the soldiers and masses of the country, and are engaging in banditry. [...] The barbarians should promptly return to their own countries. If they take this new opportunity and pay homage to our dynasty in the capacity of envoys of their kings, I will treat them heartily, greeting them and sending them off cordially. All the runaways from our dynasty shall be granted a pardon for their trespasses, be allowed to return to their original occupations and be forever treated as obedient subjects. However, should there be any who dare to disobey my order in the hope of taking advantage of the long and dangerous seaways, I am determined to dispatch troops and kill all the rebels.

This is revealing of how a land-based political power viewed the sea. According to this perspective, the *haijin* order was indispensable for maintaining the public peace within the country and for restoring diplomatic order. It is also possible, however, to get a glimpse of what lies underneath the Yongle Emperor's assertion, namely, a sense of uneasiness felt by the land-based power as it watched how the maritime region was developing at the time. Our aim in this book is to portray what was actually happening in the maritime region during this period.

We have been accustomed to looking, half consciously, at the past from the perspective of land-based political powers. We wonder, however, whether the same phenomena, if considered from the perspective of the maritime region, might appear differently. We want to reassess the existing East Asian history written from the standpoint of land-based political rulers, and write, instead, a new history of East Asia that encompasses both its land and sea areas by capturing the region in its entirety. We place the sea at the center of our view and take a fresh look at the region's history from the perspective of those living on the sea. This is the basic position that informs this volume.

As we have pointed out numerous times above, the maritime region is not readily visible from the terrestrial world. An authentic and convincing historical narrative ought to be supported by historical materials, but, unfortunately, there are few extant records written by seafarers, pirates or others who lived on the sea. Most of the old documents and records available today were written from the perspectives of, and according to the world-views of, those living on land. We believe, however, that as long as we probe into the available historical records with a full understanding of our research objectives and meticulously reorganize the pieces of information presented in those records, we may be able to gain a clear understanding of the actual situation in the maritime region and of its relationship with the "terrestrial region". Did those living in the maritime region behave in the same way as those living on the land, identifying themselves with the ruling power and keeping at a distance from "strangers"? How did fishermen and seafarers who "shed sweat and blood for their families" relate to pirates and soldiers who thought nothing of killing human beings? When history centers on a maritime region or becomes "history from a maritime perspective", we will be able to answer these questions.

## The stage for this volume's drama, and the breakdown of acts

### *What is "maritime East Asia"?*
Various maritime regions have made an appearance in world history: the South Pacific Ocean dotted with islands interconnected via outrigger canoes; the seas of Northwestern Europe crisscrossed by Viking long ships[10] and commercial ships and warships belonging to the Hanseatic League[11]; and the Indian Ocean, where dhows with lateen sails and large, multi-decked galleons rode the monsoon winds[12]. The theatre presented in this volume is the "maritime region" of "East Asia" that stretches to the east of the Eurasian continent.

Let us begin by explaining how the term "East Asia" is used throughout this volume. Although commonly used in Japan as a comprehensive name referring to an expanse of terrestrial areas including Mainland China, the Korean Peninsula and the Japanese Archipelago, its implications are far from uniform and it carries diverse connotations. Recently, a proposal has been proffered calling for the creation of an "East Asian

---

10 The Vikings were seafarers who raided and traded from their Scandinavian homelands across wide areas of Europe during the eighth to eleventh centuries.
11 The Hanseatic League was a commercial and defensive confederation of merchant guilds and their market towns that dominated trade along the coast of the Baltic Sea during the twelfth to sixteenth centuries. At its peak, the league encompassed more than 200-member cities of North Germany and neighboring areas.
12 The trade winds are also called "monsoons", meaning "seasonally prevailing winds". In the Indian Ocean the trade winds blow predominantly from the southwest in the months from May to September and from the northeast from October to April.

Union", a regional union similar to the European Union (EU). However, there are some who consider Southeast Asian countries as part of "East Asia", while others insist that the region should be defined much more broadly in order to include India and Australia. In Japan, the term "East Asia" is sometimes used to connote a sense of repentance for the foreign policy of the Japanese empire, especially so by a group of historians who, reflecting on the country's imperialist policy (namely, the Greater East Asia Co-Prosperity Sphere), draw attention to the importance of maintaining amicable international relations in the region. There are also instances where "East Asia" is used to denote a cultural sphere in which Chinese characters have been used and which has been under the influence of Confucianism.

Geographically, Asia is sometimes divided into four segments along the four cardinal points of north, south, east and west, with the eastern segment further divided into two parts, southeast and northeast. In this context, the latter two parts are deemed to constitute East Asia. There is yet another view that divides China into two along a horizontal, east-west line, emphasizing the similarity between the southern part of China and Southeast Asia. In the Republic of Korea, it is customary to refer to China, Korea and Japan collectively as Northeast Asia, while in Japan, too, the term Northeast Asia is often used in archeology and several other academic disciplines. Thus, the geographical space connoted by the term "East Asia" varies significantly depending on the views and beliefs of the people using it.

The "maritime region" that forms the main stage for this volume is made up of a series of oceans along the eastern tip of the Eurasian continent, stretching vertically from north to south, with both the East China Sea and the Yellow Sea lying at the center, and extending northward to the Sea of Japan and the Sea of Okhotsk and southward to the South China Sea. Here we call this expanse of sea waters along the east of the Eurasian continent and its peripheries the "East Asian maritime region" or "maritime East Asia", while giving due consideration to the historicity and cultural implications of the term "East Asia".

This does not mean, however, that this volume focuses exclusively on the East Asian maritime region. Pieces of aromatic *byakudan* (Cn. *baitan*; white sandalwood) that were dedicated to Hōryūji Temple in Nara in the mid-eighth century and have been kept there since carry inscriptions and pyrographic marks thought to be the names or trademarks of merchants. These pyrographic marks have recently been a subject of controversy between the long-cherished view that claims they refer to the Sogdians[13], who were actively engaged in commercial activities throughout Central Eurasia, and a new perspective that identifies them as referring to Chinese traders. It is, however, an indisputable fact that the inscriptions are written with Pahlavi letters, a script in use in the Iranian highlands. When we talk about products of this sort, we must also consider the sea world of the Indian Ocean south of Eurasia. Furthermore, when discussing particular maritime regions in the sixteenth century and beyond, when human history unfolded on a global scale, we must keep in mind the developments in the various other maritime regions around the world. Unlike land, all the seas in the world are connected. It is important to make it clear from the outset that the geographical expanse of the maritime region dealt with in this volume expands and contracts depending on the subject matter and period under discussion. Put another way, what is called the "East Asian maritime region" here signifies a space where we can get a clear picture of the interlacing series of human activities when gazing out from a position at the center of the East China Sea, though the view and expanse may vary from one period to the next.

This volume does not devote equal attention to all the seas of East Asia. As you will notice by reading the chapters that follow, the Sea of Okhotsk and the Sea of Japan are not often referred to, and in terms of the East China Sea and the South China Sea, a greater emphasis is placed on the former. There are several reasons why the space devoted to discussions of the various seas is unequal. One is a vestige of Japanese historiography, which, as pointed out above, has identified East Asia as a cultural sphere or a framework of international relations.

Secondly, few histories have been written that center on the East China Sea or the Yellow Sea. With regard to the South China Sea, the Sea of Okhotsk and their vicinities, about which research findings have been accumulating for some time in academic disciplines such as philology and archeology without being premised on the existence of modern national borders or nationalities, progress has been relatively steady in capturing the image of

---

13 Sogdians were from oases in Sogdiana or the Sogdian region of Central Eurasia. They spoke the Sogdian language, an Iranian language, and used the Sogdian alphabet, a descendant script of the Aramaic alphabet used in West Asia. Throughout the first millennium C.E., they acted as major players in the east-west trade along the Silk Road.

Prologue                                                                                                               13

a history viewed from the sea. By contrast, in the area surrounded by the East China Sea and the Yellow Sea, historical studies have been divided along the borders of modern nation-states and compartmentalized into studies of Japanese, Chinese and Korean histories, with the result that the history of the seas has been examined only as a sideline within each of these distinct national frameworks. The sea has been treated as an appendage of the land, and historical studies of the sea have verged on becoming a competition to find evidence to prove how a particular country has been more actively involved in the sea than others. However, these exigencies of historical studies in Japan have been changing rapidly over the past two to three decades. Studies focusing on themes such as the "history of the Asian maritime region" and "interactions in the East Asian maritime region" have become more robust, beginning to produce diverse research findings that focus attention on the East China Sea as a major arena. One reason why this volume attaches special importance to the East China Sea in narrating the history of maritime East Asia is because we hope to capitalize on these recent findings and to demonstrate the possibility of looking at history in radically different ways than from the nation-state-centered view.

In order to avoid confusion between a nation-state in the modern and contemporary era and a political entity in pre-modern times, we have made it a policy not to employ, as far as possible, "Japan", "China" and "Korea", and other regional names to denote political entities. This means that proper nouns such as "Japan", "China" and "Korea" as used in this volume refer to regional spaces such as the Japanese Archipelago, Mainland China and the Korean Peninsula, while the political powers reigning over land areas are referred to by terms such as "dynasty", "imperial court", "political power" or "regime". Words such as "Nihon-jin" (Japanese nationals) and "Kōrai-jin" (Goryeo nationals) are used respectively in the sense of "a person/persons in Japan" and "a person/persons in Goryeo", but not in the sense of "a person/persons belonging to a country called Japan" and "a person/persons belonging to a country called Goryeo". Aside from these, the names of ethnic groups who inhabited the northeast region of China are also used, such as the Jurchens[14] and Mongols. The term "*zhongguoren*" (Chinese

---

14 The Jurchens or Jurcheds, respectively expressed in Chinese characters as "女真" or "女直", were a Tungusic people of Northeast Asia. They practiced hunting and gathering activities in addition to dry-field and livestock farming and received

nationals) is also very ambiguous because it is sometimes used today to refer to either "Chinese national(s)" or "Han Chinese including ethnic Han Chinese living abroad". Throughout this volume we will primarily use the term "*huaren*" (ethnic Chinese, or a person/persons of Chinese descent), by paying attention to the ethnic characterizations shared by a group of people that are common and distinctive, such as language, culture, customs and so on; as much as possible, we will use more concrete regional terms such as "*Fujianren*" (people of Fujian) and "*Guangdongren*" (people of Guangdong). Furthermore, depending on the context, we will sometimes use the terms "Chinese" or "Han Chinese" when discussing Northern China or referring to people living in Mainland China.

### *A panoramic drama in three acts*

In attempting to describe East Asian history from a maritime perspective, this volume adopts a somewhat distinctive descriptive style. Instead of narrating a history in chronological order, as is often the case with history books, we focus our attention on three specific periods, presenting a conceptual reconstruction of the defining features of the maritime region and the surrounding areas in each period. We have taken this approach in the hope of presenting readers not with an abstract overview, but with the concrete and panoramic perspectives made possible by placing them as close to the center of the maritime region as possible and allowing them to look around in every direction. Unfortunately, space and time do not permit a treatise on all periods in the same manner. We have thus adopted a policy of choosing three "centuries" when the historical features of the maritime region were most pronounced and offering concrete descriptions of the salient characteristics and diversities of each period. A similar approach is often adopted in dramatic plays. This book may well be regarded as something similar to a three-act historical drama viewed from the sea.

The three "centuries" are as follows:
   Part 1:  The Open Sea, from 1250 to 1350
   Part 2:  Competing for the Sea, from 1500 to 1600
   Part 3:  The Compartmentalized Sea, from 1700 to 1800

---

strong political and cultural influences from the Mongols. They established the Jing Dynasty during the twelfth century, and the Qing Dynasty during the seventeenth. During the Qing Dynasty, the dynasty's name was changed to the Manchu Dynasty.

Each part is titled with an expression that, in our view, sums up the key feature of the maritime region in that period. The three "centuries" do not constitute three separate segments of one continuous history of the same space. Rather, we hope to present three different panoramic depictions of the same space by looking out from the center of the maritime region. Naturally, the illustrations differ in size and pattern; even if one stands in the same place at the center of the maritime region, the scenes that develop around one will vary significantly from one period to the next. At the same time, it is necessary to demonstrate similarities between certain patterns in each of the three parts, as well as to find out where and how they differ. In describing the three "centuries" by looking at maritime history, we have tried, as much as possible, to adopt the same perspective, the same yardstick and the same descriptive style. More specifically, the three parts are organized as follows.

Each part begins with a chapter presenting a "General Overview" which sums up the main developments and key features of the maritime region during the century in question. This is followed by a discussion focusing on "people". This section groups people who were connected to the maritime region in each period into three categories: 1) those involved in, or closely affiliated with, political powers; 2) those involved in sailing and maritime trade; and 3) those living along the coasts. The discussion then proceeds to clarify what roles and functions the people of each group performed in facilitating the historical developments of the maritime region in the period. We also mention major port towns that served as the arena for maritime interactions in each period, the realities of trading activities carried out in these towns, the way in which people from "outside the country" were living there and any characteristic features regarding how such foreigners were administered by the authorities. The discussion then turns to "goods" in order to clarify the economic features of the East Asian maritime region in each period by focusing on the diversity and epochal characteristics of goods transported by sea in that period. The last theme of the discussion is "information", which pivots around various facets concerning the reception or rejection of "information" in a broad sense, including technologies, learning, fine arts, religious beliefs and systems of thought. This final section examines the relationship between each of these factors and the history of maritime East Asia.

## The drama's synopsis

The historical locus of each of the three "centuries" is defined in the opening chapter of each part – the "General Overview" of the period concerned. However, in order to make these overviews more easily understandable, it seems worthwhile to present a chronological overview of the history of maritime East Asia, including the history of each of the three periods under discussion here. Such an overview may be likened to the scenario of a play, intended to help audience members gain a more accurate and profound understanding of the characters' lines and actions represented on the stage, and thereby helping them enjoy the performance more deeply. We ask our readers to take what follows in this introductory chapter as a body of fundamental knowledge that will prove useful in their enjoyment of the panoramic drama that will begin shortly.

Pre-modern people often understood the world on the basis of their self-centered world-view. In China, this was systematized in the form of the Sinocentric view of the world, a view that consisted of the middle kingdom and barbarian states (*Hua-Yi zhi bian*). According to this view, the "tribute" system constituted the basis of the world order presided over by the *tianzi* or Son of Heaven (alternatively, the Emperor), who was vested by Heaven with the task of governing the Earth. The tribute system required the ruler of a barbarian state[15], out of deference to the Emperor of China, to dispatch an envoy bearing a tributary gift. The Chinese emperor, on his part, would reciprocate by granting a return gift far more valuable than that presented to him.

This was the logic of the Chinese court. Outside of this system, however, from early on a number of maritime merchants visited numerous Chinese ports attempting to earn profits by engaging in various commercial activities. During the Tang Dynasty (618–907 C.E.), various Muslim maritime merchants who came from the South China Sea and Indian Ocean were designated by the court as "*fanke*", or "barbarian guests", who had come in admiration of the emperor's virtue. In Guangzhou and other major port cities, they lived in areas called "*fanfang*" (barbarian

---

15 Barbarians (蕃夷) were those people who were regarded, in the Sinocentric world-view, as living on the peripheries of China without being fully bathed in the emperor's virtue.

quarters). Maritime merchants from areas adjacent to the Yellow Sea and East China Sea were called "*Xinluo shanke*" (merchants from Silla), and were accommodated in *Xinluo-fang* (quarter for traders from Silla) established on the Shandong Peninsula and elsewhere. It is reported that *Bosituan*, a kind of *fanfang* for the accommodation of Persian traders, was established in Ningbo, in central Zhejiang Province. The southern-most *Xinluo-fang* was located in Taizhou in the southern part of Zhejiang Province. Thus, the spheres of activity for maritime merchants from South and North Asia overlapped somewhere near Hangzhou Bay.

Beginning in the ninth century, during the final days of the Tang Dynasty when the Japanese Buddhist monks En'nin and Enchin went there to study, the activities of Han Chinese maritime merchants in the East Asian maritime region rapidly gained momentum. In the East China Sea, they replaced traders from Silla, and in the South China Sea too, they began to compete aggressively with Muslim maritime merchants. Seeking to take advantage of growing maritime trade activities, the Song Dynasty (960–1279 C.E.) opened *shibosi* (maritime trade supervisorates) in major ports in order to administer maritime merchants and earn revenue by charging taxes on their goods. The Song Dynasty was fully aware of the importance of maritime trade, and this period saw a large number of Chinese traders advance into and live in major port towns throughout East Asia, including Hakata in Japan and Gaegyeong (alt. Kaesong), the capital of Goryeo, with Yesung Port on its outskirts, as well as other major ports of Southeast Asia. The Song China merchant Sha Kokumei (Cn. Xie Gouming) who settled in Hakata during this time is well known in Japan. The ships of these maritime merchants that sailed across the East China Sea carried not only articles of commerce, but also an increasing number of Japanese and Goryeo Buddhist monks traveling to temples in China to study.

The Song Dynasty period, characterized by active maritime trade primarily carried out by Chinese maritime merchants, was followed by the period featured in Part 1 below, i.e., the era of "The Open Sea", when the Mongols grew powerful and expanded southward, destroying Nangsong and placing the whole of Mainland China under their control. Part 1 explains in detail various facets of maritime East Asia that were powerfully shaken by the rise of the Mongol-led Yuan court.

By the mid-fourteenth century, when the Yuan Dynasty[16] was in its final days, the unifying forces of land-based political powers in various parts of East Asia had begun to wane. As the Yuan Dynasty's authority diminished due to recurrent civil wars and infighting within the imperial court, autonomous powers equipped with military strength, called "*junfa*" (military cliques), emerged in various areas of China. In Goryeo, the intensification of factional rivalries led to a succession of enthronements and dethronements of kings. The Japanese Archipelago was experiencing the *Nanbokuchō jidai* (Northern and Southern Courts period), characterized by a series of drawn-out upheavals. In contrast to the weakening of land-based political authorities, autonomous powers in various coastal areas and islands in and around the East China Sea became increasingly active. On the coast of China, rebel leaders such as Fang Guozhen and Zhang Shicheng instigated uprisings. In the Japanese Archipelago, maritime powers in various regions were divided into camps upholding the banners of the Southern or Northern Courts, repeatedly coming into conflict. Some of these maritime powers sailed as far as the Korean Peninsula and the coast of the Shandong Peninsula, acting as a destabilizing factor in the East China Sea. These groups were known as "*zenki wakō*" (the "early Wokou", a term traditionally translated as "Japanese pirates").[17]

The Hongwu Emperor, who established the Ming Dynasty by driving out the Mongol rulers, attempted to disentangle the chaotic state of affairs that prevailed in the final years of the Yuan Dynasty by reestablishing social order under a centralized system of government. With regards to the maritime region, which had been heading toward increased autonomy, he took steps to reinvent the tributary system, which had become an empty

---

16 Officially called the Great Yuan, the Yuan Dynasty was the empire founded by Qubilai Qa'an, who became the Mongol Emperor in 1260, and his descendants. Although the territory under the direct control of the dynasty was limited to Eastern Eurasia, centered on the Mongolian Plateau and China, several independent Mongol governments on the western frontiers are reported to have recognized its suzerainty.

17 The early Wokou were groups of Japanese pirates active along the coasts of Korea and China during the latter half of the fourteenth century. Primarily from the islands and coastal areas of northern Kyushu, such as Tsushima, Iki and Matsura, opinions vary regarding their social and ethnic characteristics. These groups are distinguished from the "later Wokou" active in the sixteenth century, to be discussed in Part 2.

shell, linking it with the *haijin* (maritime prohibition) policy and thereby instituting a system that would enable the dynasty to manage both foreign policy and maritime trade in a unified manner. He also attempted to divide and exterminate various autonomous maritime powers by implementing policies such as the *kongdao* policy, designed to evict inhabitants from ocean islands. Exemplified by the Ming Dynasty's *haijin* policy, there was a tendency in the East Asian maritime region in this period for land-based political powers to be sensitive about political and social developments in the maritime region, and willing to turn to policies characterized by intrusion and control. This was radically different from the way things stood in the Indian Ocean region, where land-based political powers were less concerned with the sea world. A major characteristic of maritime East Asia was that it often became a "sea of politics".

The latter half of the Ming Dynasty is the focus of Part 2: "Competing for the Sea". It was also the period when a network of maritime regions on a global scale was forged and shaped by Spanish and Portuguese seafarers. Part 2 explains the dynamic developments in the East Asian maritime region that occurred as a consequence of the maritime powers' reactions to the crumbling of established systems and the control imposed by the Ming Dynasty, as well as to the entry of new powers from the Iberian Peninsula.

The first half of the seventeenth century marked a major turning point in the history of maritime East Asia. In the Japanese Archipelago, the Tokugawa Shogunate came to power by wielding its mighty military strength and finally uniting the country, bringing an end to a long period of local rulers vying for authority. With regards to the maritime region, the shogunate installed a substantial system that combined maritime prohibitions with centrally administered trade. In Mainland China, the Qing Dynasty of the Jurchens or Manchus (est. 1644) established a strong regime of control, replacing the Ming Dynasty that had suffered from internal strife. Meanwhile, developments were unfolding in the maritime region where some forces were moving toward unification, while others were moving toward greater independence. The leading figures in these developments included Mao Wenlong[18], who gathered maritime forces in the northern part of the Yellow

---

18 Mao Wenlong (1576–1629) was a military commander of the Ming Dynasty, who advanced into the border areas between the Ming and Korea and fought against the Houjin (later the Qing Dynasty). He was, however, assassinated by a hard-line Ming commander for forming a maritime military clique and refusing to follow orders.

Sea, and Zheng Zhilong[19] and Zheng Chenggong[20], who were active in the south with the backing of maritime forces based in the East and South China Seas. In particular, Zheng Chenggong grew increasingly influential in the latter half of the seventeenth century when he moved his base to Taiwan and exerted significant influence on various areas along the central and southern coast of Mainland China. Indeed, the latter half of the seventeenth century seems to have been a time when the strength of the maritime region grew to the maximum extent possible. In its efforts to curb the rise of these independent maritime forces, the Qing regime issued a *qianjie ling*, an order prohibiting people from living in coastal areas and from going to sea, and attempted to destroy Zheng's kingdom in Taiwan from within. It was not until 1683 that the Qing Dynasty managed to successfully launch an assault on Zheng's headquarters in Taiwan[21].

After this victory, the Qing Dynasty issued a *zhanhai ling* (an edict for the development of the seas) and lifted the ban on overseas voyages by ordinary people. A large number of merchant ships operated by Han Chinese soon began to crowd the waters of the East and South China Seas to such an extent as to pose a serious problem for Nagasaki, Japan. The port, still under the system of centrally administered trade, was visited by a great number of Chinese ships, far in excess of its administrative and geographic capacity. Among the Europeans, Portuguese and Spanish traders became less and less visible in East Asia due to their close ties with Christian missionaries, a group deemed troublesome by most governments in the region, and were replaced

---

19 Zheng Zhilong (1604–1661) was from Quanzhou in Fujian Province. Leading a large armed fleet of maritime merchants, he controlled maritime trade along the coast of Fujian Province. After the fall of the Ming Dynasty, he defected to the Qing Dynasty in 1646, but was eventually executed by the Qing because of his son Zheng Chenggong's continued resistance against that regime.

20 Zheng Chenggong (1624–1662) was born in Hirado, Japan, to Zheng Zhilong and his Japanese wife. Even after his father surrendered to the Qing Dynasty, he continued to resist the regime by basing himself in Amoy. In 1661, he expelled Dutch colonists from Taiwan and relocated his headquarters there but died of malaria the following year.

21 A son of Zheng Chenggong, Zheng Jing succeeded his father's regime in 1662. He took part in several battles during the Ming-Qing transition, leading his navy on the side of the Ming. In 1681, Zheng Jing named his eldest son, Zheng Kezang, as his successor before his death later that year, however, Zheng Kezang was quickly toppled in favor of Zheng Keshuang. Zheng Keshuang surrendered to the Qing military in 1683.

Prologue                                                                                   21

by the Dutch East India Company (VOC)[22] that began to systematically engage in commercial activities. As the only European nationals allowed to participate in the Tokugawa Shogunate's centrally administered trade system, the Dutch merchants made large profits. In this way, formidable land-based powers began to flex their muscles in the latter half of the seventeenth century. Consequently, the forces in the maritime region, having had their autonomy gradually undermined, were left with no choice but to put themselves under the control of these land-based political regimes.

Part 3, "The Compartmentalized Sea", describes the situation in the maritime region when the great waves of change gradually subsided after the tsunami of the previous century. The inquiry in this final part reveals some of the early indications of what later developed into salient features that characterize this region today. At the end of the century dealt with in Part 3, the East Asian maritime region faced a new "modern" era symbolized by the Opium War.

Presented above is a preview of how this volume proceeds, but please be patient and wait a little longer for the curtain of the main drama to rise. Before you can begin to appreciate the tangible developments that unfolded over the three "centuries", we must provide you, the audience, with background information about the scenery and some of the large props involved in the dramatic production – namely, the realities of the seas, the winds, the ships and their voyages. The movements of people, goods and information were greatly affected by the natural environments of the seas of East Asia and its vicinity and were sustained by shipbuilding and sailing techniques, so please take in this "curtain-raiser" before the main act begins.

## Maritime environments and ships

### Seas and winds on the eastern fringe of Eurasia

*The shapes of the seas*
When viewed from a satellite, our globe presents a beautiful contrast between seas and landmasses. The point of contact between the Pacific

---

22  The VOC was established in 1602 through the unification of six trading companies in various parts of the Netherlands. In the East Asian maritime region, it established its base in Batavia, and was engaged in trading activities across virtually all the sea waters of the region extending from the Indian Ocean to the East China Sea.

Ocean, the largest body of salt water on Earth, and the largest continental landmass on Earth constitutes the stage for the presentation of our drama. On closer inspection, the Pacific Ocean and the Eurasian continent are not directly touching each other but are separated by a picturesque arc of island chains formed by the Kuril Islands, the Japanese Archipelago, the Nansei Islands (alternatively, the Southwest Islands, or the Ryukyu Islands), the Philippine Islands and so on. These island chains stretching along the western fringe of the Northern Pacific Ocean were formed along the borders between tectonic or lithospheric plates that make up the surface of the Earth. Consequently, the seabed on either side of each island chain takes on drastically different features. On the Pacific Ocean side before it makes contact with the island chains, an expansive seabed with an average depth of 4,000 meters falls at a sharp angle, forming trenches of approximately 8,000 meters in depth, and then sharply rises up again, creating gigantic walls 6,000 meters in height. By contrast, on the Mainland China side, the seabed gently bows, producing approximately 3,000-meter-deep oceanic basins, and then forms a gently-sloping continental shelf that stretches toward the continental coastline in some places and climbs steeply in others.

These island chains look as if they were supported by a series of stone pillars, consisting of the Kamchatka Peninsula, Sakhalin Island, the Korean Peninsula and Taiwan Island. At the same time, these peninsulas and islands simultaneously play the role of partitioning the epicontinental sea that lies between the Pacific Ocean and Mainland China, forming four bodies of water: the Sea of Okhotsk, the Sea of Japan, the Yellow Sea/East China Sea[23] and the South China Sea. These four bodies of water are not fully closed off from each other, connected as they are by the Soya Strait, the Tsushima Strait and the Taiwan Strait. They are also accessible from the Pacific Ocean through large and small openings between islands. From above, the four seas look as if they were plazas and courtyards surrounded and protected by large corridors made up of various types of buildings.

---

23 The East China Sea, the Yellow Sea and the Bohai Sea are often treated separately but given the fact that the waters of these seas are connected, we will treat them here as constituting a single body of water, lumping them together and referring to them as the Yellow Sea and the East China Sea.

The coastline on the eastern edge of the Eurasian continent is unique among continental coastlines on Earth, in the sense that the waters stretching along it are made up of a very long chain of ocean waters surrounded by peninsulas and islands. The chain of the four seas extends as long as 8,500 kilometers from just below the Arctic Circle to just south of the equator, while the land corridor stretches further toward both North America and Oceania. The topography of the East Asian maritime region has had significant impacts on the movements of people, goods and information, and on the pattern of interactions in the eastern part of Eurasia.

### *Characteristic features of the four seas*
The four seas that stretch from north to south do not serve as stages of equal importance in this volume. The East China Sea features most frequently as the main locus, though this differs depending on the period. Next in significance is the South China Sea. The Sea of Japan makes an appearance from time to time, but the Sea of Okhotsk that lies to the north of it is hardly mentioned at all except in Part 3. Needless to say, this bias results from the structure and substance of this volume as outlined above, namely a bias inherent in the script adopted here. It should be kept in mind, however, that ships sailing from Ningbo to Hakata were carrying *sumu* (sappan wood) and spices from around the South China Sea, while sea-otter fur produced in the Sea of Okhotsk was carried aboard ships sailing from Hakata to Ningbo. Even when some of the four seas are not explicitly referred to in the following pages, they are by no means unrelated to the story presented here. Let us take a brief look at the salient geographic features of the four seas.

The Sea of Okhotsk, northernmost among the four seas, lies between the Kamchatka Peninsula to the east, the Eurasian continent to the north and Sakhalin Island to the west, and faces the Kuril Islands that stretch to the south. Roughly in the shape of a dust-pan, the sea covers 1.5 million square kilometers, with a mean depth of 838 meters. The seabed becomes deeper in the north-south direction, beginning with a continental shelf stretching along the northern coastline that turns into an ocean basin of 1,000 to 1,600 meters in depth in the central part, becoming a much deeper ocean basin with a maximum depth of 3,700 meters in the southern part. The seabed in the vicinity of the Kuril Islands measures as much as 1,000 to 2,000 meters in depth. The maritime region has virtually no other significant islands aside from those mentioned above and is only studded with small and medium sized islands near its northern coastline.

The sea derives its singular nature from the Amur River that empties into the western quadrant. The river feeds large amounts of freshwater and accompanying nutrients into the sea. This has the effect of reducing the concentration of saline in the water, causing it to become frozen at a higher temperature than otherwise; as a result, sea ice covers more than seventy percent of the sea's surface in mid-winter, drifting onto the coast of Hokkaido. Moreover, the convective mixing of sea water that occurs concurrently as it freezes has the effect of stirring and propelling nutrient sediments to the surface, causing huge outbreaks of plankton, which in turn nurture the rich aquatic resources of the sea and create a paradise for marine animals clad in beautiful fur. Given the harsh environmental factors of the northern sea, such as rough weather and ice formation that prevented maritime transportation, for long periods the maritime region provided only limited numbers of littoral peoples with fishing grounds. Consequently, the development of large port towns along its coast was very limited.

The Sea of Japan, surrounded by the Eurasian continent, Sakhalin Island, the Japanese Archipelago and the Korean Peninsula, covers approximately one million square kilometers, and is the smallest of the four seas. Characterized by its large mean depth of 1,700 meters, the sea is shaped like a tube pan, so to speak, with its central area known as the Yamato Bank (400 meters in depth) surrounded by the Japan Basin (3,000 meters) to the north, the Yamato Basin (2,500 meters) to the southeast and the Tsushima Basin (2,500 meters) to the southwest. The continental shelf occupies very small areas in the northeastern and southwestern parts of the maritime region. Except for Geoje Island, Ulleungdo Island and the Liancourt Rocks (Jp. Takeshima, Kr. Dokto) located in the western part of the sea, most of the islands are small and scattered near the coastlines, with relatively larger islands limited to Oki, Sado and Rishiri near the coasts of Japan. Another salient feature of the sea is its closed nature, in the sense that it is connected with other waters only through the five narrow and shallow channels of Mamiya, Sōya, Tsugaru, Kanmon and Tsushima. The limited amount of sea water flowing in and out means that tidal changes are relatively small, an important characteristic of the Sea of Japan. In the virtual absence of tidal variation, tidal flats do not develop on the coasts. Along the coast on either side of the Tsushima Strait located at the southern tip of this sea, which constitutes an important waterway connecting the Korean Peninsula and the Japanese Archipelago, there developed a series of important port towns that served as bases for maritime interaction known as the Sampo (Three Port Towns)[24], including Pusan on the Korean Peninsula and Hakata and Shimonoseki on the Japanese Archipelago. A number of port towns for coastal trading also developed in various inlets facing the Sea of Japan along the Japanese Archipelago from Hokkaido to Hakata.

The waters covering the East China Sea (approximately 1.25 million square kilometers) and the Yellow Sea (approximately 0.4 million square kilometers) are surrounded by the Eurasian continent, the Korean Peninsula and Kyushu, and face the Nansei Islands that stretch into the south. If combined with the Bohai Sea, with its surface area measuring approximately 0.1 million square kilometers, the East China, Yellow and Bohai Seas total an area of approximately 1.75 million square kilometers, thus forming the second largest body of water among the four seas. The seabed of this maritime region looks quite similar to that of the Sea of Okhotsk, sloping down from the continental shelf in its northern part toward the 2,000-meter-deep sea basin situated near the Nansei Islands, called the Okinawa Trough. The most salient feature of this sea is its shallowness. The Okinawa Trough is only 200 to 300 kilometers in width, and the continental shelf with a depth of 200 meters or less makes up more than ninety percent of the sea area. The sea is much shallower in the northern part, with the mean depth of the Yellow Sea measuring forty meters and that of the Bohai Sea only ten meters. The shape of the maritime region's seabed may be likened to that of a Japanese teppanyaki spatula (like a metal pizza peel).

With the exception of the Nansei Islands, the islands in the maritime region are concentrated along the coastal areas. They are numerous, partly because the waters are relatively shallow. The coasts along the southwestern part of the Korean Peninsula and the Zhoushan Islands at the mouth of Hangzhou Bay take on the appearance of island-studded seas. Expansive tidal flats are formed in some of the enclosed bays on the western coasts of the Korean Peninsula, where the tidal variation reaches almost ten meters. Aside from these, there are several islands of relatively large size located some distance from the shore, such as Tsushima, the Gotō Islands

---

24 Sampo signifies the three port towns in the southeastern part of the Korean Peninsula where residential quarters for Japanese, called the Japan House (Wakan in Japanese, or Waegwan in Korean), were established, namely Busanpo, Naeipo and Yeompo.

and Jeju-do. People active in the maritime world in this region often used these islands as their strongholds.

We must not neglect the significance of the Chang Jiang River. Having discharged, together with the Huai River (Cn. Huaishui), huge amounts of silt for centuries, it has been a major factor responsible for creating enormously large sandbars on the coast between the mouths of the two rivers. The estuaries of the two rivers have also poured massive volumes of freshwater into the maritime region. The vast expanses of brackish water expelled by the two rivers combine with sea waters flowing from the Nansei Islands and the Taiwan and Tsushima Straits, forming mixed bodies of water in this sea that create diverse maritime ecological systems, including marine resources that are equally as rich but quite different from those of the Sea of Okhotsk.

Many rivers, including the Chang Jiang River, empty into this maritime region from the continent. As such, quite a few port towns developed along the Chinese coast as riverine ports and were located upstream from the mouths of these rivers. Shanghai in Jiangnan (lower Yangtze Delta) and Ningbo, Fuzhou and Quanzhou in Fujian are all examples of such riverine port towns. When the tide was coming in, ships arriving from the outer seas could ride the rising tide in the rivers and sail upstream directly to the port towns. Although this fact tends to be neglected, the rivers flowing into the East China Sea were performing important roles in connecting maritime and terrestrial transportation. Spanning across the western part of the Japanese Archipelago for a few hundred kilometers, the Seto Inland Sea shares similar characteristics with the rivers in Jiangnan and Fujian. The existence of inland waterways such as these, connected with the outer sea waters, may be counted as another salient feature of this maritime region.

Located farthest south, the South China Sea covers approximately 3.6 million square kilometers, an area more than twice as large as that covered by each of the other three seas. With a mean depth of 1,200 meters, its seabed is shaped like a combination of a frying pan and a stew pot, consisting of wide continental shelves that stretch out in the southwestern and northern parts and a huge sea basin that forms a crevasse in the eastern part, extending to the 5,000 meters-deep Manila Trench. The sea is a composite mixture of waters with diverse features: the northwestern part hemmed in by the continent and peninsulas; crescent groups scattered around the expansive sea waters; and a southeastern part made up of islands, channels and straights, notably the broad Luzon Strait, the Malacca Strait with its long, narrow shape and Hainan Island that protrudes out into the sea in the shape of a lump. Facing onto the Andaman Sea in the west and the Sulu and Java Seas in the east, this sea is also characterized by its open shape.

Most of the South China Sea is located in the tropical zone. Coral reefs flourish in the island areas, while expansive mangrove forests grow in saline continental seashores. Tidal flats featuring these mangrove forests and shallow sea shelves are ecologically productive and inhabited by many species of shrimp, fish and shellfish, in turn attracting people who earn their living by fishing these fertile waters.

Several major trading posts exist along the coasts of this sea. Along the continental seashore, just as in the case of the East China Sea, large port towns developed on the banks of major rivers in inland basins upstream from their estuaries, such as Guangzhou, Phnom Penh and Ayutthaya. Some port towns, such as Malacca and Hoi An[25], developed at the mouths of rivers. Since the mid-sixteenth century, when European maritime merchants began to advance into the area, port cities (*gangshi*) such as Macao, Manila[26] and Batavia[27] were established in locations facing the sea to serve as their trading posts. Moreover, the island areas of Southeast Asia to the south of the Philippines were inhabited by a large number of people who lived on the sea.

## *Knowledge of winds*

Various winds blow in each of the four seas. The Sea of Japan, for example, is mostly affected by prevailing westerlies, and westerly or northwesterly winds are customary throughout the year. By contrast, the East and South China Seas are characterized by the seasonal or

---

25  Hoi An is a port town in central Vietnam that flourished from early on as a trading port. There was a Japanese settlement in the town during the early half of the seventeenth century.
26  Manila used to be a trading post for Muslim chieftains in the southern part of Luzon Island, but in 1571 Miguel López de Legazpi, the first Spanish Governor-General of the Philippines, made it the colonial capital. Subsequently, galleons sailed back and forth crossing the Pacific Ocean between Manila and Acapulco in Spanish Mexico.
27  Batavia, in the western part of Java Island, is the former official name of Jakarta. The Dutch East India Company founded it as a trade and administrative center in the early seventeenth century.

monsoon winds that affect regions to the south, wherein the wind direction varies depending on the season. Seafarers who maneuvered their ships there had thorough knowledge of when and how the wind directions changed.

A navigation instruction manual titled *Shinan Kōgi*, authored in 1708 by Ryukyu scholar Tei Junsoku by compiling the stock of knowledge shared by mariners of South China, points out:

> After the Seimei festival [Cn. Qingmingjie] in early April, *ziqi* [terrestrial energy] moves from south to north, causing a southerly wind to blow constantly. After the *sōkō* [Cn. Shuangjiangjie; the frost's descent] in late October, the terrestrial energy moves from north to south, causing a northerly wind to blow constantly.

During the summer, high temperatures inland and atmospheric pressure over the Pacific Ocean in the north cause cool air from the oceans to move towards the Asian continent from the southeast. Conversely, during winter, northeasterly and northwesterly winds blowing out from the cooled-down continent prevail.

Seasonally reversing winds have left strong imprints on the environments surrounding the sea and have significantly affected the livelihoods and cultures of the people living there. In regions located in the tropical or subtropical zones, where the year is bisected into the rainy and dry seasons, the word "monsoon" has become synonymous with the rainy season. In the temperate zones featuring intervals of seasonal reversal, there emerged a view that further divides these two seasons into four. However, there are differences regarding the seasons across these temperate regions. People living in the area from the northern part of the South China Sea to the southern parts of the East China Sea and the Sea of Japan share a long spell of rainy weather in the early summer called "*baiu*," though with slight differences in terms of the precise beginning and end of that season. Despite having no first-hand experience of *baiu*, people living along the Yellow Sea and the northern part of the Sea of Japan are nonetheless aware of it. During this season, the latter area is affected not by the usual southeasterly wind blowing from the Pacific Ocean, but rather by a dry southwesterly wind that comes all the way from the Indian Ocean and crosses the Himalayas and inland areas of China. Thus, the rainy season and its effects have much to do with the differences in vegetation and farming practices in the two areas.

Winds were not limited to seasonal ones. *Shinan Kōgi* describes as follows:

> Enormous and violent winds are called *ju* [颶; Jp. *gu*], meaning blizzards or windstorms, and excessively strong winds among these are called *tai* [颱], meaning typhoons. A *ju* always develops very suddenly, while a *tai* develops gradually. A *ju* starts to blow and then ceases all of a sudden, but a *tai* continues for a day and a night, or for several days on end. Generally, *ju* occur mostly in February to May, while *tai* are concentrated in the June to September period. There also takes place in October a phenomenon commonly called *jiujiangfeng* [winds of September], with a northerly wind starting to blow violently and continuing for a few months on end. While the *jiujiangfeng* is blowing, it is sometimes reinforced by the occurrence of a *tai*, which erupts very suddenly like a *ju* in the spring. A ship may be able to cope with a *ju* if it encounters one while at sea, but there is nothing that can be done to cope with a *tai*. Given that, unlike seasonal winds, *tai* and *ju* do not occur on a periodical basis, mariners should sail their ships by availing themselves of the intervals between winds.

Typhoons that develop during the summer and autumn, windstorms caused by low atmospheric pressure and unexpected whirlwinds also posed serious threats to ocean-going vessels.

Careful observation of the skies, atmospheric assessment and the use of folklore regarding weather to make predictions were indispensable in protecting a ship from unexpected windstorms. The same navigational instruction manual provides its readers with pieces of folklore alongside more empirical advice:

> If clouds start to gather in the east, an easterly wind is certain to blow. and if clouds start to gather in the west, a westerly wind is certain to blow. The same rule holds true for clouds gathering in the south and the north. […] If fragmented clouds gather, cling to each other, and surround the sunlight, a wind will start to blow. If the movement of the clouds is fast, a strong wind will blow, and if the sun or the moon twinkles, a strong wind will blow. If the sunlight shining on overhanging clouds is red, if Venus can be seen during the daytime, and if the Orion constellation glitters these are all signs of a strong wind.

In other words, when the air current is moving fast or when the atmosphere is unstable, it is necessary to take refuge or make sufficient preparations early.

> In the afternoon of a spring or summer day when the skies are burning hot, it is certain to become cloudy and blow violently, accompanied by roaring thunder and lightning. [...] A day with strong sunlight seldom fails to be accompanied by a heavy squall. In order to detect whether a day is going to be calm, one must get up early. [...] As soon as you get up, look carefully in all directions, and if the sky color is bright and clear, you should weigh anchor and set sail right before the dawn. If the sky color remains unchanged and a gentle breeze is blowing at about eight o'clock in the morning, you should keep the ship moving forward, regardless of whether the wind is fair or against you.

This teaches the reader that even a tail wind is bound to develop into a vicious wind that will cause mountainous waves if it is excessively strong.

According to the statistics of Japan's Meteorological Agency, the number of days per month when waters of the East China Sea become rough with wave heights of four meters or more (based on five years of data beginning in 2004) are: 8.3 days for the January–March period; 1.2 days for the April–June period; 6.1 days for the July–September period; and 8.0 days for the October–December period. This means that the East China Sea is calmest from spring to the first half of summer but could pose a threat to ships going to sea in the latter half of summer with unruly winds and waves generated by typhoons, as well as in the late autumn when the waters are also rough due to the northwesterly seasonal winds.

### *The effects of ocean currents*
Turning to the ocean currents that flow in the East Asian maritime region, the Kuroshio Current or Black Tide is by far the most important. Approximately 100 kilometers wide, the warm Kuroshio Current is the largest of its kind in the Pacific Ocean and extends several thousand kilometers from the Philippine Islands up to the east coast of the Japanese Archipelago. As such, it has far-reaching effects not only on the marine climate and resources of the region, but also on the ecological systems of the region's coastal areas. However, past travelers and inhabitants of the East Asian maritime region were not as familiar with the Kuroshio Current because the sphere of activities for ships sailing in the region

was mainly confined within the epicontinental sea surrounded by arcs of islands. Needless to say, the Kuroshio Current passes through the corridor in the southeastern part of the East China Sea but does not reach the sea's shallow waters. Part of the current stretches north along the trench wall on the outer rim of the Ryukyu Arc, and in waters off the coast of Shikoku Island merges with the other half of the current flowing out of the corridor from the East China Sea. The portion of the Kuroshio Current that flows into the East China Sea is reduced by approximately half of that flowing in the Pacific Ocean both in terms of volume and velocity. When Chinese envoys on their way to Ryukyu used the expressions "*heishui*" (black water) and "*heishui gou*" (black-water trench), they did so without being aware of the diverging patterns in the flow of the Kuroshio Current, instead seeking to emphasize the difference in the depth of the waters over the continental shelf and over the Okinawa Trough. An exception can be found near the Tokara Islands situated close to the exit from the East China Sea corridor, where the Kuroshio Current gathers momentum as it turns east and starts to head toward the point of junction between the two parts of the Kuroshio Current. This rapid current has been likened to the *rakusai*, the torrential waterfall adjacent to the seashore often mentioned in classical texts or described as the *Tensui ga watashi* (the Channel of Tensui), which refers to an infamously perilous crossing for ships. Although some records state that the meeting place of the two portions of the Kuroshio Current could be crossed without incident, the situation seems to have differed significantly depending on external factors such as the season and winds. Considered from a different angle, it seems possible to say that precisely because the Kuroshio Current in the Pacific Ocean constituted an insurmountable obstacle for pre-modern navigation, the sphere of activity for ships had to be confined within the epicontinental sea surrounded by the arcs of islands.

As it moves into the East China Sea, a portion of the Kuroshio Current further branches off into the Sea of Japan and is referred to as the Tsushima Current. This warm current is responsible for causing heavy snowfall in various parts of Japan facing the Sea of Japan by supplying large amounts of vapor to the northwesterly seasonal wind blowing across this sea in winter. Furthermore, until the latter half of the seventeenth century, it had been rather common for cargoes from the Korean Peninsula, the northern shores of Kyushu or the San'in District to be transported by boat to Wakasa Bay before being unloaded there and shipped overland to Biwako Lake; from there, they would be shipped by water over the lake and then down the Yodo River to Kyoto, Osaka or other towns in the Kamigata region[28]. It was much faster to ship goods via this route to the Kamigata region by riding the Tsushima Current to Wakasa Bay rather than to sail through the Seto Inland Sea where no rapid sea current flows.

## Ships and navigation

### *Chinese ships*
What sorts of vessels actually sailed in maritime East Asia? Did the construction and function of ships or methods of navigation differ significantly from one period to the next or from one locality to another? Unfortunately, many details about the ships in the East Asian maritime region remain unknown, because these ships have not been studied as intensively or thoroughly as European ships. Presented here, therefore, is a brief synopsis of what is known about Chinese and Japanese ships. The following descriptions are focused primarily on vessels used in maritime trade. Needless to say, many other types of ships that are not the focus here were also in use, such as riverboats, warships and fishing boats.

The ships used in the coastal areas of Mainland China during the periods discussed in this volume are broadly divided into two categories. The first group consists of flat-bottomed *shachuan* (sand ships) used to sail in shallow waters such as rivers, canals and coastal waters. Characteristically, they were built so as to navigate the shallow waterways and move easily over the waves. Originally, marine traffic was rather scarce in the coastal waters north of the Chang Jiang River, where many shoals are scattered intermittently along the coastline making it difficult for many ships to pass through. However, during the Yuan and Qing Dynasties, respectively dealt with in Part 1 and Part 3 of this book, marine traffic in the form of flat-bottomed ships flourished. Some of these *shachuan* set out on ocean voyages and were recorded among the Chinese ships that visited Nagasaki during the Edo period (1600–1867).

The second group consists of *jiandichuan* (sharp-bottomed ships) with sharp v-shaped hulls resistant to waves and capable of sailing in deep seas. These ships were mainly built in areas south of the mouth of the Chang Jiang River and were used for ocean voyages. As early as the ninth century,

---

28  A classical designation to express the present-day Kansai region, including Osaka, Kyoto etc.

Chinese maritime merchants were beginning to navigate these ships along the coast of Mainland China, passing through the South China Sea and farther into Southeast Asia. It was also from around the ninth century that maritime merchants based in Jiangnan began to cross the East China Sea with these sharp-bottomed ships and commenced trade linking Mainland China with the Japanese Archipelago. Though collectively called "sharp-bottomed ships", this group can be divided into several sub-varieties, such as *fuchuan* (warships) and *niaochuan* (bird ships). *Niaochuan* built in Fujian Province were known for their proficiency in sailing rapidly in open seas, and a large number of them were used for marine transport to and from distant places. Unfortunately, concrete details about various sub-varieties of sharp-bottomed ships and the differences among them remain unknown.

Chinese ships are commonly called "junks". Although usually expressed in Chinese characters as *rongke* (戎克), the term "junk" is considered to have originated from the Chinese term "*chuan*" (boat, ship), with the Chinese word morphing into "*jong*" in Malay and "*junco*" in Portuguese before becoming "junk" in English.

Ships classified as junks share two features. One concerns the ship's structure: a junk is equipped with bulkhead plates. Bulkhead plates fitted horizontally between the planks of the hull of a ship were effective in improving the ship's strength in the lateral direction and in preventing leakage. The number of bulkhead beams varied depending on the ship's size, but typically ten or more of them were installed into the ship's hull. Another salient characteristic of junks was that they were equipped with rectangular sails called "*peng*", made of bamboo sticks woven in a wickerwork pattern, with bamboo twigs with leaves still attached inserted into this pattern. Each sail weighed a considerable amount and while hoisting them required much time and labor they could be taken down easily, which was convenient when coping with sudden changes in the weather while at sea. It also did not cost much to modify the sail aesthetically. If we define a ship equipped with these two features as a junk, then the emergence of this type of ship dates back to sometime between the eighth and ninth century. While ships built on the coast of Mainland China before that time cannot be classed as junks, some ships built outside China by non-Chinese people can be regarded as such. Moreover, both merchant ships and warships, regardless of their use, can be considered junks after the ninth century. In this way, the term "junk" is extremely ambiguous.

The ambiguity of junks extended beyond its use as a category. Other than the above, there were no common patterns that extended to other aspects of ships referred to as "junks", such as size and design, shape of anchors and paddles or number of sails. Nonetheless, insofar as merchant ships are concerned, there were some vague standards that seem to have remained more or less unchanged throughout the three periods under discussion in this volume. This is because the junk-building technique was basically established during the Song Dynasty of the eleventh and twelfth centuries, and the essential features of that technique were retained until the nineteenth century. However, the construction technique was refined and improved in various ways with the passage of time. One concrete example of this was the partial adoption of the design of European ships from Portugal and the Netherlands that sailed in maritime East Asia, which included a sail at the bow and a high-rise superstructure at the stern.

A vessel excavated in Quanzhou, Fujian Province, is an example of the type of ships built in the period covered in Part 1 of this volume. Spanning a length of thirty-four meters and a width of eleven meters, the ship had an estimated carrying capacity of approximately 200 tons. The previously mentioned shipwreck in the early fourteenth century, discovered off the coast of Sinan in the southwestern part of the Korean Peninsula, was approximately the same size as the Quanzhou ship. On the other hand, fleets of ships dispatched by the Ming Dynasty to Southeast Asia and the Indian Ocean in the early fifteenth century under the command of Zheng He[29] are known to have included a gigantic ship called *baochuan* (treasure ship). According to one view, this ship was as long as 150 meters, but more recent studies suggest that it is quite unlikely that a wooden junk of such a huge size could have been built at the time. It seems more reasonable to think that the ship was at most seventy meters in length.

As for the eighteenth century, the period covered by Part 3 of this volume, the picture scroll entitled *Tōsen no Zu* (Drawing of Chinese

---

29 A total of seven expeditions to the South China Sea and the Indian Ocean were undertaken in 1405–1433 by Zheng He, a eunuch born into a Muslim family in Yunnan. These voyages were aimed at enticing local rulers to establish tributary relations with the Ming Dynasty and engaging in maritime trade. One detachment of the fleet reached as far as the east coast of Africa.

Ships), housed in the Matsura Historical Museum on Hirado Island, Nagasaki Prefecture, presents vivid depictions of vessels from this period. A total of eleven Chinese ships, including some from Ningbo, Nanjing and Guangdong, are drawn in the scroll and accompanied by detailed measurements. Aside from the Nanjing ship with the characteristics of a flat-bottomed *shachuan*, the other ten ships are all sharp-bottomed *jiandichuan*. Among these, a ship from Taiwan is described as having a length of approximately thirty-two meters. The lengths of the nine other vessels differ slightly from each other, but do not deviate greatly from that of the Taiwanese ship.

As such, it seems safe to say that the smallest junks making round trips between Mainland China and the Japanese Archipelago throughout the three periods under discussion in this volume were approximately thirty meters long and had a loading capacity of about 200 tons. The types of wood often used in constructing these ships were as follows: heavy and corrosion-resistant pine for the keel and other components of the bottom of a ship; camphorwood, which holds nails well, for the beams; and light and buoyant cedar for the exterior planks. Moreover, as a means of preventing leaks, each joint between adjacent exterior plates was stuffed with hemp, to which was then applied a coating of paste made by mixing lime or oyster lime with tung oil (Cn. *tongyou*, Jp. *tōyu*).

### Ships of Japan

Not much is known about the ships that were used along the coast of the Japanese Archipelago. Concrete information available about ships that sailed to Mainland China only dates back to the fifteenth century. During the Nara (710–794) and Heian eras (794–1183), a series of envoy ships were dispatched from Japan to the Tang Dynasty, but no information remains about the hull structures of these vessels. Although we can assume that during the period discussed in Part 1 there were some ships built in Japan sailing between Mainland China and the Japanese Archipelago alongside Chinese junks that visited Hakata and other ports in Japan, there is no information about their size or design.

Some information is available about envoy ships dispatched during the Ming Dynasty in the fifteenth and sixteenth centuries. In addition to members of the official delegation, it was common for an envoy ship to Ming China to carry a large number of merchants. Including both the passengers and the crew, these ships are thought to have held between 150 and 200 people. As such, they had to be large ships. Rather than building a ship specifically for the occasion, trading ships already in service along the coast of the Japanese Archipelago were appropriated for the delegation. The larger of the appropriated envoy ships had a loading capacity of 1,800 *koku* (270 tons), which is considered fairly large even by the standards of the late seventeenth century. By that time, structured ships or plank-built ships known as "*kōzōsen*" had come into use and were constructed with *tanaita zukuri*, a shelf-board construction method.

In 1445, a total of 1,903 ships heading toward Osaka passed through the Hyogo Kitaseki barrier station located in Tōdaiji Temple's territory facing the Seto Inland Sea. The loading capacities of 1,687 of those ships were recorded, with more than half of that number described as small in size with a capacity of 100 *koku* or less. Ships with a loading capacity of 600 *koku* (approximately ninety tons) or more numbered thirteen. It must have been exceptionally large ships like these that were appropriated for the Japan-Ming trade. The home ports for these ships were listed as: Moji in Buzen Province; Tonda, Kaminoseki and Yanai in Suo Province; Takasaki and Kamagari in Aki Province; Onomichi in Bingo Province; and Hyōgo in Settsu Province.

It is also reported that ships used by Japanese pirates known as the "later Wokou" (*kōki wakō*) were small, flat-bottomed ships of the Japanese style without keels. This type of ship was unable to traverse the waves when faced with a cross or adverse wind, and they would reportedly take nearly one month to cross the East China Sea. People of Chinese descent from Fujian were said to have later helped to reshape the flat-bottomed Japanese-style ships and remodel them into sharp-bottomed junks, thereby enabling Wokou to cross the East China Sea in far less time.

Though not directly dealt with in this volume, the seventeenth century saw an unprecedented enthusiasm for junks across the entire Japanese Archipelago. During a short period of thirty years or so in the early half of the century, a cumulative total of more than 356 *shuinsen* sailed from the Archipelago toward Southeast Asia. Many of the licensed trading ships strong enough to sail on the open sea were junks, and many of these were built in Japan while others were purchased in Fujian or Siam. Their sizes varied widely, with a loading capacity ranging from seventy-two to 480 tons. Housed in the Nagasaki Museum of History and Culture is a drawing of a ship owned by Suetsugu Heizō, the Nagasaki Daikan (local governor of Nagasaki)[30], who was also engaged in licensed red-seal ship trade, along with a drawing of a ship owned by Araki Sōtarō, a merchant based in Nagasaki. According to the restored drawings of

**Figure 1: Nanjing ship**
Source: *Ikokusen Emaki* (Scroll Paintings of Foreign Ships), vol 1., Kagoshima Prefectural Library.

---

30 The Nagasaki Daikan was the chief of locally hired officers of Nagasaki. As an assistant to the Nagasaki Bugyō (the Nagasaki Magistrate), and also as the head of local residents, not only did the Nagasaki Daikan exert great influence on the administration of the town of Nagasaki, but he also took charge of the administration of lands in the town's vicinity that were owned directly by the Shogunate. After being held by Murayama Tōan and also Suetsugu Heizō's family, the post became hereditary to Takagi Sakuemon's family in 1739.

the two ships, they were more than forty-nine meters in length and eight to nine meters in width, which means that they were much larger than average-sized junks.

Even after it implemented the policy of national seclusion (*sakoku*), the Tokugawa Shogunate did not ban the construction of large ships or ocean-going junks. Instead, it restricted the construction of large naval warships such as *atake-bune*. In fact, the Shogunate granted the requests of the Kumamoto and Sendai Domains when they asked for permission to build junks, and in 1669, it ordered Suetsugu Heizō-Shigetomo, the fourth Governor of Nagasaki, to build a *tōsen* (Tang ship). The shogunate used the ship in the exploration of the Ogasawara Islands and their vicinity in 1675, and the information obtained on this voyage later became the basis for Japan's territorial claim on the islands.

However, by the eighteenth century, the period covered in Part 3, ocean-going junks had ceased to be built in the Japanese Archipelago. Instead, this period saw dramatic developments in domestic transportation by water. Various types of ships were used, which can be roughly classified as either riverboats or seagoing ships. The seagoing vessels can be further divided into two groups on the basis of structure. One group consisted of ships of the *tanaita zukuri* type that were used in the Seto Inland Sea and the Pacific Ocean. The other group was ships built using the *omoki zukuri*[31] technique used in the Sea of Japan. Ships called "*bezaisen*"[32] had been in use before the eighteenth century in the Seto Inland Sea and the Pacific Ocean but came into such extensive use throughout the Japanese Archipelago during this century that they became almost synonymous with merchant ships. The word "*wasen*" (Japanese-style ships or Japanese junks) most commonly refers to the *bezaisen* style of ship. There were two factors that made *bezaisen* so popular. First, they could be built rather easily and at a low cost, using only ordinary wooden plates and beams with no special materials required. Second, they performed extremely well on the water. Variants of *bezaisen*-type vessels were widely used along

---

31 *Omoki-zukuri* is a technique that combines a chamfer strip at both sides of the bottom of the ship for fortification. The advantage of this is it reduces the damage when sailing on shoaly waters.
32 "*Bezaisen*" generally means small Japanese vessels with a single square sail and a flat bottom. It gradually became the predominant ocean-going vessel of the Edo period due to its speed and capacity.

the coastal waters of the Japanese Archipelago and in the Sea of Japan alike, with cargo ships called "*higakikaisen*" and "*tarukaisen*"[33] serving the former, and those called "*kitamae-bune*"[34] sailing the latter.

The hull of a *bezaisen* was built by forming a flat base structure similar to a keel, known as a "*kawara*", by joining several planks side by side; builders then connected the lowest *tanaita* to either side of the *kawara*, fitting the second *tanaita* on top of this and so on. The ship had a single mast that carried one square cotton sail hoisted at the center of the hull, a style adopted by cargo ships by the mid-seventeenth century. By the early eighteenth century, improvements in sailing techniques made it possible for *bezaisen* to navigate solely by sail without relying on oars and paddles. Moreover, the rudder gradually became larger to support larger cargoes. For example, in the latter half of the eighteenth century, large ships with a carrying capacity of 1,000 *koku,* (approximately 150 tons) had a massive rudder with a surface area of about ten square meters.

When long-distance trade thrived during the eighteenth century, increasingly larger ships were built and even *sengoku-bune*, which boasted a carrying capacity of 1,000 *koku* were not uncommon. It should be kept in mind, however, that smaller ships with a carrying capacity of 200 *koku* (thirty tons) or less formed the vast majority of cargo ships active in domestic water transport.

### Ships of the Korean Peninsula
In the Korean Peninsula, merchants of Silla were actively engaged in external trade in the ninth century, but little is known about the ships they used. The remains of several ships used in the coastal waters during the Goryeo Dynasty from the early tenth to the late fourteenth century have

---

33 A *higakikaisen* was a cargo ship carrying mixed cargo commissioned by several consigners. The term "*higaki*" derived from wicker fences made of bamboo that were erected on both sides of the ship to keep cargo from falling off, while "*kaisen*" signified cargo ships circulating along the coast. In 1730, *tarukaisen* (cargo ships exclusively for transporting saké barrels) went into service independently from *higakikaisen*, and as they eventually began to carry cargo other than saké barrels, they came into competition with *higakikaisen*.
34 *Kitamae-bune* was a collective name for cargo ships that carried products from Ezo (now Hokkaido) and the Hokuriku district to Osaka along a westward marine route. They were also called "*bezaisen*" in the northern districts. Many of the owners of these ships were based in the coastal areas facing the Sea of Japan, and they often carried out commercial dealings in the capacity of consigners.

been discovered on the western coast. Built mainly with pine wood, they had flat bottoms and bows. Instead of bulkheads and frame timbers, they were equipped with several bars called "*garyong-mok*" that were horizontally slotted in to reinforce the hull. Throughout the pre-modern period, stocky and box-shaped ships built with thick pine planks were common along the coast of the Korean Peninsula, especially on the western coast, and were common features of fishing boats, cargo vessels and warships alike. Compared with junks and *bezaisen*, these ships were relatively less efficient. Because of their shallow draft, they were also unfit for navigating in the open sea with its large waves. Nonetheless, they were suitable for sailing through shallow waters with extensive tidal flats, where they proved more competent at avoiding running aground or being overturned.

During the Goryeo Dynasty, although maritime interaction was dominated by junks operated by Han Chinese maritime merchants, ships built in Korea likely also engaged in international commerce alongside these junks. Unfortunately, no specific information about them is available. During the Joseon Dynasty from the late fourteenth to the mid-nineteenth century, maritime interactions with China were almost totally suspended, with rare cases involving ships that drifted ashore. Yet, from time to time the dynasty continued to dispatch envoy ships to Japan. Korean vessels that visited Japan during the Edo period carrying the Tongsinsa (Goodwill Missions) seem to have been ships with flat bottoms that were built in fundamentally the same way as earlier Korean vessels, with some contrivances to make the ships' hulls proficient enough for open-sea voyages. In its interactions with China during this period, the Joseon Dynasty sometimes sent missions to the Shandong Peninsula across the Yellow Sea when land transport was obstructed. Apparently, it was possible to navigate flat-bottomed ships over such a short distance with relatively calm waters.

### *Navigational skills and religious worship*
Several centuries ago it must have taken tremendous courage to traverse the vast expanse of open sea out of sight of land. Many sailors likely felt far more at ease sailing closer to shore, even if this involved the constant danger of running aground. They would have preferred to remain in coastal waters and wait for a favorable wind or an improvement in the weather, then carefully choose their route by using various landmarks to confirm their position. Firm knowledge of the ocean currents, dangerous spots in

the waters, astronomy, meteorology and geography are all essential prerequisites for crossing the ocean. A deficiency in any of these makes it extremely difficult to directly cross a vast expanse of waters such as the East China Sea.

The *kentōshi-sen*, ships of imperial embassies dispatched to the Tang Dynasty from Japan in the seventh to ninth centuries, sailed along the route that stretched from Iki and Tsushima, then proceeded north along the western coast of the Korean Peninsula before crossing the Yellow Sea to the Shandong Peninsula. The entire journey almost exclusively involved coastal navigation and was thus fairly free from maritime accidents. Because of subsequent changes in the political climate on the Korean Peninsula, the route was changed to one that directly crossed the East China Sea. However, out of a total of eight embassies dispatched along this route, only one mission managed to complete a round trip safely.

As the accumulated body of basic information necessary for navigation gradually increased and magnetic compasses came into wider use, traversing the East China Sea became less arduous. The performance of ships improved through innovations in the design of the hull, sail and rudder. Significant sailing skills that allowed the ship to make headway even in adverse or cross winds were developed and refined, making it possible for ships to sail the open sea for much longer periods of time than previously. Consequently, during the three periods discussed in this volume, it was already common practice to sail across the East and South China Seas.

Nonetheless, voyages inevitably met with misfortune from time to time. An unexpected sudden change in the weather or trouble with the hull sometimes made it difficult for a ship to stay on the water. Especially when sailing near the coast, where the gap between the ebb and flow was large, great caution was required in order to avoid running aground. According to statistics recorded in Meiji Japan during the 1880s and 1890s, Japanese-style vessels met with accidents at sea between two and four percent of the time. This accident rate is around the same for ships operated by the various East India companies of European countries during the seventeenth to eighteenth centuries. This seems to suggest that this frequency of mishap for ocean-going ships was unavoidable, regardless of regional difference.

Safe sailing was the common wish of people living with the sea. They continued to sail while praying to their gods for safety at sea and reading the portents. Such prayer and faith in their gods also served as an anchor for maritime peoples when dealing with the unstoppable forces of Nature. The focus of people's prayers differed significantly from one locality to the next or from one group of people to another. Originally, fishing people and seafarers used to pray to the ancestral deities of their native places for help. As the traffic of trade ships increased, some port towns began to enshrine voyage-protecting deities of their own, such as Zhaobao qilang-shen (a deity for sea merchants) of Ningbo and Tongyuan-wan (a deity for long-distance voyagers) of Quanzhou. There were also deities enshrined in port towns along the naval route, including Bozu-shen (Lord of the Ships), worshiped by people of Han Chinese descent on the southern coast of Hainan Island, and the Fanshen-miao (mausoleum of the foreign deity), worshiped by people of Muslim descent. Deities were also worshiped across local boundaries, such as Longwang-shen (Dragon King of the Four Seas), the apotheosis of storms and dangerous points along naval routes, and Guanyin (the Goddess of Mercy) and Shouye-shen (Night-watch God) who both derived from Buddhist scriptures. In addition to these, there were deities of navigation with close ties to state authorities who were believed to protect official envoys and warships, including Donghai-shen (God of the East Sea) and Nanhai-shen (God of the South Sea) in China and Korea, and Hachiman-shin (God of War) in Japan. These deities were mostly enshrined in places closely related to navigation: atop mountains clearly visible from the sea; on small islets at the mouths of ports where tidal currents were complex; inside ports and at wharves where ships dropped anchor; and near the wellsprings of rivers and streams. While on board, seafarers prayed in the morning and evening to charms, talismans or painted images that were pasted or hung on the ship's hull. Larger sea-going ships sometimes even had a small altar set up in the captain's cabin in which the statue of a deity was enshrined.

Well-known Japanese guardians of sea travel included the deities of the Sumiyoshi-jinja Shrine, Konpira-gū and Kan'non (Cn. Guanyin). Even modern visitors to local port towns across the country will undoubtedly find shrines or temples for safe navigation standing quietly near the seashore. In times past, people whose livelihoods were closely related to the sea likely frequented these shrines or temples, dedicating *ema* to the deities and earnestly praying for safe passage.

The Chinese sea goddess and protector of seafarers Mazu (Jp. Maso), meaning "mother-ancestor", is well known for expanding from being a local deity to one worshiped throughout much of maritime East Asia. According to legend, the goddess was born with spiritual powers to the Lin family on Meizhou Island near Putian in Fujian Province during the Song Dynasty. First revered by local seafarers, the worship of Mazu spread as they became more active along coastal areas of China. Mazu-miao (Mazu mausoleums) were built in one port town after another, and the practice of installing a small statue of Mazu onboard a ship also proliferated. At times, she was syncretically associated with well-known Buddhist and other religious figures, with worshipers asserting that she was a reincarnation of Guan-yin or a daughter of the Dragon King.

During the Song Dynasty, Mazu was a goddess of navigation worshiped only in the southern part of Fujian Province. However, during the period discussed in Part 2 of this volume, she became a deity worshiped countrywide and was given the title of Tianfei (Queen of Heaven) by the Emperor of the Yuan Dynasty in commemoration of her distinguished service during the subjugation of the Southern Song and her role as protector of maritime travel. During the period covered by Part 2, the worship of Mazu spread to various parts of East Asia alongside a legend that resounded in the hearts of seafarers: after using her spiritual powers in an attempt to save her father and brother when they met with disaster at sea, Mazu was only able to save her father, so she threw herself off a cliff into the sea out of grief for her brother. During the period covered by Part 3, Mazu was moreover given the title of Tianhou (Empress of Heaven) by the Kangxi Emperor[35] of the Qing Dynasty in commemoration of her distinguished service in defeating the Zheng clan's administration in Taiwan. During this period, the worship of Mazu developed in the Japanese Archipelago and elsewhere in unique ways. Even today, we can see Maso-dō (Mazu temples) erected in the compounds of Kōfukuji Temple and Sōfukuji Temple in Nagasaki, both of which are *tōdera* (Chinese temples founded by Chinese merchants). Upon entering these halls, we see shelves fixed to the wall on either side for enshrining Mazu statues. When entering Nagasaki, Chinese ships temporarily deposited their Mazu statues on the shelves in these halls, and then returned them back to the ships before leaving port. Mazu mausoleums and halls that still survive in

---

35 The fourth emperor of the Qing Dynasty, Aixin-Jueluo Xuanye (1654–1722), reigned from 1661 to 1722. He stabilized the Qing Empire by suppressing the Sanfan (Three Feudatories) in South China and the Zheng clan in control of Taiwan, by driving Russia out of the Heilong-jiang region in North China and by subordinating North Mongolia to Qing rule.

various coastal areas of the East Asian maritime region may be regarded as witnesses of the history of maritime interactions.

Now, the stage seems set, and it is time for the drama to unfold. The curtain is rising for the main part of a three-act drama traversing three periods of the East Asian maritime region. We sincerely hope you enjoy the story to your heart's content.

# Part 1
# The Open Sea, from 1250 to 1350

**Figure 2: Map of maritime East Asia, 1250–1350**

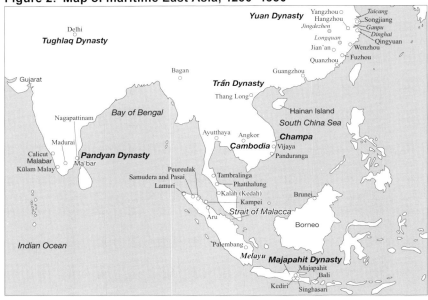

## 1.1: General Overview

In East Asia, the century from 1250 to 1350 witnessed the collapse of the Southern Song Dynasty and its replacement by the hegemony of the Yuan Dynasty of the Mongol Empire. This period corresponds to the latter half of the Goryeo period in Korea and from the middle Kamakura to the first half of the Northern and Southern Courts period in Japan.

The characteristics of maritime East Asia of this period are best understood through the keyword "open". This "openness" can be roughly described by reference to the following elements.

Firstly, interactions in maritime East Asia in this period consisted mainly of maritime trade. However, these interactions were not confined to the East and South China Sea regions. They opened out into the wider world and became part of more extensive webs of interaction that spread across the eastern and western parts of the Eurasian continent and the Indian Ocean.

Secondly, ethnically and religiously diverse "outlanders" actively traveled between regions, established communities in various locales and integrated into local societies. Their networks constituted the foundations upon which maritime interactions were built.

Thirdly, the various levels of political power of each coastal area took relatively relaxed and flexible approaches toward regulating seaborne trade. In some cases, these authorities actively protected and promoted trade. Trade and other interactions were actively conducted even in circumstances where political tensions existed between countries.

This chapter surveys the distinctive nature of these three characteristics through a study of representative examples, revealing a macroscopic image of the East Asian maritime world of this period.

## Maritime East Asia opens to Eurasia and the Indian Ocean

An outlander named Marco Polo[1] depicted maritime East Asia as it was 700 years ago. He left us a record of his experiences, documenting his departure from Venice, crossing of the Eurasian continent and arrival in China. On his return journey, he traveled the South China Sea, crossed the Indian Ocean and passed through the Persian Gulf toward the Mediterranean Sea by ship. He saw with his own eyes the greater part of maritime Asia[2] at that time.

> You must know that the sea in which these islands [island of Chipangu] lie, is called the Sea of Chin, which means the sea opposite Manji, for in the language of the islanders, Chin means Manji. This sea stretches to the east. According to the good sailors and pilots that navigate it, and who know the truth, there are 7448 islands in it, the majority of which are inhabited. [...] When the ships of Zaitun [Quanzhou] and Kinsai [Hangzhou] sail thither, they obtain great profit and gain, but they toil a whole year on their voyage, for they go in winter and return in summer, as only two kinds of wind blow there – one which carries them out, and one that brings them home again: one blows in summer, and one in winter. [...] Moreover, I will add that this sea, though I have said that it is called the Sea of Chin, yet is nothing but the Ocean Sea. They call it the Sea of Chin, just as we speak of the Sea of England, or the Sea of Rochelle; in the same way do they speak in these parts of the Sea of Chin, the Sea of India, and so on. But in every case they are all parts of the Ocean Sea.
>
> (Marco Polo 1994: 276)

In this passage, Marco Polo mentions "the Sea of Chin" in his chapter concerning Chipangu, namely, Japan. Some say that Polo's use of the phrase "the Sea of Chin" shows that he confused the present-day East China Sea with the South China Sea. However, it is more appropriate to understand the phrase as encompassing both the East and South China Seas within a single oceanic region, since Polo's knowledge was based on Islamic and

---

1 Marco Polo (1254–1324) was a Venetian merchant who traveled to China at the time of the Yuan Dynasty, served Qubilai Qa'an and recorded his travels in *Description of the World*.
2 This chapter provisionally uses the phrase "maritime Asia" to denote the maritime region that spreads from the East China Sea and its neighboring seas toward the Indian Ocean.

## 1.1: General Overview

Ptolemaic geographical conceptions[3] associated with the western part of Eurasia, rather than Chinese ones.

Polo's understanding of the unity of the China Sea and Indian Ocean worlds is evident in his description of seasonal monsoons. Monsoons are a natural phenomenon distinctive of not only the East and South China Seas, but also the Indian Ocean. Furthermore, the timing of monsoons determines the movement of ships connecting these seas together. Polo's description presupposes that "the Sea of India" extends from the area beyond "the Sea of Chin".

In fact, Quanzhou, which Polo describes as Zaitun, located in the Fujian region of China and the largest trading port of maritime Asia at that time, was directly connected to the Indian Ocean. This port enjoyed a level of prosperity that can be regarded as unparalleled even on a global scale. Let us turn again to Polo's description.

> At the end of the five days, one reaches a very large and noble city, called Zaitun. Here is the harbor whither all the ships of India come, with much costly merchandise, quantities of precious stones of great value, and many fine large pearls. It is also the port whither go the merchants of Manji, which is the region stretching all around. In a word, in this port there is such traffic of merchandise, precious stones, and pearls, that it is truly a wondrous sight. From the harbor of this city all this is distributed over the whole of the province of Manji. And I assure you that for one shipload of pepper that goes to Alexandria or elsewhere to be taken to Christian lands, there come a hundred to this port to Zaitun. For you must know that it is one of the two greatest harbors in the world for the amount of its trade.
> 
> (Marco Polo 1994: 263–264)

Polo's account states that an endless stream of merchant ships from India docked at the port of Quanzhou and that merchants flocked there from across South China. This shows that the South China Sea connected maritime East Asia and the Indian Ocean as a nodal region and that Quanzhou was the nodal point connecting sea and overland

---

3 The geographical concepts of ancient Greece and Rome, as represented by the astronomer and geographer Ptolemy (circa. second century), were later accepted and further developed under the Islamic society of West Asia and North Africa, from where they were transmitted to Medieval Europe.

routes. Marco remarked that Quanzhou was "one of the two greatest harbors in the world", which was no exaggeration. Ibn Battuta[4], a Muslim from Morocco and the most famous traveler in the Islamic world, made a similar evaluation in his account of his journeys from 1325–1354.

> When we had crossed the sea the first city to which we came was Zaitun. There are no olives in it, or in the whole of China and India, but it has been given this name. It is a huge and important city in which are manufactured the fabrics of velvet, damask, and satin which are known by its name and which are superior to those of Khansā and Khān Bāliq. Its harbor is among the biggest in the world, or rather is the biggest; I have seen about a hundred big junks there and innumerable little ones. It is a great gulf of the sea which runs inland till it mingles with the great river.
>
> (Ibn Battuta 1994: 894)

Ibn Battuta crossed the sea as an envoy of the Tughlaq Dynasty located in Delhi, India. He arrived in China in the 1340s and also returned to the Maghrib region (northwestern Africa) by ship. As one of many Muslims who plied the seas of maritime Asia, his travelogue shows that the South China Sea's role as a nodal region enabled interconnectivity between maritime East Asia and the Indian Ocean.

The hegemony of the Mongol Empire made much of this situation possible. Rising to power on the Mongolian Plateau at the beginning of the thirteenth century, by the time of Marco Polo, the Mongol Empire had expanded from Korea in the east to West Asia and the Russian Plain in the west. As a result, a period of political stability known as the "Pax Mongolica" extended over a wide area. The circulation of people and goods as well as the transfer of culture and information linking the Eurasian continent and the Indian Ocean peaked under its aegis. The period of the thirteenth to fourteenth century became one of the most

---

4  Ibn Battuta (1304–1368) was an Islamic legal scholar. He departed from Morocco on a pilgrimage to Mecca in 1325 and is thought to have later traveled as far as China via West Asia, Central Asia, India, Sumatra and Java. He wrote *A Gift to Those Who Contemplate the Wonders of Cities and the Marvels of Traveling*, usually abbreviated as *The Travels* (*Rhila*).

active periods in terms of the interactions between the eastern and western parts of Eurasia, as the area around the Mediterranean Sea and the Islamic World were connected to East Asia by Central Eurasian and Indian Ocean intermediaries.

For example, according to a merchant handbook entitled *La Pratica della Mercatura* / The Practice of Commerce written by Francesco Balducci Pegolòtti of Compagnia dei Bardi, an Italian company based in Florence, the Mongol Empire stationed Mongolian guardsmen along the roads it maintained along the trade route from the Mediterranean to China via Anatolia, guaranteeing safe travel day and night except in cases of rebellion or a change of government.

Although the maritime routes were neither ruled nor regulated by the Mongol Empire, the pre-existing monsoonal traffic network continued to function and exhibited stability that roughly correlated with the "Pax Mongolica". Ibn Battuta commented on one of the key players who contributed to that stability. According to his account, Abyssinians (Ethiopians) were famous for being "guarantors of safety on this sea; let there be but one of them on a ship and it will be avoided by the Indian pirates and idolators" (Ibn Battuta 1994: 800).

In this way, the stability of and connections among the overland and sea routes made it possible for the east-west traffic of the time to flourish. This age culminated in the structural interconnection of the Eurasian continent with maritime Asia. Under the land-based Mongol hegemony, multiple cores of maritime interactions, including the East and South China Seas, the Indian Ocean and the Mediterranean Sea, were linked to form a large circulating current in conjunction with the trunk lines of the Eurasian continent. From a standpoint emphasizing the transportation and exchange of people and goods, this space can be called the "Pan Eurasian Interaction Sphere". Maritime East Asia at this time constituted part of this interaction sphere. The region not only consisted of the East and South China Seas, but also maintained close connections to the Indian Ocean, open to East and West Eurasia.

## Agents of diffusion and coexistence

Marco Polo and Ibn Battuta represent but two of the myriad individuals with diverse origins and religions who traveled maritime Asia in this period. Some entered local governments while at the same time establishing communities in those regions. Concentrating their communities in coastal areas, they inspired additional outlanders to come and provided facilities for their reception, stimulating maritime interaction. Particularly remarkable in this regard were Muslim and Chinese maritime merchants.

For example, following the description of Quanzhou cited above, Ibn Battuta explained as follows:

> The Muslims live in a separate city. On the day I arrived I saw there the amir who had been sent to India as ambassador with the present, had been in our company and had been in the junk which sank. He greeted me, and informed the head of the customs about me, and he installed me in handsome lodgings. I received visits from the qāḍī of the Muslims, Tāj al-Dīn of Ardabīl, a distinguished and generous man, from the Shaikh al-Islām Kamāl al-Dīn 'Abdallāh of Iṣfahān, a pious man, and from the important merchants, among them Sharaf al-Dīn of Tabrīz, one of the merchants from whom I borrowed money when I arrived in India, and the one whose dealings were best. He knows the Qu'rān by heart and recites it very often. As these merchants live in infidel country they are delighted when a Muslim arrives among them. They say: "He has come from the land of Islam," and give him the legal alms due on their property so that he becomes as rich as one of them. Among the pious shaikhs there was Burhān al-Dīn of Kāzarūn who had a hospice outside the town and to whom the merchants make the oblations made to Shaikh Abū Isḥāq of Kāzarūn.
>
> (Ibn Battuta 1994: 894)

In this account we can see how religious groups, government officials and merchants collaborated to establish communities that supported maritime interaction. Ibn Battuta mentioned the name of some of the people who took care of him in Quanzhou, including the *sāhib dīwān* (head of customs), *shaykh* (elders), the *qāḍī* of the Muslims (judge) and important merchants. Each Muslim community in maritime Asia included elders and judges, who provided leadership in religious matters and legal judgments. Ibn Battuta's use of the term "*sāhib dīwān*" here likely refers to a Muslim who held an important position in the local government of the Yuan Dynasty. Ibn Battuta's account also shows that merchants played extremely important roles when Muslim communities received outlanders. When merchants crossed the seas and forged links with communities in distant lands, it was the centers of worship located in each locale that supported much of their interaction. The religious order of Shaykh Abū Isḥāq of Kāzarūn[5], which Ibn Battuta mentions above, established hospices in a string of port cities extending from the Persian Gulf to the South China Sea. Hospices served as lodgings and houses of worship for maritime merchants from China, India and other lands. Muslim communities across maritime Asia were thus connected by both commercial and religious networks.

Although they differed in several respects from their Muslim counterparts, from the ninth century such communities were also established by Chinese maritime merchants in ports of call on the coasts of the East and South China Seas.

Chinese sea merchants often cooperated with local merchants and seafarers and worked as diplomatic and commercial intermediaries between the governments of the places they lived in or visited and China. Their activities allowed local societies to accumulate the technology and knowledge required to expand into the maritime world, thereby laying the foundation for later maritime interactions by the people of each society.

In this way, the multi-layered, complex structures and diverse networks of coastal societies transcended local political boundaries and spread over ever widening areas. These networks were linked together, making possible and stimulating maritime trade and other forms of exchange.

## The leniency and flexibility of political powers

In maritime East Asia at the time, political states and other political authorities attempted to regulate people's activities in the maritime region primarily through the administration of port cities.

---

5 The Kāzarūn religious order was a Ṣufi order established by Shaykh Abū Isḥāq (963–1033) of Kāzarūn, Persia. Talismans issued by this order were used by sailors and merchants to pray for safe voyages and prosperous trade.

For example, in Song-Yuan China, an office known as the *shibosi* (maritime trade supervisorate) operated in major port cities. Maritime trade supervisors inspected and managed arriving and departing merchants, ships and commodities. From the latter half of the thirteenth century, merchants involved with maritime trade in the South China Sea and Indian Ocean (the Nanhai trade) also fell subject to regulation by the Yuan Dynasty's highest levels of regional administration, known as *xingsheng* (branch secretariats), as well as the *xingquanfusi* (branch of supervising money bureau)[6]. Involvement by these offices enabled investment by the *ortuy* (mercantile association sponsored by the Yuan Dynasty). However, these institutions were unable to rigorously control the activities of ships beyond their ports and did not restrict the freedom of action enjoyed by maritime merchants. Even though strict rules were formally established, in actual practice, the institutions came to approach the management of overseas trade flexibly, or at least acted with a certain degree of leniency.

Furthermore, the control over ports exercised by the dynasty did not necessarily inhibit maritime interactions. Ibn Battuta, providing a Muslim's perspective, wrote that the Yuan Dynasty's control over trade and ports was more rigid and strict than that of other areas. He observed that this severity helped make the trade routes secure. That is, in the background of the prosperity of the flourishing seaborne traffic in maritime East Asia, political authorities supported the trade by assuming risk management and providing security.

By 1345, when Ibn Battuta arrived in China, the Yuan Dynasty had changed its posture toward maritime interactions from a passive to an active stance. Whereas in earlier years China had restricted its activities to receiving traveling merchant ships, conducting inspections and imposing taxes, by this time the number of cases in which government officials directly provided capital to merchants and had them carry out public trade on their behalf increased. This shift from a

---

6 Mongol and Turkic rulers entrusted the management of capital to partners, known as "*ortuy*" merchants. During the Mongol Empire, this role was performed mainly by Muslim and Uigur merchants. During the Yuan Dynasty, the *xingquanfusi* oversaw investment in overall management of the privileged merchant associations. A branch of the *xingquanfusi* was established at Hangzhou and Longxing to administer *ortuy* affairs in South China.

passive to an active posture is not unrelated to the unprecedented expansion of trade encompassing the entire Eurasian continent that Mongol hegemony made possible. This trend was also spurred on by the Yuan Dynasty's recruitment of many commercially connected Uigurs[7] and Muslims from West and Central Asia as officials in its finance ministry.

Interaction in maritime East Asia was also significantly impacted by political tensions among states in the region. In 1305, a merchant ship

**Photo 1: Stone carving of ancient Arabic writing in Quanzhou**
Source: Enomoto Wataru.

---

7 The Uigurs were Turkic nomads who originally inhabited the Mongol Plateau and who, after displacing the Eastern Turks (Tujue), ruled that region from 744 to 840. When the Uigur regime collapsed, a part of these people migrated south and settled in the Tarim Basin, becoming active as merchants. Under the Mongol Empire, they widened their sphere of activity by becoming officials and merchants in many lands. The term "Uigurs" as it is used today is a collective term that has been newly applied in the twentieth century to Turkic Muslim inhabitants of East Turkistan.

carrying Ryūzan Tokken, a Zen monk from the Shimōsa region in Japan, arrived at Qingyuan (present-day Ningbo, Zhejiang Province) from Japan. He was on his way to study with a monk named Dongyan Jingri[8] at Tiantong Temple in Qingyuan, one of the five most prestigious Zen temples in China. Tokken had formerly been a pupil of Yishan Yining of Engakuji Temple[9] in Kamakura. Yishan was a Chinese monk who had been sent to Japan in 1299 as a Yuan Dynasty envoy demanding tribute from the ruler of Japan, but he was taken into custody by the Kamakura Shogunate. In recognition of his high status, he was not executed, as previous Yuan envoys to Japan had been. He was later released, and then headed various Zen temples in Kamakura and Kyoto, accepting many Japanese monks as his pupils. Tokken presumably heard about contemporary China while studying under Yining and had set his heart on studying there.

Tokken's travels did not go smoothly. The first of the several hardships he experienced occurred at the time of his arrival in China. According to Tokken's biography, the Yuan government had at that time raised the tax rate on Japanese ships and prohibited the disembarkation of merchants and monks. This ban on disembarkation is also confirmed by Yuan Dynasty documents, which show that there were provisions prohibiting Japanese from entering the inner city upon the arrival of Japanese ships, while nevertheless ordering the continuation of trade. To evade this prohibition, Tokken entered the city unbeknownst to government officials by climbing over the wall of the inner city, but was subsequently captured by the master of the house into which he had stolen. However, when Tokken explained his aspiration to continue his religious studies, the master was impressed and begged officials to exempt Tokken from their law, enabling him to finally reach Tiantong Temple.

Although the Yuan court found trade with Japan appealing, it approached the Japanese who arrived by ship cautiously. Shortly after Tokken's arrival,

---

8 Dongyan Jingri (1221–1308) was a priest of Linji (Jp. Rinzai) Chan (Jp. Zen) Buddhism in Yuan Dynasty China. A native of Douchang, Nankang-lu, he became the forty-seventh head priest of Qingyuan Tiantong Temple.
9 Engakuji Temple was endowed in 1282 by Hōjō Tokimune, eighth regent of the Kamakura Shogunate and founded by the Southern Song monk Wuxue Zuyuan. In recognition of this political patronage and religious importance, Engakuji temple held the second rank in the Five Mountains (Gozan) system into which Kamakura Zen temples were organized.

the court found further reason for concern. In 1309, Japanese merchants indignant over what they saw as unfair practices of Qingyuan's trade administrators set official buildings on fire using sulfur, which they had brought as merchandise. The fire spread through Qingyuan's densely populated city and caused extensive damage. The Yuan government enacted emergency security measures, while merchant ships returning to Japan brought rumors of a third Mongol invasion. The Kamakura Shogunate responded by ordering temples and shrines to pray for the defeat of foreign invaders. The Yuan court suspected Japanese monks resident in China of involvement in the incident, ordering their arrest at temples in various locations. Monks suffered banishment and even at times execution. Tokken himself was sent to Luoyang, where he spent a number of years. Similar roundups of Japanese occurred occasionally thereafter.

Much of Yuan officials' concern regarding Japan derived from wariness about possible counteroffensives from that country in the wake of the empire's two failed invasions of Japan in 1274 and 1281, which will be explored in greater detail below. Yuan also dispatched troops to Java, Champa[10] and the Trần Dynasty[11] of North Vietnam. These states all refused demands to send tribute and disobeyed requests for military cooperation. Such foreign wars fought by the Yuan added a distinctive feature to the conditions of maritime East Asia in this period.

However, despite these political and military tensions, once the wars ended, Yuan trade with these regions thrived. According to some

---

10 The name "Champa" denotes polities of the Cham people who inhabited the central and southern part of Vietnam from about the second century. Chinese historical sources record the name in various ways, including Linyi, Huanwang, Zhanpobai and Zhancheng. In 1471, the Cham capital Vijaya was captured in an attack by the Later Leê Dynasty of North Vietnam and the surviving Cham were conquered by the Nguyễn Dynasty at the end of the seventeenth century. Under Nguyễn rule, Champa continued to exist in the form of vassal states, which retained certain autonomous powers until 1832.
11 The Trần Dynasty (1225–1400) originated as a coastal maritime power and ruled North Vietnam after the Lý Dynasty. The Trần initiated development of the Red River Delta. At the end of the thirteenth century, they repelled attacks by the Yuan Dynasty, but declined at the end of the fourteenth century after failing to defeat Champa.

estimates, maritime interactions flourished more in this period than in any other age. In fact, the fourteenth century saw the largest confirmed number of Japanese monks cross the sea to Mainland China in the entire pre-modern period. This indicates that the merchant ships used by monks sailed between Japan and China at a nearly constant frequency.

Japan assumed a similar attitude toward the Yuan Empire: maintaining military alertness while permitting trade to continue. There is little evidence that either Japan's imperial court (the aristocratic government) or the shogunate (warrior government) attempted to restrict ships engaged in overseas trade. Moreover, both the court and shogunate themselves became involved in the trade with the Yuan as patrons in order to raise the capital required to construct and maintain temples and shrines. Maritime interactions were "open" in the sense that political authorities across maritime East Asia exerted only lenient, flexible control over ports while becoming increasingly active in trade. Authorities maintained and even extended their involvement in trade even with the existence of ongoing political and military tensions.

## Two arenas of maritime East Asia

Having outlined the open nature of interaction in maritime East Asia, let us now sketch its spatial contours as a region in this period, consisting of two parallel arenas of interaction.

The first arena extended westward from the South China Sea to the Indian Ocean. In this area, part of the trunk line of the "Pan Eurasian Interaction Sphere" made possible by the Pax Mongolica, Muslim, Chinese and other maritime merchants of various ethnicities and religions engaged in multilateral trade. This multilateral trade network continued to function even after several of the regimes that succeeded the Mongol Empire in various regions collapsed in the latter half of the fourteenth century[12]. It was only in the mid-fifteenth century,

---

12  After the Mongol conquests, Činggis Qan's sons and grandsons established several successor regimes: the Yuan Dynasty, the Ilkhanate, the Qipchaq Khanate (Golden Horde) of Činggis Qan's son Joči and the Čagatai Khanate of Central Asia.

when the Oirat Mongols[13] expanded their sphere of influence on the Mongolian Plateau and the Ming court grew less receptive to maritime interaction, that the integrity of the Pan Eurasian Interaction Sphere gradually eroded.

The second arena centered on the East China Sea, extending from the Yellow Sea to the South China Sea. This arena developed around a central axis linking South China, particularly Zhejiang and Fujian Provinces, Japan, Korea and insular Southeast Asia. Prior to thirteenth century, Chinese maritime merchants played key roles. Then, from around the fourteenth century, local merchants in each area began to take center stage. After the latter half of the fourteenth century, these local merchants formed domains of trade that variously competed and overlapped with the networks of Chinese maritime merchants. In this period, the policies of political authorities on the rim of this network profoundly influenced the conditions of maritime exchange. In particular, the Ming Dynasty, which succeeded the Yuan, enacted the maritime restriction system (*haijin*) that limited external relations in the maritime region to tributary relations. The acceptance by neighboring countries of Ming regulations increasingly demonstrated the impact of the projection of a land-based state logic onto maritime interactions. On the other hand, in reaction to such policies, the resistance to state control among maritime actors gradually increased.

These two arenas were not clearly spatially divided by the extents of the South and East China Seas, but they overlapped each other along the axis formed by the nodal areas of both seas, such as the Zhejiang-Fujian region, the Ryukyu Islands and Vietnam. The difference between the two lay in the identities of the agents of maritime interaction. Whereas those of the first consisted of a diverse group of maritime merchants that included Muslims and Chinese, Chinese maritime merchants seized the

---

13  The Oirats were a powerful nomadic tribe who inhabited a region stretching from the northwest of the Mongolian Plateau to southern Siberia at the time of the founding of the Mongol Empire. They gained influence through marriage with members of Činggis Qan's line. The Oirats retained immense power even after the collapse of the governments established by members of Činggis Qan's family. In the fifteenth century, they unified the Mongolian Plateau under the leadership of Esen Taiš, and by the seventeenth century, ruled a vast region stretching from west of the Mongolian Plateau to eastern Turkestan as the Dzungar Khanate.

initiative in the second. This pattern continued for some time in maritime East Asia, even after the disintegration of the Pan Eurasian Interaction Sphere. However, after the middle of the fifteenth century, Chinese maritime merchants became dominant in China trade connecting the regions north of the Strait of Malacca. As these merchants strengthened their cooperative connections, the East and South China Seas increasingly constituted a single sphere of maritime trade.

# 1.2: The Background to Maritime Interaction and Its Agents

This chapter briefly explains the economic, social and political structures that existed in the various lands connected to the East Asian maritime world in the period from 1250 to 1350 and introduces the major figures involved in maritime interactions at the time, as well as the groups and institutions to which they belonged. Subsequent chapters provide more detailed descriptions of the situation in maritime East Asia outlined in Chapter 1.1.

## Societal movements surrounding maritime East Asia

From the eighth or ninth century, during the Tang Dynasty, South China began to develop as a result of canal improvements and the expansion of available farmland, causing a large-scale migration of people. As a result, the economic hub began shifting toward southeast coastal areas such as Zhejiang, Fujian and Guangdong. This transition continued during the period from 1250 to 1350.

During the Yuan period, these areas fell within the administrative jurisdiction of the Jiangzhe Branch Secretariat and Jiangxi Branch Secretariat. The former accounted for thirty-seven percent of the tax income of the Yuan Dynasty at the time, while the latter accounted for ten percent. Thus, these two regions accounted for almost half of the total tax income of the empire. This data fits into a broader trend in the history of Chinese society in which the center of gravity shifted from North China to South China and from inland areas to the coast.

In the meantime, North China, near the political heart of the Yuan Dynasty, experienced a population decline as a result of the desolation that accompanied the interregnum between the Jin Dynasty and the Yuan Dynasty. For example, Shandong's population was between ten and 12.5 million in the twelfth century, at the end of the Northern Song Dynasty and the beginning of the Jin Dynasty. However, the Mongol invasions and the ensuing disorder caused significant devastation such that at one point the population fell as low as 4.5 million. Although the cultivation of farmlands and the development of salt fields and mines were promoted as a means to rebuild Shandong in the latter half of the thirteenth century, the population remained at around eight million even into the first half of the fourteenth century. Overall decline in the north is further evidenced by the fact that coastal traffic was taken over by shipping concerns from South China.

Under these circumstances, commerce and distribution continued to develop in accordance with a pattern that existed before 1250. Under Yuan rule, the northern and southern regions of China, which had previously been politically divided, were connected by new and improved means of overland and water transportation. The development of maritime traffic was particularly remarkable. Tax grain collected in South China, a farm belt, was transported by sea to the Yuan capital, Daidu (present-day Beijing). During this period in Chinese history, sea routes were very important for both domestic and international traffic, including interactions with outlying regions through the East and South China Seas.

In Japan, large-scale improvements in agriculture occurred from around the tenth century. These improvements enabled aristocrats as well as large shrines and temples to transform much of Japan's productive land into *shōen* (private estates)[1] by the thirteenth century, and as a result farming was intensified and productivity improved owing to the propagation of double cropping and dry-field farming techniques. Estates were also dedicated to the production of handicrafts. Agricultural surplus and artisanal production helped stimulate the development of a commercial commodity economy.

New transportation networks linked urban centers, the two large cities of Kyoto and Kamakura, and connected them to rural areas. Among these networks were *kaisen* (shipping organizations) that plied the seas between ports. *Shuku* (post stations) consisting of inns and other facilities along major land routes arose at important traffic nodes. Commercial agents (*toi/toimaru*) based at important distribution nodes professionally

---

1 *Shōen* were territories from which all or part of the tax and labor services owed to the provincial governor's office were exempted by order of the imperial court or provincial governor. Many of these were established by a process of commendation (*kishin*) through which the territories gained the proprietorship and protection of influential families and institutions such as the imperial family, the Fujiwara family of imperial regents, powerful temples or shrines, the Kamakura Shoguns and the main line of the Hōjō family of shogunal regents. In exchange for this protection, estates became part of the economic base of those families and institutions.

## 1.2: The Background to Maritime Interaction and Its Agents

transported, stored and carried out consignment sales of rice and other commodities. To regulate and tax this traffic, the imperial court, the Kamakura and Ashikaga Shogunates, estate proprietors, powerful religious institutions and other authorities all erected barriers and charged tolls. Copper coins imported from China played an important role as a means of exchange in trade and payment. Bills of exchange also came into use.

The Hōjō family[2], which seized de facto power in the Kamakura Shogunate, actively worked to gain control of Japan's major transportation and distribution hubs. By the end of the Kamakura period, the Hōjō counted many of these locations among their territorial holdings. The imperial court of Kyoto also directed its attention to transportation and distribution networks. It began to actively bestow the power of collecting *tsuryō* (port tolls) on large temples and shrines. Buddhist orders also came to focus their attention on the transportation and distribution hubs in conducting their activities. For example, in the middle of the thirteenth century, Saidaiji, a temple of the Precepts (Ritsu) School of Buddhism founded by Eison[3], expanded its activities to post stations and ports around the country while parlaying connections with the Hōjō.

In this way, the wealth generated from the transportation and distribution of commodities increased in importance in Japan at the time. Flourishing overseas trade can be regarded as part of this trend. The fact that a large number of the pirates and other so-called "*akutō*" (evil bands)[4] that became a problem at the time were also engaged in the transportation and distribution of commodities appears to be related to this trend. In addition, this commercialization in the central part of the archipelago contributed to

---

2 The Hōjō were originally a local elite family from Izu who served as functionaries in the Izu provincial governor's office. As the natal family of Hōjō Masako, the main wife of the first Kamakura Shogun, Minamoto no Yoritomo, the Hōjō became powerful vassals during the Kamakura period. Following the death of Minamoto no Yoritomo, the main line of the Hōjō family, the Tokusō, held de facto power in the Kamakura Shogunate.

3 Eison (1201–1290) was from Yamato Province and was a central figure in the movement to revive the monastic precepts in Nara's Buddhist community. He restored the Saidaiji Temple in Yamato, and the Ritsu school of Buddhism spread across Japan from the late Kamakura period onward.

4 The term "*akutō*" denoted groups of powerful local elites who resisted authorities, such as estate proprietors and shogunate from the mid-Kamakura through the era of the war between the Northern and Southern Courts.

the deepening of economic ties with the foreign lands of Ezo (present-day Hokkaido) and Ryukyu.

In Korea, after the twelfth century, swampy lowlands were developed by improving irrigation and introducing new strains of rice, which resulted in the enhancement of agricultural productivity. After the thirteenth century, influential families began to vigorously engage in commercial activities. They established *nongjang* (large estates) in the provinces and the markets of the royal capital flourished.

The largest mode of commodity distribution in Korea at the time was the *joun* (water transportation system) used to send grain tax via sea and river to the royal capital. This task was originally carried out by workers organized out of *jochang* (storehouses) located in thirteen shipping ports around the country. After the twelfth century, as many people became displaced, disturbances broke out and the local government system was reorganized, these storehouses partly or completely lost their function. Each district and county assumed the operation of storehouses in their locale. Still, it can be said that this decentralization broadened the range of people involved in water transportation and promoted the development of the commodity distribution economy. Further, the destabilization of society shook the status hierarchy, giving opportunities for some of those engaged in commerce to enter the political world, which resulted in members of the Goryeo court orienting themselves toward commerce.

In Southeast Asia at that time, aside from a few exceptions such as Java and the Red River basin in North Vietnam, population density remained extremely low. Distributed among these sparsely populated islands and coastal areas were small-scale port polities that were extremely dependent on trade[5]. Among the exceptional cases in mainland Southeast Asia, the Trần Dynasty of Đại Việt in North Vietnam engaged in large-scale, state-driven civil engineering works such as the development of the Red River Delta. This development enabled the population to increase, and the resulting population pressure created conditions that facilitated Đại Việt's continuous push southwards over several centuries.

---

5 Port polities were states that emerged throughout Southeast Asia in trading ports located in the estuaries of rivers and in straits. In estuarine port cities, rulers based their power on the exchange of goods produced in mid- and up-river hinterlands for commodities brought by foreign merchants.

In addition, prior to 1250, Champa in South-Central Vietnam existed as a polity in part by functioning as a way station for seaborne trade. In inland areas, various authorities of Thai descent were dominant. In Chinese documents, they appear as "Xian". They established a series of governments within the territories of present-day Myanmar and Thailand and came into conflict with Cambodian and Vietnamese groups. In the wake of these conflicts, they advanced into coastal areas and confronted the Melayu, who had advanced north from Sumatra. In later years, some groups of Thai descent would found the entrepôt of Ayutthaya[6].

In the meantime, the name San-Fo-Chi[7] began to disappear from the historical records of the thirteenth and fourteenth centuries. The San-Fo-Chi had established dominion over an area extending from the central region of the Malay Peninsula to Sumatra, including the Strait of Malacca, one of the great hubs of global trade. In place of the San-Fo-Chi, maritime trade centered on individual port polities including Melayu in southern Sumatra as well as Lambri (Lamuri), Samudera and Pasai in northern Sumatra. This seems to be due to the fact that, as the direct sea route between Mainland China and India developed, the Strait of Malacca lost its exclusivity as a way station, leading to a decrease in the recognition of San-Fo-Chi as a regional concept. Indeed, Tambralinga, which was located in the central part of the Malay Peninsula and which had been a part of San-Fo-Chi, began to develop as an independent force on the sea.

As a result of these changes, Java became the largest center of maritime trade in insular Southeast Asia. It functioned as a transshipment center and became predominant in terms of agriculture and handicraft production due

---

6 Ayutthaya (1351–1767) was a kingdom that had as its capital the port city of Ayutthaya, located in the lower Chao Phraya River basin. Promoting trade on the basis of a royal monopoly, its influence extended as far as Cambodia, present-day Northern Thailand and the Malay Peninsula.

7 In the past, San-Fo-Chi has been identified as the kingdom of Srivijaya in the seventh through ninth centuries. Other scholars hold the view that this was a collective name for a group of trading states active in the Strait of Malacca located on the coasts of the middle and southern Malay Peninsula, the Strait coast of Sumatra and the western parts of Java and Borneo. However, the most promising theory is that San-Fo-Chi is the transliteration into Chinese characters of the sounds of "Zābaj" in Arab historical sources, or the "Javaka" and "Savaka" found in Indian stone inscriptions.

to its large population. The Singhasari[8] and Majapahit Kingdoms[9], which ruled Java at the time, exerted their political and military influence over the wider region. They dispatched military expeditions into Sumatra and Bali and their influence reached as far as Borneo and the Malay Peninsula.

## People traveling the sea and those facing the sea

### Maritime merchants and sailors

The central roles in the interactions in maritime East Asia were played by the people making the voyages and those engaging in the trade that connected distant lands. Among them, Chinese merchants played both roles as they sailed across the East and South China Seas and the Yellow Sea. More specifically, key figures included the owners of trading vessels who may or may not have necessarily participated in the voyage, as well as the head merchants (*dougang* or *gangshou*) actually responsible for ship navigation and commercial transactions on behalf of patrons and their subordinate bands of merchants. In the Yellow Sea and the East China Sea in the ninth century, Silla maritime merchants connected Japan, Silla Korea and Tang China. However, they largely disappeared after the assassination of Jang Bogo[10], who had brought the various Silla sea merchants under his sway, and at this point Chinese maritime merchants came to the fore. In the South China Sea, it was also during the Tang Dynasty that Muslim merchants reached the coasts of South China. Muslim forces temporarily withdrew to Southeast Asia in the

---

8  The Singhasari Kingdom (1222–1292), based in the wet-rice agricultural region of eastern Java, advanced policies to expand overseas and engage in the spice trade and other forms of maritime trade. It was succeeded by the Majapahit Dynasty, which continued to develop overseas trade connections.

9  The Majapahit Kingdom (1293–early sixteenth century) also based itself in the wet-rice agricultural zone of eastern Java. The dynasty promoted external trade, controlling the production and distribution of Javanese rice and spices from the Maluku Islands.

10  Jang Bogo, also known as "Gungbok", came from a commoner background in Silla Korea. He traveled to Tang China early in the ninth century where he served in the military. After returning to Silla, he established and was appointed commander of the Cheonghae garrison, from which he controlled the sea-lanes around the southwest coast of Korea and actively engaged in trade with China and Japan. However, in the mid-ninth century he came into conflict with the Silla court and was assassinated.

wake of the disorder brought about by the Huang Chao Rebellion[11], which broke out at the end of the ninth century. As a result, from the tenth century, Chinese maritime merchants filled the void left by the Muslim merchants and began to trade with countries along the South China Sea and the Indian Ocean (the Nanhai trade). Chinese maritime merchants continued to operate in this way after that, including during the period between 1250 and 1350.

Meanwhile, in the region extending from the South China Sea to the Indian Ocean, Arab and Persian Muslim merchants played the most active role. In addition to the Muslims who had established communities in the trading ports of Fujian and Guangdong by the first half of the thirteenth century, newly arrived Muslim seafarers, as well as Hindu, Jewish and Christian maritime merchants, were also present. They connected East Asia with the coastal areas of Southeast Asia, South Asia and West Asia. Some of them sailed on behalf of patrons in the various polities of the South China Sea and the Indian Ocean.

In contrast, local merchants from Japan, Goryeo Korea and Southeast Asia did not play prominent roles in foreign trade. However, they did participate in this trade as members of the commercial organizations subordinate to Chinese and Muslim merchants. These opportunities allowed local merchants to accumulate know-how concerning navigation and commercial transactions. In addition, the crews of ships engaged in foreign trade often consisted of peoples with diverse places of origin, including the offspring of mixed parentage. As an example, it seems to make sense that people from Japan and Korea would have been part of crews of trading vessels under the Chinese head merchants, and would have offered their knowledge and techniques regarding navigation and commercial activity in their homelands.

Merchant ships and the networks of maritime merchants were utilized by religious travelers to cross the sea. Those who crossed the Yellow Sea and the East China Sea were mainly Buddhist monks, especially Zen monks. Their sphere of activity covered South China, North China, Japan and Korea. In the South China Sea, Buddhist monks and pilgrims were joined by a variety

---

11  The Huang Chao Rebellion was a popular uprising that occurred in Tang Dynasty China in 874. It was incited by Wang Xianzhi, a salt merchant, and later taken over by Huang Chao, who was also a former salt merchant. The activities of the rebels enveloped a large part of South China, and at one time even captured Chang'an and Luoyang. However, after those conquests, the uprising quickly dissipated and Huang Chao was murdered in 884.

of other religious travelers, including *'ulamā* (Muslim scholars) and Ṣufis. It was also not unusual for religious travelers to invest heavily in overseas trade.

Official envoys dispatched by the governments of various regions were also important voyagers. At that time, diplomatic networks often intersected and overlapped with commercial networks. From as early as the tenth century through the first half of the thirteenth century, maritime merchants supported diplomacy by carrying envoys, conveying documents and messages and collecting information. The Yuan Dynasty often used the Muslim and Uigur merchant networks to send envoys to Southeast Asia.

In some cases, individuals were chosen as envoys because their religion corresponded to beliefs practiced in the country they were to be sent to. For example, the Yuan court often dispatched Muslims to Southeast Asia. For envoys to Buddhist countries in Southeast Asia, the Yuan sometimes appointed Uigurs, many of whom were Buddhist. Furthermore, when the Yuan Dynasty attempted to demand tribute from Japan in 1299, they sent Yishan Yining, a Zen priest, as chief envoy. Accompanying this embassy was Xijian Zitan[12], a priest who had sojourned in Japan and had acquaintances in the temples of Kamakura.

Paralleling the establishment of long-distance trade and interstate diplomacy, maritime exchange occurred at interpersonal, local levels. Among the central figures in this activity were fisher folk, the inhabitants of small islands and those engaged in coastal transportation and short-haul trade. Note that the bearers of local maritime traffic were not necessarily small-scale traders. In particular, some of those who worked in the maritime transportation of tax grain, which was carried out on a large scale in China under the rule of the Yuan Dynasty, also engaged in overseas trade at the same time.

## People in port cities

Port cities functioned as the linchpins of interregional maritime trade and attracted outlanders, mainly maritime merchants and other voyagers. These

---

12 Xijian Zitan (1249–1306), a native of Taizhou, Zhejiang Province, was a founder of the Daitsū Branch of Rinzai Zen. When, in 1271, the eighth regent of the Kamakura Shogunate, Hōjō Tokimune, sent an emissary to the Zen monk Shifan in China, Xijian Zitan was dispatched by Shifan to Kamakura. After returning to Japan on another visit with Yishan Yining, he became head priest at Engakuji and Kenchōji Temples.

outlanders settled in port cities and developed relationships with an array of business acquaintances – both official and private investors, supporters and suppliers – including religious institutions that supported the maritime activities of the outlanders both materially and spiritually.

Among the groups of outlanders, Muslims formed their own communities in the coastal cities of South China. After the expansion of the Mongol hegemony to coastal areas of China, they were joined in the business of overseas trade by Muslims and Uigurs, who were mostly Buddhist, from Central Asia. In Hakata, Japan, lived communities of Chinese merchants including those called "Hakata head merchants". These Chinese and Islamic networks and communities spread widely among the port cities lining the South China Sea and the Indian Ocean.

Coastal areas including port cities often fell under the jurisdiction of local authorities who variously oversaw overseas trade and regulated maritime interactions. In East Asia, where centralization was relatively strong, the institutions that directly administered trading ports were, in most cases, not independent regional authorities, but instead, at least nominally, operated as agencies established by central governments.

In Yuan China, the coastal areas were governed through several levels of administration answerable to the Yuan court. Civil officials staffed *xingsheng* (branch secretariats), the highest level of local governance, as well as subordinate levels including *lu* (routes), *fu* (prefectures), *zhou* (subprefectures) and *xian* (counties). Inspection of local governments was conducted by the Censorate, and local governments housed garrisons of Yuan soldiers, ordered hierarchically in *wanhufu* (myriarchies) and *qianhusuo* (chiliarchies). To administer maritime trade, the Yuan continued a Song Dynasty practice of establishing *shibosi* (maritime trade supervisorates) in designated trading ports. In addition, during parts of the Yuan period, the *xingquanfusi* (branch of supervising money bureau), which supervised the Yuan's sponsored merchants (*ortuγ*), also administered maritime trade with the Southeast Asian and Indian Ocean worlds.

In Japan, from the seventh through the thirteenth centuries, the Dazaifu (the regional government in Kyushu)[13], located just south of the port of Hakata,

---

13 The Dazaifu was located in present-day Dazaifu City, Fukuoka Prefecture. It was ancient Japan's imperial headquarters (regional government) for administering Kyushu, Iki and Tsushima, handling both diplomacy and the internal affairs of Kyushu. It also functioned to control trading activities with China and Korea.

administered overseas trade and functioned as the principal initial locus for foreign diplomatic contact. After the Mongol Invasions in the latter half of the thirteenth century, the Kamakura Shogunate established the office of Chinzei Tandai (Kyushu Shogunal Deputy). Based in the port of Hakata, this shogunal deputy supervised administrative, judicial and military affairs as well as mobilized warriors to guard the coast. After the establishment of the Ashikaga Shogunate in 1336, these functions were taken over by the Chinzei Kanrei or Kyushu Tandai (the Ashikaga Shogunate's Deputy).

In Korea, after the founding of the Goryeo Dynasty, trading vessels from China regularly arrived at Yeseong Port, the official port for the royal capital of Gaegyeong (present-day Gaeseong). On the southern coast of Korea, a guesthouse was established in Gimhae in order to receive embassies from Japan. However, after Goryeo was incorporated into the Mongol Empire and participated in the invasion of Japan, the reception and guesthouse systems were abolished. By the end of the thirteenth century, the Yuan and Goryeo had established military installations such as the *zhenbian wanhufu* (frontier defense command myriarchy) at important strategic locations along the coast in order to guard against any threat from Japan.

In Southeast Asia, although much remains unknown about the histories of particular cases, many of the port cities located on islands and along the coasts developed the characteristics of state-like political units. Some became aggressively mercantilist, at times coercing merchant ships to conduct trade. There are even cases in which port polities plundered ships.

## Land-based political authorities

Inland from the port cities that housed the participants in maritime interaction extended wide-ranging political authorities: Song and Yuan Dynasty China, the imperial court and warrior governments (the Kamakura and Ashikaga Shogunates) in Japan, Goryeo Korea and, in Southeast Asia, states such as Champa and Java. In addition, in the latter half of the fourteenth century, regional authorities in Ryukyu began to establish a kingdom based in part on their engagement in overseas trade. These states and other regional authorities became, at least in name, the central actors in maritime East Asia responsible for "administering" maritime interactions.

# 1.3: Increased Openness
## Maritime Merchants Expand Maritime Interactions

Interactions in maritime East Asia thrived during the period between 1250 and 1350. The core of this activity centered on the coastal region of South China. The structural conditions that led to this prosperous trade were not generated during this period, but instead evolved out of overseas trade patterns that developed in and after the eighth and ninth centuries. At the same time, the interruptions brought about by the Mongol conquests rendered a simple resumption of the pattern of trade that had existed prior to 1250 impossible. After their conquest of South China in the 1270s, the Yuan court adopted two seemingly contradictory positions. The first sought to facilitate further maritime interaction by actively promoting maritime trade and is evidenced by the formation of an extensive, pan-Eurasian network of land and sea routes. In contrast, the second sought the expansion of Mongol hegemony, which led to political and military conflicts, generated tensions with surrounding countries and to a certain extent placed constraints on maritime interactions.

In the past, the trend has been to stress only one of these two aspects. In order to understand the whole picture, however, both elements should be taken into consideration. This chapter begins by examining the first aspect, that is, the elements of Yuan administration that facilitated maritime interactions in East Asia during the period 1250 to 1350, and the actual circumstances of the exchange carried out under these conditions. In doing so, it is important to recognize that the conditions of maritime exchange in this period reflected both transformations brought about by the Mongol conquests and continuities predating the 1250s. As such, when necessary, this chapter will consider the conditions of maritime interaction prior to the thirteenth century.

## Political authorities' flexible, lenient administration

The overall pattern of trade during the period 1250 to 1350 exhibited considerable continuity with previous centuries. Maritime merchants traversed the seas of East Asia to visit ports designated for foreign trade by the governments of China, Korea and Japan, who then oversaw the trade carried out in those ports. The administration of maritime interactions in this period was limited to these ports, and it can be characterized as flexible and lenient.

In China, the Yuan Dynasty maintained the Song Dynasty system for managing maritime interactions – the *shibosi* (maritime trade supervisorates). Trade with Korea and Japan was handled primarily by the *shibosi* in the port of Qingyuan. And, as had been the case during the Song period, trade with the lands of Southeast Asia and the Indian Ocean (the Nanhai trade) was handled primarily by *shibosi* in Quanzhou and Guangzhou.

In order to engage in foreign trade, a maritime merchant affiliated with the Yuan court was required to secure guarantors and to apply for embarkation at the local office of his *benguandi* (hometown of registration)[1]. The trade supervisor of the port from which the merchant wished to sail would then be notified by the local registration office. After confirming and registering the number of ships, the number of crew, ships' fittings, cargo and destinations, the *shibosi* would issue an official exit permit (*gongping*, also known as *gongju* or *gongyan*) that recorded these details as well as laws concerning trade. In principle, the merchants were required to return to the same port from which they sailed. When the maritime merchant returned to the port, the trade supervisor would check losses of crew members and ship's fittings against the records drawn up before departure and collect tax after conducting a complete assessment of the cargo stowed in the ship's hold. After taxation, the remaining commodities were divided among the financiers and others who had a claim on the proceeds of trade. Some investors were members of the Yuan court. In

---

1 The *benguandi* is the place-name recorded in the family registration system as the location to which a person officially belongs. In China, tax payments and requests for permission to travel were made at the local government office in the place of registration.

order to absorb the potentially vast profits of overseas trade into the state treasury, they implemented procedures for an imperially financed overseas trade system (*guanben chuan*).

Even though this strict system for administering trade did not always function perfectly, it helped prevent tax evasion as well as stem the outflow of prohibited goods, including weapons, gold, silver and copper coins. To some extent this system enabled the Yuan to regulate the activities of maritime merchants. The *shibosi* continued to inspect and assess tax on the cargo of arriving foreign ships and to inspect departing foreign ships.

In Japan, the port of Hakata continued to be the main point of contact for foreign relations, as it had been from the latter half of the eleventh century. During the Heian period, the Dazaifu administered Hakata on behalf of the court. During the Kamakura period, the Mutō family, *gokenin* (vassals) of the Kamakura Shoguns, established a *shugosho* (provincial constabulary office) at the Dazaifu and enhanced their actual control over the Dazaifu by hereditarily taking the title of Dazaifu Junior Assistant Governor (Dazai Shōni). In so doing, they involved themselves in the management of Hakata. The Kamakura Shogunate established the Chinzei Tandai (Shogunal Deputy in Kyushu) in Hakata at the end of the thirteenth century, which was then replaced by the Chinzei Kanrei (Kyushu Tandai) after the Ashikaga ascended to power in 1336. The Chinzei Kanrei oversaw the comings and goings of ships from Hakata in this period. For example, in 1350 the Chinzei Kanrei reported to the shogunate in Kyoto the arrival of a Yuan ship carrying Japanese Zen monks.

Organs of state thus exercised some authority over the port of Hakata and were capable of handling the arrival of foreign embassies and the outbreak of wars with foreign countries. However, in the Kamakura and Muromachi periods, neither the Mutō family nor the various deputy shogunal officials comprehensively controlled or monopolized foreign trade. They lacked a centralized system for managing overseas trade through which they could officially authorize or prohibit it, or purchase or even pay for commodities. In contrast, during the ninth through twelfth centuries, the imperial court had operated such a system through administrators in Dazaifu.

Instead, merchant ships were dispatched individually by large temples and shrines as well as influential people connected to the shogunate and imperial court with bases in or around Hakata. For example, the Ashikaga

Shogunate authorized the mission of the Tenryūji ship in 1342, which was dispatched for the purpose of constructing the Tenryūji Temple[2] in Kyoto. The so-called "Sinan Wreck"[3], which was discovered in coastal waters off the southwest coast of Korea, is considered to have been a trading vessel dispatched to China by Tōfukuji Temple in Kyoto in 1323. With the support of patrons (including prestigious court nobles, the Kujō and Ichijō families), Tōfukuji monks dispatched the ship through Jōtenji Temple, a Tōfukuji branch temple located in Hakata.

As the Yuan court did not limit the amount of trade or the number of ships from each country, authorities in Japan did not necessarily see the need to monopolize the right to dispatch trading vessels. Incentive to monopolize trade only arose after the 1370s, when the Ming court adopted a restrictive trade system that recognized as legitimate only those ships bearing the credentials of the King of Japan.

The Goryeo court also attempted to channel foreign trade into designated ports. As was the case prior to 1250, maritime merchants who departed from Mainland China toward the Korean Peninsula usually sailed for Gaegyeong, the royal capital of Goryeo. It is probable that Yeseong Port, the officially designated port for Gaegyeong, continued to serve as the main entryway. Although the means by which foreign trade was managed at Yeseong remains unclear, there are cases from the early thirteenth century in which Goryeo officials conducted inspections of trading vessels. During the period between 1250 and 1350, sea merchants from South China, who had been sailing to Korea for some time, were joined by merchants from the areas around Daidu, which, as the capital of the Yuan Dynasty, had grown into a commercial center. A Chinese-language primer (*Nogeoldae*, completed in the latter half of the fourteenth century) that was used in Goryeo contains stories depicting society in China under the Yuan Dynasty. One tale

---

2 Tenryūji Temple is a Zen temple in Kyoto. In recognition of its political and religious significance, Tenryūji held the first rank in the Kyoto Five Mountains System (Kyoto Gozan) into which Kyoto Zen temples were organized. Its head patron was the first shogun of the Muromachi Shogunate, Ashikaga Takauji, and its founding priest was Musō Soseki. Its construction was completed in 1345.

3 In 1976, the remains of a sunken ship were discovered off the coast of Sinan, Jeollanam-do, in the Republic of Korea. In addition to the ship's hull, a large amount of cargo was salvaged, including ceramics and wooden shipping tags. An investigation of the wreckage revealed that the ship was a Chinese junk engaged in Japan–China trade in the first half of the fourteenth century.

describes how a Goryeo merchant found a ready ship that would enable him to sail from the official port of Daidu, Zhigu (present-day Tianjin), bound for Gaegyeong. Trade linking Japan and Korea centered on the port of Gimhae (Gimju), located on the southern coast of Korea opposite Tsushima, until the middle of the thirteenth century. After the Yuan launched military expeditions against Japan in 1274 and 1281, Japanese trade with Korea changed drastically.

As the foregoing discussion shows, only a limited number of ports in China, Korea and Japan, such as Qingyuan, Guangzhou, Quanzhou, Hakata and Yeseong, served as hubs of foreign trade. Central political authorities could to a certain extent regulate foreign trade by controlling these port cities, especially in cases when the trading partner was a contingent of large-scale ships.

However, even under the sophisticated *shibosi* systems of the Song and Yuan Dynasties, it proved impossible to control to any real extent the activities of merchant ships when they sailed outside hub ports or to regulate their activities in ports beyond dictating procedures for entering and exiting them. The fact that the Yuan Dynasty's regulations for maritime trade stipulated penalties against smuggling by merchant ships before they returned to their designated port suggests that, in practice, the ships never ceased visiting ports outside the control of the *shibosi*. Furthermore, the *shibosi* system was without a doubt insufficient for dealing with the situation in the East China Sea, which was infested with rampant piracy, including the large-scale depredations of the Wokou in the latter half of the fourteenth century. When confronted with the problem of the Wokou, the early Ming court found the *shibosi* system obsolete as a means of regulating people engaged in maritime activities and abolished this system for administering maritime trade that had persisted throughout the Song and Yuan Dynasties.

In fact, violence was prevalent outside the major, officially administered entrepôts, and authorities who wished to dispatch foreign trade ships needed to be able to ensure the safety of those vessels. In some cases, local people looted merchant ships, especially those that drifted ashore. In particular, state control was diminished in archipelagic regions such as the Ryukyu Islands and Jejudo Island to such an extent that maritime merchants' fear of such regions might be the root cause of legends telling of "cannibal islands". In Japan, the customary local practice that treated ships cast adrift or wrecked (*yoribune*) as the property of local residents was widely accepted. Central authorities in China, Japan and Korea all took precautions by establishing systems in which local officials could crack down on illicit violence. China and Korea protected merchant ships when political conditions permitted, and in some cases even recaptured and returned pirated ships to their homelands. However, rather than any preemptive action, it was often the case that investigations and searches for lawbreakers were only conducted after an incidence of robbery or piracy came to light. Thus, it is hard to say that the safety of merchant ships was ever fully guaranteed. In Japan, as piracy and civil war erupted in the fourteenth century, it became essential to guarantee the safety of merchant ships. In 1325 for example, in dispatching trading vessels to China for the purpose of restoring the Kenchōji Temple[4] in Kamakura, the Kamakura Shogunate ordered vassal samurai in Hizen and Satsuma to provide protection.

In this way, apart from Southeast Asia and the Indian Ocean, whose circumstances remain unclear, specific systems were instituted in trading ports across maritime East Asia for the purpose of managing foreign trade. However, the control was limited to only single *points*, namely, inside the ports. There was essentially no way to restrict the behavior of ships once they reached the open sea. In fact, there is little indication that political authorities sought to take the sweeping actions necessary for resolving this situation. Instead, the institutions managing maritime trade in this period functioned as a stimulus for maritime interactions, which is why "lenient" and "flexible" characterize the administration of the East Asian maritime world in this period.

## "Outlanders" crossing borders

Of the several important ports in maritime East Asia from the eleventh to the fourteenth centuries, a string of port cities on the coast of South China functioned as trading hubs, including Qingyuan (known as Mingzhou until the end of the twelfth century), Quanzhou and Guangzhou. The period from 1250 to 1350 witnessed considerable continuity with earlier centuries

---

4 Kenchōji Temple is a Zen temple founded in 1253 by Hōjō Tokiyori, fifth regent of the Kamakura Shogunate, with the monk Lanxi Daolong of the Southern Song as founding priest. In recognition of this political patronage and its religious importance, Kenchōji held the first rank in the Five Mountains System into which Kamakura Zen Temples were organized.

*1.3: Increased Openness* 77

in the important roles played by foreign sea merchants and other outlanders from an array of ethnic and religious backgrounds.

During the Song Dynasty, maritime interaction in the South China Sea was dominated by Muslim (mostly Arabic and Persian), Indian and Chinese sea merchants. The port city of Guangzhou had contained a residential quarter for Muslim merchants since the Tang era. In the Song, the Muslim quarter came to be known as a "*fanfang*" (foreigner ward), which was permitted a certain degree of self-governance under the leadership of a *fanzhang* (chief foreigner). Although not on the scale of the Muslim diasporas in the South China Sea ports of Quanzhou and Guangzhou, the East China Sea port of Qingyuan housed an enclave of Bosituan, who are presumed to have had some relationship with Persian people.

Communities of Muslim and Chinese maritime merchants were also widespread in Southeast Asia and the Indian Ocean. They could be found in many lands, including Champa (present-day South-Central Vietnam), Cambodia, Brunei, Phatthalung (Southern Thailand), Nagapattinam (on the Coromandel Coast of India) and Kūlam Malay. Their continued presence contributed to the establishment of Muslim governments and Chinese diasporas in these regions in later years.

In Japan, sea merchants from "Silla" (Korea) and "Tang" (China) began arriving in Hakata to trade in the ninth century. From the eleventh through the thirteenth centuries, Chinese maritime merchants based themselves in Hakata under the leadership of the Hakata "head sea merchants". During the period when the Dazaifu administered foreign trade in Hakata through the first half of the twelfth century, the community of head sea merchants was confined to a district located along the south shore of Hakata's western inlet. This is the so-called Chinese (Tang) Quarter of Hakata Port (Hakata-tsu Tōbō, though some scholars regard it as a facility that housed Song Chinese as well). By the latter half of the twelfth century, the Chinese quarter had spread across the city of Hakata with intermixed Chinese and Japanese residents. These Chinese sea merchants relied upon domestic Japanese political and religious authorities to invest in and protect their trading voyages, and to, by providing them with property and other resources, ensure that they could establish bases for their activities.

For example, much of the eastern half of Hakata was occupied by two powerful Zen temples, Shōfukuji and Jōtenji, founded in the late twelfth century and the first half of the thirteenth century by Zen monks Eisai[5] and En'ni[6] respectively upon their return from periods of study in China. Eisai and En'ni also established close relationships with the Hakata head Chinese sea merchants. The sea merchants seem to have been followers of Zen and the connections with Eisai and En'ni enabled them to play important roles in the founding of both Shōfukuji and Jōtenji. Shōfukuji is thought to have been constructed on the site of a cemetery for Song Chinese, which in later years was known as Sōjin Hyakudō (The 100 Song Chinese Mortuary Chapels). The construction of Jōtenji was funded by Xie Guoming, a Hakata head Chinese sea merchant with whom En'ni enjoyed a close association.

In Korea, before Goryeo became a vassal state of the Yuan, Chinese people resided in the royal capital, Gaegyeong. The Goryeo court provided guest-houses in the inner city of Gaegyeong for maritime merchants, at least during the eleventh and twelfth centuries. Some maritime merchants stayed in Korea for several years and married into Korean families. In the middle of the thirteenth century, during the wars against the invading Mongols, the Goryeo court moved the capital to Ganghwado Island, after which the situation of Chinese merchants in Korea becomes unclear. However, before that, it is evident that Chinese sea merchants established bases of operation on the Korean Peninsula.

Most of the sea merchants traversing the East China Sea between the eleventh and thirteenth centuries were Chinese. Even though after the twelfth century phrases such as "Japanese merchants", "Japanese ships", "Goryeo merchants" and "Goryeo ships" appear in Chinese historical sources, these phrases often indicate that the visiting merchants and trading ships sailed from ports in Japan or Goryeo, rather than that the ships were of Japanese or Korean origin or that the merchants were ethnically Japanese or Korean. Nevertheless, the crews of trade vessels dispatched to China during the Southern Song Dynasty by the *kenmon* (influential families and powerful

---

5 Eisai/Yōsai (1141–1215) was a native of Bitchū Province (present-day Okayama). Resident in Song Dynasty China from 1168 to 1187, he laid the groundwork for what would become the Rinzai Zen school of Buddhism in Japan. He is also known for bringing the customs of Song Chinese-style tea-drinking to Japan. In addition to Shōfukuji Temple, he also founded Kenninji Temple in Kyoto and Jufukuji Temple in Kamakura.

6 En'ni (1202–1280) was a native of Suruga Province (present-day Shizuoka) and traveled to Song Dynasty China in 1235. Returning to Japan, he founded Jōtenji Temple in Hakata and Tōfukuji Temple in Kyoto.

institutions) of Japan[7] included many Japanese seafarers among a majority of Chinese sailors and officers. Although Song Chinese officials treated these ships as Japanese merchant ships, as explained in the Prologue, in general, the ethnic identities and other affiliations of the maritime merchants did not necessarily correspond to those of the owners or other authorities who dispatched the ships. This ambiguity in sea merchants' identities and affiliations differs significantly from modern conceptions of nationality and ship registration. Indeed, it was this ambiguity that helped shape the openness that characterized maritime East Asia in this period. Moreover, some of the Chinese maritime merchants active in Japan were actually of mixed Japanese and Chinese parentage. Any ethnic categorization of maritime merchants thus has only limited utility.

**Figure 3: Reconstruction of Hakata**

Source: Ōba (2008).

---

7 "*Kenmon*" is a historical term suggested by Japanese historian Kuroda Toshio (1926–1993). This concept consists mainly of the imperial family, influential aristocrats, important temples and shrines and heads of warrior families. They possessed considerable social privilege in Japan's late classical and medieval periods.

In its fundamental structures, the situation described above continued in the period 1250 to 1350, aside from the changes among the Hakata head sea merchants that occurred as a result of the Yuan's attempts to invade Japan.

In the South China Sea region, Chinese maritime merchants' settlements across Southeast Asia during the Song Dynasty began a process of community formation that continued in the period 1250 to 1350. During the Song-Yuan transition, newcomers known as "Xintangren" ("New Chinese", literally "new Tang people") arrived in Cambodia, which suggests that the flows of people continued.

Muslim merchants continued to wield considerable clout as well. At the end of the thirteenth century, for example, the influence of Muslim sea merchants contributed to the founding of the first Muslim kingdom in Southeast Asia, Samudera and Pasai, composed mainly of port cities on Sumatra. The enterprises of Muslim merchants in Southern Chinese ports such as Quanzhou and Guangzhou also prospered in this period. As we saw in Chapter 1.1, Ibn Battuta left a detailed record of the Islamic communities in Quanzhou. In China under the Yuan, Mongols connected the upper echelons of the government with Semu people[8]; especially Muslims and Uigurs who were involved in commerce migrated to these areas in several ways, including by accepting appointments as regional and local officials. In their new homes they became important mediators between the merchants with whom they associated and the Yuan government, which was the merchants' most important customer and protector. Sometimes these Muslims and Uigurs even spoke to government officials on behalf of merchants. By exploiting this function as mediators under the Yuan, the Semu established a network that stretched from Central Eurasia to the coast of China. The growth of Muslim influence in China can be seen in the increase in mosque construction. As hubs of maritime trade linking the South China Sea to the Indian Ocean, Quanzhou and Guangzhou housed mosques during the Song Dynasty. However, by the time of the Yuan, mosques could also be found in trading ports such as Hangzhou, Qingyuan and Songjiang in the Zhejiang area.

---

8 The term "Semu people" refers to "various types of people", specifically indicating residents of regions governed by the Yuan Dynasty other than Mongols, Han peoples (residents of North China under the former Jin Dynasty), Southerners (residents of South China under the former Southern Song Dynasty) and Koreans. Many of those referred to by this name originated from Central or West Asia.

The prevalence of Islam in China during the Yuan can also be seen in the development of networks of orders of Ṣufi mystics in the interior of the country. The *shaykh* (elders) and *qāḍī* (judges) of the Muslim communities in China were often wealthy merchants with close connections to the Ṣufi orders. Ṣufi orders established networks centered on hospices, which they erected across Eurasia to provide both spaces for religious practice and resources for travelers. Open to both general travelers and merchants, hospices became hubs in trans-Eurasian networks combining travel, religion and commerce. The activities of Kubrawī Ṣufi orders[9], for example, ranged from Persia and Central Asia to North China. Additionally, as we saw in Ibn Battuta's description of a Muslim community in China in Chapter 1.1, the order of Shaykh Abū Ishāq of Kāzarūn based itself in ports from the Persian Gulf to the coast of South China, attracting seafarers as believers. Through the same areas, the intercession of the saint Khidr from Southeast Asia, who was believed to protect navigation, also became popular.

Thus, as we can confirm in the previous centuries, even during the period from 1250 to 1350 in maritime East Asia, "outlanders" with diverse ethnic and religious backgrounds played important roles in their communities spreading across the region, in many cases integrating into local societies. Maritime merchants played integral roles as key intermediaries in establishing social networks with local authorities and religious orders.

## Closer relationship between political power and commerce

In contrast to earlier centuries, the period 1250–1350 witnessed considerable symbiotic collaboration between political authorities and maritime merchants. In Yuan Dynasty China, merchants themselves even became integrated into the state's institutional framework for managing overseas trade.

The aforementioned imperially financed overseas trade system is a representative example of this mutually beneficial relationship. The Yuan court was a primary investor in these voyages and divided the profits with the maritime merchants. Central figures in this trade were the *ortuy* merchants, whose sponsorship by the Yuan court enabled them to engage

---

9 The Kubrawī orders were Ṣufi orders founded by Shaykh Najmuddin Kubra in the thirteenth century. They established *khānqā* (hospices) with facilities for both travel and religious devotion in cities in the Eastern part of Eurasia.

in trade from a privileged position. These associations were largely composed of Muslims and Uigurs, who received investment capital from members of the royal court, imperial family and the Yuan officialdom. The *xingquanfusi* (branch of supervising money bureau) oversaw these merchants as well as the *shibosi*. This bureau thus both could intervene in court-related overseas trade enterprises and connected the Yuan court to the wealth generated by trade with the South China Sea and the Indian Ocean. Furthermore, in some cases, the *ortuy* merchant associations connected themselves to the commercial activities of Islamic, Christian and Buddhist religious organizations. These religious organizations were supervised by particular ministries and officials of the Yuan government, who were also in a position to speak for the interests of each religious group. As a result, administration of the *ortuy* required adjusting policy depending on the interests of ministries, officials and religious organizations.

The *ortuy* were also involved in the 'procurement of treasure for the royal court of the Yuan Dynasty' (*zhongmai baohuo*). As part of such dealings with the royal court, maritime merchants escaped from taxation by 'presenting tribute to authorities at court' (*bai jian/cheng yang*). In fact, maritime merchants had long used gift-giving to secure personal relationships with officials of the *shibosi* and other offices, enabling them to conduct illegal activities such as tax evasion and the smuggling of prohibited articles. In China in this period, political authorities in the central government and port cities who administered trade through the *shibosi* system and the maritime merchants who carried out the trade became symbiotically linked and dependent on each other.

In governing South China, the Yuan attempted to regulate the inhabitants while incorporating some into the lower echelons of local administration, outsourcing a number of governmental functions. Perhaps most famous in relation to maritime activities were Zhu Qing and Zhang Xuan. During the Southern Song Dynasty, they had been pirates and salt smugglers (defying the Song salt monopoly). During the early Yuan period, they were appointed as officials in charge of maritime transportation. The Yuan made use of their nautical expertise to have tax grain transported from South China to the Yuan capital at Daidu. As was the case with the Song Dynasty's system for contracting out shipping duties (*gangyun*), many of those hired for official purposes often operated *sihuo jiadai* (private shipping enterprises) and other commercial activities at the same time.

Many who owned ocean-going ships, had a crew of mariners and were versed in navigation techniques accepted positions in marine transportation, some of whom used *bojiaoqian* (shipping fees) paid by the government as capital for engaging in overseas trade. The Yin of Taicang, a prosperous Yuan port city, conducted trade with Goryeo in this way. Local gentry from the coastal regions of South China played central roles in foreign trade as figures who were both appointed to official posts to administer trade and who undertook official trade on behalf of the state. The Yang family of Ganpu actively engaged in maritime transportation with prominent individuals by variously accepting positions as *shibosi* (maritime trade supervisorate), engaging in trade in the Indian Ocean as an *ortuy* merchant and serving as envoy to the Ilkhanate of Persia[10]. The case of the maritime merchant Pu Shougeng[11] of Quanzhou, who will be discussed in the next chapter, demonstrates that in actual practice the *shibosi* of the Southern Song period required the incorporation of local elites in order to function. This tendency became more conspicuous in the Yuan period.

In Japan in this period, foreign trade often took the form of authorities in Kyoto and Kamakura, as well as powerful temples and shrines, fitting out and dispatching merchant ships. In several well-known examples, these patrons used the pretext of raising funds for the construction of temples and shrines to dispatch trading ships to China. Those who took charge of the voyage were known as "*gōshi*" (head merchants), who, in return for their appointment, paid a fixed share of the proceeds from the voyage to their patrons. This method for outfitting foreign trade likely represented a continuation of practices that began prior to 1250. In historical sources, temples such as Tōfukuji in Kyoto appear prominently, but they are gradually eclipsed by warrior families with connections to the Kamakura and Muromachi Shogunates, including the main line of the Hōjō regents of the Kamakura Shogunate (known as the Tokusō family), the Kanesawa, a branch line of the Hōjō regents, and

---

10 The Ilkhanate (1261–1353) was a Mongol regime established by Hülegü in West Asia, a younger brother of the Mongolian Emperor Möngke Qa'an and Qubilai Qa'an. It governed an area centered on Persia that stretched from the Āmū River to Iraq and Eastern Anatolia.

11 Pu Shougeng was a Muslim merchant based in Quanzhou who engaged in maritime trade. He became an influential political figure in Quanzhou at the end of the Southern Song Dynasty as Tiju Shibo (Chief of the Maritime Trade Supervisorate). Both the Yuan, intent on conquering South China, and the resisting Southern Song forces sought his assistance, but Pu decided to stand with the former.

the Ashikaga Shoguns themselves. This shift to warrior predominance was facilitated by the Kamakura Shogunate's assumption of control over the port of Hakata in order to defend against the threat of Mongol invasion. In Hakata, the shogunate strengthened surveillance over overseas trade, which enabled its members to participate in overseas trade after military tensions eased. In particular, the shogunate gained significant access to the port after the Hōjō regents established the Kyushu Deputy Shogunate to oversee Hakata at the end of the thirteenth century, and they appointed members of the Hōjō family hereditarily to that position.

For example, the Kanesawa family, based in Kanesawa in Musashi Province, frequently engaged in overseas trade. In 1306, a ship dispatched for the purpose of building the Shōmyōji Temple[12] in Kanesawa returned home. When this ship arrived at Hakata, Kanesawa Masaaki, the then Kyushu Shogunal Deputy, arranged to have his trade goods transshipped onto vessels to carry them from Hakata to Kamakura via the Seto Inland Sea. At the same time, he sent a letter to his cousin in Kyoto, Kanesawa Sadaaki, a member of the main line of the Kanesawa family and Rokuhara Tandai (Kyoto Shogunal Deputy[13]), to inform him about the shipment. This example shows that by holding the post of Kyushu Shogunal Deputy, the various branches of the Hōjō family were able to assemble a smooth-functioning, long-distance trade network connecting Hakata, Kyoto and Kamakura that enabled them to engage in overseas commerce. Others who had relations with the shogunate developed similar networks linking influential connections among acquaintances, relatives and local agents.

When we turn our eyes to the situation in Korea, we find that in this period, the Goryeo kings became actively involved in seaborne and overland commercial activities. Maritime merchants from China and Japan often visited Korea in the period from the eleventh to the twelfth centuries, presenting commodities as tribute. Such cases appear less frequently in historical sources from the thirteenth century onwards, and some scholars argue that Goryeo turned away from commerce in this period. However,

---

12 Shōmyōji Temple was the Kanesawa family mortuary temple. It was established by the founder of the Kanesawa family line, Hōjō Sanetoki (1224–1276).

13 The position of Kyoto Shogunal Deputy was established by the Kamakura Shogunate to conduct negotiations with the imperial court, maintain order in Kyoto and its surroundings and handle judicial matters relating to all territories in the western part of Japan.

judging from the fact that maritime merchants continued to offer tribute to the kings after Goryeo became incorporated into the Yuan, and that, in some cases, the King of Goryeo held feasts for visiting maritime merchants, there is little evidence that ties between the court and commerce had been severed. In fact, there were instances where the royal family dispatched trading vessels to China, and it seems to have been possible for the royal household to organize maritime merchants. The fact that Goryeo court officials began including those of merchant descent may also signal intentions on the part of the royal authority to be more actively involved in commercial activities.

As we have seen above, the connections between commerce and political power became more conspicuous in this period than in previous times. The significant agents of overseas trade in this period included merchants who established connections with political authorities and who engaged in overseas trade on their behalf. Strictly speaking, this way of operating was not the only avenue open to these merchants, but constituted one of the various "faces" that they showed depending on the situation of those providing capital and other forms of support. In China, Japan and Korea, those in positions of political authority became more actively concerned with commerce and trade, either in an official or a personal capacity.

## Economic expansion and spheres of foreign trade

The Mongol hegemony in Eastern and Western Eurasia brought about political stability, enabling the growth of vast networks of exchange. The Mongols supported these networks with a system of *jamči* (postal relay stations) and other institutions. From the beginning, a number of Uigur and Muslim merchants from Central Asia affiliated themselves with patrons in the Mongol court and royal family as *ortuy*. When the Yuan extended their dominion over South China in the latter half of the thirteenth century, they connected the Central Eurasian trade network to China and the South China Sea, which made possible the linking of maritime and land-based networks of exchange across Eurasia. The Yuan Dynasty actively requested tribute from the countries of Southeast and South Asia, sometimes resorting to coercive measures that required military force. One reason for these measures was the Mongols' awareness of the lucrative maritime trade coursing the South China Sea and Indian Ocean networks in the holds of junks and dhows. In the tenth century, the trading sphere of South China Sea junks intersected with that of Indian Ocean dhows at the port of Kalah, located near the Strait of Malacca. Around the twelfth century, the port of intersection shifted to areas such as Ma'bar, Malabar and Gujarat on the south and west coasts of India, enabling merchants to extend their connections in West Asia as far as the coasts of the Persian Gulf and the Red Sea via intermediaries such as the ports of Kūlam Malay and Calicut. The aforementioned Ibn Battuta and Marco Polo also traveled this route. Much of the traffic between the Yuan Dynasty and the Ilkhanate as well as Europe used sea routes and often employed the networks and resources of maritime merchants. The famous expeditions of Zheng He[14] in the early fifteenth century were made possible by navigational expertise accumulated in this period.

Even if the discussion is limited to China, the Yuan Dynasty's political unification of North and South China for the first time in four centuries is of great significance. While the Yuan established its political centers at Daidu in North China and Shangdu in the south of the Mongolian Plateau, it attached great importance to connections made possible by sea routes and canals. Financially, the Yuan depended on tax grain transported from the coastal areas of South China. Although the Yuan at first attempted to use canals to transport tax grain, in the end they settled on a system for conveying tax grain by sea, which became fully operational by the fourteenth century. This was a point of difference between the Yuan and the Song and Ming Dynasties, which mainly used canals for transportation (though the Ming did so because of the rampant piracy that plagued the end of the Yuan period). The transportation of tax grain during the Yuan Dynasty began as tax grain was gathered and stored prior to being shipped at the port of Liujia in Taicang located near the mouth of the Yangtze River. From Liujia, the main route for the grain took it to Zhigu on the Gulf of Bohai by sea, and thence to Daidu by canal, forming an immense commodity distribution line running through North and South China. As part of their new commitment to maritime transportation, the Yuan bestowed the title of "Queen of Heaven" (Tianfei) on Mazu, a goddess of the sea indigenous to the Fujian region, thereby granting her the protection of the realm and enabling the erection of shrines for the worship of Mazu

---

14 Zheng He, a eunuch from a Muslim family in Yunnan, led seven expeditions to the South China Sea and the Indian Ocean between 1405 and 1433. Zheng He's voyages set out to entice local rulers to establish tributary relations with the Ming Dynasty, and also engage in maritime trade. One detachment of the fleet reached as far as the east coast of Africa.

along the coast of China, including in the north. As a result, the worship of Mazu began to spread to various areas of China and even started to appear across maritime East Asia.

China's maritime shipping routes included a branch route that headed from the Shandong Peninsula to the Liaodong Peninsula and then on to Korea. The Yuan used this to send military provisions and emergency food aid during crop failures and other disasters. This sea-lane also served as the main artery by which the Yuan took in the provisions it had compelled Goryeo to send. Furthermore, although it was only a temporary measure, at the end of the thirteenth century, the Yuan set up *shuizhan* (relay ports) along the west coast of Korea in order to carry various commodities it had requisitioned from that country. In this way, the political integration of Goryeo into the Yuan incorporated the Korean coast into the Yuan's official networks for the seaborne transportation of people and goods. The Yuan sentenced criminals to exile on Korean islands. Moreover, Jejudo Island was directly ruled by the Yuan for a time and, even after it was returned to Goryeo, the island continued to house

**Figure 4: Map of great canals and sea-lanes of the Yuan Era**

pastures for the Yuan imperial household run by Mongol herdsmen. The degree to which the Korean coast and China developed unprecedented, close connections is demonstrated by the existence of a plan for Emperor Toɣon Temür of the Yuan to escape to Jejudo Island in the last days of the Yuan period.

At the same time, private travel increased in addition to the human traffic of maritime merchants, including the illegal trafficking of children from North and South China who were taken from their homes under the pretext of adoption and then taken to Korea and other places. In the latter half of the fourteenth century, sea people from the Zhoushan Islands in Zhejiang fleeing from Ming troops sailed far over the sea to hide in the southeastern coastal area of Korea, likely because prior interactions had generated a social environment that enabled the local society to accept these people.

In contrast, in the case of Japan, repeated requests for tribute and attempted invasions met with failure, and diplomatic relations between the Yuan and the archipelago never officially normalized. As a result, the Yuan never extended its official maritime networks to Japan. Nonetheless, as will be explained in the next chapter, while official interstate relations between the Yuan and Japan were rife with political and military tension during this period, trade between China and Japan and the interpersonal connections that came with it flourished.

In the Ryukyu Islands, the results of archaeological excavations have revealed increased amounts of Chinese ceramics in sites from the latter half of the thirteenth century. In particular, large amounts of crude earthenware from Fujian, which were found in only small amounts on the Amami Islands and other regions in Japan north of Kyushu, have been unearthed in the Okinawa and Sakishima Islands. This suggests the possibility that an independent commodity exchange network linked China and Ryukyu, which perhaps set the stage for the trade between the two that flourished in the following period.

# 1.4: What Conflicts with the Mongols Wrought
## Isolationism Within Openness

As the Mongols expanded their dominion politically and militarily, maritime interactions in East Asia in the period 1250–1350 reached peak "openness". At the same time, the responses of each country to the stimulus of Mongol expansion generated seeds of isolationism within this openness. In contrast to the previous chapter that explored dimensions of maritime interactions that expanded and developed on foundations laid in the pre-1250 period, this chapter focuses on factors that hindered interaction and set the stage for the representative manifestation of isolationism in maritime East Asia: the *haijin* (maritime prohibition policy) enacted by the Ming Dynasty in the late fourteenth and the fifteenth century. As this chapter's focus is on war and diplomacy between states, the narrative is not directly concerned with the maritime activities of sea merchants and other such figures, but rather focuses on the histories of land-based political authorities. However, although large-scale political authorities such as the Yuan court or the Kamakura Shogunate were far removed from the events in the East Asian maritime world, the various levels of local authorities on the coast that actually carried out diplomatic and military activities also tended to be the major actors engaged in overseas exchange. These included the court of Goryeo, the countries of the South China Sea and the Indian Ocean and the local civil and military officials in the Yuan Dynasty, among others.

## Mongol plan and military activities (1): Invasion of Japan

By the time of the reign of its fourth emperor, Möngke (1251–1259), the Mongol Empire had acquired a vast territory extending to North China and the Liaodong region of China in the east and Persia and the Russian Plain in the west. However, when Qubilai established the Yuan Dynasty in the wake of his victory in the war of succession following the death of Möngke, he shifted the political center to North China, which was his sphere of influence. Mongol leaders in Central Asia, Persia and the Russian Plain seceded and formed virtually autonomous governments.

In this way, the Yuan established direct control over Eastern Eurasia and extended its influence to the east and south. Between the 1260s and 1270s, it subjugated Goryeo on the Korean Peninsula, ensuring its influence over that region, and suppressed the resistance of the Southern Song's remaining forces, successfully taking control of South China. In doing so, the Yuan arrived at the gateways to maritime East Asia.

From that point, the Yuan endeavored to continue its advance into the maritime world. In 1266, it began working through Goryeo to instruct Japan to present tribute. The Yuan also dispatched numerous envoys to countries of South and Southeast Asia (the region called "Nanhai") in 1281 and 1282, including Cambodia, Tambralinga, Java, Ma'bar[1], Kūlam Malay, Samudera and Pasai, Siam, Peureulak, Aru and Kampei. Two explanations have been offered for these actions: first, they fulfilled a political aspiration to extend political influence and second, they had an economic rationale, aiming to gain control over trade and the wealth it generated. Both cases required the Yuan to take control of the "paths of the sea", namely maritime interaction.

However, Japanese authorities rejected the Yuan's request, and requests for tributary relationships with the countries of the South-China Sea and Indian Ocean were obstructed because Champa in South-Central Vietnam began to resist. As a result, the Yuan went to war with Japan and Champa, and then with Java in 1292–1293, which had also rebuffed demands to send tribute.

These wars differed in one respect from the large-scale foreign conquests engaged in by the Mongols up to that point. Normally, in a large-scale campaign, forces would have been composed of personnel levies from various territories ruled semi-autonomously by descendants and relatives of Činggis Qan as well as other noble houses. This policy was adopted in consideration of the division of spoils in the wake of a conquest. In contrast, these wars exhibited little of the character of campaigns conducted with the full force and will of Mongol rulers as

---

1 Ma'bar refers to an empire that ruled the southern tip of the Indian sub-continent from the late twelfth through the middle of the fourteenth century. To distinguish it from a forerunner that existed prior to the tenth century, Ma'bar is also known as the Second Pandyan Dynasty. "Ma'bar" can refer either to the name of the dynasty or the region.

a collective. These were, so to speak, wars commanded by the emperor and his court. Further, these wars were carried out by local forces from the coastal areas of South China and Korea that served as advance bases, as well as garrisons on the front line that had been used in the conquest of these regions. Indeed, the usual Mongol practice was to redirect the military power of a conquered region on to the next target of conquest. So, from the standpoint of the wider Mongol Empire, these wars prosecuted by the emperor and his court were only local conflicts. Still, it was the first time in the history of Eastern Eurasia that a large number of soldiers from the continent had been dispatched to distant lands across the open sea.

However, the Yuan Dynasty did not possess the capacity to ensure that its will was conveyed directly to the lowest level of administration and executed faithfully. The preparation for and execution of wars was determined more or less autonomously by front-line military forces in the regions concerned. This autonomy both contributed to the war effort and hindered and obstructed it, depending on the variety of intertwining calculations and interests concerning the Yuan, including resistance, active and passive cooperation and political and economic exploitation. Internal political conditions were complicated for those who were invaded as well as the invaders.

When the Yuan proceeded to invade Japan, the local authority in Korea was still the Kingdom of Goryeo, which contained a complicated mix of positions regarding the Yuan. In the latter half of the twelfth century, military officials seized de facto power over the government. The descendants of these generals led the war against the Mongols in the first half of the thirteenth century. This military government continued to rule in Korea even after Goryeo was incorporated into the Yuan Dynasty in 1260 and maintained an atmosphere of resistance against the Mongols. As a result, Goryeo was initially uncooperative in regard to the Yuan's attempt to instruct Japan to send tribute. When the first envoys were dispatched in 1266–1267, the Goryeo Minister Yi Jangyong explained to Hindu, an envoy from the Yuan, about the dangers of the voyage to Japan and the meaninglessness of negotiating with that country, eventually succeeding in persuading him to abandon the attempt. Further, contrary to Qubilai's prior warning against justifying the cancellation of the embassy on the bases of "intemperate wind and waves" and "non-communication with Japan", Yi Jangyong did, in fact, justify its cancellation citing these very reasons. At that time, the gateway for Goryeo's diplomatic and trade relations with Japan was located at Gimhae on the southeastern coast of the peninsula. While Goryeo led the Yuan envoy to Geojedo Island, located to the west of Gimhae, it demolished the guest-houses it had erected there for receiving people from Japan in order to conceal its relations with that country.

In his rage over the failure of his envoy and Goryeo to execute his orders, Qubilai demanded that the Goryeo government convey a letter from the Yuan Emperor to Japan. As a result, Ban Bu was dispatched to Japan at the end of 1267. When he arrived in Japan, Ban Bu sent a letter to the chief of the Dazaifu[2]. Ban worded this letter in such a way that placed the Yuan in an inferior status to Japan and disclosed that Goryeo had hindered the Yuan's plan to invade Japan, requesting that it handle the situation prudently.

After that, the relationship between Goryeo and the Yuan deteriorated. In 1270, the Goryeo military government collapsed and Goryeo was under pressure to improve its relationship with the Yuan for security reasons. As part of that, Goryeo began to cooperate in plans to invade Japan, though it remained somewhat unenthusiastic, as seen in its attempt to reduce the costs it would have to bear for the invasion.

In the period between the first invasion in 1274 (Jp. the Bun'ei Campaign; Kr. the Gapsul Campaign) and the second in 1281 (Jp. the Kōan Campaign; Kr. the Sinsa Campaign), Goryeo proposed dispatching more troops and took other measures to present a more actively cooperative position towards the war. However, anticipating that renewed hostilities with Japan were unavoidable, Goryeo attempted to take the initiative in planning and executing the military operations, thereby protecting its own interests against the demands of and interference by the Yuan.

In the meantime, after the collapse of Goryeo's military government, the Sambyeolcho (Three Patrols)[3], an assemblage of elite Goryeo military units that had carried out the war against the Mongols for many years, escaped to Jindo Island, located off the southwestern coast of Korea, then to Jejudo Island in the sea south of Korea. From there, they continued to resist both the Yuan and their home country's government in Gaegyeong until 1273. This resistance inhibited the ability of the Yuan and Goryeo

---

2 This was most likely a member of the Mutō house who hereditarily bore the title of Deputy Assistant Governor of the Dazaifu (Shōni).

3 The Sambyeolcho was an elite military force composed of three different units: two platoons of the Night Patrol (Yabyeolcho), the left and the right, which were originally assembled as public security units, and the Army of Transcendent Righteousness (Sinuigun), which was composed of a select group of soldiers who had escaped after being taken captive by the Mongol army.

to gain control of the southern coast of the peninsula, which delayed the attack on Japan. At the same time, the Kamakura Shogunate was facing growing political instability, which burst into violence in an incident known as the "Nigatsu Sōdō" (Second Month Disturbance) in 1272[4]. As a result of the Sambyeolcho's activity along the Korean coast, the Kamakura Shogunate gained sufficient time to prepare its defenses. In addition, in this period the Sambyeolcho sent envoys to Japan to call for an alliance against the Yuan, and there is also evidence that the Southern Song dispatched Japanese monks studying in China as secret messengers to Japan. However, the Japanese Shogunate refused to commit itself to either of these overtures, which rendered both attempts at alliance moot.

In Japan, the Yuan admonishments to send tribute met with strong opposition from both the imperial court and the Kamakura Shogunate. At the same time, there is evidence that the Dazaifu, emissaries' gateway to and from Japan, had prepared their own embassy to the Yuan court, reciprocating the arrival of the Yuan envoy Zhao Liangbi in 1271. In 1269, Goryeo sent back Tsushima islanders, who had been captured by Yuan and Goryeo envoys, bearing two letters. The Yuan secretariat, the central administrative organ of the Yuan court under the emperor, sent the first letter and a Goryeo regional governor, the Superintendant for Gyeongsang Province sent the second. Japan's imperial court drafted a strongly worded refusal to the secretariat's letter, but it prepared a friendly reply to the Superintendant's. Although neither of the replies was actually sent, it appears that the "favor" the Goryeo envoy Ban Bu had secretly shown to Japan was certainly conveyed to Japanese authorities.

From the period before 1250 until the eve of war, diplomatic and trade networks linked Japan and Goryeo across the Korea Strait. The Mutō family, who held the title of Deputy Assistant Governor of the Dazaifu, traditionally the actual authority in charge of the Dazaifu, helped maintain the network from the Japanese side. Since assuming the post in the late twelfth/early thirteenth century, the Mutō had conducted negotiations with Goryeo concerning issues of commercial intercourse and the suppression

---

4 The Second Month Disturbance (Nigatsu Sōdō) was an internecine struggle within the shogunal regent's family, the Hōjō. The main line of the Hōjō, the Tokusō, defeated two brothers, Tokiaki and Noritoki, belonging to a powerful branch family, the Nagoe, as well as Tokisuke, an elder half-brother of the reigning shogunal regent Tokimune.

of the Wokou. In 1263, shortly before the Yuan first instructed Japan to present tribute, a trading vessel that the Mutō had some hand in dispatching to Song China was wrecked on the coast of Korea and received protection and assistance from Goryeo. This network was also used in an attempt to avoid coming into contact with the Mongols. The arrival of a Japanese ship[5] at Gimhae in 1272 can be regarded as part of the ongoing trade relationship between Japan and Goryeo that had continued through the first half of the thirteenth century. However, Jo Ja'il, the Gyeongsangdo Provincial Commissioner of Inspection who tried to conceal the fact of the arrival of this Japanese ship, was executed by the Yuan. Tensions were already beginning to heighten.

In preparation for both attacks on Japan, Happo (present-day Changwon) on the southeastern coast of Korea served as an advance base. The squadrons of ships built or commandeered in Korea set out to attack Japan from this location carrying conscripted Korean sailors. The degree to which Koreans were familiar with the navigation required for the voyage to Japan is unclear, though they had sufficient expertise to sail ships carrying political embassies when necessary. Much of the trade between Japan and Korea in the period between the tenth century and the first half of the thirteenth occurred when Japanese ships sailed to Korea. In addition, the 1273 attack on Jejudo Island to destroy the "three patrols" in advance of the attacks on Japan served as a rehearsal for the Yuan and Goryeo in sending large numbers of military forces across the open sea. In the attack, they demonstrated sufficient capability to achieve success. Although also including a poorly trained labor force conscripted in short order, the preparations for and execution of the invasions required the large-scale exploitation of the techniques and knowledge of both Korean officials and subjects involved in maritime activities.

For the second attack on Japan in 1281, a Song general who had surrendered to the Yuan, Fan Wenhu, mobilized the naval might of the Southern Song, including experts in shipbuilding and navigation technologies and knowledge, as well as the manpower to sail the ships. Their major port of departure was Qingyuan and its environs, although some argue that the Mongol forces set sail simultaneously from multiple locations including Qingyuan. In comparison to the forces from Korea, the

---

5  The number of ships is uncertain.

fleet setting forth from South China contained a much smaller proportion of newly wrought warships from Quanzhou, Yangzhou and other areas. In addition to warships confiscated from the Southern Song's navy, the South China fleet included many commandeered private ships and even those designed for use on rivers (*yanjiang-chuan*). Naturally, manpower for the invasions was drawn from those with experience in sailing on the trading vessels that traveled between Japan and China, because engaging in a military campaign across the sea was an unknown experience even for the former Southern Song naval forces.

## Mongol plan and military activities (2): Invasion of the South Seas

Shortly after the first invasion of Japan, the Yuan began dispatching diplomatic missions and military forces to the region known as the South Seas (Nanhai), a broad maritime region encompassing lands in the South China Sea and Indian Ocean. Integral to the diplomatic and military activities of the South Seas was the connection between Soɣatu, the Mongol general who initially led the invasion, and Pu Shougeng, a Quanzhou-based Muslim merchant thought to have been of either Arab or Persian descent.

After participating in the conquest of Hangzhou and its environs as commander of the naval forces seized from the Southern Song, Soɣatu proceeded to the south in 1277 as the *xuanweishi* (pacification commissioner) for Fujian, where he led the campaign to eliminate Song resistance. In Quanzhou, he rescued Pu Shougeng who had sworn allegiance to the Yuan. In the following year, Soɣatu was named an overseer for the Quanzhou branch secretariat, the highest level of local administration for that region. In that capacity, he received orders from Qubilai Qa'an to instruct countries along the South China Sea and Indian Ocean coasts to send tribute. He undertook this task together with Pu Shougeng, requiring access to his network of Muslim merchants to succeed.

Their activities entailed not only delivering the Yuan's admonishments that local governments should offer tribute, but also attracting merchant ships to return to China. This latter element accorded with Pu Shougeng's commercial interests in reviving foreign trade, which had come to a standstill in Fujian and Guangdong, and particularly in Quanzhou, as a result of the Yuan's war against the Southern Song. As a result, there were some situations in which Soɣatu and Pu Shougeng were the central figures on the scene rather than the

Yuan court, who actively directed the planning and execution of expeditions admonishing countries to send tribute, and even times when the Yuan court had to restrain their initiative. The Yuan dispatched several other expeditions to instruct countries along the South China Sea and Indian Ocean coasts to send tribute. The leaders of and participants in these embassies were often chosen because of connections they had to either Soγatu or Pu Shougeng, including Yang Tingbi, who was sent to Kūlam Malay and other lands, as well as Meng Qingyuan and Sun Shengfu, who were sent to Champa from 1279 to 1283.

By 1281, the Yuan court had become actively involved in planning an invasion of the South Seas region. Rival factions in the court competed over rights to the lucrative maritime trade of the South China Sea and Indian Ocean regions, causing changes in the personnel who would lead the diplomatic and military activities. In 1281, a Champa Branch Secretariat office was established as the headquarters of the offensive, and preparations for war were completed under the direction of Soγatu, Liu Shen, a naval commander who had played an active role in subjugating the Southern Song, and Yigmiš, a Uigur trade administrator in the Yuan court.

As the court made preparations for war, it also intensified diplomatic pressure on the countries along the South China Sea and Indian Ocean coasts. Several envoys who seem to have been Muslims were dispatched to the region: Sulaymān was sent to Melayu in 1280, Shams al-Dīn was sent to Melayu, Cambodia and Tambralinga in 1281, and 'Abd Allāh was sent to the Pandyan Dynasty port of Ma'bar in 1282. At that time, Muslims from Central Asia, who connected with merchants, had arrived on the southern coast of China in large numbers and played prominent roles in the Yuan government. Mangγutai, the Mongol official in charge of Fujian, appears to have had connections with a Muslim of Central Asian origin named Shihāb al-Dīn, who controlled the rights to profits by the *ortuγ* (merchant associations). This connection seems to have influenced Mangγutai to exploit his access to naval power to extend his influence over the harbors of Fujian.

Both the demonstrations of military force and the embassies carrying inducements for the lands of the South Seas to offer tribute failed due to resistance from Champa. The Yuan then opened hostilities against Champa and the Trần Dynasty of Vietnam, which had refused to cooperate with the Yuan in an attack on Champa. Soγatu died in battle during this campaign. After the war ended in 1287, Qubilai shifted his policy vis-à-vis the countries along the South China Sea and Indian Ocean coasts to peaceful commerce.

Soγatu's army was taken over by a Uigur official named Ariq Qaya, and those who had engaged in the campaign ceased dealing with policies related to the countries of the South China Sea and Indian Ocean.

As for Pu Shougeng, during the period from 1280 to 1284, he became the de facto authority over Quanzhou. However, in 1285, new personnel arrived to take over the Fujian Branch Secretariat. Those connected to Soγatu were dismissed and Pu Shougeng lost his patronage at the Yuan court, though he is considered to have remained a locally influential person for years after.

The Yuan also launched a military invasion of Java, which held an important position as a collection and distribution center for the spice trade. After repeated refusals to its admonitions to send tribute, the Yuan dispatched an army from Quanzhou in an attempt to invade Java in 1293. Just prior to the expedition's departure, the Lord of Kediri overthrew the King of Singhasari, ruler of much of Java. Raden Wijaya, the king's son-in-law, who had been driven from the court, joined forces with the invading Mongol army and settled the situation. Wijaya subsequently expelled the Yuan forces, who had now fulfilled their role, and established the Majapahit Dynasty.

## Local states' responses to the Mongols

The expansion of Mongol hegemony applied various forms of pressure on the lands surrounding maritime East Asia. In some places, this pressure created opportunities for political change. In China, the emergence of the Yuan brought about the dissolution of local warlord power that had grown after the end of the Jin Dynasty, and, to a certain extent, centralized parts of the Mongol Empire, restricting the autonomy of members of the nobility and Mongol royal families who had grown powerful in certain regions. The Yuan's policies for overseas expansion can be seen as part of this trend. In Korea, the government ruled by military officials that had long held de facto power was overthrown and the royal family of Goryeo, which enjoyed a close relationship with the Mongols, was restored to rule. King Jayanegara of the Majapahit Dynasty of Java also strengthened an unstable powerbase by establishing a close relationship with the Yuan. He actively dispatched envoys to the Yuan court, and even visited it himself, though he was murdered upon his return to Java. In Japan, the Kamakura Shogunate continued to refuse to establish diplomatic relations with the Yuan. Instead, the main line of the Hōjō family and hereditary regents for the shogun, the Tokusō house, exploited the continued military tensions to increase its autocratic rule.

Invasion and rule by foreign peoples awakened anti-Mongol consciousness and new self-awareness among the inhabitants of the coasts of maritime East Asia. These new forms of consciousness manifested in various ways. For example, in South China, there is a scene in *Canjunxi* (The Adjutant Play; a comical and satirical drama) performed in Hangzhou in 1279 in which the abbot of a temple gives a scolding as follows: "One who is as noble as a god of the bell [*chung shen*] should not be expected to kowtow that easily". This appears to satirize *shidafu* (scholar-officials)[6], such as Fan Wenhu, who had surrendered to the Yuan, with a play on words using "*chung shen*" (the god of the bell) in place of "*chung shen*" (loyal retainers). In addition, to some extent memories of the Song imperial family, which was wiped out by the Yuan, helped unify parts of China. *Chuogeng Lu* (Records Compiled After Returning from the Farm)[7], an account from the end of the Yuan period, celebrates the "noble deeds" of Tang Jue and Lin Jingxi, who collected the remains of an emperor of the Southern Song whose imperial mausoleum was dug up at the beginning of the Yuan period. Han Shantong, one of the leaders of the Red Turbans[8], a rebel army that rose up at the end of the Yuan period, claimed to be a "grandchild of Huizong, the eighth Emperor of the Song Dynasty".

In Korea, after the subjugation of Goryeo by the Yuan, the various manifestations of overt resistance to the Mongols, including the utilization of Buddhism for the purpose of defending the country, largely came to an end. However, some elements in Goryeo continued to adhere strongly to their own "state's traditions" (*guksok*) so as to differentiate themselves from the "universal" system of the Yuan. The most important

---

6 *Shidafu* were persons of the Chinese intellectual class and bureaucrats who had passed the Chinese civil service examination.
7 *Chuogeng Lu* is a miscellany composed by the literatus Tao Zongyi between the end of the Yuan Dynasty and the beginning of the Ming Dynasty. It was compiled by a man known as Nancun, a native of Huangyan in Zhejiang Province.
8 The Red Turbans (1351–1366) was the name of a popular uprising that challenged Yuan supremacy in China. The movement spread from the Anhui and Hubei regions to South China. The name originates in the red headdress worn as a symbol of the uprising. They based their power in popular religious groups such as the Bailianjiao (White Lotus Society).

## 1.4: What Conflicts with the Mongols Wrought

among these traditions was the myth of Dangun, which is now claimed to be a tale relating the origin of the Korean people. Although the origin of the Dangun mythology is considered to extend further back in time, the oldest forms of the myth that can be confirmed at present are found in two histories completed in the latter half of the thirteenth century, *Jewang-ungi* (Songs of Emperors and Kings) by Yi Seunghyu[9] and *Samguk-yusa* (Memorabilia of the Three Kingdoms) by Iryeon[10]. The former distinguishes the genealogy of successive monarchs of Korea from the successive emperors of China, including the emperors of the Yuan Dynasty, and places Dangun at the head of Korea's royal genealogy. Although these projects did not necessarily constitute resistance to the Mongols, these histories do suggest an attempt on the part of the Goryeo elite to articulate a "we consciousness" that distinguished the people and political systems of Korea from those of China.

In Japan, there was an increase in belief in Japan as a land of the gods. These ideas actually predated the Mongol invasions, becoming prominent in response to the emergence of a government led by warriors in the Kamakura period as those who sought to maintain an emperor-centered political system emphasized the sacredness of the lineage descended from Amaterasu Ōmikami (Japan's sun goddess) lineage. The Mongol invasions provided an external stimulus that facilitated the promotion of this belief. A draft of the Japanese imperial court's reply to the official letters from the Yuan Dynasty's Central Secretariat in 1269 is notable for explicitly emphasizing to foreign countries that the rulers of Japan were the descendants of Amaterasu Ōmikami and that the country enjoyed divine protection. These ideas were propagated to additional levels of society after the appearance of so-called "*kamikaze*" (divine winds) (typhoons that facilitated the repulsion of the Mongol invasion forces). This strain of thought reached its apogee in *Jinnō Shōtōki* (*A Chronicle of Gods and*

---

9 *Jewang-ungi* is a historical epic poem that relates the lineages of the successive emperors of China and kings of Korea. It was compiled by Yi Seunghyu (1224–1300), a native of Gari-hyeon, Gyeongsan-bu, who went under the pen name of Dongan Geosa.

10 *Samguk-yusa* is a collection of historical records of ancient Korea and Buddhist tales focused on the history of Silla. It was assembled by Iryeon (1206–1286), a native of Jangsan-gun, Gyeongju, and a high-ranking Seon (Cn. Chan, Jp. Zen) Buddhist monk.

*Sovereigns*) by Kitabatake Chikafusa[11] in the fourteenth century, which opens with the passage, "Great Japan is the divine land. The heavenly progenitor founded it, and the sun goddess bequeathed it to her descendants to rule eternally. Only in our country is this true; there are no similar examples in other countries. That is why our country is called the divine land" (Kitabatake 1980: 49).

In the lands of Southeast Asia too, the impact of the Mongols can be seen in a rise of "we consciousness" that manifested in systematized forms of history. The Trần Dynasty of Đại Việt formalized its history, royal authority, territory and religion all at the same time. In 1272, Lê Văn Huru compiled the official history of the Trần Dynasty, the *Đại Việt sử ký*. In 1299, "the gods of the mountains and rivers" were enshrined around the country. In 1329, *Spiritual Powers of the Việt Realm* (*Việt điện u Linh Tập*) compiled the stories on the origins of the gods that were given titles by the king after the repulsion of the Yuan and were to be enshrined by the state. It is said that the creation of poetry in the national language (Chữ Nôm poetry) began during the war against the Mongols. In Java a court official compiled a chronicle of kings entitled *Desawarnana* (*Nagarakertagama*). In mainland Southeast Asia, where Theravada Buddhism was influential[12], the original versions of the Buddhist and dynastic chronicles of the early modern era were also first completed by the fourteenth century.

## Thriving trade amidst tensions in the East China Sea

From the point of view of people in the modern age, it would not have been surprising if, having gone through two military conflicts that left political enmities unresolved, Japan and the Yuan had terminated the trade between their two lands. In fact, they did no such thing. Although trade was temporarily suspended during and immediately after the invasions, it later became as prosperous as it had previously been. Some

---

11 Completed in 1339 and revised in 1343, *Jinnō Shōtōki* by Kitabatake Chikafusa relates the deeds of the Japanese emperors from the mythological age to the Emperor Go-Murakami. It argues for the legitimacy of the Southern Court in the conflict between the Northern and Southern Courts. Kitabatake Chikafusa (1293–1354) was a court noble who played a central role in the leadership of the Southern Court.
12 In Southeast Asia, Theravada Buddhism (the so-called Hinayana (Lesser Vehicle) of Buddhism) became the major religion of Thailand, Myanmar, Laos, Cambodia and other lands.

even consider that it became more active than at any time before or since. The same was true in terms of Yuan maritime trade in the South China Sea and Indian Ocean. Whether it is the case that the trade was active regardless of the warfare, or whether, from a historical viewpoint, a confrontation between political powers would not necessarily affect private trade, this situation has implications for the study of international relations today. The structures and characteristics of the trading system did not change drastically from the situation prior to 1250. In China, Qingyuan remained the gateway, where trade was controlled by the *shibosi* (maritime trade supervisorate), while in Japan, Hakata remained the major gateway, even though Qingyuan and Hakata represented the launching point and target, respectively, of the two invasions of Japan.

At the same time, the two military encounters also sparked transformations that helped generate the types of maritime interaction characteristic of the next period of maritime East Asia.

In Japan, having already suffered from invasion, the Kamakura Shogunate implemented precautionary measures to prepare for possible further invasions by the Yuan. A plan to launch a retaliatory attack to "punish foreign countries" (i.e. the Yuan and Goryeo) was never implemented. Instead, from 1272, the shogunate successively rotated its vassals to perform *ikoku keigo banyaku* (guard duty against foreign invasion) along the northern coast of Kyushu. In 1276, it ordered the construction of a defensive wall, the remains of which still exist along the coast of Hakata bay. As an additional defensive measure, signal beacons began to be installed in 1294. The shogunate established the office of the Chinzei Tandai (Shogunal Deputy in Kyushu) in the 1290s to serve as the institutional nucleus of the defense system. This office was maintained until the downfall of the Kamakura Shogunate in 1333.

It is unclear how much these security measures affected the management of diplomacy and foreign trade. At least, it appears that shipping traffic was suspended in tense situations such as when envoys arrived from Yuan or Goryeo. It is presumed that the Chinzei Tandai and other authorities made preparations to restrict the arrival and departure of ships as necessary, though it is unclear whether they constantly maintained this state of readiness.

Chinese maritime merchants remained the main carriers of trade between Japan and China at that time. Travelogues of Japanese monks and other records indicate that these merchants sailed back and forth frequently, except for brief periods such as during diplomatic crises or episodes of actual warfare. However, the composition of the Chinese maritime merchant bands changed from what it was prior to 1250. At this point, the communities of Chinese maritime merchants based in Hakata led by those known as the Hakata *gangshou* (head sea merchants) become less visible in the historical record. Although it is unlikely that the descendants of the *gangshou* all disappeared, no Chinese appear in records related to the founding of Myōrakuji Temple[13] in Hakata in the first half of the fourteenth century, in contrast to the prominent place of Chinese sea merchants in the cases of Shōfukuji and Jōtenji Temples founded earlier.

One reason for this change was the war with the Yuan, which caused, in 1281, the shogunate to instigate the issuance of an edict expelling newly arrived foreigners. It is possible that the heavy shipping traffic between Japan and China was in fact a consequence of new conditions in Japan that made it difficult for newly arrived foreign maritime merchants to reside for long periods in the archipelago, causing a new trend in which sea merchants operated trading vessels in shorter, but more frequent cycles. Without replenishment by newcomers, the Chinese communities of northern Kyushu lost distinctive ethnic identities and were soon assimilated into the local society. However, from a different point of view, the new pattern of trade showed that shipbuilding and navigation technologies as well as the political, economic and social structures necessary for smooth commercial dealings that sufficiently preserved profitability had reached a point such that stable maritime interaction and commerce could occur even without merchants who built bases in overseas trading hubs and stayed for long periods (*zhufan* type trade).

In Yuan China, even as it established policies that emphasized openness in and the development of trade, the Yuan court took a vigilant stance regarding trade with Japan. After subjugating South China, the Yuan established a garrison known as the *yanhai wanhufu* (coastal myriarchy) in the port of Qingyuan charged with guarding the coast from Shandong to Fujian. This institution inherited aspects of the coastal defense system related to armaments and personnel that had been in place since the

---

13 Myōrakuji Temple began when Getsudō Sōki founded Sekijōan Hermitage in 1316 at Okinohama in Hakata. The name was later changed to Myōrakuji. The temple was involved in diplomatic and trade relations with Ming China and Joseon Korea.

Southern Song. In particular, it employed local elites with influence in maritime regions, such as Pu Shougeng of Quanzhou and the Yang family of Ganpu. The Yuan increased its garrisons in the Zhejiang region, which contained the ports of entry for most Japanese arrivals, by establishing the Zhedong *douyuanshuaifu* (circuit military command) in 1303 and the Dinghai battalion *qianhusuo* (chiliarchy) in 1304. As in the case of Ryūzan Tokken, mentioned in Chapter 1.1, Japanese were prohibited from entering the cities of the ports where their ships were moored. Merchant ships from Japan were prohibited from visiting around the time of the war with Japan and immediately after the riots by "*woshang*" ("Japanese merchants") (not necessarily ethnically Japanese merchants). The effects of a 1335 Yuan ban on Japanese ships can be seen in the sudden disappearance of Japanese Buddhist monks traveling to China from historical records, who until then had traveled to that country frequently on trading vessels. This state of affairs continued until 1342, when trading vessels were dispatched from Japan to finance the building of Tenryūji Temple.

**Photo 2: Remaining defensive stone walls in Hakata Bay**
Source: Saeki Koji.

Needless to say, these precautionary measures on the part of the Yuan were brought about by the failures of embassies admonishing Japan to send tribute, the invasions of Japan and Yuan perceptions of Japan as a potentially hostile force. A vicious cycle worsened this already tense situation after eruptions of violence on the part of "*woshang*" intensified the Yuan court's sense of caution toward Japan. An account in the first half of the fourteenth century, *Ma Yuanshuai fangwo ji* (Record of the Defense Against the Japanese by Marshal Ma) by Yuan Jue, contains an episode that describes how trade with Japanese merchants at Dinghai, an outport of Qingyuan, occurred under heavy guard.

Japan and China were able to engage in trade even while such tensions existed. However, what should be emphasized here is the fact that trade flourished regardless of the political and military situation. That the forms of "open" trade that had been practiced from the period before 1250 were maintained and even expanded under these constraints should be interpreted as a manifestation of the resilient nature of the "open" maritime interactions.

In much the same way, maritime trade in the South China Sea and Indian Ocean continued to flourish even after the Yuan withdrew its forces, though it also suffered comparatively less from warfare. The Yuan did briefly prohibit sailing to the South China Sea at the time of the expedition to Java in 1293, but they did not take military precautions or restrict trade as was the case regarding Japan. The Yuan had no military conflict with most of the countries along the South China Sea and Indian Ocean coasts, excepting Champa, the Trần Dynasty and Java, and the possibility that the Yuan might have been directly invaded by these states was rather remote.

In contrast, tensions between Japan and Korea escalated. At the time of the second invasion of Japan, the Yuan had established the office of the Eastern Conquest Branch Secretariat in Goryeo as the headquarters of the military forces setting out from Korea, with the King of Goryeo serving as its head. After the second invasion, the Yuan reestablished this office on a number of occasions whenever further military action against Japan was planned. From 1287 on, it became a permanent institution run by the King of Goryeo and the highest level of Yuan local government administering that land. However, as suggested by the continuous use of its name, the Eastern Conquest Branch Secretariat appears to have remained unchanged as an institution designed to oversee military action along the Yuan's eastern frontier, particularly against the hostile country of Japan. In 1294, the death of Qubilai led to the abandonment of invasion plans, and the institution was expected to play a defensive role to counter any threat from Japan.

In addition, after the second invasion, *zhenbian wanhufu* (frontier defense command myriarchies) were established to protect the port of Happo and the coast of Jeolla Province. In 1301, the Tamna Commandery was established on Jejudo Island. In this way, the Yuan constructed a defensive network against Japan all along the southern coast of the Korean Peninsula. These institutions were all overseen by the King of Goryeo, the head of the Eastern Conquest Branch Secretariat, and their offices were all staffed by Goryeo government personnel. The Kings of Goryeo thus took responsibility for the defense of the Yuan's eastern border and emphasized the importance of this role when appealing to the Yuan regarding Goryeo's interests.

In the end, Japan never launched a large-scale counteroffensive against either Goryeo or the Yuan, although Goryeo would have likely obtained information about Japanese invasion plans. At least, at that time, small-scale incidents involving the Wokou occasionally occurred in coastal areas of Goryeo, which some scholars supposed to correlate with a Japanese plan to "punish foreign countries". In addition, from 1350 the Wokou began striking Korea in large-scale raids (known as the first wave of the Wokou). Military threats from Japan were not necessarily inconceivable from the standpoint of Goryeo.

Meanwhile, the trade between Japan and Korea that had continued until the mid-thirteenth century appears to have been forced into cessation at the outbreak of war. Although there were some cases in which individuals labeled "Japanese" (*wae'in*) were shipwrecked in or otherwise reached Korea, it appears that formalized trade relations ceased completely, in contrast to the relations between the Yuan and Japan where both sides, though vigilant toward each other, continued to receive the other's ships. However, when considering the fact that the Goryeo court regarded itself as the linchpin for the Yuan's defense against Japan on its eastern frontier, and they used this position as grounds for advocating Goryeo's interests to the Yuan court, it is not surprising that Japan is frequently described in the official records of Goryeo as a security threat. It is even possible that Goryeo's official position was only a pretense. As such, it is possible that some of the "Japanese" who appear in historical sources as castaways or pirates were actually intending to conduct trade. There were not enough such cases to leave clear traces in the historical record, but it is unlikely that commercial interactions stopped completely. When considering the first wave of the Wokou in the latter half of the fourteenth century, this relationship between maritime activity and the Goryeo court's official responses will be worth examining.

This chapter has explored how, in maritime East Asia between 1250 and 1350, the Mongol Empire expanded militarily while trade between Japan and China as well as the maritime trade in the South China Sea and Indian Ocean flourished. Some argue that, with regard to the latter, the Yuan considered military action part of the measures necessary to promote commercial intercourse. These military and commercial activities created a huge network of interaction extending east and west across the Eurasian continent, both on land and sea, which enabled the movements of people, objects and information between distant lands in an unprecedentedly direct manner and on an unparalleled scale. The structures for managing maritime interaction retained the relatively relaxed and flexible character that they had possessed before 1250. Indeed, the "openness" that defined the operation of maritime interaction in the period prior to 1250 peaked in this period.

In the East China Sea region, maritime trade also occurred amidst political and military tensions. However, in contrast to the South China Sea and Indian Ocean, maritime interaction in this region both extended "the openness" of earlier periods and exhibited signs that political authorities were attempting to establish institutions through which they could insert themselves directly into the patterns of trade in the maritime world. Politics thus began to interfere with the voyages of trading vessels, terminating trade relations between Japan and Korea for example. Although the direct causes and motivations differed, the maritime prohibitions enacted in the early years of the Ming Dynasty were an extension of this type of political intervention in the interactions in the maritime world.

# 1.5: Traffic in Goods and Technology
## Expanding the Field of Interaction and Mutual Exchange

The East Asian maritime world served as a medium for the exchange of goods and the transfer of technology in the period 1250 to 1350. Through these interactions, maritime East Asia generated new cultural forms and traditions in the countries surrounding it. In order to illuminate the distinctive characteristics of these forms of maritime exchange in this period, this chapter mainly focuses on the case of Japan, taking advantage of an abundance of extant, reliable historical documents and materials concerning sea-based intercultural exchange. Japan's separation from continental Asia by the ocean made it necessary for foreign interactions to be carried out via sea routes, thus the bulk of historical sources are relevant to the study of maritime exchange.

Direct and bilateral interactions between Korea and China also increased significantly in this period. The most advanced cultures and technologies from China, including Zhu Xi Neo-Confucianism, Buddhism, gunpowder, agricultural manuals, currency and calendars, were actively introduced to Korea, as were cultural elements from further north and west, including Mongol customs and Tibetan Buddhism. However, Korea is not only connected to the Eurasian continent by land routes, but was also linked to North and South China by sea routes, as previous chapters explained. It is difficult to determine whether a particular element of foreign culture was transmitted via land or sea, no matter whether the artifact, idea or technology originated in a northern, southern, inland or coastal area of the continent. In particular, in a case where transmission by both land and sea routes occurred, the question of which route was actually taken is meaningless unless one knows the differences in the quantities and qualities of the goods conveyed by each route. Similar difficulties arise in considering the case of West Asia and mainland Southeast Asia, which are also connected to China by land routes.

On the other hand, it is all the more necessary that we include these complex situations in our analyses, since it is possible that they were relevant to maritime interactions. Particularly when dealing with the situation in coastal areas, maritime interactions cannot be understood without considering intersections with terrestrial developments; neither can be studied in isolation.

This chapter explores how goods and technologies coursed the seas of East Asia between 1250 and 1350 and drove Japanese maritime intercultural exchange, turning attention to the situation in other lands when necessary. The analysis reveals two important trends. First, in contrast to earlier centuries, the circulation of goods between the southeastern coast of China and neighboring countries demonstrated significant bidirectionality, meaning that goods flowed in and out of the countries surrounding maritime East Asia. Second, the social stratum of people involved in "cultural" transmission across maritime East Asia expanded to a much greater degree than before.

The goods discussed in this chapter do not constitute an exhaustive list, and are only representative examples. Readers should bear in mind that various kinds of goods in addition to those introduced here, including textile products, medicinal substances, spices, various metal and non-metal materials and handicrafts, were also traded in maritime East Asia during this period.

## Goods flowing out of China

From 1250 to 1350, the demand for goods originating in China from those living in neighboring lands was stronger than in previous periods, and this period saw a significant growth in the demand.

Each of the lands in maritime East Asia in this period evinced distinctive economic circumstances, which become visible when exploring the situation regarding currency, in particular the reception of currencies from China that circulated in vast quantities across Eurasia at the time.

The Mongol Empire cast silver ingots in a distinctive shape, known in Mongolian as *süke* (axe) and in Persian as *bālish* (pillow). The Mongols introduced this currency after the expansion of their empire across much of Eurasia caused the economic spheres of China, Central Asia and West Asia to become more closely interlinked than ever before, which necessitated a universally accepted standard unit of exchange. These silver ingots found use not only in land-based trade in Central Eurasia, but also as capital invested by members of the *ortuy* (merchant associations) in South Seas maritime trade, bringing this currency to the South China Sea and Indian Ocean.

A variety of currencies circulated in the Southeast Asian ports that served as intermediary way stations along seaborne trade routes, including tin coins issued by local governments, Chinese copper coins brought by maritime merchants from China and Muslim dinar coins. Later, counterfeit Chinese copper coins minted in local areas and gold and silver coins issued by local governments also appeared.

In Japan, the monetary economy developed rapidly from the mid-twelfth century. By the latter half of the thirteenth century, it had become common for estates to pay a variety of taxes using copper coins, which had previously been paid in kind or corvée commuted. However, in this period neither the

**Photo 3: Yuan silver ingot**

Source: Collections of China Finance & Taxation Museum.

imperial court nor the military governments (the Kamakura and Ashikaga Shogunates) issued their own currencies. Instead, the rapid development of a cash economy was facilitated by the importation of large amounts of copper coins from China (known as *toraisen*), especially those minted in huge quantities during the Northern Song period. Excavations of medieval sites across Japan have unearthed hordes of Song Dynasty copper coins. In Ryukyu too, masses of unearthed Chinese coins suggest that Chinese currency imports reached one of several peaks in the thirteenth and fourteenth centuries, raising the possibility that direct trade was conducted with China at that time.

Korea was the exception to this situation. Although Goryeo had issued its own iron and copper coins on several occasions after the end of the tenth century, they were not in extensive circulation, and Chinese copper coins were not imported in quantities sufficient for the development of a cash economy. Instead, the means of exchange were limited to commodities such as rice, cloth and silver. From the twelfth century, the government issued standardized *eunbyeong* (silver coins) for use in large-scale domestic transactions and trade with China, but their use ceased at the beginning of the fourteenth century. Paper bills issued by the Yuan (*jiaochao*) were used in transactions with China and for donations to temples, but there was little domestic circulation of these bills in Korea. Further, the commutation of corvée labor or taxes in kind into cash did not occur in Korea in this period.

Ceramics were another commodity produced in China that was exported to maritime Asia in vast quantities, and large volumes of these products were imported into Japan. Among them were the celadon wares produced in Longquan (in Zhejiang), the *yingqing* (shadowy blue wares) of Jingdezhen (in Jiangxi), dark-glazed bowls known as *tenmoku* in Japanese and counterfeit wares produced in several areas within China, such as Fujian and Guangdong. The importation of these ceramics was stimulated by new sources of domestic Japanese demand at that time: the diffusion of tea-drinking, the increase in the consumption of *karamono* (continental luxuries) by new warrior elites and the urban development of the warrior capital of Kamakura and other cities. As mentioned above, the influx of Chinese ceramics into Ryukyu also increased in this period. Among the ceramics imported in large quantities into Ryukyu was roughly made white porcelain from Fujian that has rarely been found in other areas of Japan, which suggests independent interactions between Ryukyu and China. In Korea, local porcelain production techniques, mainly of the famous Goryeo celadon, had already taken root by this period. Goryeo celadon was even exported to China.

The production of porcelain began in Korea around the tenth century, when the technology was introduced from China. In Japan, however, production only became possible much later, by the end of the sixteenth or beginning of the seventeenth century, after porcelain making technologies and craftsmen seized in Korea by Toyotomi Hideyoshi's invasion forces[1] arrived in Japan. As a result, in earlier periods, Japanese artisans devised ways to imitate celadon and white porcelain using special techniques in glazing and other processes. The invention of these imitation techniques shows the degree to which Chinese ceramics were in strong demand and highly valued. The imitation of Chinese ceramics also occurred in Vietnam, Siam and Burma, beginning around the fourteenth century when local production of ceramics gradually developed in Southeast Asian states. By the fifteenth century, ceramics produced in Southeast Asia began to be actively exported and have been found in excavations in the Japanese port of Hakata.

Silk, both in the form of high-quality fabrics and thread used as raw materials, was imported into Japan from China from ancient times, and these imports continued during the thirteenth and fourteenth centuries. However, this neither led directly to improvements in existing local silk fabric production techniques nor to the local production of goods equivalent to those imported from China. Local silk production techniques in Japan did not sufficiently develop to equate with silk goods produced in China until the fifteenth to sixteenth centuries. This shows us that as in the case of porcelain, the process of moving from the imitation of Chinese techniques to transforming local methods of production was not simple or straightforward. As Korea also depended on maritime merchants from South China for high-quality raw silk, we may presume that Korea was in a similar situation to

---

1 Toyotomi Hideyoshi, who unified Japan under his rule at the end of the sixteenth century, launched an invasion of Korea when the Joseon court refused to cooperate with his plans to conquer Ming China. Japan waged two campaigns in Korea, in 1592–1593 and 1597–1598. In Korea, Japanese forces mobilized by *daimyōs* from across Japan battled the Joseon court's official army, "righteous army" irregulars and relief forces dispatched by Ming China. In Japan, this war is known as the "campaigns of Bunroku and Keichō", in Korea as the "Imjin War" and in China as "the Korean War" (Chaoxian zhiyi).

Japan in terms of this technology. Furthermore, the imitation of Chinese silks also occurred in West Asia.

One of the Chinese products that originally did not attract as much attention was a new strain of rice known as "Champa Rice", or, as it was known in Japan historically, "China Rice" (*Daitōmai*), a variety of the Indica Rice native to Southeast Asia. It was suitable for early-season cultivation and for planting in low-yield paddy fields with poor soil fertility, and was thus often planted in newly developed paddy fields in swampy lowlands. It was introduced into China in the eleventh century and widely cultivated, particularly in South China.

In Japan, the establishment of regular Champa Rice cultivation in the fourteenth or fifteenth century is considered an important landmark in the history of rice agriculture in that country. Champa Rice was used, for example, to help in the development of swampy lowlands on the Tsukushi plain in Kyushu. The first appearance of the variety in historical sources is in a document from 1308, which shows that it had been introduced prior to this time. The importation of this seed variety was made possible by the trade actively moving between Japan and China, and it is likely that sea merchants or Zen monks traveling on merchant ships brought it into the country from South China in the thirteenth century or earlier. It appears that similar varieties were used in the development of swampy lowland regions in Korea after the twelfth century, as explained in Chapter 1.2, which, as was suggested by the case of Japan, further indicates that South China represented the route of transmission for Champa Rice. The case of Champa Rice highlights the importance of a perspective that includes maritime interactions when considering the history of agricultural technology, an area in which developments are often assumed to be indigenous.

## Goods flowing into China

The conquest of large swaths of Eurasia by the Mongol Empire energized not only the traffic of goods flowing out of China, but also that flowing into it. This commodity trade had gradually begun developing in the eighth or ninth century, when maritime merchants appeared in maritime East Asia. However, the commodity trade in this period differed from that in earlier ones in that the goods brought in from foreign countries affected the lifestyles and cultures of not only the elite strata of society, but also those of a wide range of status groups across society.

For example, the techniques involved in Islamic miniature paintings and the production and use of cobalt dye were introduced from West Asia and brought together in Jingdezhen, enabling the invention of its famous blue-and-white ware. Although this variety of porcelain was exported to Japan and Korea, where it has been found in excavations and as heirlooms, much of the production was designated for export to the west of China, including to West Asia.

Another influence from West Asia was its cuisines, brought into China not only by Central Eurasian land-based merchants, but also by seafarers across the South Seas. West Asian ingredients were fused with traditional local recipes to generate a new culinary culture, which then appeared in cookbooks and domestic encyclopedias such as *Yinshan-zhengyao* (Proper and Essential Things for Food and Drink) and *Jujia biyong shilei* (Collection of Necessary Matters Ordered for the Householder). There was also a heavy influx of *material medica* for Islamic medicine, influencing medical practices in China.

**Photo 4: Jingdezhen's blue-and-white ware**
Source: Shanghai Museum.

The "sulfur road" connected China to the rest of Eurasia via sea-lanes in this period, providing support for the development of gunpowder and firearms in that country, which began during the Song Dynasty. Sulfur is a key ingredient of gunpowder, but it was not found in China in large amounts. Instead, vast quantities of the substance were shipped from Japan, Java and West Asia.

Chinese society in southeastern China grew considerably from the Southern Song onwards, causing a rapid increase in the consumption of timber. The supply of wood for building material and fuel caused rapid deforestation mainly in the Zhejiang region where the capital was located. As a result, China turned to a new source for the supply of timber: overseas trade. For example, wood from Suō Province in Japan began to be imported into China during this period.

An exploration of goods flowing into and out of China highlights the bidirectionality of the interactions in maritime East Asia between 1250 and 1350.

## The spread of the lifestyle of South China

Japanese trade with China flourished during the period 1250 to 1350, when a large number of monks belonging to the Zen and Ritsu schools of Buddhism[2] traveled to Mainland China by taking advantage of trading vessels. We can also presume that many Japanese people other than monks crossed the sea in this period. In contrast to the official state-sponsored embassies to Tang China composed of aristocrats and high-ranking bureaucrats, in this period a large number of Japanese people from a variety of statuses and affiliations traveled to China. Through their interactions the everyday culture of commoners in China, particularly those of the ports of South China – Japan's diplomatic and commercial gateway to that country – was brought to Japan in a variety of forms.

For example, Buddhist monks and merchants likely brought foodways of China back to Japan, such as *shōjin ryōri*, a vegetarian cuisine based on the Buddhist philosophy that prohibits the killing of animals, and dim sum. These had a significant influence on Japanese culinary culture. In

---

2 The terms "Zen" and "Ritsu" are often paired, as both Zen and Ritsu Buddhist schools expanded their influence in Japanese Buddhism during the Kamakura and Muromachi periods.

the first half of the fourteenth century, Emperor Go-Daigo[3] reportedly enjoyed meals that included these "Chinese style dishes" (*karayō no zen*). Legend has it that noodles and *manju* (steamed buns) were introduced into Japan by monks crossing the sea in the Kamakura period through Hakata, the largest port involved in trade with China at that time and Japan's gateway to the world. Although these stories that attribute such deeds to famous historical monks must be taken with a grain of salt, it is highly probable that the newest Chinese cuisines were in fact introduced into Japan by Japanese monks who traveled to China in the Kamakura period.

Another example of the diffusion of culinary culture is the custom of tea-drinking. The tea culture of South China, in which a certain species of tea plant, tea utensils and a specific brewing method are combined, was adopted in Japan, leading to the characteristic Japanese tea ceremony culture in later years. Tea also began to be experimentally cultivated in Persia in this period. Although tea plantations did not take root in West Asia until the seventeenth century when the production of black tea began, the tea culture of China first reached the opposite edges of Asia – Persia and Japan – centuries earlier, during the period 1250 to 1350.

Korea, by contrast, as a result of having been incorporated into the Mongol Empire, received from Mongol China elements of the culinary cultures of the west and north, such as grape wine and distilled spirits. Although there are no historical documents showing an explicit record of transmission by sea, when considering the fact that Goryeo seaborne trade with China was ongoing, it appears that there were cases similar to the one in which Hyeso, a twelfth-century monk, purchased a large quantity of sugar confectionery from Song maritime merchants.

Among the everyday cultural materials shipped to Japan from China that gained widespread popularity were Buddhist paintings, specifically the so-called "Ningbo Buddhist paintings". Study of these paintings has revealed that religious, intercultural exchange at the time occurred on much wider and deeper scales than was previously thought. Ningbo Buddhist paintings were produced in Qingyuan (present-day Ningbo), one of the

---

3 Emperor Go-Daigo reigned from 1318 to 1339. In 1333, he overthrew the Kamakura Shogunate, establishing a new government known by its reign-era name, Kenmu. Soon after, he came into conflict with Ashikaga Takauji and in 1336 retreated to Yoshino (present-day Nara Prefecture). It is from this time that the rupture between the Northern and Southern Courts began, which lasted until 1392.

most important trading ports in China. These paintings were the products of professional painters who made a living meeting the heavy demand from local temples and ordinary people in their region. Once brought across the sea to Japan, these paintings exerted various types of influence on Buddhist painting and sculpture there. Further, recent studies have revealed that these imported Buddhist paintings actually included some paintings inspired by Manichaeism[4], which was spreading in the coastal areas of South China at that time. To give another example of religious exchange, the miniature paintings of the West Asia region that had such an impact on the formation of Jingdezhen blue-and-white wares were themselves actually influenced by painting styles of the Song and Yuan periods.

Japan also quickly received new forms of medical knowledge, medicines and techniques developed in China from the Song through the Jin and on into the Yuan periods. The first to absorb these new medical practices were not the official physicians connected to the imperial court or the shogunates, but rather local medical practitioners and monk-physicians. They were able to acquire and learn from imported Chinese medical texts that discussed a large number of practices that had been recently developed in the Zhejiang region. In other words, the importation of medical knowledge and techniques from the Zhejiang region was one significant effect of the establishment of that region as the juncture in the maritime trade networks linking Japan and China. Among the Chinese medical books used in Japan at the time was Xi Fanzi's *Maijue jijie* (Collection and Commentary on the Secrets of the Pulse), written in South China during the Southern Song period. This book was also introduced to the Ilkhanate in West Asia at around the same time. This extensive distribution of Chinese medical books vividly illustrates the active interactions linking the eastern and western regions of Eurasia in this period. In addition, some stories relating the introduction of what in later centuries became known as *kanpōyaku* (Chinese medicine) cite the thirteenth and fourteenth centuries as the period of their importation to Japan. Regardless as to whether or not the stories are true, it seems that the

---

4 Manichaeism is a religion founded by Mani, a native of the Persian Sasanian Empire, and teaches a dualistic cosmology of good vs. evil and light vs. darkness. Combining elements of Judaism, Zoroastrianism and Christianity, and integrating aspects of these religions with aspects of Buddhism and Taoism, Manichaeism spread widely across the Eurasian continent. It is thought to be almost extinct today.

transmission of the latest medical practices of China at that time played a certain role in the background to these stories.

China's intellectual culture was also in the process of being accepted by neighboring countries including Korea, Japan and Vietnam, particularly Song period Neo-Confucianism, the reinterpretation of Confucianism by Zhu Xi and others during the Southern Song period.

As was the case with other types of cultural exchange, Japanese Zen and Ritsu monks who traveled to Song and Yuan China during the Kamakura

**Figure 5: Ningbo Buddhist painting**
Source: Lu Xinzhong, Nirvana painting, Nara National Museum, Japan.

period, as well as the Chinese Zen monks who came to Japan, played important roles in the introduction of new intellectual trends to Japan. Along with Buddhist scriptures and books on Buddhism, Zen and Ritsu monks brought back a large number of tomes on Neo-Confucianism. They interpreted these Neo-Confucian works following an intellectual current prominent in Tang and Song Dynasty China that sought to unify Confucianism and Buddhism as well as to fuse Zen and Confucianism. They argued that Buddhism was superior to Confucianism and Zen Buddhism to Neo-Confucianism, while also finding the teaching of Neo-Confucianism useful for gaining patronage for the promotion of Zen Buddhism. By the first half of the fourteenth century, they had found such a patron in Emperor Go-Daigo, who showed an interest in Chinese culture and so authorized lectures on Confucian texts.

In conjunction with the introduction of new Chinese schools of thought into Japan by Zen and Ritsu monks, Buddhist temples in Japan began printing and binding books in this period, a trend that later blossomed into the Five Mountains editions (*Gozan-ban*) of Buddhist and Chinese texts[5]. This was an epochal moment in the history of books in Japan: the transition from complete dependence on imports to the beginning of domestic publication. The important roles played by Japanese Buddhist monks in the introduction of printing from China can be seen in the history of one of the first temples to begin the publication of books, Sennyūji Temple in Kyoto, which also produced a large number of monks who traveled to Song China, including Shunjō[6], the founder of the temple.

Korea also had a long history of actively importing books from Song China via the sea-lanes. The surviving evidence almost exclusively concerns books brought into Korea in conjunction with the comings and goings of envoys. An account of foreign trade during the Southern Song period written in the first

---

5 *Gozan-ban* books were woodblock printed editions of Zen works, Buddhist sutras, the recorded sayings of former Zen masters, anthologies of poetry and other works. Zen monks of the Kyoto Five Mountains System and other temples crafted these printed editions from the end of the Kamakura period through the end of the Muromachi period.

6 Shunjō (1166–1227), a native of Higo (present-day Kumamoto), was a scholar-monk of Ritsu, Tendai and Zen Buddhism. Traveling to Song Dynasty China in 1199, he studied at Tiantaishan, Jingshan, Simingshan and other temples. Returning to Japan, he served at Kenninji Temple in Kyoto and Sōfukuji Temple in Hakata, among others. He later founded Sennyūji Temple in 1218.

half of the thirteenth century, the *Zhufanzhi* (Record of Foreign Countries), lists among the articles exported to the Korean Peninsula publications from Jian'an in Fujian, a location famous for its publishing business. This record suggests that books were brought into Korea through maritime trade in the Song Dynasty, and this situation presumably continued during the period between 1250 and 1350. The Chinese-language primer *Nogeoldae* used by Koreans referred to in Chapter 1.3 includes a list of goods that the Goryeo merchants appearing in this book brought back to their home from the Yuan capital of Daidu. This list contains various titles including Confucian books such as Zhu Xi's *Sishu-jizhu* (Collected Commentaries of the Four Books), political and historical volumes such as the *Zizhi tongjian* (Comprehensive Mirror for Aid in Government) and *Zhenguan-zhengyao* (Essentials of Government of the Zhenguan Period), as well as a work of fiction, *Sanguozhi pinghua* (Records of the Three Kingdoms in Plain Language). We can thus conclude that these titles were sometimes actually shipped across the sea to Goryeo from the port of Zhigu.

## From the importation of "civilization" to that of "culture"

This exploration of the history of Sino-Japanese relations suggests that in maritime East Asia the period from 1250 to 1350 witnessed the completion of a shift in the focus of sea-based exchanges of culture and knowledge from a civilization-based exchange centered on North China to a culture-based exchange centered on South China.

Until the eighth or ninth century, Sino-Japanese relations occurred mainly via official, 'diplomatic missions to Tang China' (*kentōshi*). These envoys brought back to Japan the civilization that had developed around the large cities of North China. Here the term "civilization" denotes ideas, texts, artifacts, institutions and technologies that were both foundational to local cultures and expressed a global universality transcending their areas of production. Representative examples include Buddhism and the Chinese system of government based on criminal and administrative codes that served as the basis for Japan's foundational, imperial-bureaucratic Ritsuryō government. Japanese, chiefly members of the upper echelons of society such as aristocrats, bureaucrats and high-ranking clergy, modified elements of this "civilization" and produced "culture".

In subsequent periods, private trade involving a broader swathe of peoples in both Japan and China flourished and became the central mechanism linking the two countries. As a result, in the main gateways to maritime interactions – the port cities of South China and environs – individuals from across different levels of society were responsible for the development of culture imported into Japan. Here the term "culture" denotes the manners and customs, thoughts, lifestyles and technologies indigenous to people who lived in a relatively small area. Also included are various commodities, culinary cultures, folk manners and beliefs. In other words, the culture belonging to a wide range of Chinese society, including the lower classes, began to be imported into Japan, where, correspondingly, individuals from a wider range of social strata were responsible for its reception and transmission, enabling it to take root.

Cultural exchange between China and Japan in the period between 1250 and 1350 exhibited dimensions that both continued and developed the pattern of exchange from earlier periods. In fact, at the core of practices such as Japanese tea ceremony, ink painting, Noh and Kyōgen that have developed since the Muromachi period and that later came to be known as "traditional Japanese culture" are various elements that were brought into Japan in this period through maritime interactions with China. These elements were derived from the culture that was blossoming in South China, especially the coastal area of Zhejiang frequented by trading vessels.

This history of Japan's cultural exchange with China also resembles the exchange that occurred between Korea and China. Although interactions with North China also occupied an important place in Korea's interactions with China, given that under the close political relationship between the two countries the traffic between them was more direct and of a larger scale than that between China and Japan, the ties between Korea and South China generated by exchange in some varieties of culture were likely even stronger than those that existed in the case of Japan. For example, Buddhist cultural connections between Japan and Korea developed as a result of the intermediary role played by South China.

# Part 2

# Competing for the Sea, from 1500 to 1600

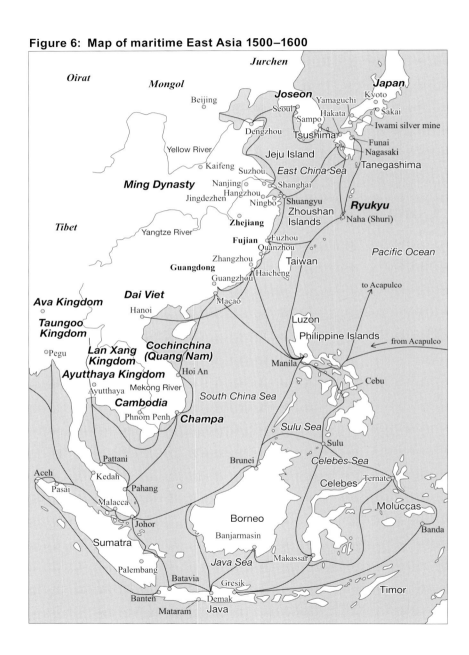

Figure 6: Map of maritime East Asia 1500–1600

## 2.1: General Overview

### From Pires to Carletti

In 1512, Tomé Pires, an apothecary from Lisbon, Portugal, arrived in Malacca, which had been conquered in 1511 by Portugal. During his two-and-a-half year stay in Malacca (My. Melaka), where he served in various capacities in the Portuguese factory, Pires avidly collected information about various parts of Asia. He recorded this information in *Suma Oriental* (1515), the most detailed and systematic description of maritime Asia at that time. It includes considerable amounts of rather specific information not only on the region around the Indian Ocean and the South China Sea, but also on China and Ryukyu.

Drawing on what he heard from Chinese traders about a place that lay even further east than China, Pires describes Japan (Jampon) as follows:

> The island of Jampon [Japan], according to what all the Chinese say, is larger than that of the Lequíos [Ryukyu], and the king is more powerful and greater, and is not given to trading, nor are his subjects. He is a heathen king, a vassal of the king of China. They do not often trade in China because it is far off and they have no junks, nor are they seafaring men.
> 
> (Pires 1944: 131)

This is all the information provided by Pires on Japan, aside from a statement that seafarers from Lequíos (i.e. Ryukyu) bring Japanese products to Malacca. Although Christopher Columbus had reached the Americas twenty years prior in pursuit of the golden island of "Zipangu", presumably Pires did not recognize "Jampon" as this island.

In 1597, about eighty years after Pires' stay in Malacca, Francesco Carletti, a Florentine merchant, arrived at Nagasaki. He had left Europe for Peru then boarded trading vessels to travel from Acapulco to Nagasaki via

Manila. The following year, he left Nagasaki for Macao, and completing his round-the-world voyage via the Indian Ocean, returned to Europe in 1606. Later, in a book dedicated to the Grand Duke of Tuscany Cosimo II de' Medici, he summarized what he had seen and heard during his voyages and stressed the benefits of trade with Japan, saying:

> Very good business is done between that country and other lands. But there is a very lack of vessels ready to make long voyages, though the Japanese make them in every way, and at much risk, to diverse places. […] I say that Japan is one of the most beautiful and best and most suitable regions in the world for making profit by voyaging from one place to another. But one should go there in our sort of vessel and with sailors from our regions. And in that way, one would very quickly make incredible wealth, and that because of their need of every sort of manufacture and their abundance of silver as of the provisions for living, as I already have said.
>
> (Carletti 1964: 129, 132)

The Japan that Pires had heard of was a faraway island country that had few exports, no ships capable of traversing the open ocean and little overseas trade, aside from that which it sent through Ryukyu. Eighty years later, however, based on his experiences actually circumnavigating the globe and engaging in trade, Carletti emphasized that Japan was the most promising trade partner in the region because of its strong demand for foreign products, its high silver production and its active overseas commerce. To understand what led to this drastic change in accounts of Japan in the space of a mere eighty years, we must examine the political and economic situation in maritime East Asia during this period.

    The sixteenth century witnessed several transformations on a world-historical scale as part of the so-called "Age of Exploration" that distinguished it from anything that came before. From the thirteenth through the sixteenth centuries, seaborne trade in maritime East Asia experienced a cycle of openness, followed by control, and then openness again. The trade networks of Muslim and Chinese maritime merchants expanded across maritime Asia in the era of the "Open Sea" in the thirteenth and fourteenth centuries. However, by the late fourteenth century, maritime trade in East Asia was limited to state trade under the Ming tributary trade-maritime prohibition system. The tributary trade area of the Ming Dynasty was rapidly extended by the naval expeditions of Zheng He in the early fifteenth century from the East and South China Seas to the Indian Ocean. The tributary system, however, began to stagnate in the mid-fifteenth century and almost broke down in the sixteenth after a long, continuous decline. Maritime merchants then once again came to play a major role in seaborne trade. At the same time, in the sixteenth century, a wide variety of regions around the globe, including the New World, were linked together to form a worldwide economic system. The remarkable difference in circumstances in maritime East Asia at the beginning and at the end of the sixteenth century demonstrates that the seas of this region stood at the forefront of this worldwide transformation.

In 1500, there were only a limited number of routes by which maritime trade could travel in the East China Sea. Trading ships sailing from the Japanese Archipelago had only three overseas destinations: Ningbo in China, Sampo (the Three Ports)[1] in Korea and Naha in Ryukyu. Japan maintained largely stable, continuous trading relations with Korea, but had been permitted by the Ming court to send tributary trade embassies to China, in principle, only once per decade. Trade via Ryukyuan intermediaries supplemented some deficiencies. However, in contrast, the South China Sea region in the same period had already entered what historians have

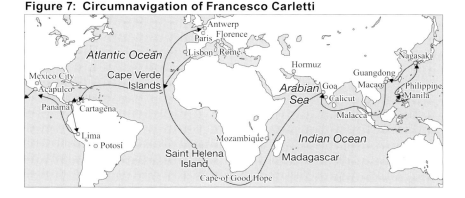

**Figure 7: Circumnavigation of Francesco Carletti**

---

1 "Sampo" is a collective term for the three ports of Naeipo, Busanpo and Yeompo in Gyeongsang-do in the southeast of the Korean Peninsula, where the Joseon court allowed Japanese people to reside and trade.

termed an "Age of Commerce", characterized by prosperous cross-cultural maritime trade. Maritime merchants from West Asia and India created a trade network centered on Malacca that linked port polities across Southeast Asia and the Indian Ocean region, and Chinese maritime merchants expanded their enterprises that enabled them to participate in this Southeast Asian trade illicitly. In stark contrast to the vibrant South China Sea trade, maritime trade in the East China Sea remained largely stagnant.

In 1600, however, trade in the East China Sea region flourished. A large quantity of Chinese products, including raw and woven silks, were carried to Japan by Portuguese traders operating between Macao and Nagasaki and via Chinese sea merchants' smuggling vessels. In exchange, they sought Japanese silver that then flowed into Chinese markets. Dutch vessels also came to Japan in 1600 for the first time. Adding to the networks of Arab, Persian and Indian traders, Chinese maritime merchants expanded their trade networks to encompass the entire South China Sea region. Particularly significant to regional trade was their cargo of enormous amounts of New World silver shipped from Manila to China[2]. At the same time, the Portuguese sought to develop Asian interregional trade linking the South China Sea with the Indian Ocean and East China Sea. Their efforts were contested by bourgeoning Dutch merchants attempting to advance into these waters. Moreover, Japanese maritime merchants were beginning to make voyages across the South China Sea to various parts of Southeast Asia. Both the East and the South China Seas witnessed a boom of maritime trade during this period.

This second part of the book deals with developments in maritime East Asia during the hundred years of the sixteenth century that saw a period of global transformation. The East and South China Sea regions became more integrated in this century as a result of the rapid increase in the movements of people, goods and information between these two areas. Chinese sea merchants as well as Europeans and Japanese developed trade networks and navigation practices that linked the South and East China Seas to a degree unparalleled in earlier periods. This part of the book explores how the East and South China Seas became more closely

---

2 Silver extracted from Latin America under Spanish rule, such as from Peru and Mexico. Especially after the 1570s, extraction at the Potosí silver mine increased sharply. The silver was then transported across the Atlantic Ocean to Europe and across the Pacific Ocean to China via the Philippines.

interconnected, eventually resulting in the formation of the single region of "maritime East Asia".

Underlying the structure of maritime interactions in both the East and South China Sea in this period were centrifugal trends that generated a multicentered region. As a prelude to our exploration of these changes, this chapter presents an overview of the establishment of the tributary trade-maritime prohibition system by Ming China in the late fourteenth century, and its evolution during and after the fifteenth century.

## Tributary trade-maritime prohibition system in East Asia

In 1368, the Hongwu Emperor[3] of the Ming Dynasty unified China in the midst of the general crisis of the fourteenth century. At the time, there were sharp population declines throughout Eurasia due to natural disasters, famines and widespread epidemics. Economic activity stagnated, long-distance trade declined and there were repeated episodes of political turmoil and warfare. The dissolution of Mongol rule occurred amidst political instability across East Asia. In Japan, after the Kamakura Shogunate was overthrown, the Northern and Southern Courts continued to compete for the throne; on the Korean Peninsula the Goryeo Dynasty's control wavered; and Vietnam's Trần Dynasty was in decline. Domestically, the Hongwu Emperor attempted to address the instability and fluidity that wracked Chinese society in the political turmoil of the last years of the Yuan Dynasty by reestablishing a system of centralized rule. In terms of China's foreign affairs, he established state control over both diplomacy and trade by combining the "tributary" system and the *haijin* (maritime prohibition) policy.

The Hongwu Emperor both actively dispatched emissaries to neighboring countries to encourage them to pay tribute to the Ming Dynasty and repeatedly issued a maritime ban strictly prohibiting his subjects from traveling abroad. Further, in 1374 he abolished the *shibosi* (maritime trade supervisorate) system that had served as a gateway for foreign trade in

---

3 The Hongwu Emperor reigned from 1368 to 1398. His personal name was Zhu Yuanzhang, and his Chinese reign designation was Taizu as founder of the Ming Dynasty. Born into a poor farming family in the Huaihe River basin, he rose to power by joining and then becoming a leader of the Red Turban rebellion. Founding the Ming Dynasty with Nanjing as its capital, he drove the Yuan Dynasty back to the Mongolian Plateau and unified China.

earlier periods. As a result, by the late fourteenth century, Chinese overseas trade became limited to the state trade that occurred under the tributary trade-maritime prohibition system, which enabled the Ming government to monopolize both diplomacy and trade.

In the first half of the fifteenth century, during the reigns of the Yongle Emperor and the Xuande Emperors (1403–1435), the Ming extended its tributary networks to the Indian Ocean, North Asia and even Central Asia by means of seven naval expeditions to the South China Sea and Indian Ocean led by Zheng He and to Inner Asia by land-based trade. Table 1 shows the geographical structure of the Ming tributary system in the first half of the fifteenth century, divided into maritime Asia and inland Asia.

Nominally, the tributary system operated as a means of exchange in which various tributary states sent tributary goods to the Ming Emperor, who gave them imperial gifts in return. In reality, however, trade in supplemental commodities brought by envoys and merchants accompanying the tributary mission were of much greater significance. The Ming court had priority access to purchase those supplemental goods, after which the court administered markets where private merchants were allowed to trade for any remaining goods. In principle, trade between Ming China and neighboring countries was limited to tributary trade, and trading without tribute was not permitted, maintaining the principle of "no trade without tribute". In 1403 the Ming government reopened the *shibosi* to help oversee the tributary trade system, but not private foreign trade. Thereupon, countries in Southeast Asia and the Indian Ocean came to engage in tributary trade with the Ming through the Guangzhou Supervisorate. At the same time, Ryukyu engaged in tributary trade through the Quanzhou Supervisorate (later Fuzhou) while Japan did so through the Ningbo Supervisorate.

Around the time of the establishment of the tributary trade-maritime prohibition system, the political chaos of the fourteenth century in each of the countries of East and Southeast Asia was gradually resolved through the establishment of centralized authorities. In Korea, the Goryeo Dynasty was replaced by the Joseon (Yi) Dynasty in 1392[4]. In that same year in Japan

---

4 The Yi (Joseon) Dynasty (1392–1897) was founded by Yi Seong-gye, who played an important role in driving out the Red Turban Army and the Wokou. As well as paying tribute to the Ming Dynasty, he also conducted diplomatic relations on an equal footing with the Ashikaga Shogunate and the Ryukyu Kingdom.

## 2.1: General Overview

the Ashikaga Shogunate brought an end to the war between the Northern and Southern Courts. In 1429, the Chūzan Kingdom unified the Ryukyus and situated itself as an intermediary connecting the East and South China Seas through maritime trade. In Vietnam, the Lê Dynasty regained its independence from temporary Ming rule in 1428[5]. In Siam (present-

**Table 1: Tributary system in the first half of the fifteenth century**

| Region | Tributary | Tribute route |
|---|---|---|
| *Maritime Asia* | | |
| East Asia | Joseon Dynasty, Korea | Liaodong: Fenghuangcheng (via Shanhaiguan) |
| | Japan (Ashikaga Shogunate) | Zhejiang: Ningbo Maritime Trade Supervisorate |
| | Ryukyu Kingdom | Fujian: Quanzhou Maritime Trade Supervisorate |
| Southeast Asia | Vietnam (temporarily annexed to the Ming) | Guangxi: Zhennanguan to Pingxiang |
| | Mainland and archipelago states | Guangdong: Guangzhou Maritime Trade Supervisorate |
| Indian Ocean | India, West Asia and East Africa | Guangdong: Guangzhou Maritime Trade Supervisorate |
| *Inland Asia* | | |
| North Asia | The Mongols and the Oirats | Shanxi: Datong (via Juyongguan) |
| | The three Uriyangkhad commanderies | The North Zhili: Xifengkou |
| | The Jurchens (Jianzhou, Haixi, Yeren) | Liaodong: Kaiyuan (via Shanhaiguan) |
| Central Asia | West and East Turkestan and West Asia | Hami (via Jiayuguan) |
| Southwest Highlands | Tibet, Amdo and Khams | Shaanxi, Sichuan |
| | Southwest aboriginal officers (*tusi*) | Sichuan, Yunnan, Guizhou, Guangxi, etc. |

---

5 The Lê Dynasty (1428–1789) was founded after Lê Lợi drove the Ming troops out of Vietnam. Setting up a centralized, bureaucratic system similar to that of China, it expanded its territory into central Vietnam, but in the sixteenth century the throne was usurped by the Mạc clan.

day Thailand), the Ayutthaya Kingdom expanded its power through the development of the Chao Phraya Delta and foreign trade[6]. The Sultanate of Malacca and the Majapahit Kingdom on Java also promoted tributary trade with the Ming[7]. The Sultanate of Malacca maintained its prosperity through the wealth delivered to its ports by merchant ships and its powerful navy. The Sultanate was originally founded by a Hindu Malayan, but the royal family quickly converted to Islam, eagerly welcoming Muslim maritime merchants from India and West Asia. Malacca became known as the largest "emporium" in Southeast Asia, dealing in products from across the South China Sea and Indian Ocean, and the language in the regions surrounding the Sultanate of Malacca became the lingua franca of the Malay world, later becoming the basis for the modern Malayan and Indonesian languages.

The restoration of long-distance trade in East Asia was also in part due to a warmer climate in the first half of the fifteenth century, which gradually stabilized agricultural production. In Ming China, agricultural recovery provided increased tax revenues, which enabled further mine development that led to a rise in silver production. These financial gains supported large-scale state projects, including the naval expeditions of Zheng He and the relocation of the capital from Nanjing to Beijing. As Ming China grew more powerful, neighboring countries enhanced their regional importance by entering into tributary trade relationships with China and, at times, even securing Ming political backing. Furthermore, entering into tributary trade with the Ming Dynasty stimulated East and Southeast Asian countries to open up additional commercial and diplomatic relations with other countries. Generally speaking, around 1400, the Ming tributary trade-maritime prohibition system enabled the growth of centralized political authority in the countries of maritime East Asia and inhibited the autonomy of coastal regions.

---

6 Ayutthaya (1351–1767) was a kingdom that took as its capital the port city of Ayutthaya, located in the lower Chao Phraya River basin. Promoting trade on the basis of a royal monopoly, its influence extended as far as Cambodia, present-day Northern Thailand and the Malay Peninsula.

7 The Majapahit Kingdom (1293–early sixteenth century) based itself in the wet rice agricultural zone of eastern Java. The empire promoted external trade, controlling the production and distribution of Javanese rice and spices from the Molucca Islands.

## Political turbulence and economic development

However, as early as the mid-fifteenth century, the Ming tributary trade-maritime prohibition system began to show signs of weakening. From the 1430s, the economic burden of supporting huge state-driven projects created financial problems for the Ming government and impoverished rural communities. With the climate again cooling across Eurasia in the 1440s, China was frequently hit by famine and natural disasters. In Inner Asia, the Oirats joined with a group of Muslim merchants and requested an expansion of their tributary trade privileges. When the Ming court rejected their request, the dissatisfied Oirats invaded in full force in 1449, capturing the Zhengtong Emperor. Following this event, known as the "Tumu Incident", the Ming court completely shifted its foreign policy to a defensive posture and strove to restrict its tributary trade with the various countries of maritime Asia. In the mid-fifteenth century, deliveries of tribute from the Indian Ocean ceased almost entirely, tribute from Southeast Asia decreased significantly and Japan was limited to sending tribute once per decade. Losses from the decrease in tributary trade were offset for a time by Ryukyuan intermediaries trading between Ming China, Southeast Asia and Japan. However, tribute from Ryukyu also decreased sharply after the 1460s.

Fifteenth-century Japan also experienced a series of famines and popular uprisings in the lead up to the outbreak of the decade-long Ōnin War that began in 1467, which hastened the decline of Japan's centralized authority under the Ashikaga Shogunate. After the Ōnin War, two provincial feudal lords of Western Japan, the Hosokawa and the Ōuchi, held sway over Japan's trade relations with Ming China. In 1523, a violent conflict erupted between tributary embassies sent by the two feudal lords in Ningbo (the Ningbo Incident), after which the Ōuchi monopolized Japan's trade with Ming China. Japan–Korea trade gradually came to be dominated by the Sō clan of Tsushima[8]. However, in 1510, Japanese merchants and residents in the three ports allotted by the Joseon court to Japanese for settlement and

---

8 Tsushima was the contact point for Japan's diplomatic relations with Korea and was also a base of the early Wokou. The Joseon (Yi) Dynasty permitted trade with the maritime forces of Tsushima, including the Sō family. By the latter half of the sixteenth century, the Sō clan came to virtually monopolize trade with the Yi Dynasty.

trade in Korea launched an uprising (the Three Ports Uprising), leading the Joseon Dynasty to restrict trade with Tsushima considerably. Tsushima managed to maintain the scale of trade by dispatching imposter embassy missions that used the names of powerful authorities in Japan such as the "King of Japan" (Ashikaga Shoguns).

In the late fifteenth century, when the climate began to recover from its cooling period, East Asian economic activities revived and the population began to grow again. China's population had decreased dramatically due to a series of natural disasters and wars that constituted the "crisis of the fourteenth century", with the result that the total population of the Ming Dynasty in the late fourteenth century stood at a mere sixty million. North China suffered particularly seriously from devastation and depopulation. Even though the region's population continued to increase after the beginning of the fifteenth century and topped the 100 million mark by the early sixteenth century, disparities between North and South China were not easily overcome.

During the Ming Dynasty, wealth and population were concentrated in the southeastern region, including the lower Yangtze region, Zhejiang and Fujian, to an extent unequalled at any other time in the history of China. In the Yangtze Delta region in particular, the available paddy land had been nearly completely developed by the sixteenth century, and there was a rapid increase in the number of peasants engaged in the production of goods such as raw silk, silk, cotton yarn and cotton fabric as side occupations. In rural areas, many *shizhen* (market towns) emerged as bases for the production and distribution of these goods. In large cities such as Suzhou and Songjiang, quality fabrics were produced. These products were distributed throughout China and also exported to markets overseas by merchants of Huizhou[9] and Shanxi[10]. The flood plains along the middle of the Yangtze River, where the development of paddy fields had started in

---

9 The Huizhou merchants were a merchant group native to the Huizhou basin of southern Anhui Province. Also known as "Xin'an merchants", they became prominent as salt merchants in the late fifteenth century. Centering their activities in the Yangtze Delta region, they pioneered the distribution of merchandise in the Yangtze River basin and along the Grand Canal.
10 The Shanxi merchants were a merchant group native to the Fenshui River basin in Shanxi Province. They gained prominence at the beginning of the early Ming Dynasty by delivering military food supplies to the North and selling salt. They based themselves in North China from which they expanded their sphere of activity.

full swing around this time, became China's largest breadbasket, replacing the Yangtze Delta region.

In the Japanese Archipelago, the population grew gradually during the fifteenth century. In the sixteenth century, warlords and other regional lords embroiled in conflict in various parts of the country made strenuous efforts to develop their territories. In particular, they began to open up paddy fields in alluvial plains and to reclaim land in marshy coastal areas, paving the way for the Age of Reclamation in the seventeenth century. The factor that proved pivotal for these paddy-field reclamation projects was the new variety of Indica rice, proficient for cultivation in reclaimed or marshy fields, that was introduced from Southeast Asia and known as "Champa Rice" (*zhancheng mi*) in China and "Great Tang Rice" (*daitō mai*) in Japan. Commodity distribution and transaction volumes also increased, with the tandem growth of Kyoto at the center of an archipelago-wide commercial sphere and castle-town markets at the center of commercial spheres in warlords' territorial domains. The total population of the Japanese Archipelago in 1600 is estimated to have reached at least twelve million, approximately thirty percent of which was concentrated in the Kinai region of Kyoto and its environs. On the Korean Peninsula, too, the expansion of paddy lands increased in this period through the development of mountain fields and the reclamation of land along the western coast. The production of cotton cloth also spread across the peninsula during the fifteenth century. This product saw wide use as a clothing material, constituting a currency, and it became an important article of export to Japan.

## Centrifugal trends leading to a multicentered age

By the sixteenth century, all of the countries in East Asia had come to a turning point in agricultural production. They had reached the limits of growth based on older forms of paddy fields, consuming most of the available space in alluvial fans and river valleys, and shifted to expand the acreage into deltas, alluvial plains and marshy, coastal lowlands. Regions leading the development of lowland areas, such as Southeastern China, the Kinai region of Japan and Southern Korea, experienced increased agricultural production and population growth, which together helped create "peasant communities" composed of relatively autonomous peasant families engaged in labor-intensive agriculture. By contrast, in much of Southeast Asia, except for the Red River Delta in Northern Vietnam and the island of Java where intensive paddy rice cultivation was developed, slash and burn farming in forests and extensive rice farming in flood plains constituted the main forms of agriculture. Southeast Asia's total population around the year 1600 has been estimated at approximately twenty-three million, a large portion of which was concentrated in several paddy rice cultivation areas.

In sixteenth-century East Asia, the developed regions where agricultural improvements and population growth occurred also experienced a shift towards a market economy and increased participation in overseas trade. This economic transformation and boom in foreign trade empowered coastal regions in East Asia, which from the end of the fifteenth to the sixteenth century gradually demonstrated their autonomy. Chinese maritime merchants in Fujian Province, for instance, engaged in a lucrative smuggling trade in the South China Sea region. In Guangdong, foreign ships visited Guangzhou for mutual trade (*hushi*) outside the tribute system. Local authorities tacitly consented to such activities and collected tariffs. In Western Japan, *daimyōs*[11] and autonomous seafaring bands teamed up with Chinese maritime traders and began to engage in smuggling and piracy in the East China Sea. Ryukyu, whose tributary trade with China had been in decline since the latter half of the fifteenth century, shifted its trading focus to Japan and the smuggling activities of Chinese sea merchants. As a result of these changes, the Ming Dynasty could no longer continue to exert unitary control over foreign trade by means of the tributary trade-maritime prohibition system.

The disintegration of a regional order centered on the Ming court accelerated the growth of local autonomy in maritime East Asia and contributed to the emergence of a multicentered region. As Japan became more decentralized in the mid-sixteenth century, various maritime powers based in the west of the archipelago expanded their participation in illicit trading and raiding enterprises in the East China Sea. In Vietnam, the Lê Dynasty gradually lost power in the late fifteenth century, though

---

11 The word "*daimyō*" generally signifies territorial lords in Japan's feudal system. However, its character differs significantly depending on the period. In Part 2 of this book, *daimyō* takes on the special meaning as a Sengoku (Warring States period) *daimyō*. Sengoku *daimyō* can broadly be characterized as (1) having an independent region-state style of governance as a supreme ruler, and (2) spending their lives mainly on battlefields to expand or maintain their territories.

it continued to fight on even after the Mạc Dynasty was established in 1527. In Java, after the decline in power of the Majapahit Kingdom in the late fifteenth century, many port polities[12] competed to fill the void. In the context of this region-wide turmoil, Portuguese forces captured the Sultanate of Malacca in 1511, forcing their way into the maritime trade networks of Southeast Asia. Portuguese merchants and military moved east from Malacca through the Java Sea to the Molucca (Maluku) Islands and then sailed further north through the South China Sea, reaching the coast of China. As a consequence, some of the Muslim maritime merchants relocated their bases from Malacca to neighboring port cities, so Malacca's function as a collection and distribution center for goods shifted to entrepôts on the Malay Peninsula and present-day Indonesia.

Although these changes in the maritime regional order first emerged in the South China Sea region, by the 1540s they had spread to East Asia. At that time, Chinese merchants induced the Portuguese to trade at the port of Shuangyu in the Zhoushan Islands, where some Japanese also joined in smuggling activities. This is the beginning of what some historians have termed the "Age of the Wokou" in maritime East Asia. "Wokou" (Jp. *Wakō*; Kr. *Waegu*) is a term used in the historical records of China and Korea. The Japanese themselves at the time used a variety of terms to identify the groups engaged in piracy in foreign regions, including *kaizoku*, *akutō* and *bahan*. As explained in Part 1, mainly Japanese were involved in these practices in the fourteenth century, as the term "Wokou" denotes. After the middle of the sixteenth century, however, both Chinese and Japanese took part in activities labeled by Chinese and Korean officials as "Wokou", and the number of Chinese involved exceeded that of Japanese. Then in the mid-sixteenth century, while the collaborative Wokou (later) engaged in by Chinese and Japanese on the southeast coast of China, Han Chinese fugitives joined Mongol forces in launching wide-ranging incursions that pillaged across northern China. In the late 1560s, the Ming court finally significantly altered the tributary trade-maritime prohibition policy and allowed Chinese maritime merchants to sail from Fujian to various parts of Southeast Asia. Along the northern border, the Ming concluded peace

---

12 Port polities were states that emerged throughout Southeast Asia in trading ports located in river estuaries and in straits. In estuarine port cities, rulers based their power on the exchange of goods produced in mid- and up-river hinterlands for commodities brought by foreign merchants.

negotiations with Altan Khan of the Mongols that permitted tributary trade to Beijing and opened four *mashi* (horse markets) along the Great Wall, where Mongol tribes and Chinese merchants were allowed to engage in mutual (i.e. non-tribute) trade.

## Three spheres of competition

In the sixteenth century, the Age of Commerce in the South China Sea reached its peak and the boom in maritime trade extended to the East China Sea. The connections generated by Chinese, Portuguese, Japanese and other maritime merchants gradually integrated the two seas into a single maritime region. However, as the rest of Part 2 of this book shows, this integration was also facilitated by various groups of people involved in the maritime world coming into competition with each other and, along with their commodities, currencies, cultures and technologies, moving across borders. There were three overlapping spheres of competition, as outlined below.

First, there was competition between the Ming government, which attempted to maintain centralized control over diplomacy and trade through the tributary trade-maritime prohibition policy, and Chinese sea merchants and foreign powers who opposed that policy with a view to promoting more open maritime trade. This competition first manifested in the late fifteenth century in the South China Sea in the form of smuggling by Chinese merchants and mutual trade with foreigners off the coast of Guangzhou. In the mid-sixteenth century, illicit commerce and raiding by multiethnic Japanese pirate bands intensified in the East China Sea. This competition was, however, resolved in the late 1560s as the Ming government eased its maritime prohibition policy and removed the ban on Chinese merchants trading in the South China Sea.

The second realm of competition occurred in the wake of the appearance of Portuguese and Spanish ships in Asian waters. Portugal attempted to control the main maritime commercial networks in Asia by seizing the key ports that served as trade hubs, including Hormuz, Goa and Malacca. Muslim merchants contested Portuguese dominion by establishing new bases of trade and shipping routes. Portugal and Spain also competed against each other in the Molucca Islands over the spice trade. In the East China Sea region, this second realm of competition intersected with the aforementioned first realm concerning China's tributary trade-maritime

## 2.1: General Overview

prohibition policy. Portugal sought access to the Chinese market, while the Ming government sought to exclude the Portuguese from its ports. This last situation was also resolved by the mid-sixteenth century.

Third, there was also increased "competition" among East and Southeast Asian countries during the sixteenth century. All across the East and South China Seas new powers benefitted from the trade boom and sought to keep a firm grip on profits from maritime trade. Political authorities combined the profits of maritime trade with military power derived from the acquisition of European firearms and warred with each other. For example, in Southeast Asia the Taungoo Kingdom in Burma (present-day Myanmar) fought the Ayutthaya Kingdom in Siam in a war that lasted through the second half of the sixteenth century[13]. In East Asia, the Toyotomi regime put an end to political division and strove to establish a centralized system of government in Japan, and also mobilized a large army carrying new firearms that it used to invade Korea. Japan's invasion of Korea also drew Ming China into the conflict, which became the largest war in that century.

The following chapters of Part 2 survey maritime East Asia during the sixteenth century through a lens focused on the intersections between these three "spheres of competition". However, as is evident from the descriptions by Pires and Carletti cited at the outset of this chapter, the sixteenth century was a time of unparalleled transformation and change in maritime East Asia, making it difficult to treat this hundred years as a single period. It seems, therefore, more appropriate to discuss the developments in the East Asian maritime region by roughly dividing the century into halves. For that reason, the chapter structure of Part 2 differs from that of the other two parts.

Chapter 2.2 deals with how competition intensified in the South China Sea in the early sixteenth century as a result of the weakening of the tributary trade-maritime prohibition system and the arrival of Portuguese forces. It shows how the competition expanded into the East China Sea in the mid-sixteenth century and led to the Age of the Wokou. Chapter 2.3 surveys how the Age of Commerce manifested across the East Asian maritime world. After the Ming government relaxed its maritime

---

13 The Taungoo Kingdom (1486–1752) expanded its influence in Southern Burma from the late fifteenth century. In the late sixteenth century, the Taungoo King Bayinnaung conquered Northern Burma and subjugated the Ayutthaya Kingdom. Its capital was the port city of Pegu on the Bay of Bengal, from which it sponsored overseas trade.

prohibition policy in the late 1560s, the burgeoning commercial activities of sea merchants set an increasing number of goods and people in motion. Maritime East Asia was linked to the global market and became one of its central nodes. Chapter 2.4 takes up topics such as religion, art, handicrafts, printing and publishing and information and military technology. It does so in order to explore global movements of people and goods – cultural exchange and knowledge transfers within maritime East Asia as well as between maritime East Asia and the rest of the world – and looks at how culture and knowledge from different regions interacted.

## 2: The Age of the Wokou
### Transformations in the Structure of East Asian Trade

### The Wokou

On the twenty-fifth day of the twelfth month of the thirty-eighth year of Jiajing (1559), a prisoner was executed for treason at the gates of the city of Hangzhou. His head was displayed at the Dinghai barrier on the shore near Ningbo, and his wife and children were given as slaves to meritorious subjects of the dynasty. Before his arrest, he declared his innocence and even submitted a petition to the emperor in order to plead his case. Although this type of document is extremely rare, we are able to read it today because its content was included in a woodblock-printed account of the affair.

A summary of the prisoner's plea is as follows:

> I am a merchant from Huizhou Prefecture and engaged in my business in Zhejiang and Fujian Provinces, sharing profits with my men and defending the coastal frontier for the sake of your majesty, but I never did ally with the pirates, nor comitted any act of disturbance. When Japanese pirates raided China, Ryukyu and Korea, I went to Japan as a messenger of peace out of true-hearted loyalty to your majesty and appealed to the lords of many countries on their land to halt their acts of aggression. I humbly request that your majesty trust me and please allow me to trade with the Japanese. I will persuade the Japanese lords never to behave in a disorderly way. Then, it will become possible to subdue enemy forces without bloodshed.

The man's name was Wang Zhi[1], and he is usually treated as the standard bearer of the episodes of violence known to historians as "Jiajing-era

---

1 Wang Zhi (?–1559) built up his wealth by smuggling from a base in the Zhoushan Islands. He had many Japanese under his command and moved his base to the

Japanese Piracy". At the time, invasions by the Wokou represented a serious problem for Chinese coastal areas. In addition, although unofficial voyages between Japan and China were banned, many Chinese, including Wang Zhi, secretly sailed to Japan. We will return to Wang Zhi again later in this chapter. Here, let us give a basic definition as to who the Wokou were.

The term "*wokou*" is usually defined as pirates who went to China or Korea from Japan for the purposes of trade and plunder. Literally, the characters used to write "Japanese pirate" mean "barbarous acts committed by Japanese" or "invaders from Japan". However, the term "*wokou*" (Cn.), or "*waegu*" (Kr.), was not used by Japanese people at the time. Rather, it was the Chinese term that originally began to appear in historical documents of Korea in the late Goryeo Dynasty in the form of an expression meaning "Japanese invaded [a certain area]", and eventually became part of everyday language in Joseon Korea and Ming China in the form of the noun "Wokou" (Japanese pirate).

This chapter deals with accounts of Wokou who raided areas from the Yangtze Delta region to Guangdong from the 1550s onward. As many Chinese historical sources indicate, however, the majority of the pirates originated from Chinese coastal areas, such as Jiannan, Zhejiang, Fujian and Guangdong, and participants from the Japanese Archipelago were, in fact, a minority.

Certainly, various anti-government forces acting along the southeastern coastline of China included among their ranks some born in the Japanese Archipelago who spoke Japanese as their mother tongue and identified as Japanese natives. The term "*wokou*" came to popularly mean "Japanese pirate" perhaps because these Japanese became known for wielding their Japanese swords while serving in the vanguards when their bands plundered locals and fought against government forces.

However, the concept of "*wokou*" was often interpreted so broadly by contemporary as well as latter-day writers that not just Chinese merchants but even Portuguese private traders could be regarded as members of Japanese

---

Gotō Islands and Hirado (present-day Nagasaki Prefecture) due to attacks by Ming naval forces. He surrendered to the Ming in response to a call to swear allegiance to the Ming Emperor by Governor-General Hu Zongxian, but was considered to have been a mediator principally responsible for Wokou and was executed by decapitation. Chinese historical records mention Wang Zhi as a pirate, but today there are also views that evaluate him in a more positive way by acknowledging his contribution to the development of responsibility in continuing Sino-Japanese trade in this period.

## 2.2: The Age of the Wokou

pirate bands depending on how the historical documents are read. Japanese pirate bands were far from monolithic, and factions with various overseas connections often feuded and competed with each other. In addition, in order to truly understand the Wokou phenomenon, we must explore the histories of merchants, pirates, military forces and fisher-folk in China, Japan, Korea and Ryukyu. We also need to emphasize the Portuguese impact on their commercial and military activities in the wider context in which the Wokou operated. In this chapter on the "Age of the Wokou", while understanding that Wokou engaged in acts of excessive violence, their history can be used to sketch the contours of maritime East Asia in the early to mid-sixteenth century. Although we might single out any number of ethnic groups, classes or occupational groups, it is the outlaw pirate-traders, occasionally called "Wokou" in Chinese chronicles, who had the most dramatic impact on maritime East Asia during this period.

## Pirates and naval forces

The Yangtze Delta region was the Chinese coastal area most heavily devastated by the Wokou in the sixteenth century. Some port towns in the several prefectures around the Yangtze estuary, such as Zhelin in Songjiang, Zhapu in Jiaxing and Nansha of Chongming County in Suzhzou, were captured temporarily by *wozei*[2] and many *shizhen* (market towns) often became battlefields. However, a considerable amount of the devastation in the Yangtze Delta region attributed to Wokou attacks was actually caused by secondary rebellions reflecting internal contradictions in Ming society that followed in the wake of pirate attacks. The rich could flee into large, fortified cities, while the poor, such as peasants, *dianhu* (tenant farmers)[3]

---

2  The term "*wozei*" literally means "Japanese robbers". It signifies Japanese nationals with criminal characteristics who were persecuted by Chinese authorities. However, at the time it was common for armed groups composed of Chinese, along with a comparatively smaller number of Japanese, to be known collectively as "pirates" using a variety of expressions including "*wozei*", "*wokou*" and so on.

3  *Dianhu* were peasants who borrowed land for cultivation from a landlord. However, the statutory *dianhu* status included a wide range of social strata because of the complex situations that developed regarding land tenure. For example, there were frequent cases of tenants managing agriculture on borrowed land, leasing the land to third parties or transferring it to a fictitious name to escape labor services imposed on owned land.

and *shamin* (boat people)⁴, often took the side of the invaders, passing on food and information to pirate bands, and sometimes rose up against the government authority and joined the rebels. The government forces were not necessarily reliable. Mercenary soldiers conscripted from places such as northern Jiangsu, Hunan and Guangxi were often considered to be more unruly and troublesome than the invaders and were more detested by locals.

Coastal prefectures and counties in Zhejiang and Fujian Provinces were also assaulted year by year by Wokou in the 1550s. However, the government authorities and residents of these provinces were never mutually cooperative, and rather blamed each other for the raiding. Government vessels were built too poorly for practical use and local private ship-owners fled to avoid military service. Mariners who had been employed from elsewhere to serve on warships maintained secret contact with pirates from their home area, resulting in leakages of confidential information. The line separating government and rebels was quite ambiguous.

Such ambiguity between officialdom and rebels was also observed outside China, for example in Japan. According to historical materials, pirates were generally regarded as a threat to maritime safety, and it was necessary to suppress them. However, they also played essential roles in protecting ships en route from enemy attacks. In medieval Japan, the "protection" of pirates themselves was often necessary in order to secure the sea-lanes and to help ships avoid "pirate" attacks. This protection encompassed a wide range of services from guard duty to navigation. Seafarers providing these "protection" services charged fees that they called "*sekisen*" (tolls) and "*reisen*" (honoraria). If it were felt that the payments were inadequate, those providing protection would turn predator. The various families who went by the surname Murakami used these pirate and protection practices to establish themselves as powerful seafaring forces, controlling much of the main trade artery of Western Japan, the Seto Inland Sea. Although later

---

4 *Shamin* were people who inhabited the sandbars in the area of Chongming Dao Island in the Yangtze estuary during the Ming and Qing Dynasties. Many were natives of other regions who had migrated to the area, where they sailed flat-bottomed boats known as *shachuan* (sand boats) appropriate for navigating the shallows. They engaged in fishing, commerce and shipping. Among these were people who conducted illicit trade in contraband and robbed and pillaged to make a living, and thus they were viewed by government officials as a hotbed of pirates.

chronicles record that the Noshima Murakami[5] participated in Japanese pirate attacks overseas, there are no primary historical sources to support that claim. In fact, during the sixteenth century, Tsushima Island, a hotbed of Japanese piracy during the fourteenth century, was attacked by pirates from Iki Island and by ships that were most likely pirate ships from the Seto Inland Sea (*kami-zokusen*).

In addition, although often labeled pirates, the Noshima Murakami and other such groups were not full-time raiders. They engaged in a wide variety of activities, including shipping, trading and fishing in addition to violence. Their bands were composed of a diverse array of seafarers from the lower strata of society, who historians have labeled "*umi no zōhyō*" (maritime privateers). With medieval Japan beset by endemic famine, crop failure and warfare, battlefields became important sites for earning a living. As a result, it is likely that for such "maritime irregulars" Japanese pirate raids in China represented an opportunity for finding employment overseas. Chinese sources identify Kyushu and the Seto Inland Sea regions as Wokou homelands. However, it is likely that such attribution of pirates from Japan participating in Wokou attacks on China during the sixteenth century referred mostly to "maritime irregulars" from Western Japan, rather than the highly organized pirate bands and naval forces of local lords.

By the mid-sixteenth century, there is also evidence of Wokou incidents in Ryukyu. In 1556, a faction of Wokou who had assaulted the Chinese coast and then fled raided Naha Port. In response to this incident, the Kingdom of Ryukyu, based in Shuri Castle next to Naha Port, reinforced the port's military defense line. Ryukyu constructed a military road and a *gusuku* (fortress) armed with Chinese-style firearms. Cases of Wokou attacking Naha Port went beyond bands returning from China. In the second half of the sixteenth century, merchants sailing in armed bands

---

5 The "Murakami families" refers to three families who bore the family name Murakami and who were based on the three islands of Noshima, Kurushima and Innoshima in the Geiyo Islands (present-day Ehime and Hiroshima Prefectures). They were an autonomous naval force active in the Seto Inland Sea. The family engaged in the protection of shipping on behalf of the Muromachi Shogunate and the military governors of Iyo Province, the Kōno, among other powerful patrons. After the Toyotomi government issued its anti-piracy edict, the Noshima and Innoshima Murakami families became vassals of a powerful *daimyō* of Western Japan, the Mōri, while the Kurushima Murakami became a small-scale *daimyō* in Kyushu.

from Japan to trade with Ryukyu were feared to be Wokou. Although the actual identities of these seafarers are unknown (in terms of geographical context), they are likely to have included pirates from the Shichitō-shū (Seven Islands band) of the Tokara Islands, who traded between Satsuma in the south of Kyushu and Ryukyu. The Tokara Islands were located in dangerous waters near to where the Black Current intersected with the Nansei Islands, requiring skillful navigation. Pirates thrived in such chokepoints.

On the Korean Peninsula, after its founding the Joseon court established a navy based on the naval forces the Goryeo court had raised in order to fight off the Wokou, which had inflicted considerable suffering on Korea in the fourteenth century. However, by the mid-fifteenth century, the combination of a policy of appeasement had largely eliminated the threat posed by Wokou and the naval defense system gradually became a shell of its former self. As a result, by the late fifteenth century, reports of Korean pirate activities began to appear. Bands of *sujeok* (sea bandits) were first mentioned in 1474 during the reign of King Seongjong[6] (r. 1469–1494), which seem to have consisted of people from Jeju Island as well as a small number from the southwest coast of Jeolla Province. During and after the reign of King Jungjong[7] (1488–1544), water bandits had expanded their operations northwest, basing themselves in Haerangdo, Ganghwa Island and Hwanghae Province. According to the *Veritable Records of the Joseon Dynasty*, people from these regions often dressed like Japanese and raided inland villages, attributing the raids to Wokou. It would have been very

---

6  King Seongjong (whose name was Yi Hyeol) reigned from 1469 to 1494 as the ninth king of the Joseon Dynasty. A follower of Confucianism, he placed importance on culture and rites. Under his rule, the *Gyeongguk daejeon* (Joseon Code of Law), *Dongguk tonggam* (Comprehensive Mirror of the Eastern Kingdom), *Tongguk yeoji seungnam* (Augmented Survey of the Geography of Korea), *Dongmunseon* (Anthology of Korean Literature), *Haedong chegukki* (Record of Countries to the East) and other important works of the dynasty were produced.

7  King Jungjong (whose name was Yi Yeok) reigned from 1506 to 1544 as the eleventh king of the Joseon Dynasty. He usurped the throne by ousting the previous king, Yeonsan-gun, in a *coup d'état*. His rule was characterized by incessant political strife and a series of diplomatic and military crises, including the 1510 Japanese riots in the three ports and invasions by Jurchens from the north.

difficult to distinguish between Korean water bandits and Wokou. In the early sixteenth century, a series of events occurred that made coastal defense once again an urgent priority for the Joseon court, including an uprising of Japanese people in the three ports, attacks by Wokou and frequent arrivals of Chinese smugglers. In response, in 1510 the court established the Bibyeonsa (Border Defense Council), a temporary military administrative office, and in 1554 it became a permanent organ intended to strengthen the naval defense system.

In the early Joseon Dynasty, seafaring people who pursued livelihoods on the coast and on islands were mobilized to crew naval vessels. Many of these mariners were in fact "boat people" who lived most of their lives with their families aboard ships. In the sixteenth century, however, the authorities increased the number of men conscripted into the navy, causing streams of those with seafaring backgrounds to desert. To replace them, the government conscripted people from mountainous regions. The desertions were in part made possible by networks of *pojagin* (abalone harvesters). The impact of this group is vividly seen in their mobilization for the navy led by Admiral Yi Sunsin against Japan during the Imjin War[8] of 1592–98 (known in Japan as the campaigns of the Bunroku and Keichō eras). On the one hand they provided valuable navigational services, while on the other they were involved in various illegal activities, including helping soldiers to desert.

These abalone harvesters occupied a middle ground between the Korean navy and Wokou because of their expert navigational knowledge, especially of the dangerous seas around the Korean Peninsula. For example, individuals identified as "Japanese" captured abalone harvesters from islands off the southwest coast of Korea (Heuksando and Chujado), brought them to their base and treated them warmly in order to induce the harvesters to act as guides for their piracy activities.

---

8 The Imjin War (Imjin Waeran) is the Korean name for the war of invasion of Korea by the Toyotomi government of Japan. The first and the second wars together are known as the Imjin (1592) and Jeongyu (1597) Waeran. In addition, these wars are known as the "Korean Campaign of the Wanli Emperor" (Wanli Chaoxian zhanzheng) in China and in Japan by such names as "Advance into China" (Kara-iri) and the "Korean campaign" (Kōrai-jin).

One well-documented abalone harvester who acted as an agent of the Japanese was Sahwadong[9] from Jindo, a small island off the southwest coast of Korea, who was kidnapped by Japanese and brought to the Gotō Islands off the coast of Korea. He guided Wokou invading the Korean island of Sonjukdo in 1587. At the time, he is reported to have said to the Korean official captured by the Wokou, "Gotō is a good place to live. Taxes are burdensome in Joseon, where the government takes all of our abalone". In the second half of the sixteenth century, the sea people inhabiting the southern coast of the Korean Peninsula and its islands were at times incorporated into the Korean navy, and at other times became part of Japanese pirate bands.

## Arrival of the Portuguese

The trade networks of maritime East Asia were anchored by the hub-ports of Naha (Ryukyu Kingdom) in the east and Malacca in the west. However, the Sultanate of Malacca was destroyed by the Portuguese. This incident redrew the political map of maritime East and Southeast Asia.

Since the era of the "Open Sea" discussed in Part 1, the Strait of Malacca had been integral to interregional connections, housing many port polities. However, conflicts among Java, Siam and other maritime powers rendered political stability impossible until the sudden rise of the Sultanate of Malacca at the beginning of the fifteenth century. In the first half of the fifteenth century, Malacca grew rapidly as a base for Zheng He's expeditions to Southeast Asia and the Indian Ocean. Then, when Ming foreign trade waned by the mid-fifteenth century, Malacca devoted its resources to expanding trade in the Indian Ocean region. The sultan's family converted to Islam, and as they conquered port towns on either side of the Straits of Malacca, they promoted the Islamization of the region. Islam spread to port towns along the coastline of the Java Sea, and from there to other islands of Southeast Asia, including the Moluccas. Then, having grown into an archetype of the

---

9 It is said that Sahwadong was from Jindo Island in Cholla Province. In 1587, he acted as a guide for a Japanese pirate raid off the coast of that province. In response to a request by Toyotomi Hideyoshi that the Joseon court dispatch an envoy, the court in turn requested the extradition of Sahwadong, who at the time was on Gotō Island. With cooperation from the Matsura family of Hirado, Sahwadong was handed over to the Korean side in February 1590 and the dispatch of an envoy was achieved.

Southeast Asian emporium, gathering in and redistributing commodities, Malacca was attacked by and fell to the Portuguese fleet in 1511.

The Portuguese fleet extended its power in an attempt to secure the sea-lanes connecting Portugal and East Asia by conquering and fortifying a string of key trading ports. They made inroads into the Moluccas, founding a factory (trading post) on Ternate Island in 1513, and in 1515 occupied Hormuz, located at the mouth of the Persian Gulf. As a chief producer of cloves, nutmeg and mace, the Moluccas were an irresistible target for those seeking to control the spice trade.

At the same time, the various political authorities competing for hegemony in maritime East Asia found the Portuguese and other European forces highly valuable due to their military power. The political authorities found the new styles of firearms carried by the Europeans to be extremely useful tools for extending political influence. In return for providing firearms, the Portuguese sometimes gained permission from the local authorities to set up trading bases. For example, the Kirishitan (Christian) *daimyō* Ōmura Sumitada[10] donated the port of Nagasaki to the Jesuits in order to welcome Portuguese vessels. Not only Europeans, but also Chinese, Persians, Japanese and others found employment in Southeast Asian countries as officials and mercenaries. It should be noted, however, that at the time of the sixteenth century, with the exception of Malacca and the Philippines, in much of Southeast Asia it was local governments rather than Europeans who retained the political initiative. Europeans could only secure certain privileges, including the construction of trading bases or factories in the port towns, through negotiations with the political authorities that controlled the port cities. The "European invasion and colonization of Asia" as it is usually understood was still a long way off.

For instance, even with their control over the Strait of Malacca, the Portuguese were not able to dominate the trade networks of insular Southeast Asia. After the Portuguese occupied Malacca, Malays kept their trade routes alive by pursuing a multicentered strategy. They developed several new trading hubs, including Aceh (on Sumatra), Banten (on Java) and

---

10 Ōmura Sumitada (1533–1587) was a *daimyō* of Hizen (present-day Nagasaki Prefecture) during the Warring States (Sengoku) period. Ōmura Sumitada became the first Kirishitan *daimyō* and forced the population under his dominion to convert to Kirishitans. In doing so, he was able to convince the Portuguese to base their trade in his domain, luring them away from Hirado to Yokoseura Bay and then to Nagasaki. Facing attacks from lords in surrounding territories, he donated Nagasaki and its environs to the Jesuits.

Makassar (on Sulawesi). In addition, Chinese-Muslim merchants engaged in a wide range of activities beyond trade with China. By this period, overseas Chinese had established complex, stratified societies. According to one source, it was said on Java that "black Chinese were residents whose ancestors had come to Java, while white Chinese were newcomers".

It should also be noted that not all Portuguese maritime merchants acting in Southeast Asia were linked directly to the court of Portugal. Although voyages in maritime Asia east of Malacca were nominally administered by the captain-major (Pt. *capitão-mor*) system[11], in which the Portuguese King appointed a captain-major to lead each voyage based on military services rendered and other accomplishments, this system only operated in the major trade routes, such as that between China and Japan. Instead, in much of this region, the Portuguese fell into the category of people called "*folangji*" (Franks) by Chinese officials and were regarded as a type of pirate. The activities of these *folangji* embodied the transnational character of maritime East Asia. They often chartered Chinese junks for their private trading ventures with the majority of the crewmen comprised of seafarers and slaves from Africa, South India, Southeast Asia and China.

For a short time after their conquest of Malacca, the Portuguese, as newcomers, usually chartered Chinese junks for the pepper trade between Malacca and China. However, in maritime East Asia, east of Malacca, many Portuguese traders gradually came to buy junks, which they crewed with Chinese sailors. Then, by the mid-sixteenth century, the Portuguese began voyaging to Japan in round ships known as "*nau*" (carracks).

Portuguese shipbuilding technology changed significantly around the time when they reached the Indian Ocean. In the fifteenth century, a relatively small ship called a "caravel" was used for the voyage from the West African coast to the Cape of Good Hope. The caravel had a total length of less than thirty meters with masts less than thirty meters high. It was distinctive for being rigged with lateen sails while also bearing oars.

---

11 The captain-major system refers to the Portuguese crown's annual special appointment to command the voyage from Goa to China and Japan. It was established to help the Portuguese crown retain a monopoly over these trade voyages. At first, after initial selection by the Viceroy of Goa, this position was awarded to persons who had shown exemplary service to the court. However, rights to the position eventually came to be sold by auction in order to raise funds for military expenditure required by the colonies in the Indian Ocean. Rights to the position were also resold by wealthy merchants.

## 2.2: The Age of the Wokou

However, after rounding the Cape of Good Hope, the Portuguese were influenced by Islamic shipbuilding techniques and developed a large ship with a load capacity that averaged about 400 tons. It had a deep, rounded bottom with three to four masts and was square-rigged. This type of ship was called "*carraca*" in Portuguese and Spanish, and "carrack" in English. In Portuguese, in particular, it was also called "*nau*", which simply means "ship". The term "*nau*" is often used synonymously with "carrack", but the latter, if distinguished from the former, refers to a ship with a hull reinforced with iron ribs. The ship traveling from Macao, as seen in folding screens depicting Iberian merchants and missionaries (*Namban byōbu*; see Chapter 2.4), is a large carrack/*nau*-type vessel. From the second half of the sixteenth century, an improved version of the carrack appeared, known as the galleon. A large version of this galleon (with a load capacity upwards of 1,500 tons) was used for the trade route between Manila and the Americas, which will be explained in detail in Chapter

**Figure 8: Portuguese carracks, galleon, square-rigged caravel and galleys**
Source: D. João de Castro (1541).

2.3. The galleon had a longer hull and shallower draft than the carrack, and its most important distinguishing feature was its enhanced military capability. Naval conflict in Asian waters increased in the seventeenth century with the arrival of new European powers, chiefly Britain and the Netherlands. From the Indian Ocean to the China Seas, much of this warfare was prosecuted using galliots. The galliot was, however, not the carrack/*nau*-type ship that had evolved in the Indian Ocean in the early sixteenth century, but a reversion back to the small, lateen-rigged ship with oars.

## The rise and fall of Shuangyu

The port of Shuangyu, located off the coast of Ningbo in China's Zhejiang Province, is the paradigmatic example of smuggling ports in East Asia in the early sixteenth century. Liampo, the name used by the Portuguese for Ningbo, contained a secret enclave for the Portuguese in Chinese waters. It occupied a strategic point along the coastal shipping routes of South China that connected the provinces of Guangdong and Fujian with Zhejiang and Jiangsu, as well as the sailing route between southern China, Ningbo and Japan. The smuggling trade based out of Shuangyu engaged in by Portuguese private traders not only tied together the Chinese coastline and Western Japan, but also united the South and East China Seas as a space for maritime interaction. As a result, the Ryukyu Kingdom, which had formerly functioned as a link between the two seas, was surely headed for decline.

The process by which Shuangyu, formerly an unknown islet, was suddenly catapulted into the role of an international trading port is reported to have begun when a trader from Fujian Province known by the surname Deng brought his clients from southern sea countries to the islet and made it a base for the smuggling trade. It was at this time that the Portuguese, who were expelled from the waters around Guangzhou by the Guangdong authorities, first moved north to Zhangzhou and Quanzhou in Fujian and then to Ningbo in Zhejiang. It is likely that the Portuguese activities had a decisive impact on the development of the port. Later, the four brothers of the Xu family (Xu Song, Xu Dong, Xu Nan and Xu Zi), who had been active around Malacca, became prominent partners of the Portuguese. The brothers, from She County, Huizhou, were part of the prominent and extensive merchant networks based in Huizhou. Shuangyu soon took on

2.2: The Age of the Wokou

a character of multiethnic hybridity, which is richly documented in both Chinese and European sources.

Portuguese sea merchants found Shuangyu an ideal trading port at which to obtain products from southern China. Fernão Mendes Pinto, who wrote *Peregrinação* (Pilgrimage), a grandiose autobiographic account of voyages and explorations across maritime Asia, was one such maritime trader. Although Pinto's descriptions contain many exaggerated accounts and fictional elements, the social and geographical backdrop of the narrative is deemed to faithfully portray the conditions of maritime East Asia that he experienced.

Japanese traders also eagerly participated in this international trade market with silver as their merchandise (Japanese silver is discussed in detail below). In 1548, ships dispatched by the Ōuchi, a powerful *daimyō* family in Western Japan, that carried the last Japanese official tributary embassy to Ming China with tallies of seal impressions and serial numbers[12], were received at the port of Ningbo. However, around the same time, several other powerful *daimyōs* such as (assumedly) Ōuchi, Ōtomo, Sagara and so on, also sent fleets carrying tributary trade embassies, though none of those illegitimate envoys was successful enough to be admitted. Beginning in the 1540s, many groups of Chinese maritime merchants also came to Kyushu to trade. At first, there were few Portuguese ships going directly to Japan, so even the famous Jesuit missionary Francis Xavier[13], who introduced Christianity to Japan for

---

12  In order to ascertain the veracity of tributary missions, the Ming court required missions from Siam, Champa and Cambodia to carry credentials known as tally sheets (Jp. *kango*, Cn. *kanhe*) from 1383. Tallies bore divided impressions of the seal and serial numbers affixed by the Ministry of Rites, which supervised the reception of tributary missions. The seal and serial numbers were collated by the maritime trade supervisorate in the entry ports and the Ministry of Rites in the capital. It was compulsory for the names of the messengers, the tributary goods and other cargo to be listed in the blank space on the tallies. Later, this credentialing system was further applied to some of the other tributary states including Japan (in 1404), but the rest, including Korea, Vietnam and Ryukyu, were exempted from this requirement.
13  Francis Xavier (Sp. Francisco Javier, 1506–52) participated in the founding of the Society of Jesuits, and from 1541, carried out missionary work centered on Goa, India. After landing in Japan at Kagoshima in southern Kyushu in 1549, he proceeded with missionary work in Hirado, Yamaguchi, Kyoto, Bungo and other locations. Voyaging to China to conduct missionary work, he fell ill and passed away on Shangchuan Island off Guangdong.

the first time, voyaged to Japan in a Chinese ship. His missionary work in Japan, however, helped raise Portuguese interest in the archipelago, and Portuguese ships began sailing on the Japan–China shipping lanes to engage in trade. From that time on, the people of Kyushu began to see the *kurofune* (black ships) painted with tar, which are vividly depicted on the folding screens portraying Iberian merchants and missionaries with Asian and African crews, including slaves.

The smuggling trade network that formed around Zhejiang and Fujian soon also extended to the Ryukyu Kingdom and impacted it profoundly. The expansion of the smuggling trade inevitably undermined the foundation of the Ryukyu Kingdom, whose prosperity was due to the tributary relationship with Ming China. In 1542, Ryukyuan officials became embroiled in a conflict with private trade ships based in Fujian and Guangdong. As a result of this incident, the fact that the Ryukyu government had permitted smuggling by Chinese merchants was openly revealed before the Ming court. The incident showed that the Ryukyu Kingdom had been forced into a situation in which it could not survive without establishing connections with the smuggling networks of Chinese sea merchants. As the tribute system diminished in importance, Ryukyu's trade with Japan took on greater significance for the kingdom. Major Japanese trade partners also shifted from the Ashikaga Shogunate to the Hosokawa family in the second half of the fifteenth century, and to the Ōuchi family in the first half of the sixteenth. The Shimazu and Tanegashima families became major trade partners with the Ryukyu Kingdom in the second half of the sixteenth century.

The prosperity of Shuangyu, a prominent smuggling base offshore of Ningbo and an ideal location for approaching the Yangtze Delta from the Zhejiang-Fujian region, abruptly ended when the Ming court launched an intensive crackdown on smuggling. Portuguese merchants relocated their base for a time to Wuyu off the coast of Zhangzhou, then, from 1554–1555 to Shangchuan[14] (São João) and Langbaiao (Lampacau)[15] off

---

14 Shangchuan Island is located in the sea south of present-day Taishan City in the southwest of Guangzhou. Driven out of the Zhejiang region by the Ming army, the Portuguese temporarily made this island their main base around 1550. Due to the similar pronunciation, the Portuguese also called this island São João (Saint John). It is also the place where Francis Xavier died from illness.
15 Located west of Macao, Lampacau is a port now identified with present-day Nanshuizhen, Zhuhai City. During the Ming Dynasty, the shallow seas in the area were dotted with sand banks of different sizes, and smuggling activities were

the coast of Guangzhou, until finally, in 1557, they arranged to settle in Macao in return for paying the Guangdong provincial government for lease and anchorage. The captain-major granted the right of navigation for trade with Japan and China by the Portuguese King was regarded as the leader of the Macao community. He performed services as an official on behalf of the king, safeguarding the Portuguese living in maritime East Asia and supervising their activities. Sometimes local captains were appointed separately by public opinion. It is, however, mistaken to conclude from these facts that the Portuguese ruled Macao as a colony. They had merely "rented a space" in Macao, indicative of the distinctive characteristics and limitations of European power in maritime East Asia at the time.

One important aspect that must not be forgotten in understanding the maritime activities of coastal residents and smugglers is the patronage offered by the local gentry (*xiangshen*)[16] and the local authorities on the Chinese coast. Merchants developed smuggling and trade networks by relying on the huge ships and capital invested in their operations by the local gentry and local authorities as patrons. A mutually beneficial relationship evolved between merchants and local elites; merchants received the protection offered by the prestige of local officials, while the local gentry depended largely upon the financial resources of merchants as a source of revenue. In order to suppress particular pirate bands, government officials charged with coastal and maritime safety sometimes employed rival pirate groups as privateers, authorizing them as militia ships. Of course, those naval forces appreciated the protected status given to them by the authorities.

This practice of hiring naval forces is part of a wider trend in the mid-Ming period in which military and police institutions had begun to privatize. The system of military colonies that supplied soldiers for

---

carried out by merchant ships of various nationalities that docked at the port. In 1554, the Portuguese, prior to settling at Macao, were permitted by the Guangdong authorities to trade at this port.

16 The gentry in China were local elites who held a status that made them eligible to serve in the bureaucracy during the Ming and Qing Dynasties, including those who were on a leave of absence due to illness or mourning, or who had retired. They were recognized as holding special privileges, such as exemptions from labor service, and were treated deferentially by the local administrator. During the late Ming Dynasty especially, the personal prestige and repute of the local gentry frequently surpassed that of the local magistrates appointed by the court.

the empire began to fail, leading to the employment of mercenaries. The core of China's coastal military forces also changed from state-owned military ships to the mobilization of private ships, shifting the burden of coastal defense to the private sector.

It was Zhu Wan[17], Governor of Zhejiang with military jurisdiction over the Fujian coastal region, who was able to navigate this set of conditions and put an end to the prosperity of the smuggling trade at Shuangyu. In order to carry out a purge of pirate activity, he incorporated large-scale private ships along with their crews into the government's navy. In the fifth month of 1548, his fleet struck Shuangyu Port and destroyed it completely. By early spring of 1549, his government forces had attacked and devastated several other smuggling ports. Zhu's coercive measures, despite outstanding success, provoked a fierce backlash from the local people. As a result, he was dismissed from office and committed suicide by drinking poison.

In fact, smuggling occurred even within the naval forces under Zhu's command, because the warships he had mobilized were not only official navy ships but also private vessels that had been used for illicit trade. That is, many of those "militia ships" serving under Zhu had previously been pirate-traders who had simply cleverly switched over to the government's side just a few days before the campaign began. It was no longer possible for Zhu to ban overseas trade as he had planned, even through the use of forceful suppression.

## Wang Zhi's potential

After the fall of Shuangyu, Wang Zhi from Huizhou (mentioned at the beginning of this chapter) took control of the illicit trade network. It is said that he amassed a huge fortune by building a large ship in Guangdong and trading at ports in Japan, Siam and other Southeast Asian countries. As is well known, in 1543 a junk carrying Portuguese anchored at Tanegashima in Japan, resulting in the introduction of European arquebuses to that

---

17 Zhu Wan (1494–1549) was an official born in Suzhou. Dispatched to suppress piracy on the coasts of Zhejiang and Fujian, he mobilized private ships from Fujian and brought them to Zhejiang to destroy the smuggling ports. This policy was militarily successful, but aroused conflicting arguments among factions in the bureaucracy leading to his resignation and subsequent impeachment, after which he committed suicide.

country. The owner of this junk was reportedly Wang Zhi himself. In addition, some accounts relate that it was Wang who first involved Japanese in the Shuangyu-based trade network. The source of his power was in trading with the Japanese and Portuguese, and, after engaging in fierce conflicts with fellow sea merchants, he rose to such great heights that people would say, "No other pirate is as powerful as Wang Zhi".

In the process of establishing maritime supremacy, Wang Zhi enjoyed support from local officials such as the Haidaofushi[18](Coastal Defense Circuit Vice Commander) of Zhejiang and the Zhifu (Prefect) [19] of Ningbo. His band included a considerable number of Japanese, whom he led in campaigns to establish order. Conversely, there was a case in which, at the command of local authorities, Wang purged some of the Japanese members of his band. Wang achieved supremacy through "cooperation" with local government forces.

In response to Wang's growing power, Yu Dayou, a highly respected and famous general, insisted most aggressively that he be eliminated. In 1553, Yu launched a surprise attack on Wang's fleet anchored at Liegang Harbor on Jintang Island on the opposite northern bank of Ningbo, driving him east across the seas. Yu held Wang responsible for a large-scale Wokou raid on Huangyan County, Taizhou, around the same time. After the battle at Liegang and the pirate attack on Taizhou, Chinese annals record incessant Wokou incursions over several years. This peak of raiding, known as "Jiajing-era rampant Japanese Piracy", exposed a contradiction distinctive to the maritime prohibition system: not only could no one control the pirates in Wang's absence, but government forces' attacks also fueled piratical violence.

---

18 *Haidaofushi* was the name of a bureaucratic post in the Ming and Qing eras. Coastal defense was administered by maritime circuits tasked with maintaining order and carrying out policing functions in the coastal areas of provinces. *Haidaofushi* duties were typically carried out by a vice commissioner who served under the surveillance commissioner, the top judicial and surveillance officer of the province.

19 *Zhifu* (prefects) were the chief officers at the head of prefectures, the local government administrative unit. Throughout China's successive dynasties, the most basic administrative units to which bureaucrats appointed by the emperor traveled were known as *xian* (counties). The appellation of the unit superior to the county differs according to the era, but in the Ming and Qing eras provinces were generally divided into administrative units known as *fu* (prefectures), each with several *xian* under its jurisdiction.

After being expelled from China, Wang Zhi once more resided in Japan for several years and was based in Hirado and the Chinese community in Fukue in the Gotō Islands. It is said that there were 2,000 Chinese in Hirado and Gotō at the time, and most were certainly led by Wang. He is reputed to have fit himself out like a king. He sailed aboard a huge warship that itself carried more than 300 subordinates, employed battle flags and dressed in silk damask and other luxurious garments reportedly with his hair tied up in a topknot like one of the Japanese warlords.

A plan to once more employ Wang Zhi to help resolve the Japanese pirate problem was devised by Hu Zongxian[20], supreme commander of Jiannan and Zhejiang. Some scholar-officials in the coastal region believed that a good way to restore order on the coastline was to negotiate with those with actual power in Japan. It had become clear to them that the Ashikaga Shoguns, officially recognized as kings of Japan by the Ming Dynasty, lacked the ability to deal with the piracy situation. Instead, they hoped to gain access to a powerful *daimyō* in Kyushu, such as the Ōtomo family. In 1555, Hu Zongxian appointed Jiang Zhou[21] and Chen Keyuan, who were from Ningbo and once suspected of collusion with the Japanese, as emissaries to Japan. They traveled to Kyushu, carrying Hu's letter encouraging Wang to return to his former allegiance, together with a letter from Wang's family. In 1557, Jiang Zhou and Wang returned to Cen Harbor in Zhoushan Island across from Ningbo.

---

20 Hu Zongxian (1512–1565) acceded to the post of Governor-General of Jiannan and Zhejiang by joining the faction of Yan Song, who occupied the center of power at the Ming court. Excelling in Machiavellian scheming and the frequent object of suspicion for financial misconduct, Hu assembled a staff of talented officials with a variety of practical skills and succeeded in largely eliminating the threat posed by the Wokou. After the downfall of Yan Song, Hu was imprisoned for his connections with him and died in prison.

21 Jiang Zhou (?–1572) traveled to the Gotō Islands in Hizen (present-day Nagasaki), in 1555 in an attempt to persuade Wang Zhi, a Wokou leader, to surrender to the Ming authorities. He then traveled to the court of Ōtomo Sōrin in Bungo (present-day Ōita Prefecture), and also sought the cooperation of the Sō, lords of Tsushima, as well as the Ōuchi family in the suppression of the Wokou. He returned to China along with Wang Zhi in 1557. The knowledge gained from his experiences in Japan was used by Zheng Ruozeng to help compile his *Riben tuzuan* (Atlas of Japan) and *Chouhai tubian* (Illustrated Compendium of Maritime Defense) that had a significant impact on the Chinese perception of Japan.

Though hesitant at first, Wang finally accepted Hu's call for disarmament and surrender, believing in Hu's honeyed words: "If you return to China, you will not be punished. The maritime prohibition policy will be relaxed to authorize private trade". Hu, as a local official, seems to have initially intended to make a serious effort to pardon Wang. However, when rumors flew about the court that Hu Zongxian was attempting to cover up Wang Zhi's crimes in return for a bribe, Hu immediately withdrew his memorial to the emperor, which had recommended pardoning and recruiting Wang, and instead submitted a new one recommending severe punishment. As a result, Wang was executed by decapitation at the end of 1559.

Wang's explanation of his actions that opened this chapter is too one-sided to be taken at face value, but his request "Please allow me to trade with Japan. I will persuade Japanese lords never to behave in a disorderly way" is hard to dismiss as disingenuous. If he had wanted to contribute to the Ming Dynasty, he had no choice but to request that the court "authorize private trade". Hu's plan was based on the same way of thinking. If China's political influence was to extend over the East China Sea, there was virtually no other imaginable scenario. The option for China to actively seek negotiations with Japan, approve official trade as in the past and thereby bring order to the maritime region once more was almost completely closed by the death of its agent Wang Zhi.

## Maritime East Asia's economy and Japanese silver

Along the Chinese coast in the sixteenth century, the production of commercial crops such as cotton and hemp and the manufacture of goods by artisans such as raw silk and silk fabric increased dramatically, leading to a significant growth in China's commercial economy, especially in the cities. The percentage of those abandoning agriculture in favor of another industry rose sharply, and a considerable portion of these people came to make a living from maritime commerce or fishing. However, these changes exacerbated the gap between rich and poor. While cities and market towns absorbed rural populations, conflicts over increased tax burdens arose one after another in farming communities, causing even more people to abandon their farmlands and take to the seas.

People had different reasons for hiding on the small islands scattered around the sea and came from different places. They included migrants from inland areas trying to escape burdens such as taxation and corvée labor service, seasonally hired sailors drawing nets aboard ships, scholars who had failed to pass the examinations to enter into government service and social advancement, fugitives, armed merchants engaged in smuggling and illicit trade and pirates making a living by raiding passing ships. These groups were joined by Portuguese and Japanese seafarers. In this non-state environment, they did not hesitate to use force to resolve conflicts over business problems, and raided coastal towns when resources ran low. According to one account, they even captured a government patrol boat and held the crew for ransom.

As these pirates and smugglers became stronger, peaking in the 1550s, a seaborne commercial network was formed. One important catalyst of this commercialization was Japanese silver, especially that extracted from the Ōmori silver mine in Iwami[22].

The Ōmori silver mine is thought to have been discovered by Hakata merchant Kamiya Jutei[23] in 1526. In 1533, Kamiya brought from the port of Hakata Korean mining experts to introduce the Korean cupellation process for refining silver, called *"haifuki"*[24]. As a result, silver output grew dramatically, enabling Japan to gain a strong position in the maritime East Asian trading sphere. Domestic demand for silver was low at the time, so most of that produced flowed overseas as export or payment for imported goods. For example, in the Japan–Korea trade

---

22 The full-fledged development of the Ōmori silver mine (Iwami-Ginzan) occurred in the first half of the sixteenth century, and it is said to have provided one-fifteenth of silver produced in the world at the time. Possession of the mine became the cause of fierce battles involving the Ōuchi, Amago, Mōri and other powerful local lords, with the Mōri family gaining the final victory. After the unification of Japan, the mine fell under the control of first the Toyotomi and then the Tokugawa. It reached the zenith of its production in the first half of the seventeenth century.
23 Kamiya Jutei was a member of a powerful merchant family of Hakata, the Kamiya. He had a deep connection with both the Iwami silver mine and Shōfukuji Temple in Hakata. It was previously thought that he was the son of Kamiya Kazoe Kazuyasu, but historical records of the time prove that he was from a different family.
24 *Haifuki* is a method of silver extraction developed in Japan from the sixteenth century and beyond. Lead is first added to the silver ore, and hot air is blown into the mixture to melt them together. Next, the craftsmen put the argentiferous lead (mixture of lead and silver) on a bed of the hardened ashes of bones and pine needles. When hot air is blown into the argentiferous lead, it becomes oxidized. As the lead oxides have low specific gravity and low surface tension, they are absorbed by the ashes and the pure silver remains.

after 1538 considerable amounts of silver were exported to Korea by Japanese, replacing copper as the chief precious metal exported. In 1542, an imposter envoy pretending to be from the King of Japan (Ashikaga Shogun), but who was actually sent from Tsushima, arrived in Korea with 80,000 taels (Jp. *ryō*, Cn. *liang*) of silver (one tael equaled approximately 37.5 grams of silver). This incident upset the Korean government because the continuous import of such an amount of silver could empty the state store of cotton bolts used as currency for official trade. These large amounts of silver flowing into the Korean Peninsula were then brought into China to feed the high demand for silver there, especially via the Liaodong Peninsula and other parts of China's northeastern frontier.

However, beginning in 1541, Japanese and Chinese maritime merchants actually began buying back silver from Korea to sell directly themselves to buyers in South China. In the mid-sixteenth century, Chinese merchant ships from South China bound for Western Japan were occasionally thrown off course by adverse winds and landed on the Korean Peninsula.

In exchange for silver, Japanese and Chinese sea merchants brought back from China commodities that included raw silk, silk fabrics, bronze coins, Chinese lacquerware and ingredients for Chinese medicine – almost the same commodities, in fact, sought from China in periods both before and since. One distinctive feature of the trade at this time was the importation into Japan and Southeast Asia of a large amount of privately minted, counterfeit coins from Zhejiang and Fujian[25].

As mentioned earlier, in the sixteenth century, Portugal and Spain took the lead in gaining entry into the maritime East Asian trading sphere. One reason they did so was because after the Ottoman Empire[26] conquered Constantinople, the former center of Eastern trade, capital invested in

---

25 Privately minted coins were minted and circulated without permission from the state. Private minting was a serious crime generally carrying the death penalty. Private coins minted in Japan were particularly known as "*mochūsen*" (counterfeit coins).

26 The Ottoman Empire (1299–1923) was a multiethnic state that arose in Anatolia in the late thirteenth century. At its height, it controlled West Asia, central and eastern North Africa and southeastern Europe. The royal house was descended from Osman I (1259–1326), a chief of Turkic tribes. From the seventeenth century onwards, the empire slowly declined as a result of the rise of Western Europe. After World War I, the empire was dismantled, leaving only the territory of the present-day Republic of Turkey.

Genoa and other Italian city-states based along the Black Sea shifted to the Iberian Peninsula. The Portuguese and Spaniards in maritime Asia sought nutmeg, cloves, pepper and other spices valued highly by both Europeans and Chinese people. Though much pepper was transported to Europe, as is well known, demand was also quite high in China, particularly for that produced in Java and Sumatra. For example, it is said that pepper collected in and shipped from Malacca quadrupled in price when sold in China. There was high demand for the nutmeg, cloves and other spices produced in the Moluccas in both China and Europe. In returning from Malacca, Chinese maritime merchants took on board items such as pepper, cloves, Indian textiles, saffron, coral, minium (used as a vermilion pigment), mercury, opium and other aromatic medicines, iron, saltpeter and twisted cotton yarn. The Portuguese succeeded in establishing a foothold in interregional trade in Asia by trading in these commodities.

## Attempts to secure authorization for *hushi* (mutual trade)

Until the early sixteenth century, the Ming Dynasty's tribute system had functioned in the East Asian region as a common institutional framework for international relations. In many cases, those responsible for actually taking charge of the delivery of tribute were members of Chinese diasporas overseas. When overseas Chinese became involved, their familiarity with the meaning and structures of tribute facilitated the operation of the system. Overseas Chinese who had left China as smugglers and reentered the country as interpreters were treated as special members of the foreign embassy.

Private overseas travel and contact with foreigners were, in principle, prohibited in Ming China, but in coastal provinces such as Guangdong, Fujian and Zhejiang, there was no end to the number of people who left the country illegally, chasing the prospect of success abroad. It became common for local authorities to give tacit acknowledgment of such practices. Those traveling overseas illegally also helped to draw foreign merchant ships to the seas near China. In contrast to the Ming government's strengthening of its exclusionary stance toward foreign countries, private activities in the South China Sea actively fostered international connections in the early sixteenth century.

Foreigners who arrived on China's southeastern coast on non-tribute ships took refuge on offshore islands to avoid interference from Chinese officials. Many of the local people who supplied them with food and water were coastal residents who made a living as fishermen or who worked in the shipping trade. Among them were well-known populations of boat people, such as the Danjia (Tankas)[27] in Guangdong and the Shamin of South China. In the sixteenth century, however, when there was substantial growth in the commercial economy, coastal waters became important routes for the distribution of goods in China and many coastal inhabitants came to be involved in some capacity in the transportation of commodities.

As foreign trade became more active in maritime East Asia, there were some in the various countries across the region who advocated adapting to the new economy in order to capture some of the wealth being carried by the trade, even in China where private interactions with foreigners had been declared illegal. Outside the framework of officially sanctioned tributary trade, non-tributary, mutual trade expanded gradually in coastal areas. As pointed out in the previous chapter, under the tributary trade-maritime prohibition system, only those traders who visited China accompanying tributary envoys were allowed to engage in mutual trade with Chinese merchants. However, from the middle of the Ming Dynasty, in Guangdong, China's major gateway for trade in the South China Sea region for centuries, avenues for mutual trade were gradually opening to foreign vessels unrelated to tributary envoys.

Many of the foreign vessels that sailed to Ming China from the south landed in Guangdong. According to Ming law, only tributary missions could be publicly received by the *shibosi* (maritime trade supervisorate), but in fact it is clear that many of the foreign vessels sailing to Guangdong were not tribute-trade ships. Therefore, the authorities accepted such private trade ships at their discretion and allowed them to engage in trade

---

27 *Danjia* is a name that refers to boat people who once lived along the Guangdong coast. Many were engaged in fishing and shipping. They did not intermarry with ordinary Chinese people on land and are said to have belonged to separate administrative structures than the rest of China. Historically, the Han people have considered Danjia as having a separate ethnicity. However, since the time of the Republic of China, they have been found to be linguistically and physically indistinguishable from ethnic Han Chinese and a policy of permanent settlement has been promoted to date.

to some extent. In these cases, *choufen* (import duties)[28] were imposed on trade, with the revenues earmarked for local military expenses. Although the approval of mutual trade was nothing but an expedient measure taken by the authorities for financial reasons, in the end, official approval for mutual trade opened a "tiny crack" in the Ming Dynasty's tributary trade-maritime prohibition system. As mentioned in the next chapter, this crack gradually widened from the 1570s onward.

---

28 *Choufen* was a tax on commerce imposed by the Chinese government. The tax was levied on goods transacted at specific markets by groups or individuals, and was assessed after exempting a certain proportion of the total amount of the commodity and collected either in kind or in the form of copper cash or silver taels. From the Southern Song onwards, these taxes were levied at coastal trading ports and at government-run markets located on the land-borders with foreign groups.

# 2.3: The Age of Maritime Merchants

## Trade friction with China in 1591

In April 1591, the Spanish Governor of the Philippines[1], Pérez Dasmariñas[2], issued an ordinance prohibiting the natives from wearing clothes made in China. In reply to a subsequently conducted survey, a village chief in central Luzon answered as follows:

> This witness stated that since the Spaniards have become established in these islands, he has noticed how the Chinese have come hither, in larger numbers every year, eight ships at least coming annually from China; and in some years this witness has seen as many as twenty to thirty, all laden with cotton cloths and bolts of silk. And when the natives of these islands and of this province saw all these cloths brought by the Chinese, they made less exertion to weave their own; but to avoid even that little work, all the natives began to clothe themselves with the said stuffs from China, discarding entirely their own, which they formerly wore. And so far has this continued to the present day, that all alike – without distinction of chief from timagua, or of timagua from

---

1 Spain began attempting to conquer the Philippine Islands in the mid-sixteenth century and Spanish rule in the Philippines was established in 1571, with Manila as its capital. The Governor of the Philippines ruled as a representative of the King of Spain, presiding over the administration, finances and military affairs of the colony.
2 Gómez Pérez Dasmariñas y Ribadeneira was the seventh Governor of the Philippines, in office from 1590 to 1593. His tenure is notable for having to deal with a demand from the ruler of Japan, Toyotomi Hideyoshi, that the Spanish Philippines submit and send tribute. He was murdered in a mutiny of Chinese rowers while on an expedition to the Molucca Islands.

slave – dress in these stuffs, making it impossible to judge their rank from their dress.

In July 1592, Dasmariñas reported to the King of Spain, Philip II[3], on the ban on wearing Chinese clothes as follows:

> With your Majesty's permission, I must state that I regret the trade of these Chinese, for it seems to me injurious. It might be forbidden on the ground of the great sums of money which they take from these islands to foreign countries. The most of the trade is in cotton stuffs – the material for which they take from this country in the first place, and bring it back woven. [...] The rest that they bring is silks, very poor and sleazy, except some silk which is brought in raw or spun into thread. This last, I fear, exceeds in quantity that brought from the Spanish kingdoms; and would interfere with your Majesty's royal revenues from the silks of Granada, Murcia, and Valencia.
>
> (Blair and Robertson 1903–1909, Vol. 8).

In spite of this ban, silver continued to flow from the Philippines to China in huge quantities, and with Chinese commodities flooding into the Philippines, Dasmariñas's efforts ended in futility. The massive influx of cheaply produced Chinese goods caused the decline of local industry. This phenomenon, which occurred in the Philippines more than 400 years ago, is also evident in various places in the world today. Since the era of the "Open Sea" of the thirteenth to fourteenth century, Chinese goods, such as raw silk, silk and ceramics, were shipped not only to the East and South China Sea regions but also to the Indian Ocean region. In the late sixteenth century, however, maritime East Asia was now also being incorporated into the emerging global economic system. As a result, what happened in China had the potential to affect the global economy, including the Pacific and Atlantic regions. The inexpensive raw silk produced by Chinese farmers as a side-business flowed into the

---

3 Philip II, King of Spain, reigned from 1556 to 1598. He was the second of the Spanish Hapsburg kings. He succeeded his father, Charles I, to the throne, and in 1580 he also succeeded to the throne of Portugal, thereby coming to rule over a vast colonial empire encompassing parts of the Americas, Africa and Asia.

Philippines, resulting in the loss of market share by the silk weavers of Granada[4], Spain, on the other side of the world.

Cotton cloth exported from China to the Philippines was not a luxury item used solely by the privileged classes, but a daily commodity also used by farmers and slaves. The main trade goods in the era of the "Open Sea" tended to be expensive, luxury items, though some relatively cheap, bulky commodities were also shipped as ballast. In the sixteenth century, however, more daily commodities such as cotton fabrics and food for mass consumption increased in importance as trade goods.

## Restructuring the system of trade in East Asia

"The Age of the Wokou" in maritime East Asia dawned with the smuggling trade on Shuangyu in the 1540s and peaked in the 1550s. Although it gradually declined in the 1560s, Portuguese and other foreign ships were permitted to conduct mutual trade in Guangdong in the 1550s under the supervision of local authorities. In 1557, the Portuguese secured a trading base in Macao. Once a trade route other than for tributary trade was officially acknowledged, it became impossible to return to the tributary trade-maritime prohibition system that had existed in the past.

In the sixteenth century, the tributary trade system gradually became progressively unable to regulate trade not only in maritime Asia but also in inland regions. From the mid-sixteenth century onward, the Mongols often invaded North China, calling for increased trade privileges and even besieging Beijing in 1550. Many Chinese on the northern frontier fled to the Mongols to engage in agriculture or smuggling. In the wake of this catastrophic situation, in the late 1560s to early 1570s, the Ming government significantly relaxed the tributary trade-maritime prohibition policies adopted in the early Ming period and restructured the foreign trade system to open up avenues for legalized, private trade in both maritime and inland areas.

Around 1570, a new trade system replaced the tribute system in both maritime and inland regions of Asia in which various types of trade

---

4 Granada was capital of the Nasrid Dynasty, the last Muslim emirate on the Iberian Peninsula. It is well known for its palace of the Nasrids, the Alhambra. Even after the fall of the Nasrid Dynasty, many Muslim weavers continued to live in Granada, which became the center of silk production in Spain.

routes came to coexist based on the relationships between Ming China and each of its individual trading partners. Here, we will refer to this new trade system simply as the "1570 system". The tribute system was based on the principle of "no trade without tribute", whereas the 1570 system was characterized by the coexistence of tribute and trade, which actually allowed both tributary and non-tributary trade (mutual and voyaging trade), depending on each situation.

In the late 1560s, the Ming Dynasty relaxed the maritime prohibition policy considerably and permitted Chinese maritime merchants to sail from the port of Haicheng[5], located in Zhangzhou Prefecture in the south of Fujian Province, to Southeast Asia. This enabled Chinese merchants to voyage legally to Southeast Asian countries upon receipt of a *wenyin* (sailing license) from the Fujian provincial government and the payment of a set fee. This seaborne trade facilitated by Chinese merchant ships traveling to Southeast Asia was sometimes called "*wangshi*" (voyaging trade), in contrast to the *hushi* (mutual trade) conducted by foreign ships sailing to Guangdong. This easing of trade restrictions was not applied to Japan, and traveling to that country was still banned. However, the demand for Japanese silver led many Chinese merchants to engage in smuggling along the Kyushu coast. Furthermore, the intermediary trading hub of Ryukyu, which had already been on a long-term trend of decline since the late fifteenth century as a result of smuggling in the South and East China Seas, now suffered a decisive blow due to the lifting of the maritime prohibition policy. Chinese maritime traders now openly engaged in trading activities in the South China Sea. State-sponsored trade between Ryukyu and Southeast Asian countries ended in 1570, increasing its dependence on trade with Japan.

In 1571, the Spanish began construction in the colonial city of Manila[6], giving them a terminus for a trans-Pacific trade route between Mexico and the Philippines. At the same time, the amount of silver being extracted from

---

5 Haicheng was a port town on the southern coast of Zhangzhou Bay, an important port city in southern Fujian Province. Originally a smuggling port known as Yuegang, it became a base for Japanese pirate forces in the mid-sixteenth century. In the 1560s, the Ming Dynasty established Haicheng County in the area, permitting Chinese maritime merchants to sail to Southeast Asia from the port.

6 The City of Manila was formerly a trading port of the Muslim emirs of southern Luzon Island. In 1571, the first Governor of the Philippines, Legazpi, militarily occupied the port and it became the capital of the colony. After this conquest, galleons crossing the Pacific Ocean sailed between Acapulco in Mexico and Manila.

Potosí and other mines in Spanish America was increasing rapidly. Spanish galleons began to ship large quantities of silver from Mexico to Manila, where they bought Chinese products brought in by Fujian merchants, and then shipped them back to America. Fifteen seventy-one also witnessed the first Portuguese ships sailing from Macao to Nagasaki, Japan. Portuguese ships received royal charters to sail regularly from Goa to Malacca, to Macao and to Nagasaki, linking the Indian Ocean directly with the South and East China Seas and enabling huge quantities of Japanese silver to flow from Macao into the Chinese market.

Furthermore, in 1571, the Longqing Peace Agreement was concluded between the Ming Dynasty and Altan Khan of the Mongols, under which the Ming Dynasty once more permitted the Mongols to bring tribute and established a large number of *mashi* (horse markets) along the Great Wall, where the Mongols were allowed to engage in mutual trade with the Ming government and Chinese merchants. In the same year, markets for trading with Jurchens and Mongols were opened in the Liaodong region. In the late sixteenth century, Nurhaci[7] began unifying the various Jurchen tribes and expanded his influence by dominating the trade in ginseng and marten furs.

Table 2 gives an outline of the spatial structure of the 1571 system. This table shows that neighboring countries were permitted to trade with the Ming Dynasty using any one or two of the three forms of trade (tribute, mutual and voyaging trade), or using all three, such as was the case with Vietnam and Siam. The only exception was Japan, which was totally excluded from both the tributary and non-tributary trade systems and not allowed official access to any trade route, because Chinese authorities were extremely cautious of and on guard against Japan as the base of the Wokou. Although the exchange between Japanese silver and Chinese commodities was the most profitable form of local commerce in maritime Asia at the time, profits from this flowed to the Portuguese engaged in Macao-Nagasaki trade and to Chinese maritime merchants involved in smuggling.

---

7 Nurhaci reigned from 1616 to 1626. He was a leader of the Jurchens, who was later known by the Chinese designation of Taizu as founder of the Latter Jin Dynasty. Born into the tribespeople known by the Ming Dynasty as the Jianzhou Jurchens, in 1583 he began unifying all the Jurchen tribes and founded the forerunner of the Qing Dynasty, the Latter Jin Dynasty, in 1616.

## Chinese merchants and their sphere of trade

In both maritime and inland East Asia from the 1570s onward, the mutual trade, voyaging trade and smuggling engaged in by private maritime merchants coexisted with state-managed tributary trade. As far as maritime trade in East and Southeast Asia was concerned, however, the main players at the time were no longer tributary missions and the merchants who accompanied them. Instead, trade came to center on the maritime merchants who expanded the trading ports of Haicheng, Guangzhou, Nagasaki, Macao and Manila into hubs of overseas trade.

Although this situation appears to be a return to the Open Sea period, compared to the situation in the thirteenth to fourteenth centuries, merchants came from more diverse origins and their trading sphere transcended maritime East Asia, linked as it was to the global economy. The leading roles in the trade networks of maritime Asia at that time were played by Chinese and Portuguese sea merchants, especially the shipmasters (Pt. *capitão*) who controlled navigation and trade. Of particular importance were sea merchants from Zhangzhou and Quanzhou in southern Fujian Province who, in transforming the port of Haicheng into a hub for maritime trade networks that extended over the East and South China Seas, became integral agents of the Age of Commerce.

Captains of Chinese merchant ships were called "*chuanzhu*" or "*bozhu*" (shipmasters). They played the same role as the *gangshou* (head sea merchants) during the Song and Yuan periods and were wholly responsible for navigation and trade. Shipmasters were the actual owners of ships, their agents or representatives of several joint partners. Merchants aboard a ship under a shipmaster's control were called "*keshang*" or "*sanshang*" (guest merchants). They paid the shipmasters a fee to obtain the use of part of the hold, into which they loaded their shipments. Upon the return of a Chinese merchant ship, *pushing* (government-certified brokers) would bring up the cargo. These brokers monopolized the trade in imported goods, paying taxes to the government in return. They frequently invested in voyages involving shipmasters and guest merchants.

There were broadly two trade routes for Chinese merchant ships: the Eastern Sea and Western Sea routes. The Eastern Sea route stretched from

## 2.3: The Age of Maritime Merchants

### Table 2: Spatial structure of the 1570 system

| | State | Tributary trade site | Place and type of trade |
|---|---|---|---|
| *Maritime Asia* | | | |
| East Asia | Joseon Dynasty | Liaodong: Fenghuangcheng (via Shanhaiguan) | Mutual trade in Liaodong |
| | Japan | <Terminated in 1550> | <Macao-Nagasaki trade by Portuguese> <Smuggling trade conducted by Chinese merchants> |
| | Ryukyu Kingdom | Fujian: Fuzhou Maritime Trade Supervisorate | <Smuggling trade conducted by Chinese merchants> |
| Southeast Asia | Vietnam | Guangxi: Zhennanguan | <Smuggling trade conducted by Chinese merchants> |
| | Siam | Guangdong: Guangzhou Maritime Trade Supervisorate | Mutual trade at Guangdong from the late fifteenth century |
| | Other Southeast Asian states | <No records after 1543> | Voyaging trade between Haicheng and Southeast Asia from the late 1560s |
| Europe | Portugal | <Trade negotiations failed> | Mutual trade at Guangzhou from 1557 |
| | Spain | | Voyaging trade between Haicheng and Manila from 1571 |
| *Inland Asia* | | | |
| North Asia | Mongolia | Shanxi: Datong (via Juyongguan) | Mutual trade at horse markets along the Great Wall from 1571 |
| | Uriangkhad | Northern Zhili: Xifengkou | Horse markets in Liaodong |
| | Jurchen | Liaodong: Kaiyuan (via Shanhaiguan) | Horse markets, tree markets and mutual markets in Liaodong |
| Central Asia | States of the West | Hami (via Jiayuguan) | Horse Trade Office in Shaanxi Mutual trade in Suzhou from the fifteenth century |
| South-western Highlands | Tibet Southwest Tribal Chieftains | Shaanxi and Sichuan Sichuan, Yunnan, Guizhou, Guangxi, etc. | Horse Trade Office in Shaanxi and Sichuan Trade with Chinese merchants |

Note: The information in angle brackets <> indicates forms of trade other than tribute, mutual or voyaging trade.

Fujian through the Philippines, moving south to Brunei, Sulu[8] and the Molucca Islands. However, most ships seem to have sailed for the Philippines, especially Manila. The merchants exported Chinese commodities such as raw silk, woven silk and cotton cloth to Manila, and brought to Fujian the New World silver that the Manila Galleon had transported across the Pacific. In contrast, the Western Sea route extended from Fujian and Guangdong and passed the eastern coast of mainland Southeast Asia and the Malay Peninsula, reaching Sumatra and Java. Chinese maritime merchants using this route exported Chinese products and imported Southeast Asian commodities, including pepper and other spices, medicinal substances and metals.

Although traveling to Japan was strictly prohibited, in reality, Chinese merchants frequently engaged in smuggling on the Kyushu coastline by crossing the East China Sea from Fujian. Many sailed to the Philippine Islands along the Eastern Sea route, then voyaged northward to Kyushu to engage in smuggling. In 1596, for example, Fujiwara Seika[9], who is well known as a founder of Japanese Neo-Confucianism, communicated by means of writing with the captain of a Chinese merchant ship that arrived from Luzon to the port of Uchinoura on the Ōsumi Peninsula. According to Seika, sixty Chinese were on board this ship, and the captain's son was said to be the leader of the Chinese community in Luzon.

## Maritime merchant profiles

In the late sixteenth century, Chinese merchants supplied Chinese products to all of maritime East Asia and imported New World and Japanese silver as well as products from Southeast Asia, while Portuguese maritime merchants supplied Japanese silver and Southeast Asian commodities to the Chinese market and brought Chinese products to Japan, Southeast Asia and the Indian Ocean region.

---

8 Sulu is a group of islands in the waters between Mindanao Island and Borneo Island (Kalimantan). An Islamic emirate that prospered through maritime trade with Manila and China from the seventeenth century onward was established there.

9 Fujiwara Seika (1561–1619) was a Zen monk at Shōkokuji Temple, who devoted himself to Confucianism. In 1596, he traveled to Ōsumi and Satsuma (present-day Kagoshima Prefecture), hoping to journey to Ming China and study Confucianism, but was unable to make the crossing and returned to Kyoto. He later taught the doctrines of the Zhu Xi school, commonly known as Neo-Confucianism, in Kyoto and had a large number of pupils, including Hayashi Razan.

## 2.3: The Age of Maritime Merchants

Trade activities carried out by Portuguese ships in maritime Asia can be categorized in the following three ways. The first was the ships of the captain-majors (Pt. *capitão-mor*) who were granted exclusive trade privileges by the King of Portugal for a specific trade route for a given year. A typical example is the voyage to and from Goa, Malacca, Macao and Nagasaki. This privilege was bestowed by the king as a reward for military exploits and other deeds, and then often sold to local maritime merchants. The second activity was trade authorized by the Portuguese captains of Malacca in the regions encompassing the trade routes of the former Sultanate of Malacca. These sailing rights were also often sold to local merchants. The third was purely private trade. After completing their terms of employment in either trading factories, the fortress or the fleet, many Portuguese settled in Malacca and freely engaged in trade. They often married local women, and the *mestizos*[10] born to them also acted as merchants or mercenaries.

Whereas the Portuguese expanded the trade networks connecting the Indian Ocean and the South and East China Seas, the Spanish developed a trans-Pacific trade route between America and Asia in which the Manila Galleons sailed annually from Acapulco to Manila, exporting New World silver and returning to Acapulco fully laden with Chinese products. The Manila Galleon's trade route was the economic lifeline of Spain's dominions in the Philippines. Originally, only Spanish residing in the Philippines were allowed to load products on these galleons for export to America. However, merchants in Spain, Peru and Nueva España also invested a huge amount of capital in the trading voyages of the Manila Galleons.

In addition to the aforementioned trade routes of Chinese, Portuguese and Spanish merchants, a trade network emerged connecting port cities across the seas of Southeast Asia that served maritime merchants of diverse origins. Key figures in this network were the *orang kaya* (merchant elite), of which there were three types: foreign merchants coming to various port cities to engage in trade; foreigners serving as intermediaries between the royal courts of port polities and merchants, as well as their descendants; and local influential persons involved in trade. In the early sixteenth century,

---

10 *Mestizos* is a collective name for the descendants of children born to white Europeans and local residents in Portuguese and Spanish colonies. However, in the Spanish Philippines, "*mestizos*" also referred to interracial children born from a Chinese father.

foreigners of the first type were primarily Hindu Tamils of southern India and Muslim Gujaratis from northwestern India, but later, the Chinese, Portuguese, Persians and Arabs expanded their influence, replacing the Tamils. The second type of "merchant elite" involved foreign merchants appointed as *syahbandar* (port managers)[11] by the ruler of a port polity. Major port cities employed multiple *syahbandars*, each of whom was in charge of managing trade ships from their country of origin, collecting taxes from these merchants and serving as intermediaries between the ruler and merchants.

By the late sixteenth century, Japanese also began sailing to the South China Sea. Until the fifteenth century, the destinations of Japanese ships were largely limited to Ningbo, China, the three ports in Korea and Naha, Ryukyu. However, with the integration of the East and South China Sea regions into a single trading sphere in the 1570s, Kyushu in Japan occupied the northern tip of this plane of interaction. *Daimyōs* (warlords) in Kyushu invited foreign ships to their domains for the purposes of raising funds for military campaigns and to purchase munitions through trade. In addition, Japanese maritime merchants also began to visit Manila and other port cities in Southeast Asia to import the raw silk and other goods brought by Chinese sea merchants, as well as to acquire commodities from Southeast Asia such as gold and spices. The early stirrings of what would become the system of red-seal trade ships (*shuinsen*) in the early seventeenth century were already discernable.

## The port cityscape and foreigners' settlements

As Chinese, Portuguese, Spanish, Japanese and other maritime merchants extended their trade networks over the East and South China Seas in the late sixteenth century, the hubs of their operations became large coastal port cities. In the sixteenth century in the South China Sea, various trade routes were extended in every direction and entrepôt ports developed where the trade routes intersected, attracting many maritime merchants from differing

---

11 *Syahbandar* derives from Persian, signifying a person who administers (*shah*) a port (*bandar*). These administrative officers could be found widely in the port cities of the Bay of Bengal and Java Sea. In Malacca, four *syahbandar* were appointed, each tasked with administering arrivals from different regions: Gujarat, the Indian Ocean, the Java Sea and the South China Sea.

lands. By contrast, in the East China Sea, trade was concentrated in the Macao-Nagasaki route of the Portuguese and the Fujian-Kyushu route used by Chinese smugglers. A secondary route between Kyushu and Luzon in the Philippines also came to prosper.

The relationship between the port cities and their hinterlands in Southeast Asia was also substantially different from that in East Asia (see Figure 9). In insular Southeast Asia, port polities were often established in the downstream and estuarine sections of major rivers. These port polities exported spices, rice, forest products, gold and other hinterland products (located along the mid- and upper-stream sections of the river), and supplied those inland areas with the imported goods brought to the port cities by foreign merchants. In these port polities, royal authorities based in the port towns controlled the respective hinterlands both politically and economically. In East Asia, however, inland agricultural-based political powers ruled the port towns and attempted to acquire the

**Figure 9: Port city and its hinterlands**
Source: Cited from Bronson (1977).

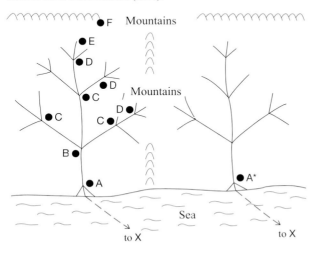

A = port city; B–D = upstream trading centers; E, F = producers; X = international markets

profits from trade by dispatching officials or governors to rule the ports. Port cities rarely became political powers that ruled their hinterlands, though some, such as Sakai in Japan, enjoyed considerable autonomy.

Those port cities that received foreign visitors from a wide variety of regions often contained foreign quarters. For example, in port polities in Southeast Asia, it was common for foreign settlements to be divided according to ethnicity. These ringed the city center, where the royal court was located. Each settlement had its own chieftain, and foreigners were allowed to live there adhering to their own religions and customs. Influential foreign merchants such as the *orang kaya*, *syahbandars* and court interpreters led the port city's trade in partnership with the court. In the Ryukyu Kingdom as well, Chinese people began to settle in Kume Village in the fifteenth century and became responsible for much of Ryukyu's diplomacy and trade. However, as the importance of trade with Japan increased in the sixteenth century, many Japanese settled in Naha and the Chinese community in Kume Village gradually declined.

In China, although the Ming court had relaxed its maritime prohibition policy at the end of the 1560s, it did not permit foreigners to settle in port cities, with the exception of Macao. In Haicheng, only Chinese merchants could enter or leave the port, and foreign ships were not even allowed entry. In Guangzhou, foreign ships were permitted to enter the port, but settlement by foreigners was prohibited. Guangzhou held Chinese product fairs in the spring and fall for export to Japan and the South Seas region, respectively. The Portuguese in Macao and other foreign merchants were permitted to enter the port of Guangzhou at this time, going upstream on the Pearl River, but were not allowed to settle. They thus seem to have stayed aboard their ships, disembarking only for the purpose of engaging in trade.

The sixteenth century also saw the emergence of a new type of port city in addition to the port towns where foreign merchants conducted trade under local rulers. In some cases, Europeans constructed new ports as bases for commerce in Asia, including the Portuguese trading base with China, Macao, and the capital of the Spanish Philippines, Manila, though these two cities also differed considerably from each other in many respects. At the center of Manila stood a walled city, known as "Intramuros", that contained a fortress around the Governor's Palace and churches and was inhabited by Spanish. On the outskirts in a swampy area along the river lay the Chinese settlement, known as the "Parian", and the Japanese quarter. In Macao, by contrast, there were as yet no fortifications in the sixteenth century. The Portuguese paid annual rent and anchorage fees to the Guangdong authorities, who in exchange for these payments tacitly allowed them to settle there.

In 1571, Portuguese ships began sailing to Nagasaki. In 1580, Ōmura Sumitada, warlord over the region, donated the city's territory to the Society of Jesus. Nagasaki soon grew into a major hub of trade in East Asia for the Portuguese, rivaling Macao in importance, and became the base for Jesuit activity in Japan. Even after 1587, when Toyotomi Hideyoshi placed Nagasaki under his direct control, he tacitly permitted the Jesuits to live in the city, where they continued to play a leading role in trade with Portuguese ships. By the 1590s, Nagasaki had become an international port; its population had reached 5,000 and included Japanese, Portuguese, Chinese, Koreans and their children of mixed descent. Adding to this cosmopolitanism, in the late sixteenth and early seventeenth century Tōjin-machi (Chinese settlements) appeared in several port cities in Kyushu. These "Chinatowns" were often situated alongside a wharf, suggesting that they developed at locations where Chinese maritime merchants

**Figure 10: Macao in the seventeenth century**
Source: António Bocarro (1635).

unloaded their goods, carried out trade with Japanese merchants under the supervision of the lords and stayed until leaving port.

## The commodities of maritime Asia

Even in the Open Sea era from the thirteenth to fourteenth century, the Eurasian and African continents had been connected by Indian Ocean trade and inner Asian caravan trade. In the late fifteenth century, the arrival of Europeans in the Americas connected another third of the world (the American continent and Atlantic Ocean) to the "Old World". Then, in 1571, when the city of Manila was built by the Spaniards and the trans-Pacific route between Mexico and the Philippines was established, the final third of the world (the Pacific Ocean) was incorporated into the global economy. As a result, some scholars date the beginning of globalization precisely as the year 1571.

In the sixteenth century, goods for mass-consumption became the dominant commodities traded in maritime East Asia. Items that had once been luxuries, such as raw silk, silk, porcelain and pepper, came into daily use by a broader range of people. As mentioned in Chapter 2.2, from the early sixteenth century onward, Chinese smugglers and Portuguese merchants brought considerable amounts of pepper and other spices, medicinal substances, minerals and fabrics produced in Southeast Asia and India to the countries of East Asia. Then, in the late sixteenth century, after the ban on Chinese maritime merchants sailing to Southeast Asia was lifted and Portugal and Spain secured bases for trade with China and Japan, both the variety and amount of commodities increased even more. The expansion of the trading sphere, the shift in trade to everyday commodities and the diversification of traders helped bring about the peak of the Age of Commerce in sixteenth-century East Asia.

Among the goods traded in maritime Asia, most popular were those introduced at the beginning of this chapter: Chinese raw silk, silk and cotton fabric. Raw silk and silk were primarily produced in the paddy-field zone of the central Yangtze Delta region, and cotton fabrics at slightly higher altitudes along the coast of the eastern part of this region. Many of the textiles produced in this region became brand-name products in demand worldwide, especially the raw silk of Huzhou, high-quality silk fabrics from Suzhou and Hangzhou and high-quality cotton fabrics from Songjiang. For example, in the late sixteenth century, Macao exported around sixty tons of raw silk annually to both Nagasaki and India, and raw silk, silk and cotton fabrics were also shipped in large quantities from Haicheng to Manila.

According to a list of exports and imports handled by the Portuguese of Macao in the late sixteenth century, raw silk, silk, gold, mercury and porcelain were exported from China (Macao) to Japan (Nagasaki), and raw silk, silk, sugar and crude drugs were exported from China to India (Goa). In exchange, a large amount of silver flowed from Japan and India into China. Indian cotton fabric was the commodity most in demand in Southeast Asia; Portuguese and Indian sea merchants supplied it to port cities around the region, and carried some to East Asia as well.

Three other important commodities in maritime East Asia in this period were copper coins, war materiel and foodstuffs. Copper coins were an important Chinese export to the rest of maritime East Asia, especially the low-quality counterfeit coins minted in Zhangzhou in the south of Fujian Province. In the mid-sixteenth century, Wokou smuggled them in large amounts to Japan. Moreover, in the late sixteenth century, after the maritime prohibition policy was relaxed, Chinese sea merchants brought these coins to various parts of Southeast Asia. Wherever these coins arrived, they played an important role in the expansion of the cash economy. The late sixteenth century also witnessed a dramatic increase in demand for war materiel, including the ingredients for gunpowder and ammunition – sulfur, saltpeter[12] and lead. Sulfur was exported from Japan, while Chinese saltpeter and lead were smuggled into Japan from Macao and Fujian. Saltpeter and lead produced in Southeast Asia were transported to Japan via Macao and Manila. Grains and processed food were also major trading goods. Rice harvested in agricultural belts in Siam, Burma and Java was exported to port cities around the region, where arable land was scarce. Wheat, as a staple food for the Spanish, and biscuits, used as food for voyages, were shipped from Kyushu to Manila.

---

12 Saltpeter is a chemical material and potassium nitrate is its main ingredient. The black gunpowder used in the arquebuses and cannons of this period is made from a mixture of sulfur, saltpeter and charcoal powder. As saltpeter is not found naturally in Japan, it was imported from China and Southeast Asia. The manufacture of artificial saltpeter spread from the end of the sixteenth century.

## The "Age of Silver" in East Asia

Demand for Chinese raw silk, silk, cotton fabric and porcelain was very strong not only in maritime Asia but also on the world market. In exchange for these items, an enormous amount of silver flowed continuously into China. Despite the massive influx, the value of silver was still higher there than in Japan or Europe in the late sixteenth century. The ratio of the value of gold to silver was one to twelve in Europe, about one to ten in Japan and about one to seven in China. Profit margins could therefore be increased considerably if silver from Japan and the New World was brought to China, where the purchasing power of silver was strong and used in exchange for Chinese goods to be shipped overseas.

Foreign silver flowed into China via three routes during the sixteenth century. Firstly, Japanese silver, extracted from the Ōmori in Iwami and other mines, flowed into China through the Portuguese Nagasaki-Macao trade and the smuggling trade conducted by Chinese merchants. Secondly, New World silver, produced from the Potosí and other mines, was transported from Mexico to Manila by Spanish galleons and shipped on to China by Fujian maritime merchants. Thirdly, part of the New World silver shipped from Mexico to Europe was invested in Portuguese trade in Asia and brought, along with Old World silver, from Goa to Macao via the Indian Ocean. In 1600, it is estimated that an annual total of fifty to eighty tons of Japanese silver flowed into China, while twenty-five to fifty tons of New World silver flowed into China via Manila. If silver shipped to Macao via the Indian Ocean is added, the total inflow of silver into China may have amounted to 100 to 150 tons per year (see Figure 11).

A considerable portion of the silver in circulation across China was collected as taxes by the Ming government. At the same time as the 1570 system began to emerge globally, the Ming court implemented a new tax system across China known as the "*yitiao bianfa*" (single whip tax reforms)[13], which required the commutation of land taxes and corvée duties into silver. This was certainly linked with the inflow of foreign silver, which entered

---

13 The *yitiao bianfa* simplified and rationalized Ming China's complicated and varied payment procedures and taxation standards. As a result of the reforms, the greater part of taxes and corvée requirements became payable in an amount of silver mainly based on the value of owned land. The reform was first begun in the southeast coastal areas in the 1560s and gradually spread throughout the country.

China along the southeastern coast in exchange for export commodities, and was then absorbed into the domestic market, especially in the downstream area of the Yangtze River. Much of this silver ended up on the northern frontier along the Great Wall. The Ming court collected large amounts of the silver spreading across China as tax revenue, which it needed to cover military expenses for campaigns in the north and as a medium of exchange for the mutual trade with the Mongols and Jurchens. Around 1600, the Ming government paid out about 150 tons of silver per year for military and trade expenses on the northern frontier. This amount was almost equal to the annual inflow of silver. However, most of the silver sent to the northern frontier flowed back into central China in exchange for military supplies and Chinese products.

The influx into and circulation of silver in sixteenth century China led to the formation of three prosperous, silver-related areas on the Ming periphery. The first was Western Japan, where silver was mined. The second was the southeastern coast of China, including Fujian and Guangdong, into which Japanese and New World silver flowed. The third was the northern frontier, where silver collected as tax revenue was devoted to military and trade expenses. Consequently, in the late Ming period, large-scale merchants in the Yangtze Delta region – particularly merchants living in urban areas – where much of the production of goods used for export was centered, enjoyed a

**Figure 11: Circulation of silver in the world circa 1600**

Source: Kishimoto Mio (1998).

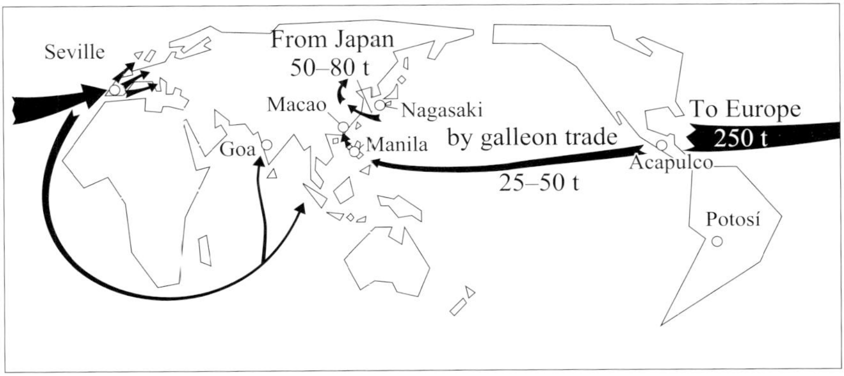

bubble-like economic boom. In addition, Western Japan, the southeastern coast of China and the northern frontier also reaped the benefits of the boom in trade brought about by the production and circulation of silver.

## "Sea of Competition" and rise of new political powers

In the East and South China Sea regions in the sixteenth century, various political powers competed for the profits of trade and to strengthen their military might by investing these profits. New forces linking trade profits with military power also gradually emerged from this sphere of "competition". One typical example was the Taungoo Kingdom in Burma. In the first half of the sixteenth century, the Taungoo Kingdom unified the whole of Burma, overrunning the central plain of the Irrawaddy River region and conquering Pegu, a center for maritime trade on the Bay of Bengal. The Taungoo transferred its capital to Pegu and moreover, extended its military influence to neighboring areas by obtaining large quantities of Western-style firearms through maritime trade and by setting up a corps of musketeers composed of Portuguese mercenaries. In 1564, the Taungoo finally captured Ayutthaya and subjugated Siam, building a powerful empire in mainland Southeast Asia.

Four years after the Taungoo's conquest of Ayutthaya, in Japan, the warlord Oda Nobunaga entered the capital of Kyoto and placed the central parts of the archipelago under his control. He expanded his power in ways similar to Taungoo, which, in order to do so had focused on controlling Pegu as a center of overseas trade, and assembled a musketeer corps. Nobunaga seized Sakai, the largest port city on the Japanese main island of Honshu and one that had maintained close connections with maritime East Asia via Kyushu. He promoted his domain's commercial economy by implementing a series of policies, including the abolition of toll barriers, removal of institutional barriers hindering the development of markets in his castle towns and standardization of official currency values. Nobunaga also assembled a large unit of arquebusiers, which he then used to advance his plans to politically unify the Japanese Archipelago.

Toyotomi Hideyoshi, whose regime succeeded that of Nobunaga, conquered Kyushu and placed Nagasaki and Hakata under his direct control in order to dominate foreign trade. He also sought to unify Japan under a more unitary, centralized rule to replace the decentralized environment in which several political centers were in competition with each other. As part of that process, his regime implemented a series of measures that included a countrywide land survey (*taikō kenchi*), the disarmament of non-warrior classes (*katana-gari*: sword seizure), the separation of the peasantry from the warrior class, the denial of the right of private redress of conflicts (*sōbujirei*) and a ban on piracy both in Japan and abroad (*kaizoku chōjirei*).

However, after the Toyotomi regime's attempt to launch state trade with Ming China ended in failure, Hideyoshi embarked on an enormously delusional expansionist foreign policy that led to two invasions of Korea, which exploded into the largest war in the sixteenth-century world. Mobilizing to the utmost limit of its authority, the Toyotomi government sent upwards of 300,000 warriors armed with state-of-the-art arquebuses to Korea. The invasions of Korea ended in complete failure because of Korean resistance and the considerable military assistance provided to the Joseon government by Ming China. These invasions had significant impacts in Japan, contributing to the self-destruction of the Toyotomi regime, and abroad, weakening the perceived centrality of Ming China in the international political order.

Maritime trade flourished in sixteenth-century East Asia. In each of the states in this region, new commercial and political forces became

### Figure 12: Japanese soldiers in the Philippines

Source: Olivier van Noort, *Description du Penible Voyage Fait Entour de L'univers ou Globe Terrestre* (1610).

powerful by dominating and extracting profits from overseas trade as well as by enhancing their military power, acquiring new firearms and naval forces for example. Many of these new powers came into conflict with each other, while also playing centralizing roles in unifying competing powers within each state. At the same time, as they pursued profit from overseas trade and military expansion, these new powers gradually detached themselves from the political order centered on Ming China. The Toyotomi regime in Japan was at the forefront of this trend. In the seventeenth century, competition among various commercial and military forces led to the emergence of particularly strong new powers who established centralized rule in their region, independent of Ming China. In two significant cases, these new powers arose in two economically flourishing regions on China's periphery: Nurhaci and his son Hong Taiji[14] in the northeastern frontier, and Zheng Zhilong[15] and his son Zheng Chenggong[16] (Koxinga) along the southeastern coast.

## The global movement of people and goods

The Age of Commerce, in which the structures of maritime trade in East Asia developed into a new system, peaked in the late sixteenth century, at the same time as the emergence of a truly global economy. Maritime

---

14 Hong Taiji (1592–1643) was the first emperor of the Qing Dynasty. The eighth son of Nurhaci, he was selected as the second emperor of the Latter Jin Dynasty, but changed the name of the empire to the Qing Dynasty in 1636, thus becoming the first Qing Emperor. He subjugated Inner Mongolia and Joseon Korea and reformed the institutional structure of the dynasty.
15 Zheng Zhilong (1604–1661) was a native of Quanzhou, Fujian Province. He led an armed fleet of sea merchants, established an alliance with the Dutch East India Company, engaged in trade with Japan and controlled maritime trade along the Fujian coastline. After the fall of the Ming Dynasty, he surrendered to the Qing Dynasty in 1646, but was executed due to his son Zheng Chenggong's continued resistance against the new empire.
16 Zheng Chenggong (1642–1662) was born in Hirado (present-day Nagasaki Prefecture) as the son of Zheng Zhilong and a Japanese mother. Following his father's surrender, he based himself in the port of Xiamen, from which he engaged in maritime trade that supported his resistance against the Qing. In 1661, he drove the Dutch from Taiwan and moved his base there, but died of illness the following year.

East Asia became linked to the world market, bringing Chinese products in particular in large amounts to various parts of the Old and the New Worlds. Even before the fifteenth century, many Chinese products had been exported by Muslim maritime merchants to the maritime region of the Indian Ocean. In the sixteenth century, however, the Portuguese supplied Chinese products directly to Europe. It is said that in the late sixteenth century, on one street in Lisbon alone, one could find at least six Chinese ceramic stores, and that at a hospital in Goa meals were usually served on Chinese dishes. In 1603, a Dutch ship captured a Portuguese merchant vessel laden with 1,200 boxes of Chinese raw silk and 200,000 individual pieces of Chinese ceramics.

As mentioned at the beginning of this chapter, Chinese raw silk, silk textiles, cotton cloth and porcelain were also exported in large amounts to the Philippines by Fujian maritime merchants, and then carried from Manila to Acapulco, Mexico, in the holds of Spanish galleons. Soon after, inexpensive, high-quality silks from China soon deprived Spanish silk weavers of the Mexican market. In Mexico, local production of raw silk declined due to the influx of Chinese raw silk, while a silk weaving industry using Chinese raw silk expanded.

Chinese products were further transported from New Spain (Central America under the Spanish rule) to Peru (South America under the Spanish rule), where the Potosí mine was situated. In Peru in the late sixteenth century, it was said that when husbands had tailors make their wives clothes out of Spanish silk, it cost more than 200 pesos, but if made of Chinese silk, the cost was only twenty-five pesos. It was also said that the citizens of Lima, the capital of Peru, wore high-quality, expensive silk clothing, and that the women of Lima enjoyed the most abundant selection of silk dresses in the world. King Philip II of Spain often imposed restrictions on the import of Chinese goods to prevent the outflow of Peruvian and Mexican silver, but such measures had little effect. Chinese products were even accepted by leaders of conquered indigenous tribes. A list of goods bequeathed by the wife of a tribal chief in 1602 included a "Chinese satin tapestry". In addition, a painting of the portraits of monarchs of the Incan Empire[17] sent to a fellow

---

17 Monarchs of the Inca Empire ruled over a vast territory in the Andes Mountains from their capital of Cuzco in Peru from the thirteenth century. Cuzco was conquered by the Spaniard Francisco Pizarro in 1533, but the descendants of the Incan monarchs continued to resist the Spanish for forty years.

Inca in Spain by members of the tribe in Cuzco was depicted on a "white taffeta cloth made in China".

This worldwide circulation of goods was mainly carried out by Europeans. Opportunities for East Asian peoples to voyage across the Pacific or Indian Ocean were limited. Nonetheless, even apart from well-known cases, such as the Tenshō and Keichō embassies, a number of people traveled from East Asia to other parts of the world in the late sixteenth and early seventeenth centuries. As mentioned earlier, there were 10,000 Chinese and 1,000 Japanese residents in Manila in the late sixteenth century; it was not unusual for some of these to travel by galleon to the American continent. An authentic remaining document states that a Portuguese merchant in Cordoba, Argentina, sold a Japanese slave to a priest in 1596. According to a census conducted in 1613 in Lima, Peru, there were thirty-eight Chinese residents and twenty Japanese in the city, many of whom were lower-class tradesmen or Spanish slaves, probably brought to America as chattel or to pay off debts. The scale of the Chinese community in Mexico City at this time can be seen in an order by city authorities in the 1630s limiting the number of Chinese barbers in the city to twelve in order to protect their Spanish counterparts.

Slaves were one of the most significant commodities in maritime trade worldwide from the sixteenth century onward, and maritime East Asia was no exception. In particular, *daimyōs* or millitary commanders mobilized for the invasions of Korea abducted and transported enormous numbers of Koreans to their domains, selling them to foreign merchants in Nagasaki and other cities. The slave trade that occurred in the wake of the invasions of Korea enabled Francesco Carletti, who was referred to in Chapter 2.1, to purchase five Korean slaves in Nagasaki. He converted them to Christianity, set four free in Goa and then embarked on his return voyage to Europe with a Korean named Antonio and a Japanese man. Their ship was attacked and seized by a Dutch vessel as they navigated the Atlantic Ocean. His Japanese companion was killed in the attack, and Carletti and Antonio were taken away to the Netherlands. Carletti later returned to Florence, and Antonio then moved to Rome.

People and goods began to move on a global scale in the sixteenth century, especially in the second half of the century, transmitting cultures, religions, artisanal methods and technologies, which variously fused into new hybrid forms and competed with each other on the global stage. Chapter 2.4 deals with some aspects of this cultural exchange, with a particular focus on the interactions between maritime East Asia and the rest of the world.

# 2.4: Development of Diverse and Hybrid Cultures

## A port city's view of maritime East Asia

There is nothing that more concretely illustrates the fruits of intercultural exchange in sixteenth-century maritime East Asia than artifacts unearthed from the port cities that once served as hubs of maritime trade. Here we discuss the Japanese city of Funai (now Ōita) in Bungo Province, Kyushu, where recent excavations have yielded abundant artifacts concentrated in a limited area that can be studied fruitfully in conjunction with a relatively rich documentary record.

Funai was a port city situated at the mouth of the Ōita River that flows into Beppu Bay on the Seto Inland Sea. A site of local political importance since ancient times, in the sixteenth century it became the base of the Ōtomo family, a *daimyō* (warlord) family who sponsored large-scale overseas trade activities. Funai was one of the foremost cities in Western Japan during that period. The city was centered on the Ōtomo mansion, which also served the Ōtomo as the political headquarters for ruling their domain. Funai was divided by four roads running north-south and five streets running east-west, and included as many as 5,000 commoners' houses. It consisted of forty-five neighborhood blocks, including a Chinese quarter (Tōjin-machi).

The variety of artifacts unearthed in Funai clearly shows the distinctive features of maritime East Asia as the Ming court's relaxation of its maritime prohibitions was accompanied by a resurgence in trading activity by Chinese maritime merchants and by the arrival of European traders in Japan. Excavations of the site of the Ōtomo mansion have unearthed gilt items, including gilded red earthenware dishes and metal fittings ornamented with gold, *tenmoku* tea bowls and other utensils used in tea ceremony, small glass dishes, lead bullets, products made in South China and Siam and other artifacts. The excavations of commoners' houses are distinctive for the considerable amount of Jingdezhen and Zhangzhou blue-

and-white porcelain[1] that has been unearthed. It is presumed that these pieces included not only commodities for trade, but also everyday articles belonging to Japanese who engaged in trade with China or by Chinese who sailed to Japan. In addition, Funai excavations have yielded Korean, Siamese and Vietnamese products, and even some of the few Burmese products ever discovered in Japan. Quantitative analysis of some of the finds suggests that trade ceramics account for more than sixty percent of the excavated items. Some of the market house remains also yielded Kirishitan[2] artifacts. Funai became an important base for Jesuit activity after Francis Xavier completed his missionary work in 1551. The Jesuits constructed a church, hospital and *colégio* (seminary)[3]. Buried remains of Japanese Kirishitans have also been discovered in church cemeteries.

In the mid-sixteenth century, a Chinese writer pointed out that "In the past barbarians entered the Chinese territory, but nowadays Chinese are rather entering the barbarian regions" (Zheng Xiao, *Huang Ming Siyikao*). Under such circumstances, Chinese established settlements in various parts of East Asia and introduced their culture into neighboring regions. In the case of Funai, Chinese sea merchants formed a loose-knit diaspora, living in a mixed residence environment with Japanese people without becoming a distinct minority group. They took advantage of their professional seafaring expertise to play important roles in the local community, and their ability to introduce advanced technologies enabled many to acquire high social standing. Moreover, they made pilgrimages to Japanese religious institutions and gave them donations, and also engaged in religious rituals in such a way as to demonstrate the fusion of different cultures, religions and beliefs.

European merchants took advantage of the Chinese maritime merchant networks in order to make inroads into maritime East Asia. Along with

---

1 Blue-and-white ware is porcelain produced by painting images on white porcelain using a blue underglaze made mostly from cobalt and then firing it after applying a transparent glaze. It is known in China as "*qinghua*" (blue flowers) due to the distinctive blue and white design.
2 In this book, when Christianity is mentioned in its general religious sense the word "Christianity" will be used, but when the faith accepted into Japan or its followers is discussed the Japanized word "Kirishitans" will be used.
3 Jesuit *colégio* were established for the purpose of training people for work in the church and to teach Western culture to Japanese people. The seminary in Funai was founded in 1580.

their commercial activities, Europeans brought their religion, culture and new technologies with them. The impact of this encounter is evident in the great variety of Christian-related relics unearthed in Funai. In addition, the Japanese side of this encounter with foreignness evinced considerable openness to accepting foreign goods, ideas and artifacts. They were open-minded and tolerant not only of Chinese culture but also of the Christianity being brought over from Europe. This openness in Funai indicates the potential for port cities, the gateways for cultural exchange, to also function as spaces for intercultural fusion and hybridity. In the sixteenth century, different cultures not only coexisted in and penetrated maritime East Asia, they also sometimes came into conflict with each other or became intermixed. Such dramatic competition among diverse cultures usually occurred at the frontiers of cross-cultural exchange: the port cities of East Asia.

Among the diverse aspects of culture, this chapter focuses on forms of culture particularly shaped by and emblematic of the multidimensional maritime exchanges in sixteenth-century East Asia: religion (seafarers' deities, Christianity), artisanal crafts and artwork (ceramics, folding screens, Namban lacquerware), technology (firearms, publishing) and information.

## Seafarers' deities and the expanding sphere of trade

Each of the peoples traveling between the port cities of sixteenth-century maritime East Asia prayed to various gods for safe passage. At this time, faith in seafarer deities such as Mazu, the Dragon King[4] and Avalokiteśvara[5] (Cn. Guanyin, Jp. Kannon) spread as a result of the active trade voyages of Chinese maritime merchants, and gradually transformed the local religious practices of inhabitants where they sailed. The worship of Mazu in particular spread widely around maritime East Asia in conjunction with the expanding trade networks of Chinese sea merchants. From its main temple on Meizhou Island, Fujian Province, worship of Mazu spread from the southern coast of Mainland China to the Ryukyu Islands, southwestern Japan and Southeast Asia as the overseas activities of Fujian ships spread.

---

4 The Dragon King, (Skt. Sāgara) rules over the other dragons. In Buddhism, this refers to the eight dragon kings, who were prayed to in order to secure safe passage.
5 Avalokiteśvara is the Sanskrit name of a bodhisattva known as "Guanyin" in China and "Kannon" in Japan who was worshiped as a guardian deity of seafarers.

Mazu worship gained new adherents as it spread by being adapted to local religious practice. In the coastal area of Zhejiang Province where belief in the Dragon King was strong, Mazu was accepted as the Dragon King's daughter, a famous figure in Buddhism for her gift of a jewel to the Buddha, her ability to change genders and achieving Enlightenment. Mazu became meaningful to yet more seafarers as she came to be construed as an avatar of a Bodhisattva, the Putuoshan Guanyin, a protective deity of seafarers who emerged in the Zhoushan Islands and spread from the central coastline of China to Korean coastal areas and Western Japan in the era of the "Open Sea" explored in Part 1. Mazu came to be commonly known as "the Bodhisattva" (*bosa* or *pusa*) in the Ryukyus and Kyushu. Worship of the Dragon King was prominent along the coasts of Shandong Province and Korea. In Shandong, the Dragon King was linked with the God of the Eastern Sea (Donghai Shen), one of the imperially recognized deities in the official religion, and became the Dragon King of the Eastern Sea (Donghai Longwang). However, among people on the coast, belief in the female version, the Dragon Princess, was more popular. In the era discussed in Part 1, Mazu had been promoted to become part of the officially recognized deities owed sacrifices and rites as a tutelary deity of seaborne shipping. She became an even more significant part of official religion and popular belief in the Ming period when she became the tutelary deity of Zheng He's expeditions and coastal defense installations. However, worship varied considerably depending on region, and even on status. For example, the Tianfei Palace built on Miao Island, situated between Shandong and Liaodong, was also known as the Temple of the Dragon Princess, the object of worship differing according to people's rank.

In Japan, Mazu worship was transmitted via and centered on Chinese settlements in Kyushu. However, the worship of gods who could guarantee safe passage was a practice found in the archipelago since ancient times. For example, pirates of the Seto Inland Sea worshipped the deities of Itsukushima[6] and seafarers from Kyushu and the Nankai region, a wide maritime belt extending from the Kii Peninsula to Shikoku, worshipped

---

6 Three chief deities are enshrined at Itsukushima Shrine (Miyajima, Hiroshima Prefecture): Ichikishimahime no Mikoto, Tagorihime no Mikoto and Takitsuhime no Mikoto. After being revered by Taira no Kiyomori and other members of the Taira family, belief in the Itsukushima deities spread to the mariners of the Seto Inland Sea and beyond.

## 2.4: Development of Diverse and Hybrid Cultures

the deities of Kumano as both Shinto deities and Buddhist avatars[7]. Later, worship of Hachiman, the God of War, grew in popularity during the long period of strife in the fifteenth and sixteenth centuries and invocations of this god began appearing on Japanese pirate flags. Depending on the region, however, belief in deities of the Munakata Shrine[8] and Itsukushima also increased.

In contrast, the Zen monks who regularly served as diplomatic envoys to Ming China beginning in the late fourteenth century prayed for safe passage to gods enshrined in localities along the sailing route from Japan to China, including the Mañjuśrī on Shika Island and Shichirō Gongen on Hirado Island. Shichirō Gongen seems to have originally been either a dragon god, a god of the sea or a temple guardian deity named Zhaobao Qilang, who was widely worshipped from Song to Ming China. Belief in Shichirō Gongen spread to and became established in Japan as a result of the active maritime trade between Japan and Song China. However, in sixteenth-century mainland East Asia, Skanda (Weituo; the Indian deity Skanda, son of Siva and general of his army) and Emperor Guan Yu, a deified hero from the Three Kingdoms period, came to be worshipped as important temple guardian deities, and the worship of Mazu as a goddess with the power to ensure safe passage spread, causing Zhaobao Qilang to wane in popularity and be forgotten. In Japan, however, Shichirō Gongen remained as a guardian deity of Zen and Ritsu temples – schools of Buddhism imported from Song China – and, as the case of Shichirō Gongen on Hirado indicates, continued to attract worshippers seeking to pray for a safe voyage. It can be said that the gods, too, were engaged in a struggle for survival.

---

7 The Kumano deities are enshrined in three Kumano Shrines in Kii (present-day Mie Prefecture): the Kumano Hongū Taisha in Hongū, the Kumano Hayatama Taisha in Shingū and the Kumano Nachi Taisha in Nachi.
8 The three deities of Munakata are three sea goddesses: Takiribime no Mikoto, Ichikishimahime no Mikoto and Tagitsuhime no Mikoto. These are worshipped at the three shrines (Okitsumiya, Nakatsumiya and Hetsumiya) at the Munakata Taisha Shrine in Fukuoka Prefecture. The Munakata goddesses were worshiped not only by seafaring groups but also by the central government as guardian deities of seafaring.

## Christian missionaries and religious conflict

In the sixteenth century, European trade activity brought the European religion of Christianity to East Asian seas. In 1547, having helped to establish a base in the Portuguese-controlled Indian port of Goa from which the Jesuits[9] could expand missionary activities into South and Southeast Asia, a Jesuit missionary named Francis Xavier sailed to Malacca, where he met a Japanese man from Satsuma (present-day Kagoshima) named Anjirō. Anjirō had come to Malacca on a private Portuguese trading ship. This encounter inspired Xavier to extend his proselytization to Japan. Since he was unable to find a Portuguese trading ship leaving for Japan, he boarded a Chinese junk owned by a Chinese maritime merchant named Aván[10], bound for Satsuma. Xavier reported in an official letter that during the voyage Aván frequently drew lots in front of an enshrined icon. This custom appears to be evidence of praying to a seafaring deity such as Mazu in order to ensure safe passage.

After being baptized, Anjirō assisted Xavier with his missionary work in Kagoshima, but withdrew from the Society of Jesus and joined a pirate band after Xavier departed from that country. According to Francisco Pérez, a Jesuit in Malacca, a Chinese junk that arrived bearing letters Xavier and his party wrote soon after reaching Japan carried four Japanese who had converted to Kirishitans while lodging in a Chinese Christian's house in Malacca. Until the 1590s, the Jesuits were the sole organization proselytizing in Japan, focusing on western parts of the country (mainly Kyushu and the Kinai region around Kyoto). In the late sixteenth century, however, members of Spanish mendicant orders[11] arrived in Japan and expanded the scope of missionary activity in Honshu.

---

9 The Society of Jesus is a religious order of priests founded in the sixteenth century by Ignatius of Loyola and seven comrades, including Francis Xavier. The Jesuits stood at the forefront of the Counter Reformation in many countries. Christianity was brought to Japan by Francis Xavier in 1549.

10 Aván was a Chinese maritime merchant who married into a family in Malacca and who traded actively from that port. He was known in Portuguese by his nickname of "Robber" (Ladrão). According to a report by Xavier, he is said to have died in Zhangzhou, China.

11 Spanish mendicant orders refer to the Franciscan Order, the Dominican Order and the Order of Saint Augustine. Originating in thirteenth-century Europe, which had been impoverished by the Crusades, these are groups of priests who aspire to live

Early on, the Jesuits followed a conversion strategy of first converting the ruling class to Kirishitans, particularly the *daimyōs* who hoped to engage in trade with foreigners, on the condition that they invited Portuguese trade ships to harbor in their domains. They then expanded their conversion efforts to the retainer bands and domanial inhabitants of the *daimyōs*. However, the *daimyōs* did not simply shift their domains over to Kirishitans in a uniform manner. For instance, in the territory of the Ōmura family in Hizen Province, Kyushu, inhabitants had made pilgrimages to worship at Ise Shrine since ancient times. However, after the conversion of Lord Ōmura to Kirishitans when it began to spread throughout the domain, the number of worshippers at Ise Shrine and subsequently the number of people receiving the holy amulet from the shrine, Jingū Taima, decreased. However, if the ruling class had converted in unison, religious friction between groups of vassals and "heretics" within the domain would have been unavoidable. Therefore, the head of the Ōmura family expanded Kirishitans slowly within his clan, for instance limiting conversion to groups of four to six members in turn. The head of the clan himself continued to receive Jingū Taima, practicing simultaneously and without contradiction both Kirishitans and Ise-Shinto (which is itself a syncretic fusion of Shinto and Buddhism). Although it is possible that this syncretism can be put down to the strategy of a particular Kirishitan *daimyō*[12], this period is distinctive for the number of cases in which religions coexisted as well as those in which they competed.

Another approach of the Jesuits was to provide avenues by which commoners could convert by operating at the grassroots level. In the domains of *daimyōs*, Jesuits organized churches, hospitals, relief houses for the poor and orphanages. In Japan, the construction of hospitals and orphanages was funded by donations from the Portuguese Jesuit Luís de Almeida, who had been a sea merchant before joining the Society of Jesus in Japan. Almeida used his property to engage in trading that raised funds for the promotion of Jesuit missionary activity. From that time on, Jesuit missionary work in Japan and China was supported by profits from maritime trade, thus the role of the Jesuit procurator in charge of economic

---

a life resembling that of Christ, taking poverty, humility and a lack of possessions as their principles. While Macao was the Jesuit's base for voyages to Japan, the base of the mendicant orders' activities in Asia was Spanish-ruled Manila.

12 Kirishitan *daimyōs* were those warlords who converted to Catholicism during the Sengoku (Warring States) period and the early Edo period.

matters became more important. When the city of Nagasaki was donated to the Society of Jesus, the annual arrival of a trade ship from Macao made it the most prosperous port city in Japan. Merchants and artisans flocked to Nagasaki from across Japan and converted to Kirishitans. By the end of the sixteenth century, the number of Kirishitans in Japan had climbed to about 300,000.

In Macao, where the Portuguese began to reside in 1557 in order to engage in mutual trade at Guangzhou, the center of Jesuit missionary activity was St. Paul's College. Some members of this school were invited to the Ming court on the pretext of teaching European science and technology. Especially prominent was Matteo Ricci[13], who arrived in China in the late sixteenth century. He endeavored to proselytize gradually while introducing European culture through exchanges with scholar-officials (*shidafu*) in the Ming court. As a result of these efforts, by the seventeenth century, Christianity had begun to gain a foothold among intellectuals and in the court; this proved instrumental in transmitting European science and scholarship to China.

The proselytization of Christianity in maritime East Asia proceeded at varying rates in different countries. Whereas Christianity won a considerable number of Japanese believers mainly in the western part of the archipelago in the latter half of the sixteenth century, it was not until the beginning of the seventeenth century that the missionary work began to pick up steam in China. However, just as it was gradually spreading across Japanese society, the religion was banned and severely suppressed after the authority of the Toyotomi regime issued proscription edicts against it in the late sixteenth century. In China, too, the Qing Dynasty increased the severity of its bans on the propagation of the Christian faith in the latter half of the seventeenth century. East Asia as a whole was heading for an age when the Christian faith would be gradually prohibited.

## A ceramics road connecting maritime Asia

Most of the large number of ceramics unearthed in Funai, Bungo Province were produced in China, indicative of the fact that Chinese ceramics were one of the most important Chinese handicrafts carried not only across Asia,

---

13 Matteo Ricci (1552–1610) was an Italian Jesuit missionary. In China he was known as Li Madou. He was permitted to reside in Beijing, where he built a base for Catholic missionary work and introduced Western scholarship to China.

## 2.4: Development of Diverse and Hybrid Cultures 193

but also to various other parts of the world. In the fifteenth and sixteenth centuries, blue-and-white porcelain, also known as "underglaze blue" ware and called *"sometsuke"* in Japanese, replaced celadon and white porcelain as the main style of ceramic produced in China. During the Ming period, official kilns for imperial production were established in Jingdezhen, and blue-and-white porcelain with delicate designs emphasizing space, in contrast with the powerful patterns of the Yuan period, began to be produced. The colors appearing in the ceramics of each period tend to reflect the trade situation at the time. In the Ming period, high-quality cobalt-blue pigment depended on imports from West Asia. For example, during the Wanli period the use of domestically produced *zheqing* (cobalt)[14] became prevalent when it became difficult to acquire cobalt from West Asia, causing the colors of wares to become darker.

Although blue-and-white porcelain was produced mainly for the imperial court and the wealthy class, the volume manufactured as a commodity in private kilns[15] began to increase in the fifteenth century and grew significantly in the sixteenth. The technical capacity of private kilns equaled that of official kilns, which then came to entrust the firing of porcelain to the private sphere. Blue-and-white wares were produced in private kilns not only in Jingdezhen, but also in places such as Zhangzhou, southern Fujian Province, where rough copies of Jingdezhen wares were produced and exported to various countries in Southeast Asia and Europe. These ceramics produced for export later came to be known popularly as "Swatow ware" in Europe and later as *"gosude"* in Japan. Another type of porcelain ware, known in Japan as *"fuyōde"* because it mirrored the form of flower petals radiating outwards, was manufactured for export in the sixteenth century and became known in Europe as *"kraak"* ware after the "carracks" used to transport it. Before long, counterfeit wares were produced in Japan, West Asia and Europe, initiating a worldwide porcelain boom.

Ming China's relaxation of its maritime prohibition system also brought about a major change in the structure of the ceramics trade in the East

---

14 *Zheqing* is a blue pigment produced in the Zhejiang region of China used as an underglaze in blue-and-white porcelain instead of Huiqing Mohammedan blue pigment imported from the west of China, or Shizi Blue and Pingdeng Blue produced in China's Jiangxi region.
15 Private kilns fired porcelain for private use in contrast to "imperial" or "official" kilns that fired porcelain for royal court and government office use. However, private kilns were also commissioned to produce official wares.

and South China Seas. In the period from the mid-fourteenth through the sixteenth century, when official-kiln fired Chinese blue-and-white ware was dominant, ceramics imitating Chinese celadon and blue-and-white ware were produced in Vietnam, Siam and Burma and exported in large amounts. In Islamic western Asia in particular, ceramics made in Siam and Burma from the mid-fourteenth century have been unearthed in more or less equal amounts to those found in China. This was particularly the case in the mid-fifteenth century when Chinese maritime trade in the South China Sea stagnated, causing the quantity of Chinese ceramics in circulation in Southeast Asia to decrease and stimulating a rise in the production of ceramics in Siam and Vietnam. However, in the late sixteenth century, the ceramics industry in Southeast Asia shifted focus to domestic demand, and production dwindled in the face of increased exports from China after the Ming court relaxed its maritime prohibitions. The removal of maritime trade bans promoted the growth of Chinese private kilns, overwhelming the Southeast Asian market, and subsequently caused Southeast Asian ceramics to lose considerable market share.

## Folding screens (*byōbu*): Mirrors of their times

In 1582, the head of the Jesuit order in Japan and representative of the Father General in Rome, Alessandro Valignano[16], departed Nagasaki on a Portuguese ship accompanied by an embassy composed of young male scions of powerful Kyushu-based Kirishitan *daimyō* bound for Rome. This was the Tenshō Embassy, named for the reign era in which it departed Japan. The embassy carried with it a painted *byōbu* given by Oda Nobunaga to Valignano that depicted Nobunaga's castle and a scene of the city of Azuchi (*Azuchijō zu byōbu*). Nobunaga had commissioned the painter Kanō Eitoku to depict Azuchi Castle, replete with its seven-story donjon, and the city of Azuchi. Eitoku epitomized the art of the late sixteenth century, especially that of the age of Nobunaga and Hideyoshi, known to art historians as the

---

16 Alessandro Valignano (1539–1606) was an Italian Jesuit missionary. He traveled to Japan three times as a *visitador* and set many kinds of regulations and rules for missionary activity in Japan to accommodate with Japanese culture. He was involved in the establishment of a school for the training of Japanese priests, the dispatch of the Tenshō Embassy of young men to Europe and the printing and publication of the "Kirishitan editions" in Japan (see below).

Azuchi-Momoyama period. He dramatically altered the graceful simplicity that characterized the Kanō-school's painting style in the early sixteenth century and innovated a new large-scale style of painting distinguished by luxuriousness and strong, bold lines. He devised works that suited the tastes of the powerful figures of his time and found favor with Oda Nobunaga and Toyotomi Hideyoshi. The original pair of Azuchi Castle screens sent from Nobunaga were presented to the Pope and exhibited in the Gallery of Maps within the Vatican. Although the current whereabouts of the screens are unfortunately unknown and the work is now sometimes referred to as the "phantom screens", the fact that Kanō Eitoku's Azuchi Castle screens were displayed at the Apostolic Palace symbolically commemorates an age in which Japanese screen paintings flooded into Europe.

Long predating the presentation of Eitoku's screen to the Pope, Japanese folding screens were artistic handicrafts with a long history of being presented as gifts as part of diplomatic relations between Japan and other East Asian countries. Many of the folding screen paintings that crossed the seas were luxurious works of art that expressed hopes for wealth and good fortune with depictions of flowers and birds and the prevalent use of gold leaf. Folding screens were both furniture and fine arts, and their rich decoration made them a prominent form of household art. These screens aroused curiosity and interest among the Jesuit missionaries who visited Japan after the mid-sixteenth century. Luís Fróis[17] wrote in his *História de Japam* (History of Japan) that, as a result of this fascination, "Some *byōbu* have already been sent to Portugal and Rome. A large number of folding screens are shipped to India every year". The continuous stream of screens exported to Europe caused the Japanese word "*byōbu*" to become part of the Portuguese and Spanish languages as "*biombo*".

At the same time, a new style of painted screen depicting Europeans became popular in Japan and was produced in large numbers: this was the

---

17 Luís Fróis (1532–1596) was a Portuguese Jesuit missionary. He traveled to Japan in 1563 and gained favorable treatment from Oda Nobunaga. He had a thorough knowledge of Japan, authoring the *História de Japam* and *Tratado em que se contêm muito susinta e abreviadamente algumas contradições e diferenças de costumes entre a gente de Europa e esta província de Japão* (Striking Contrasts in the Customs of Europe and Japan).

Namban Byōbu[18], literally "painted screens of the southern barbarians". These screens took as their subject "things Namban", especially the Europeans and the European ships that arrived in Japan in the late sixteenth and early seventeenth centuries. The word "Namban" originated in China as a derogatory term used by the Chinese to refer to foreigners to the south, based on a division of the world into civilized and barbarian. From the sixteenth century onward in Japan, however, the word came to mainly designate the Portuguese and Spaniards coming to Japan from Southeast Asia. It eventually acquired a new, less derogatory nuance signifying exotic and strange foreign things. Namban Byōbu typically consist of a pair of six-paneled painted folding screens that depict Namban people and ships then active in Japan or abroad, as well as the trade goods they carried. Prior to the sixteenth century, Japanese in this period embraced a worldview that divided the world into three realms (*sangoku*): Fusō (Japan), Shintan (China and Korea) and Tenjiku (India). The Namban world represented something new and Japanese became intensely curious about the people, goods, customs and cultures of this new world, depicting them in great detail on screens. However, although the objects of the paintings may have been novel, the style and materials used remained traditional. The style was the same as that used in the portraiture of the time. The composition of the image and the depictions of Namban people and ships are comparatively accurate, but the drawings of foreign buildings that the painters could not possibly have seen themselves were dependent on their imagination. Interestingly, where one would expect to find European-style buildings, Oriental buildings were substituted on the screens. Namban screens thus reflect the pattern of maritime interaction in maritime East Asia in the sixteenth century. The designs mix Eastern and Western elements, in that the artists used the traditional Japanese art form of the folding screen and Japanese materials and techniques to represent the newly arrived Western people and their artifacts.

---

18 Namban Byōbu are painted folding screens that depict exchanges with European-led crews who voyaged to Japan from the latter half of the sixteenth century to the first half of the seventeenth century. In the narrow sense, this term signifies a genre of painted screens that depict scenes of European ships docking and trading in Japan.

## Maritime exchange expansion and Namban lacquerware

The Portuguese had various commodities produced in a European form that were made using the local techniques and decorative methods of the Asian countries they visited. These commodities were first developed in and around Goa, an important Portuguese base in India, and the style is known as "Indo-Portuguese", signifying the mixture of Indian and Portuguese forms. These hybrid-style artisanal goods began to be produced in various parts of Asia and exported to Europe, after handicrafts and artisanal cultures of specific locales caught the eye of Portuguese merchants.

Namban lacquerware[19] is representative of the hybrid artisanal commodities developed in maritime East Asia at the time. This form of lacquerware was made in the shape of European goods but decorated using the distinctive Japanese technique of *maki-e*[20]. The designs, however, were quite different from traditional Japanese ones. Namban lacquerware was characterized by decorative patterns used to fill space and the heavy usage of mother-of-pearl inlay (a technique known as *"raden"* in

**Figure 13: Southern barbarian ship at shore**
Source: Kanō Naizen, Namban Byōbu, Kobe City Museum.

---

19  Namban lacquerware was lacquerware exported by Portuguese merchants.
20  A unique lacquerware technique carried out by sprinkling gold or silver powder on the surface of the product.

Japanese)[21]. With regard to the use of the latter, the possible influence of Yi Dynasty (Korea) mother-of-pearl inlay on Namban lacquerware has been pointed out. However, Namban lacquerware has features in common not only with crafts made in countries such as Korea and China, which traditionally had a significant impact on Japanese fine arts, but also shares features with crafts made in Gujarat in northwestern India. Similarities between Namban lacquerware and Indo-Portuguese artifacts can be seen in the use of mother-of-pearl inlay in Namban lacquerware based on the shell artistry of Gujarat and the fact that in India chests of drawers were also made according to the same standards. Objects similar to the Indian artifacts were probably produced in Japan because Europeans wanted lacquerware with an "Indian style". It can be said that Europeans usually associated the Orient with images of India instead of Japan, with which they were unfamiliar, and demanded this kind of image on all goods from Asian areas. The distinctive hybridity and diversity in Namban lacquerware that combines both Japanese and Indian elements suggests a gap between the image of Japan pursued by Europeans and the reality. This gap is revealing of the fact that juxtapositions as well as harmonization or fusions occurred when the materials and images brought by Europeans were articulated via traditional Japanese techniques.

Indeed, some Namban lacquerware includes elements not constructed in Japan, resulting less in some form of fusion or hybridity and more in the competition of heterogeneous elements. Namban lacquerware was created by mixing together Japanese elements with Indian and other elements in a wide variety of ways. It is important to remember, however, that Europeans sought home furnishings made using the distinctive methods of various lands after having compared the handicrafts of many countries. As such, Namban lacquerware emerged as a result of Europeans having judged Japanese lacquerware to be superior to that made in other countries in terms of its strength, quality and the expressiveness of its images and designs, as it made use of techniques such as *maki-e*. Namban lacquerware thus became a global commodity, becoming a forerunner of Japan's export lacquer

---

21 *Raden* is one technique used in lacquerware craftwork. Seashells such as *Turbo marmoratus* (green turban) or abalone that have iridescent surfaces are cut into shapes, which are then inlaid or affixed to a wood or lacquered surface.

industry that brought lacquer not only to Europe, but also to intermediary ports in Asia.

Objects affected by Japanese lacquerware have been made in various lands since the seventeenth century. In Mexico, for example, artisans influenced by Namban lacquerware combined oil painting with mother-of-pearl inlay. The creation of new kinds of hybrid objects in the other parts of the world influenced by Namban lacquerware, itself the product of mixing Eastern and Western elements, indicates the dynamism of maritime exchange at the time, which cannot be explained adequately as simply exchange between the Eastern and Western worlds.

## New developments in firearms technology

Ceramics, folding screens and Namban lacquerware epitomized the types of goods exported from Asia to Europe through maritime trade, whereas trade in the opposite direction, from Europe into Asia, is vividly illustrated in the form of new firearms technologies. Fifteenth-century Europe witnessed the rapid development of firearms that helped precipitate what historians have labeled a "Military Revolution". These firearms soon spread to West Asia, and, by the sixteenth century, had reach maritime East Asia, exerting far-reaching effects on subsequent historical developments.

Metal-barreled firearms first saw practical use in battle in thirteenth-century China, and from the late fourteenth century, Ming China began producing an enormous number of firearms, including portable guns and large cannons. However, from the mid-fifteenth century, as a result of no large-scale wars being fought, firearms innovation ceased and the technology stagnated. Firearms of the early Ming style continued to be produced in the early sixteenth century. Through interactions with Ming China, these firearms reached Korea and Ryukyu, and as a result of military clashes with the Ming Dynasty, they also spread to Southeast Asia. However, the Japanese Archipelago was left out of the large-scale dissemination of firearms in East and Southeast Asia, most likely because, in addition to various strategic reasons, it was impossible to procure saltpeter, indispensable for the production of gunpowder, in Japan.

As the Portuguese gradually advanced eastward in the first half of the sixteenth century, the European-style firearms they carried flowed into various parts of East Asia, such as the *folangji-pao* (Frankish cannon) and the matchlock arquebus. The *folangji-pao*, a cylindrical barreled, breech-loading cannon, was used as naval artillery mounted on Portuguese vessels, and was introduced to the Ming in 1521 after a military clash between Portugal and the Ming Dynasty in Guangdong. The *folangji-pao* was superior to conventional Chinese firearms in terms of the amount of time it took to reload in addition to its range and destructive power. The Ming exploited their expertise in firearms manufacturing techniques, accumulated over many long years, and improved the *folangji-pao* so that it could be used both for defending castles and on the battlefield. China mass-produced European guns of varying sizes during the Ming period.

Then, in 1543, arquebuses were brought to Japan's Tanegashima Island by the Portuguese. The method of manufacturing this weapon spread rapidly across the Japanese Archipelago, as Japan was in the midst of a period of endemic civil war, and firearms came to play a pivotal role in facilitating the political unification of the archipelago. The speed by which firearms technology was adapted by the Japanese is also suggested by an account that Ming China overcame difficulties in recreating the European arquebuses transmitted by the Portuguese after their attack on the Wokou enclave on the island of Shuangyu enabled them to acquire and study Japanese-style firearms. European firearms also spread from Fujian and other parts of the southeast coast to other regions of China. In 1558, China produced more than 10,000 arquebuses called "*niaochong*" (bird guns). However, these are considered to have been made by casting copper according to traditional firearms technology rather than from wrought iron. Although the short-term mass-production of the barrel of the copper arquebus was possible, it was weaker than those made from iron, likely to explode if fired repeatedly and not particularly accurate.

In Japan, where firearms manufacturing methods had remained largely unknown, efforts were made to learn the techniques from scratch by trying to reproduce the arquebuses introduced in the mid-sixteenth century as faithfully as possible. The arquebus manufacturing method thus acquired was rapidly disseminated throughout the archipelago. One factor responsible for facilitating the fast spread of firearms in Japan seems to have been the fact that saltpeter produced in Southeast Asia and China was brought to Japan by Portuguese and Chinese sea merchants. In contrast, China exploited its traditional expertise in firearms manufacturing, made improvements of its own to the *folangji-pao* and deployed a large number of large-scale cannons of varying models. Consequently, when the Toyotomi regime of Japan invaded Korea, there was a direct confrontation between Japanese-made firearms and the cannons of Ming China.

Large-scale war between the Ming military, amply equipped with various types of cannon, and the Japanese military, armed with large numbers of well-crafted arquebuses, stimulated the exchange of firearms technologies and provided both sides with opportunities to develop in this regard. The large cannons possessed by the Ming were powerful and very effective in attacking fortifications. Impressed by their effectiveness, Tokugawa Ieyasu had gunsmiths in the ports of Sakai and Kunitomo (in Ōmi, present-day Shiga) build cannons, and imported other cannons from the Dutch factory. During the siege of Osaka Castle in 1614 and 1615, the Tokugawa unleashed a fierce bombardment using more than 100 cannons. On the other hand, the highly effective Japanese arquebuses posed a serious threat to Ming forces, and the Ming government worked to acquire these weapons by having captive Japanese soldiers introduce the techniques for manufacturing the Japanese-style wrought iron weapons. Ming China even organized firearms units made up of captive Japanese soldiers, and mobilized these units in combating the rebellions of ethnic minorities in the southwest and in fighting the Jurchens in the northeast.

**Figure 14:** *Folangji-pao*
Source: Zheng Ruoceng (1562), National Archives of Japan.

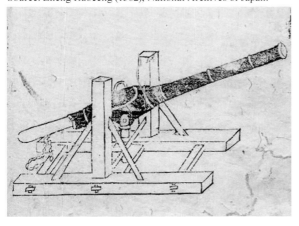

Given these developments, there was a sharp increase in Ming China's interest in firearms technologies, including those of Japanese-style arquebuses. A treatise on firearms published in the late sixteenth century, the *Shenqipu* (Record of Celebrated Materials) by Zhao Shizhen, contained illustrations of various firearms, including an Ottoman Turkish musket, which appeared to be superior to Japanese arquebuses. In Korea, which had served as the battlefield for Japan and China, Japanese arquebuses were obtained from Japanese prisoners of war and Frankish guns from the relief army dispatched by Ming China. Although in Korea the bow and arrow had been the main weapon until that time, in the seventeenth century, it acquired leading-edge arquebus technology and became one of the foremost East Asian countries producing and possessing firearms.

With frequent outbreaks of large-scale warfare in which firearms were the main weapons, the movement of peoples, including prisoners of war, facilitated the circulation and diffusion of firearms technology. As a result, the strength of the land-based empire of Ming China as a centralizing force weakened, inviting new powers to rise up and challenge it. In Ming China in the first half of the seventeenth century, Xu Guangqi and other officials with close ties to Jesuits were at the center of an effort to introduce European-style state-of-the-art firearms, and achieved a number of successes – for example, in defeating Nurhaci in battles with the Latter Jin Dynasty[22]. Subsequently, however, the Ming Dynasty was unable to make significant headway with its effort to introduce state-of-the-art firearms. In contrast, the Latter Jin succeeded in arming themselves with firearms captured from Ming China, including state-of-the-art European-style artillery known to the Chinese as the "Red Barbarian" cannon through the intermediary of Christian missionaries and others well-versed in the production and use of firearms. Consequently, the Latter Jin gradually gained an advantage over the Ming Dynasty. In maritime East Asia from the late sixteenth century onward, the ability to successfully acquire and deploy new firearms technology became a determining factor in the survival of regimes. Those societies that were able to adopt this technology smoothly would subsequently become the leading

---

22  The Latter Jin was a dynasty established when Nurhaci unified the Jurchens and is known in Manchurian as Manju Gurun (Manchuria) or Aisin Gurun. The Latter Jin attacked the Ming Dynasty and invaded the Liaodong region, changing their name to the Great Qing in 1636.

powers during the transformations that swept the international order of East Asia during the seventeenth century.

## Age of print culture and integration of printing techniques

Print culture is integral as a means for enabling societies to share information and knowledge. In maritime East Asia, a new print culture appeared in the sixteenth century, enabling the publication of books and other materials in large quantities. Because of the dominance of Chinese characters as a form of writing, woodblock printing constituted the basic form of printing in the region, with the exception of the Korean Peninsula where movable type printing was developed. The sixteenth century was a time when new publication techniques were imported from beyond the Chinese-character cultural sphere and integrated with conventional techniques.

The activities of book publishers and sellers dramatically expanded in sixteenth-century China. Although woodblock printing was widely known in the Chinese-character cultural sphere, publication activities were previously carried out mainly by central and local governments and powerful individuals. Before the sixteenth century, as well as we can ascertain, the business of both publishing and selling books only occurred in a limited number of urbanized centers. In addition, the number of book sellers involved in printing and publishing was quite limited because of the engrained culture of copying manuscripts. It was only in the sixteenth century that printed publications finally prevailed over transcriptions and books began to be published in large numbers in China as commercial publishing developed in coastal regions.

In Europe, Johannes Gutenberg[23] invented movable type printing in the mid-fifteenth century, and by the sixteenth century, his methods of letterpress printing had spread widely. The Jesuits introduced this technique into Asia in the mid-sixteenth century to aid their proselytization efforts. A printing press was brought to Asia by the Tenshō Embassy, departing from Lisbon on its return to Japan. In 1587, the Jesuit Alessandro Valignano arranged for a Latin speech made by Hara Martinho, a member of the embassy, to be printed with movable type by Japanese in Goa.

---

23 Johannes Gutenberg was a German inventor said to have been the originator of the technique of printing using moveable type. He cast type in a mold and invented a printing press to print the forty-two-line Bible, indulgences and other items.

In Japan, while under threat from the Christian missionary expulsion edict that had been issued in 1587, the Jesuits printed more than 100 titles of what are called *Kirishitan-ban* (Kirishitan editions) in both Roman letters and Japanese *kana* on the initiative of Valignano. In contrast, after a Jesuit named Matteo Ricci arrived in Macao in 1582 and entered the Ming court in 1601, he translated many books into Chinese, including his own works on Christianity and other Western academic books, and had them published using traditional Chinese woodblock printing techniques.

The Japanese invasions of Korea in the late sixteenth century dispatched by Toyotomi Hideyoshi resulted in the forced removal of a large quantity of Korean cultural items to Japan. Among these were many Korean typeset books published in Korea as well as the copper type used to produce them. In Japan, after Emperor Go-Yōzei issued a royal command in 1593 instructing that printing using movable type be carried out, the "age of old typeset editions" continued for about sixty years, during which the emperor, powerful *daimyōs* and major temples and shrines sponsored the printing of works using movable type. Although these publication enterprises were directly influenced by Korean movable type culture, they also adopted the European typesetting techniques used for the so-called "Kirishitan editions". In other words, "old typeset editions" were printed by replacing the lead type with wooden type and adapting the traditional technique for Japanese woodblock printing instead of using a letterpress.

The publication of a Chinese book in 1606 in Japan by order of Toyotomi Hideyori (heir of Hideyoshi) exemplifies the intensive hybridity that distinguished the publishing culture of maritime East Asia at the time. This book was called *Teikan zusetsu* (Cn. *Dijian tushuo*[24]), which means "the Emperor's Mirror, illustrated and discussed".

The original text published at the end of the sixteenth century was representative of the standard woodblock printing techniques of the late

---

24 *Dijian tushuo* is a book of the Ming court that describes, with illustrations, actions to be recommended or admonished in the vicissitudes of a realm's rise and fall taken from histories of the reigns of ancient Chinese emperors. The content covers a total of 117 accounts, eighty-one of which describe benevolence to be held up as exemplars (mirrors) that include the ability to make wise appointments, filial piety, mercy, frugality and the love of scholarship of emperors from the Sage King Emperor Yao to Emperor Shenzong of the Northern Song Dynasty, and thirty-six of which detail detrimental actions that are to be admonished from Emperor Taikang of the Xia Dynasty to Emperor Huizong of the Northern Song Dynasty.

Ming period. However, the edition sponsored by Hideyori was printed by fusing the typesetting of the "old typeset editions". After its introduction into Japan and subsequent publication, *Teikan zusetsu* was appreciated by the ruling class as a source of political ideology. The text included discussions and illustrations of moral exemplars, which inspired models for paintings done on the walls, sliding doors and folding screens of warrior residences newly constructed as part of a building boom that swept the country in the early seventeenth century. The use of *Teikan zusetsu* as inspiration for paintings is epitomized by the *Teikanzu* (Emperor's Mirror illustrations), painted by Kanō Tan'yū on the sliding doors of Nagoya Castle. The case of *Teikan zusetsu* shows how the rising tide of the new print culture in maritime East Asia accelerated the dissemination of information. The body of up-to-date information contained in the original Chinese edition of the book, published in the first year of the Wanli reign era (1573), soon spread at an unprecedented pace across the Japanese Archipelago.

**Figure 15:** *Teikan zusetsu*
(Ch. *Dijian tushuo*)

## Information on Japan disseminated over the sea

In sixteenth-century maritime East Asia, the flow of not only people and goods but also of information gathered speed. In particular, people overseas began to actively collect information on Japan as a global leader in silver production, a nest of Wokou, an epicenter of the invasion of Korea and the front-line of Christian missionary activity. This interest led to the production of various studies and reports.

The Ming Dynasty had hitherto not shown much interest in information on Japan. Chinese interest in the country, however, was sparked by the Ningbo Incident of 1523 (see Chapter 2.1), leading a scholar from Dinghai named Xue Jun[25] to compile *Riben kaolue* (Summarized Studies of Japan, 1523), which served as a foundation for future scholarship on that country. New information was added to these findings in the mid-sixteenth century when, in response to the Wokou who raided the coasts of China, the Ming court dispatched envoys to Japan to request that local authorities suppress piracy. Jiang Zhou led one embassy in 1555 and Zheng Shun'gong another in 1556. Both investigated a number of locations in Western Japan and brought back up-to-date information on Japan to Ming China.

Based on information on Japan provided by Jiang Zhou and others, Zheng Ruozeng published *Riben tuzuan* (Atlas of Japan) in 1561, which contained highly detailed maps, including a "Map of Japan", a "Map of Japanese Pirate Invasion Routes" and an "Illustrated Guide to the Navigational Route of an Envoy to Japan" based on Jiang Zhou's account of his voyage to Japan via Ryukyu. The image of Japan as a pirate base can be seen in the "Map of Japan", which represents the Gotō Islands, home of Wang Zhi and other pirates, as the same size as Kyushu. Zheng Ruozeng also compiled the *Ryukyu tushuo* (Illustrated Guide to Ryukyu), which contains a "Map of Ryukyu", the sole map from the sixteenth century depicting Shuri and Naha Port. Zheng Ruozeng later expanded the contents of *Riben tuzuan* by referencing some 136 maps and other books to create a comprehensive study of Wokou in thirteen volumes (*juan*), entitled *Chouhai tubian*

---

25 Xue Jun was a native of Dinghai County, China. He was well-versed in scholarship and is said to have worked as a teacher in Changzhou. He compiled *Riben kaolue* (Studies of Japan), the first scholarly work on Japan completed in the Ming period, and while the book is not considered to be an accomplished work, it had a great influence on later studies of that country.

(Illustrated Compendium of Maritime Defense) and published in 1562. This work contains a rich assortment of maps of the Chinese coast and other locales, a comprehensive chronology of Wokou raids and diagrams of ships and weaponry.

In contrast, Zheng Shun'gong[26] completed the book "A Mirror on Japan" (*Riben Yijian*) in 1565 based on information that Zheng himself collected while staying in Japan as an envoy. This book describes his voyage to Japan, the state of Wokou activity and the geography and customs of Japan. He also included maps that provide information not found in any other account. Much information about Japan was also included in *leishu* (daily-use encyclopedias). Because these were published at different times during the Ming Dynasty, we can trace significant changes that took place in the way Japanese males are portrayed. Whereas the drawings in the editions published in the early years of the dynasty portrayed Japanese males in the form of Zen monks, later editions depicted them as half-naked men carrying a sword on their shoulder. This reveals that the Wokou image had become the stereotypical representation of the Japanese man, replacing the image that had been associated since the Song and Yuan periods with the Zen monks who visited China to study.

Joseon Korea, having suffered for so long from raids by the "early Wokou", early on made strenuous efforts to collect information on Japan. The product of such efforts was a comprehensive work by Sin Sukju entitled *Haedong chegukki* (Record of Countries to the East, 1471)[27]. However, as Wokou activity had diminished by the latter half of the fifteenth century, Koreans became less interested in information on Japan. By the early sixteenth century, unable to gain access to raw firsthand information, the Korean

---

26 Zheng Shun'gong visited Japan on the order of the Supreme Commander of Zhejiang in 1556 with the aim of entering into negotiations regarding the suppression of Wokou. He stayed with Ōtomo Sōrin of Bungo (present-day Ōita Prefecture) and returned to China the following year with Seiju, a monk-envoy sent by the Ōtomo family to Ming China. He compiled *Riben yjian* (Mirror on Japan) based on his experiences sailing to Japan and his observations in that country, as well as the sources that he collected. This work had a great impact on Chinese perceptions of Japan.
27 *Haedong chegukki* was completed in 1471 by Sin Sukju at the order of the Joseon King Seongjong. It contains material on the state of affairs in Japan, Tsushima, Iki and Ryukyu, as well as the history of diplomatic relations between these lands and Korea. It also outlined rules for the reception of envoys. The book later became an essential reference for Korean diplomats.

government became dependent on whatever knowledge was brought by imposter embassies dispatched by the Sō family of Tsushima seeking to exploit the Joseon court's reception system for foreign visitors. As the "later Wokou" began to appear more frequently along the coast of Korea in the mid-sixteenth century, the Joseon court became aware once more of the need to improve their country's naval defenses against Japan. It was against this backdrop that a Korean tribute mission in Beijing obtained a copy of Xue Jun's *Riben kaolue*, which the Joseon court then had reprinted in Korea in 1530. Nonetheless, the Korean government subsequently failed to secure a reliable means of obtaining correct and up-to-date information on Japan, and this failure partly explained why Korea remained largely defenseless when invaded by the Toyotomi government of Japan.

However, the organization that had the greatest interest in Japan, strove to collect information on it and made the most detailed study of it in the sixteenth century was the Jesuits. Their motives for doing so were quite different from that of the Chinese or the Koreans. The Jesuits aimed to use the collected information not only to spread Christianity, but also to produce propaganda for consumption in Europe in order to raise funds for their missionary work in foreign countries. In addition, this information helped to satisfy the appetite of European intellectuals for knowledge of unknown lands. Information-gathering by the Jesuits was characterized by the collecting and sharing of information through the exchange of letters between members. Since Xavier's visit to Japan, reports on the development and achievements of missionary work had been sent to the Father General in Rome, and, after a process of inspection, censorship of sensitive information and receipt of final approval by the Society, these were printed and distributed widely. Apart from such public documents, confidential papers were also produced, and the information included in them was more reliable than in the letters written to encourage support for missionary work. The Jesuits' study of Japanese language, history, literature and geography was also extremely detailed, and led to the completion of works such as the first Japanese-Portuguese Dictionary, *Vocabulário da Língua do Japão* (Jp. *Nippo Jisho*)[28], and Luís Fróis's *História de Japam* (History of Japan).

---

28 The "Japanese-Portuguese Dictionary" was compiled by Jesuits to help their missionaries learn Japanese. The main dictionary was completed in 1603 and a supplement in the following year. Gathering 32,800 Japanese words, irrespective of whether they were of Japanese or Chinese origin or slang words, the dictionary

Of the three foreign collectors of information on Japan – the Ming court, the Joseon court and the Jesuits – comparison reveals that the Jesuits were exceptional in information collection and analysis, a fact reflecting their superior sources of information. For instance, Fróis obtained information from reliable sources such as the *yūhitsu* (secretaries)[29] who wrote out documents for Toyotomi Hideyoshi, and was able to include in his *História de Japam*[30] copies of vermilion seal letters issued by Hideyoshi. The Jesuits also set a high standard with their capability at systematizing miscellaneous pieces of raw data and conducting comprehensive analysis of the processed information.

## Return to the Port of Funai

During the fifteenth century, the maritime movement of people, goods and information between the Japanese Archipelago and the countries of the East China Sea took place along a limited number of routes. However, in the sixteenth century, these flows in East Asia suddenly became more active and extended much further afield. The port town of Funai, Bungo Province, introduced at the opening of this chapter, epitomized many of the trends of maritime East Asia during this period. Excavations of Kirishitan crosses and medals along with Buddhist altar fittings and statues are tangible reminders of a time when, within the urban space of Funai, Zen Buddhist temples, Kirishitan churches and a Chinese settlement existed side by side. These excavations at Funai have also uncovered the commodities of sixteenth-century maritime East Asia. Large quantities of ceramics made in Japan, China, Korea and Southeast Asia have been unearthed, along with bullets and component parts of arquebuses, a large number of Chinese coins and balance scales used to measure out amounts of silver produced in Japan.

The ruler of this cosmopolitan port city, Ōtomo Sōrin, attempted to dispatch tributary envoys to Ming China, sponsored smuggling with Ming

---

provides lexical interpretations in Portuguese as well as indicating the source, usage, related words, register and so on of entries.

29 *Yūhitsu* wrote documents on behalf of their lords.
30 *História de Japam* was written by Luís Fróis and covers the history of the Jesuit mission in Japan during the roughly forty years from the arrival of Francis Xavier to around 1592. Despite a certain bias from the missionary viewpoint, the book is highly valued as a resource due to the accuracy of its observations and sources of information as well as its detailed descriptions.

China and trade with the Ryukyu Kingdom, opened up trade with Macao through Jesuit intermediaries and even personally established trade relations with countries in Southeast Asia, including Cambodia. In his youth, he came into contact with an arquebus soon after the first arrival of the weapons in Tanegashima Island. Later, he imported large *folangji-pao* from Macao. Both Jiang Zhou and Zheng Shun'gong stayed in Bungo and gathered information on Japan under Sōrin's aegis. Furthermore, letters written by missionaries staying in Funai were disseminated across the world through the Jesuit order's information network. In his *História de Japam*, Luís Fróis gives a heartfelt description of the glories of the Kingdom of Bungo and its fall in the assault launched by the Shimazu family. Located in a small corner of the Japanese Archipelago on the eastern edge of maritime East Asia, Funai constituted a gathering space for people, goods and information voyaging across the seas.

However, toward the end of the sixteenth century, the Toyotomi government subjugated Kyushu and mobilized the Ōtomo family[31] and other *daimyōs* of Kyushu for the invasions of Korea. Afterwards, the Toyotomi expelled the Ōtomo family from Bungo on the pretext of misconduct by Sorin's heir, Yōshimune, on the battlefield in Korea. Consequently, Funai lost its character as a cosmopolitan port city in the seventeenth century, thereafter becoming just one of the hundreds of small domanial castle towns. The era when multitudes of forces in pursuit of both profits from trade and military supremacy competed with each other in various parts of maritime East Asia was gradually coming to a close. Dawning in its place was a new era in which those regimes that defeated their rivals in "competition" established unified states in maritime East Asia and exerted unitary control over the movement of people, goods and information along predetermined routes.

---

31 Ōtomo Sōrin (1530–1587), born as Ōtomo Yoshishige, was a *daimyō* of the Sengoku period, and held title to the military governorship of six provinces: Bungo, Chikugo, Higo, Chikuzen, Buzen and Hizen (parts of present-day Ōita, Saga, Kumamoto, Fukuoka and Nagasaki Prefectures). The son of Ōtomo Yoshiaki, he was a brother of Ōuchi Yoshinaga. He had established a domain in northern Kyushu, but approached the Toyotomi government when he was embroiled in a conflict with the Shimazu family who controlled southern Kyushu. He actively engaged in foreign trade and had a strong connection with Christian missionaries.

# Part 3

# The Compartmentalized Sea, from 1700 to 1800

**Figure 16: Map of maritime East Asia, 1700–1800**

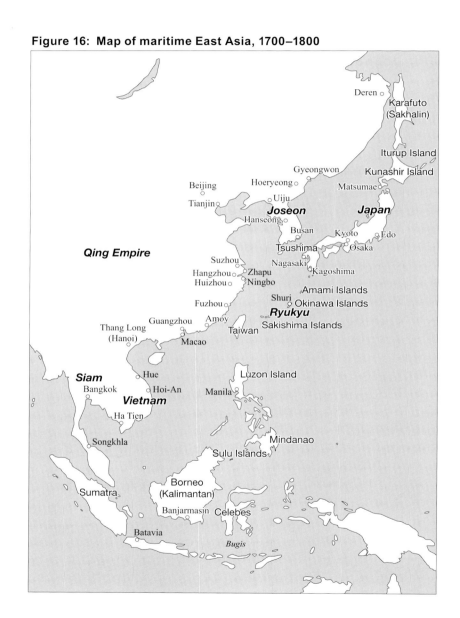

## 3.1: General Overview

### Two ships lost at sea

In the winter of 1742, during the reign of the eighth Tokugawa Shogun Yoshimune[1] (r. 1716–1745), a vessel registered in Satsuma Domain (present-day Kagoshima Prefecture) met with misfortune while sailing from Ryukyu to Kagoshima. The ship had a crew of twenty-one, including two Ryukyuan seamen hired in Ryukyu. The crew did everything possible to keep the ship under control, throwing the cargo overboard to make it lighter and even petitioning the divinities in a ritual involving cutting their hair and throwing it into the sea. All of this was to no avail, and the ship finally foundered in the raging seas. The crew managed to escape the sinking ship by moving into a small lifeboat, but one member lost his life during the transfer. The remaining twenty crewmen drifted, leaving their fate in divine hands. Fortunately, they washed ashore on an island[2].

In October 1764, when the *Ise-maru*, a cargo vessel based in the Chikuzen Domain (in the western part of present-day Fukuoka Prefecture), was sailing in the Sea of Kashima (off the coast of present-day Ibaraki

---

1 Tokugawa Yoshimune (1684–1751) was the eighth shogun of the Edo Shogunate (r. 1716 to 1745). One of the three branches of the Tokugawa house, he was the fifth head of the Kishū Tokugawa family, but became shogun by inheritance from the main branch of the Tokugawa family. He reformed the structure of the shogunate by spearheading financial and administrative restructuring in what is known as the Kyōhō Reforms.
2 This paragraph consists of information extracted from several sources. *Tsūkō Ichiran* (Directory of Commerce and Diplomacy in the Edo period), Vol. 225; *Sasshūsen Shinkoku Hyōchakudan* (An Account About a Ship that Drifted from Satsuma to Qing China); *Kyūki Zatsuroku* (Miscellanies of the Old Records of Satsuma), Appended Vol. 87.

Prefecture) carrying lumber from Tsugaru (in the west of present-day Aomori Prefecture) to Edo, she was battered by a storm. The twenty-member crew struggled desperately for hours in the raging tempest, bailing out water that was accumulating in the ship, throwing lumber overboard to lighten the ship's load and cutting their hair and casting it into the sea to invoke the divinities and the Buddha for help. Even though they made it through the crisis, their ship, deprived of its sails, rudder and anchor, drifted for around 101 days until it washed ashore on a large, unknown island[3].

Certain aspects of these two stories are ubiquitous; they could be indicative of a maritime event that occurred at any time or in any place in the world, with only minor variations in the type of vessel and the religious beliefs of the crewmen involved. However, the different ways in which the two stories unfold once the crew were washed ashore throw into relief the salient features of maritime East Asia from 1700–1800, the period under consideration in Part 3. Let us look first at what became of the crew of the first, Satsuma-based ship.

## The castaways' return home

In the first story, the surviving crew members washed ashore on an island that they guessed was part of China. They were correct in this speculation; it was one of the small islands constituting the Zhoushan Islands, scattered in the waters northeast of present-day Zhejiang Province in China. The residents of the island did not understand Japanese, but by using hand and body gestures the crew were able to convey that they were castaways, and the islanders gave them food and took care of them. Subsequently, the crew was taken to a large island called Zhoushan, where they were questioned by local officials using Chinese characters. On that occasion, Denbē, the captain of the ship, is reported to have identified himself in writing as a "resident of Japan's Satsuma Domain governed by Matsudaira Ōsuminokami", referring to Shimazu Tsugutoyo, the lord of the Satsuma Domain. The surname Matsudaira was bestowed by the shogun upon

---

3 The sources of this information are *Nankai Kibun* (Stories Told About the Southern Sea) and *Hyōryū Tenjiku Monogatari* (The Story of Ships That Drifted to Tenjiku [India and Southeast Asia]).

certain *daimyōs*[4] in the hope they would influence other lords and potential rivals in his favor. The crew were treated courteously during their stay in Zhoushan and provided daily with meals, tea and tobacco.

Before long, Denbē and his crew were shipped across the sea to China's mainland, and after traveling by land and stopping at places such as Zhenhai, Ningbo, Hangzhou, Shaoxing and Jiaxing, they were finally taken to a port town called Zhapu, one of the major ports from which the merchant ships of Qing China set sail for Nagasaki, Japan. While there, the crew members were accommodated in the residence of Sanguan, a Chinese merchant who owned a fleet of ocean-going ships that often visited Nagasaki. During their stay in his residence, they were treated cordially, fed well and supplied with clothes and bedding. Sanguan was ordered by the local officials of Zhapu to take good care of Denbē and his men and send them home to Japan; public funds would cover their living expenses and any goods the sailors required for the journey home.

In the spring of 1743, the crew left Zhapu on board a ship owned by Sanguan. After a voyage of about ten days the ship arrived in Nagasaki, where they were handed over to the Nagasaki Bugyōsho (magistrate's office). The Bugyōsho interrogated the crew members, inquired about their names and registered addresses and religious faith, making them trample on a picture of Christ to determine whether they were Kirishitans (Christians) or not (*fumi-e, e-fumi*). The crew was then questioned at length about how they came to be adrift at sea, and about their life during their stay in Qing China. When the officials found nothing suspicious about the crew, they were handed over to officials of the Satsuma Domain and allowed to return to their families.

Thus, the crew who had drifted ashore close to China was safely repatriated to Japan in an effort that involved both the ordinary local people and officials of Qing China, despite the fact that Japan had no diplomatic relations with the country. They returned to their daily lives without being charged with a crime stemming from the law that banned Japanese from traveling abroad. The Zhoushan Islands where they washed ashore were a major base of the Wokou ("Japanese pirates") during the period covered by Part 2 of this volume. Thus, if the incident had taken

---

4 In the Edo period, the character of the feudal system was further strengthened by the central regime of Tokugawa (*bakuhan* system). Each *daimyō* was forced to pledge allegiance to the shogunate and put under the total control of the central regime.

place during that time, they would have been robbed of their possessions and sold as slaves or left with no other choice but to become pirates themselves.

However, in the East China Sea of the eighteenth century, the aforementioned episode was far from extraordinary. Nearly without exception, Japanese people who drifted ashore in the territories of Qing China received favorable treatment and protection and were repatriated to Japan aboard merchant ships bound for Nagasaki. As is evident from the fact that local officials handled castaways as part of their official duties and that the cost of taking care of the Japanese castaways was borne out of public funds, rescuing and protecting foreign castaways was treated as part of the Qing government's official policy. The reverse was also the case. People of Qing China who drifted to Japan's shores were rescued and protected in accordance with the laws and regulations of the shogunal government and individual domains and were sent home in a similar way to Japanese castaways. This practice of rescuing, protecting and repatriating foreign castaways as part of institutional state policy was observed not only between the Qing government and the Tokugawa Shogunate, but also with the Ryukyu Kingdom and Korea's Joseon Dynasty. Furthermore, even between countries with no formal diplomatic exchange, such as Ryukyu and Korea, Japan and Vietnam or Ryukyu and Vietnam, the practice of mutually repatriating foreign castaways to their home countries was carried out through the intercession of Qing government officials, who were capable of making diplomatic contact with the relevant parties.

While it may seem common and universal to us today, it was not until the early eighteenth century that a policy of rescuing and repatriating foreign castaways began to be implemented almost without fail among the four governments of the Qing Empire, Tokugawa Japan, Joseon Korea and the Ryukyu Kingdom. Needless to say, victims of shipwrecks had been rescued and repatriated in earlier times, but the practice was often carried out on a unilateral basis, with the result that mutual repatriation was not guaranteed. Moreover, it was not uncommon for foreign castaways to become naturalized members of the local community, or to be enslaved. In medieval Japan, it was an accepted practice for those who found castaways to either enslave or sell them as chattels. In other words, the mutual and institutionalized practice of protecting and repatriating foreign castaways to their home countries was a salient feature that characterized the East China Sea in the eighteenth century, as opposed to the haphazard situation in earlier years.

It is also noteworthy that this mutual repatriation was not necessarily based on official diplomatic relations between the two countries concerned. It is well known that Tokugawa Japan and the Qing Dynasty had no diplomatic relations during the eighteenth century, but this does not mean that the two countries remained totally disengaged from one another. On the contrary, private trade and various other relationships existed between them on an intensive and stable basis, indicating that both Japan, ruled by a mix of central and local authorities under the *bakuhan* system, and the Qing Empire gave tacit approval to a "policy of disengagement in theory and the pursuit of interaction in practice".

While the closed and passive image of the eighteenth century in East Asia, epitomized by Japan's so-called "*sakoku*" (seclusion) policy and the Qing's "Canton System" that limited foreign trade to the port of Guangzhou, has recently been significantly redrawn, many people remain under the strong impression that this period was more "closed" than those before and after it. Despite the existence of many restrictions, it was not the case that countries in the region kept their borders shut; rather, they engaged in active relationships and interactions with each other under certain conventions, be they explicit laws and regulations or tacit understandings. Indeed, the establishment of an informal understanding among the governments regarding the mutual rescue, protection and repatriation of foreign castaways constituted just one aspect of this intercourse.

Certainly, dramatic wars or disturbances did not occur in maritime East Asia during this period, but this does not mean that interactions were stagnant or subdued. Instead, it seems more indicative of a period of stability and prosperity wherein some kind of crucial change was taking place quietly but steadily underneath the surface. It is therefore worthwhile to look more closely into the characteristics of this period in comparison with those of the previous.

## Powers around the East China Sea and "maritime peace"

As described in Part 2, the East China Sea and the regions around it were booming in the early seventeenth century, with international trade involving the exchange of goods produced in Mainland China for silver mined in Japan or America. Changes to the political order and social structure were occurring in various areas of the region, and the upheavals of the time gave rise to two new political powers. One was a central government encompassing the entire Japanese Archipelago; largely established by Oda Nobunaga, this administration was followed and expanded upon first by Toyotomi Hideyoshi and then by Tokugawa Ieyasu, the founder of the Tokugawa Shogunate. The other ascendant power in the region was the Later Jin Dynasty, which Nurhaci (r. 1616–1626) established by unifying the Jurchens in Manchuria. Both the Tokugawa and the Later Jin consolidated their respective power bases during the 1630s and 1640s. In Japan, during the reigns of Tokugawa Hidetada, the second shogun (r. 1605–1623), and his son Tokugawa Iemitsu, the third shogun (r. 1623–1651), the shogunate established a powerful system whereby the Edo-based central military government of the Tokugawa family maintained control over hundreds of *daimyōs*[5]. Hong Taiji (r. 1626–1643), the second emperor, officially adopted the name "Manchu[6]" for all Jurchens and changed the name of the state from "Later Jin" to "Great Qing".

At its inception, the Tokugawa Shogunate had been eager to negotiate for the establishment of diplomatic relations with the Ming Dynasty and to promote foreign trade using red-seal ships carrying government-issued permits. It began to reorganize its diplomatic relations during this period and to install a system of strict control over external relations, which became known in the nineteenth century as the "seclusion" system. This system of control emphasized the proscription of foreign travel by Japanese people, the prohibition of the practice and evangelization of Christianity and control over foreign trade by the shogunate and its proxies. Foreign trade and relations were also regulated by only allowing them to occur at one of the "four gateways": the port of Nagasaki, under the direct jurisdiction of the shogunal government and

---

5 Tokugawa Hidetada (1579–1632) was the second shogun of the Edo Shogunate. With his son, Iemitsu (1604–1651), the third shogun, Tokugawa Hidetada strove to establish a firm footing for the Tokugawa rule and stabilized the hegemony that had been won through the military might of Tokugawa Ieyasu, the first shogun.

6 Originally an ethnic name, "Manchu" was known to the Ming Dynasty as the Jianzhou Nüzhi (Jianzhou Jurchens) and was the dynasty name used by Nurhaci (in Manchu: *Manju Gurun*). When Hong Taiji changed the name of the dynasty to the Great Qing (in Manchu: *Daicing gurun*) in 1635, the ethnic name was also changed from "Jurchens" to "Manchu".

## 3.1: General Overview

where Dutch and Chinese merchant ships were allowed to dock; the Satsuma gateway controlled by the Shimazu family and used for their trading monopoly with the Ryukyu Kingdom; the Tsushima gateway, through which the Sō family, the lord of the Tsushima Domain, traded with the Joseon Dynasty in Korea; and the Matsumae gateway in Ezo (present-day Hokkaido), through which the Matsumae family traded with the Ainu.

The Later Jin Dynasty, later the Qing Empire, which emerged at around the same time, established a nationwide institutional framework called the "*Baqi*" (Eight Banners)[7] system, combining administrative and military organizations. Not only did the Qing exploit the Eight Banners' powerful centripetal force in order to defeat and absorb Mongol forces one after the other, it also forcibly brought Korea under its influence in an arrangement that superseded the latter's previous tributary status with the Ming Dynasty. In this way, the Qing established an international order of its own design. On the other hand, both the Joseon Dynasty of Korea, which had been invaded by Toyotomi Hideyoshi and Hong Taiji in close succession, and the Second Shō Dynasty of the Ryukyu Kingdom, which had been militarily suppressed by and put under the control of the Satsuma Domain, had no choice but to politically and diplomatically reorganize themselves in order to adapt to the new environment.

In the midst of these vicissitudes, the Ming, which had been in control of Mainland China and at the center of the international order in East Asia since the fourteenth century, collapsed in 1644 as a result of internal strife. In its wake came forty years of struggle for supremacy among various contenders: the Manchus of the newly-minted "Great Qing" who immediately advanced into Beijing; the armed rebel forces led by Li Zicheng and others who had actually defeated the Ming; the Ming loyalist regimes that remained in South China after the collapse of the Ming; the

---

7   Military and administrative organizations of the Later Jin and Qing Dynasties were known as the "Eight Banners" due to the eight patterns of the flags used to represent the eight groups. Initially, all subjects belonged to one of the banners, to which they would perform the duties of military service, labor service or tax payment. After the conquest of China the Eight Banners no longer engaged in agriculture, industry or commerce, but became a privileged class that provided bureaucrats and military personnel.

San-fan or Three Feudatories[8], most notably Wu Sangui, who defected from the Ming to the Manchus and later became a feudatory lord of the Qing; and the maritime force led by Zheng Chenggong and his family. These forces continued to fight against each other, creating and breaking a variety of alliances between them. In the course of its conquest of one rival after another, the Qing government issued the *haijin* (maritime prohibition) order to the residents of coastal areas and banned maritime activities and instituted the Qian Jie Ling (Great Clearance) that forced coastal residents to relocate to the interior, as part of its strategy against Zheng Chenggong's naval forces. In 1683, the Qing successfully took Taiwan from the Zheng family, who has used the island as their base since ousting the Dutch in 1661. In this way, the last independent maritime power that had existed since the sixteenth century was destroyed and Qing consolidation was nearly complete.

In 1684, the year following this victory, the Kangxi Emperor (r. 1661–1722)[9] of the Qing issued the Zhan Hai Ling, an order permitting overseas voyages by private merchant ships, and took steps to establish *haiguan* (customs houses) at four strategic locations along the coast in order to supervise foreign trade. These were the Jiang Haiguan in Jiangsu Province, the Zhe Haiguan in Zhejiang Province, the Min Haiguan in Fujian Province and the Yue Haiguan in Guangdong Province. Nagasaki was included among the merchant ships' overseas destinations, and stable trade relations between Japan and the Qing were thus established without any diplomatic contacts between the two central governments. Given that the Qing had already established diplomatic relations with the Ryukyu Kingdom and Joseon Dynasties as tributary states, the opening

---

8 "San-fan" refers to the Qing Dynasty forces' Han Chinese military generals including Wu Sangui, who were stationed in the South China region. When ordered to withdraw from their stationed positions, Wu Sangui, in Yunnan Province, mutinied, and in combination with local forces began a civil war known as the Revolt of the Three Feudatories (1673–1681).

9 The Kangxi Emperor (1654–1722) was the fourth Qing emperor, whose name was Aisin Gioro Hiowan-ye (Xuanye), and he reigned from 1661 to 1722. He subdued the Three Feudatories in the south and the Zheng family in Taiwan. In the north, he drove Russia out of the Heilongjiang River (Amur River) region and forced northern Mongolia to become a vassal state. He was therefore successful in putting his empire onto a stable footing.

of trade relations between Japan and Qing China marked the emergence of a situation in which maritime intercourse, both official and unofficial, was regulated by powerful land-based polities.

The period covered in Part 3 was one in which each of these regional state powers first became capable of exerting control over the various local powers within their political orbits, and second oversaw the development and management of systems for both inter-regional and international trade and transportation. Following the upheavals and changes in the political order that had characterized the sixteenth century, the seventeenth century featured four political powers with a strong grip on their territories. Two of these were newly formed – the Qing Empire and the Tokugawa Shogunate – while the other two had been forcibly reorganized – Joseon Korea and the Ryukyu Kingdom. Here, we shall call such political powers "early modern states". These powerful early modern states put an end to the situation that had existed in sixteenth-century East Asia that resembled a melting pot characterized by a mixed coexistence involving non-dominant land and sea powers vying for supremacy. Each of these states delineated and redefined their territory as distinct from that of the others, decided who their people were and faced the seas with a determination to rank on par with other states politically and economically.

At the same time, it should be kept in mind that these "early modern states", particularly the influential Qing Empire and Tokugawa Shogunate, neither remained unconcerned with nor took an entirely hostile view toward seaborne trade. On the contrary, having emerged as new military powers against the backdrop of booming international trade during the sixteenth to seventeenth century, these states had an inherent interest in maritime commerce. However, as they consolidated their power and constructed a new early modern world order, they increasingly began to place more emphasis on territorial governance than on foreign trade. Because their systems of control over foreign relations existed in close proximity to each other, armed conflicts and diplomatic issues virtually disappeared, leading to the emergence of a "maritime peace" that would become the hallmark of this era when states became able to devote their undivided attention to trade. State control extended to visitors from outside the East China Sea, so that even European ships sailing into the area during this period were obliged to abide by the rules regulating trade and diplomacy in the region.

It should be pointed out that this situation was by no means a product of the kind of "international negotiation" seen today. Rather, it resulted from complementary interactions between the systems of control over foreign relations created by the countries concerned. Each of these systems was designed by the relevant central government to be the most rational and best adapted to its own needs. This situation was possible because of tacit agreements that the central governments had engineered amongst themselves, which induced each to avoid conflict when possible. The states managed this situation in order to uphold both the logic of internal governance and the logic pertaining to international order and foreign relations. We can thus characterize the relations between these governments, adjacent to each other and each exerting strong control over its territory, as enabling them to avoid any head-on disputes. At the same time, they were not bound by official treaties of peace and amity, so they could also choose to avoid trouble by turning a blind eye to certain events on a case-by-case basis. The relationships, then, may be described as either "a compartmentalized sea" or "coexistence among neighboring governments, each ruling in its own way". One noteworthy manifestation of this coexistence was the fact that the Qing Empire and the Tokugawa Shogunate, both of which harbored self-centered visions of an international order in East Asia, carefully avoided direct diplomatic relations. This lack of official relations enabled them to prevent a clash between their respective world-views and images of the international order. Still, both states gave approval to and encouraged trans-border trade by private merchants. It was thanks to this situation in the East China Sea that Denbē and his crew aboard the storm-battered ship based in Satsuma were able to return home.

## Fate of those who drifted outside the East China Sea

In contrast to the situation in the East China Sea, which was kept in order by tacit but rather well-defined rules, what were the circumstances outside of that sea? In order to answer this question, let us see what became of the crew aboard the *Ise-maru*, the second of the storm-battered ships mentioned at the beginning of this chapter.

After enduring an exacting ordeal of approximately three months adrift at sea, the twenty crew members of the *Ise-maru* set foot on land

and felt alive once more. As they were to learn later, they had reached Mindanao Island[10], one of the islands of the Philippines. There was not a soul to be seen, but after traveling into the interior of the island for several days, they finally spotted some houses. Greatly delighted, they rushed toward these structures, but in the next instant were surrounded by more than 100 strange-looking natives carrying weapons such as guns, blowguns, spears and shields. They tried to identify themselves by writing "Japan" in Chinese characters on the sandy ground, but to no avail. They were totally deprived of their possessions. Moreover, they were taken to the headman, who made them slaves and forced them to do farm work. During their enslavement, nine members died in close succession, while four more were taken elsewhere and likely sold off as slaves. The remaining seven members were sold to the Kingdom of Sulu[11] in Borneo, where they were forced to work as seamen aboard merchant ships for approximately one year.

In 1766, two of the seven, Magotarō and Kōgorō, were taken to Banjarmasin, a port town in the southern part of Borneo Island, but Kōgorō died from a disease on the way. Magotarō, now alone, was bought by a Chinese merchant living in Banjarmasin named Taikon-guan, who was a wealthy trader dealing in silk fabric and ceramics. Taikon-guan was originally from Zhangzhou, Fujian Province. Though based in Banjarmasin, he periodically returned home to have his family registration renewed and to purchase new merchandise. Taikon-guan had many slaves, but Magotarō, perhaps because he won favor with his owner, was differentiated from the others and treated much like a member of the trader's family.

Banjarmasin was a big port housing a Dutch factory (trading post) as well as the residences of many overseas Chinese merchants like Taikon-guan. Slightly upstream from the port, the headman of the native

---

10 Mindanao Island is a large island in the southern Philippines throughout which Islam spread in the sixteenth century. The Islamic emirate in central Mindanao flourished due to maritime trade, and confronted the Spanish forces in Manila on Luzon Island to the north.
11 Sulu is a group of islands scattered in the waters between Mindanao Island and Borneo (Kalimantan). An Islamic emirate that prospered through maritime trade with Manila and China from the seventeenth century onward was established there.

people had his office, which Taikon-guan visited to conduct trade, often taking Magotarō with him. Magotarō was also sent to the Dutch factory from time to time on business errands. On these occasions, the Dutch merchants suggested that if he was willing to escape to the Dutch factory by secretly swimming across the river in the darkness of night, they would take him back home to Japan from Batavia (Jakarta) within three months. Batavia had been the base for the Dutch forces' intra-Asian trade since the seventeenth century.

Seven years passed, and Magotarō increasingly yearned for his home, so one day, he took the plunge and made a request to Taikon-guan that he be sent home. His earnest appeal was successful. Taikon-guan granted Magotarō's wish and took the trouble to consult with the owner of a Fuzhou-based ship that had sailed into port. The ship owner, after consulting with another ship owner, agreed to take Magotarō to Nagasaki on the condition that he disguise himself as a Chinese by changing his hairstyle into a *queue*[12]. Unwilling to shave his hair in the form of a *queue*, Magotarō declined the offer, thereby passing up the chance. Before long, however, he had the opportunity to travel to Batavia aboard a Dutch ship, where he was transferred to another Dutch ship bound for Nagasaki. In the summer of 1771, Magotarō finally landed in Dejima (Deshima). He was handed over to officials of the Bugyōsho (magistrate's office), and after interrogation, was allowed to return home.

In marked contrast to the account of the first group of seamen who had drifted in the East China Sea, the fate which befell the second group that washed ashore in Southeast Asia was much more miserable. Even though all the twenty-member crew managed to set foot on land again, they were immediately subjected to deprivation, enslavement and human trafficking, and their whereabouts are lost to the vicissitudes of history with the sole exception of Magotarō. As for him, it was only thanks to luck, the kindness

---

12 The *queue* is a hairstyle in which one part of the hair is allowed to grow to considerable length while the remainder of the head is shaven. This custom is widely seen among male nomadic and hunting people in North Asia. The Manchu *queue* involved growing only one part of the hair at the rear of the head, allowing it to grow long enough to braid and then hang down. With the Manchu conquest of China, Han Chinese were compelled to follow this custom as a sign of submission.

of his Chinese owner and the shipping networks of the Dutch East India Company that he was able to return home alive.

In the South China Sea, castaways were not necessarily rescued or repatriated to their home countries. On the contrary, both the castaways and their vessels were often regarded as acquisitions that belonged to the local residents or lords. However, it is not the case that the South and East China Seas were two separate worlds that had no contact with each other except for rare incidents involving shipwrecks and castaways. Magotarō was purchased by a Chinese merchant, and, after contacting a Fuzhou-based ship, he managed to return home on board a Dutch ship. In other words, Chinese maritime merchants and Dutch merchant vessels were active on a regular basis in the South China Sea, just as they were in the East China Sea; i.e. economic activities like maritime transportation and seaborne trade occurred without being divided by maritime worlds or by the political authorities in power.

Politically, however, the state of affairs in the South China Sea was different from that in the East China Sea. As can be inferred from the fact that the headman of the native people did not show any particular interest in Magotarō, the local political authorities in places where the *Ise-maru* castaways landed were not part of the cross-territorial arrangements for mutually protecting castaways outside their own territories and for repatriating them to their home countries. The crew members of the *Ise-maru* were met by tragedy not because they washed ashore on a strange, foreign land with which Japan, their home country, had no political or economic links; rather, it was because the countries facing the South China Sea, despite having economic ties with each other and with countries in the East China Sea, did not uphold the increasingly widespread, international political and institutional arrangement for mutually protecting and repatriating castaways from other countries that was already common practice in the East China Sea.

## "Difference" between East and South China Seas

Answering the question as to what differentiated the fate of one group of castaways from that of the other is tantamount to answering the question of what the differences between the East China Sea and the South China Sea were at the time. Indeed, the difference between the two seas constitutes the second characteristic of the period under study here: the disparity between the political arrangements and economic activities at play in each sea.

As noted above, the East China Sea, when viewed from a political perspective, constituted one integrated world in which the constituent central governments created a "compartmentalization" based on tacit agreements amongst them. By contrast, the South China Sea constituted a politically asymmetrical world; while in the East China Sea the Qing was the dominant power and other states functioned as its counterparts, in the South there was no political equivalent to the Qing state. When looked at in terms of the economy and trade, however, the East and South China Seas functioned harmoniously, forming one continuous arena. This much is evident from the fact that Chinese maritime merchants and European merchant ships actively traveled the waters and connected Mainland China, the Japanese Archipelago and other lands to the south and east. Thus, even though the East and South China Seas were discontinuous in terms of their political arrangements, the two seas functioned as one entity with respect to their economic and trading activities. Furthermore, such activities thrived to a greater degree in the South China Sea than in the East China Sea, and during the eighteenth century they became increasingly concentrated in the former.

The emergence of this "difference" may be partly attributable to the fact that the economic and trading activities of the South China Sea were left virtually undisturbed by the regional governments of the area, who wielded much weaker control over such activities than their counterparts did in the East China Sea. This does not mean that the Qing pursued different policies in the South and the East. In the East China Sea, even though several different states in the region each had a different foreign affairs policy, they largely shared an unconscious consensus that originated from previous relations between states. Conversely, in the South China Sea there were no government entities capable of orchestrating or enforcing policies similar to those seen in the East China Sea. Consequently, economic and trading activities in the area were left to themselves. This contrast decisively affected, for instance, the choice of location by Chinese people seeking to migrate abroad. Since overseas travel was restricted by the government, Japan and other countries in the East China Sea that maintained informal but reciprocal relations with Qing China would have been unwilling to accept immigrants. In contrast, emigrants to the South China Sea would have been free to settle in their newfound homes with no fear of forced repatriation. This led to a mushrooming of communities of overseas Chinese in various parts of the region.

Given this situation, it is no surprise that the rapid population increase of the eighteenth century saw huge outflows of Chinese people to the South China Sea region and resulted in the growth of many Chinese communities there. To return to the story of Magotarō, let us reconsider some salient facts: the residences of Chinese merchants lined the streets of the port of Banjarmasin; Magotarō was purchased as a slave by a Chinese merchant; and his owner took the trouble to approach the owner of a Fuzhou-based ship that had sailed into port to ask for his help in returning Magotarō to Japan. These all form an eloquent testimony to the degree to which interregional trade was thriving in the South China Sea and to the extent to which overseas Chinese settlers were making inroads into the region. It is also important to keep in mind how Magotarō was finally repatriated through a series of Dutch ships via Batavia. Thus, we might also conclude through this story that the Netherlands had also established itself as an important presence in insular Southeast Asia and was also engaging in stable trading activities across the South and East China Seas.

## Seas as "boundaries"

In addition to the emergence and maintenance of a "compartmentalized sea policy" among governments, the eighteenth century was also characterized by a growing definition of the boundaries of each region, leading to the creation of "insider" and "outsider" groups. The sea has a dual nature; it can be either a means to connect various regions with each other, or it can act as a boundary that separates one area from another. It was the latter characteristic that became pronounced during this period, as the sea was increasingly used to differentiate between the "inside" and "outside" of areas and groups. Jurisdiction over territories and human populations became demarcated and consolidated. The "inside", most commonly delineated by the boundary of the sea, gradually began to take shape in contrast to what was "outside". In this way, the emergence of countries, or states, constitutes the third feature of this period.

In the East China Sea during this period, when the state of compartmentalization among neighboring countries took shape, direct interpersonal contact was restricted to such an extent that it occurred only sporadically. On the other hand, goods were shipped across the seas consistently and in great volumes. These commercial products were accompanied by an active exchange of knowledge and technology through books as well as objects. Restrictions on face-to-face contact and encounters between living persons had the effect of making physical articles and information relatively more significant and valuable. Given this, efforts were made in various places to syncretically analyze and incorporate both indigenous cultural practices and those of foreign origin. Through these efforts quite a few cultural elements came to be subsequently called "traditions" peculiar to the "country" or "modern nation" concerned, despite their inherently foreign or hybrid nature. Furthermore, based upon the tacit and shared perception of the sea as a boundary, the countries in the region introduced the practice of mutual non-aggression based on reciprocal territorial recognition and created the accompanying institutional arrangements necessary for the mutual repatriation of castaways from other countries in the region.

It should also be pointed out that this policy of "sea as territorial boundary" only grew stronger and more influential in each country throughout this period. This development not only had the effect of sustaining a compartmentalization amongst the countries of the East China Sea in the eighteenth century, but inadvertently aided in preparing them for the arrival of the European-led modern era when the national borders and territories they demarcated would become essential matters of state. The eighteenth century marked the dawn of this era. Looking beyond the East China Sea to the oceans of the world as a whole, the century might be best characterized through the emergence of the Northern Pacific. It was there that European and American ships grappled with the concepts of national territories with their borders and related conventions, then brought these concepts to the East China Sea.

In the first half of the eighteenth century, Russian explorers had advanced overland to the East, crossing the Bering Strait and reaching the Aleutian Islands and Alaska in North America while simultaneously moving south along the Chishima Islands (Kuril Islands) and coming into contact with Japan. In the latter half of the century, both the James

Cook expedition from Britain, led by the famous Captain Cook[13], and the Lapérouse expedition from France, explored the Northern Pacific[14]. The latter expedition navigated north from the East China Sea and traveled the entire length of the Sea of Japan. These ships from the West competed to expand their national territories by holding land acquisition ceremonies at each of their anchorages in the Northern Pacific, giving European names to the places they "found". In the East China Sea region, where powerful land-based governments stood adjacent to each other practicing compartmentalization, this method would certainly not have been effective. Nonetheless, the notion and convention of manifest territorial division that was introduced into the East China Sea by these Russian, French and British ships heralded the coming era. While in some ways a break from the "compartmentalized sea" policy governing international trade and relations, these new concepts of territory and national rights also shared some affinity with the "rules" already operating in the region.

In conclusion, a bird's-eye-view of the East China Sea in the early modern period finds the year 1684, when the Qing Empire shifted to an open-door policy, to be a watershed moment. Thus, we will take that year as our starting point for Part 3 and cover the "long eighteenth century" rather than strictly spanning 1700 to 1800. The bulk of our discussion begins at the turn of the eighteenth century with the reigns of two rulers with strong personalities, the Kangxi Emperor and Tokugawa Tsunayoshi[15], the fifth Tokugawa Shogun (r. 1680–1709).

---

13 James Cook (1728–1779) was a British naval captain and explorer. Cook undertook three voyages of exploration to the Pacific Ocean from 1768 onwards. He was killed in a conflict with native people in Hawaii in 1779.
14 Jean-François de Galaup, Comte de Lapérouse (1741–1788?) was a French maritime explorer. In 1785, on orders from the French King Louis XVI, he embarked on a voyage of exploration of the Pacific Ocean, reaching the Sea of Japan and sailing through the Sōya Strait.
15 Tokugawa Tsunayoshi (1646–1709) was a son of Tokugawa Iemitsu. He became the adopted heir of his elder brother Ietsuna, thereby succeeding him as fifth shogun. Emphasizing scholarship and culture, he promoted politics by civilian control, and his reign was known as the Genroku era.

It will conclude in 1800, one year after the Qianlong Emperor's[16] (r. 1735–1796 retired) long reign ended with his demise and when Tokugawa Ienari[17], the eleventh shogun of the Tokugawa Shogunate (r. 1787–1837), was still in power.

---

16 The Qianlong Emperor (1711–1799) was the sixth Qing emperor, whose name was Aisin Gioro Hung-li (Hongli), and who reigned from 1735 to 1795. He overthrew the Dzungar Khanate and annexed East Turkistan, expanding the empire's territory to the maximum extent. He abdicated in favor of the Jiaqing Emperor after sixty years on the throne, just as his grandfather, the Kangxi Emperor, had done, but continued to hold real power as Taishang Huang, the retired emperor.
17 Tokugawa Ienari (1773–1841) was the eleventh shogun of the Edo Shogunate (r. 1787 to 1837). He held the position of shogun for fifty years, the longest serving shogun of the Edo period. Thereafter, he remained the power behind the scenes as Ōgosho, the retired shogun.

## 3.2: Maritime Merchants and "Compartmentalization" Among Early Modern States

### Players in the eighteenth-century maritime world

As we saw in the previous chapter, the repatriation of castaways in the East and South China Seas was often facilitated by land-based polities. The fact that Denbē and other members of the Satsuma-based ship, who were taken into protective custody by the government authorities of Qing China, and Magotarō, who experienced such hardship in Southeast Asia, were repatriated to Japan via the trade routes to Nagasaki, shows that castaways were often able to return home under the aegis of the land-based political powers of the region. This signifies that the East China Sea during this period was surrounded by powerful regional states, or "early modern states", and that people who traveled by sea had to act according to the rules established by these powers.

It should also be kept in mind that these early modern states did not directly monopolize trade by completely banning private activities. This much is demonstrated by the return of Denbē and his men aboard a Chinese maritime merchant ship, while Magotarō was repatriated to Japan on a Dutch ship. With the permission of land-based state authorities, private traders and shippers, most notably Chinese maritime merchants and European traders, were the major players in the waters of East Asia during this period. Three of the four early modern states – Japan, Korea and Ryukyu – strictly prohibited their people from embarking on overseas travel, resulting in the monopolization of the East and South China Seas by traders from other states and non-state agents. Following the removal of the *haijin* (maritime prohibitions) toward the end of the seventeenth century, the junks of Chinese merchants ventured out on the sea and came to play a central role in trade and other interactions in the East and South China Seas in the first half of the eighteenth century, turning these waters into a "sea of Chinese traders". Visits to the East and South China Seas by European merchant ships also increased after having been subdued during the early to mid-seventeenth century following the early modern states' imposition of maritime prohibitions. By the second half of the eighteenth century, European ships emerged as the other mercantile force in these waters alongside the Chinese.

Compared to the situation described in Parts 1 and 2, the emergence of Chinese and European merchants as major players in the East and South China Seas in this period highlights the absence of Muslim maritime merchants and the withdrawal of Japanese ships, whose roles came to be occupied by traders from China and newcomers from Europe. Among these newcomers, it should be pointed out that Dutch and British ships had now eclipsed the Portuguese, who had dominated shipping in Asian waters over their European rivals in the sixteenth century.

One significant difference between the East and South China Seas of the sixteenth and eighteenth centuries was that these new players chose to comply with the "compartmentalization" of local political powers instead of coming into conflict with them. Whereas previously a number of independent local forces – such as the Wokou, influential Chinese local elites and Japanese *daimyōs* during Japan's Warring States period – had struggled against each other for supremacy, each state had now managed to consolidate its political and economic power. The result was that trade, either contracted out or approved by these public authorities, prospered under their control. This does not mean that states unilaterally suppressed and regulated maritime activities. On the contrary, private merchants and shippers generally found it advantageous to live with and earn profits under official regulations enforced by a strong political entity. In the eighteenth-century world of the East and South China Seas, therefore, traders and voyagers willingly undertook overseas trade and external negotiations by working in tandem with and living under the auspices of the compartmentalization of local political powers. They were in turn assisted by agents and interpreters who took charge of the various clerical procedures required at the ports of call and who acted as mediators in trade deals.

## Seagoing junks of the Chinese maritime merchants

Let us look more closely at the lives of these traders and voyagers. The most active players at the time were the Chinese maritime merchants who

## 3.2: Maritime Merchants and "Compartmentalization" 233

sailed the seas aboard vessels called "junks". Several kinds of junks had been developed to suit the various types of seas in the region. The main type used in the East China Sea was a sharp-bottomed, ocean-going ship known as "*niaochuan*" (bird ships). The need to finance the enormous costs involved in building and maintaining large *niaochuan*, which measured forty to fifty meters long, led to the development of arrangements such as joint investment, consignment contracts and a management structure similar to that of a corporation.

More specifically, the operation of a large junk of the *niaochuan* type involved a wide range of people, such as the investors who provided the capital, the person in charge of commercial transactions or his proxy and the crew recruited by the captain. Essential to the trading process were the *chuanhu* (ship-owner) who built and owned the ship, the consigner who dealt with overseas goods and the *chuanzhu* (ship's captain or supercargo) who entered into a contract with the consigner for the shipping and trade of the latter's cargo. In some cases, the consigner himself made the voyage to conduct foreign trade in person, while in others he commissioned the *chuanzhu* to deal on his behalf. When a consigner did not make the voyage with his cargo, he was referred to as a "*caidong*", or a consigner remaining in China, while the ship-owner who acted on his behalf and conducted deals under contract during these voyages was called a "*hangshang*" or "*chuhai*" (seagoing merchant). By the mid-eighteenth century, the division of labor between consigners remaining in China and seagoing *chuanzhu* merchants had been largely established. The proceeds earned from a voyage were divided between the co-investors and the crew, with investors paid according to their shares in the investment and crew members based on their rank and functions. Moreover, crew members, including the *hangshang*, were allowed to bring a certain amount of their own cargo on board to sell at ports of call overseas.

The *chuanzhu* in charge of a merchant ship was not only responsible for operating the ship, but also for all the business he had been commissioned to conduct on the voyage. Senior crew members, who jointly commanded the ship by dividing the major tasks among themselves, consisted of a *caifu*, who acted as both deputy *chuanzhu* and accountant, *huozhang* (chief navigator), *zongguan* (chief clerk) and *duogong* (helmsman). Below these officers were a large number of lower-ranking crew members called "*mulu*" or "*shuizhu*". These included *yaban* (lookouts), *daliao* (sailors in charge of sails and masts), *touding* (those responsible for anchors), *zhiku* (those in charge of cargo management) and *zongpu* (cooks), all of whom were employed on a voyage-by-voyage basis. Roughly thirty to forty junior crew members were hired by a small junk and 100 or more by a larger ship. Including traders and other passengers, each seafaring junk carried a total of about fifty to sixty people on the smaller vessels and as many as 200 to 300 in the case of a larger ship. Passengers bound for the South China Sea typically included many workers and migrants, in addition to traders and crewmen.

Most Chinese junks trading with Japan set sail from ports in the Jiangnan area, such as Ningbo and Zhapu in Zhejiang Province and Shanghai in Jiangsu Province. For some time after the lifting of the maritime prohibitions in 1684, Chinese ships arrived in Nagasaki in large numbers not only from the Jiangnan area, but also from ports in Fujian and Guangdong. However, as the Tokugawa Shogunate imposed trade restrictions and the Qing government started to implement its own trade regulations through merchant organizations, ports in the Jiangnan area began to dominate. Particularly Zhapu, the base port for merchants in Zhejiang, established itself as the major hub for Japan trade by the mid-eighteenth century. In Japan, people who sailed from ports on the Chinese continent and their affiliated merchant ships were generally known as "Tō-jin" (Chinese or people of Chinese descent) and "*tōsen*" (Chinese ships). More specifically, Japanese people classified Chinese merchant ships by the distance between Japan and their ports of embarkation, calling ships from Jiangsu and Zhejiang "*kuchi-bune*" (ships from the gate), those from Fujian and Guangdong "*nakaoku-bune*" (ships from places of medium distance) and those from Southeast Asia "*oku-bune*" (ships from faraway lands).

In relation to these areas, Xiamen in Fujian and Guangdong in Guangzhou were both major centers of South Seas trade. Xiamen, or Amoy, had developed into the largest port of embarkation, while Guangzhou, or Canton, grew to rival Xiamen in the latter half of the eighteenth century when it was designated as the port of entry for European ships, thereby developing into a hub port for South Seas trading. Moreover, in the region encompassing the Java Sea and the Philippine Islands, trading forces such as the Sulu Kingdom and the Buginese[1] were especially active, at times competing with

---

[1] Buginese are Muslim residents of Sulawesi Island in the east of the Southeast Asian Archipelago. Proficient in shipbuilding and navigation, they were active in maritime Southeast Asia as merchants and soldiers.

## 3.2: Maritime Merchants and "Compartmentalization"

**Figure 17: Diplomacy and passage control by "early modern states"**

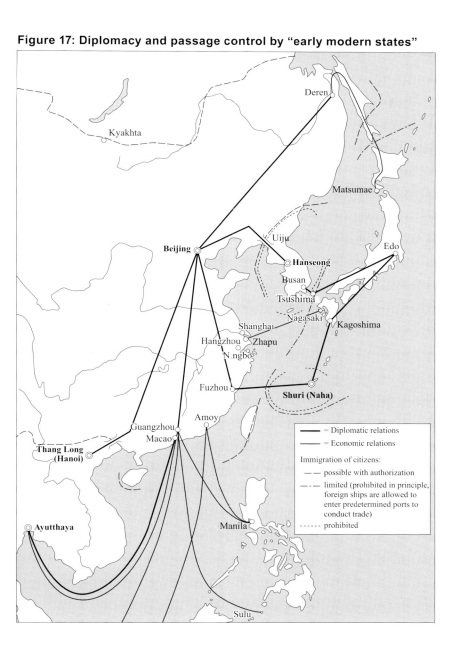

the Chinese and at other times collaborating with them. While maritime interactions in the East China Sea during the eighteenth century had become largely unilateral endeavors by Chinese agents, those in the South China Sea were two-way in nature with various traders actively taking part. It was these Chinese maritime merchants, active in the South China Sea, whom Magotarō encountered in Banjarmasin.

## Merchant groupings in trading ports

Not only did the influential merchants of Qing China directly engage in overseas trade, they also made deals with and oversaw foreign ships visiting the region. Under the Qing, no institutional distinction was made between international and domestic trade, so *yahang* (middlemen-cum-brokers), who had traditionally been active in business deals in Chinese society, also became involved in overseas trade. *Yahang* acted as mediators and brokers in overseas trade in much the same way as they did in the domestic sphere.

In addition to acting as mediators in international transactions, *yahang* also performed other services, such as securing and operating warehouses and accommodation for merchants and paying taxes for various people – though in the eyes of the local government, this was tax collection on its behalf. Local authorities, for their part, also used *guangya* (*yahang* in the service of government offices) to collect taxes on transactions, manage merchants and craftsmen and procure goods for official use. A *yahang* handling maritime trade, called a "*chuanhang*", mediated interactions between consigners and ship-owners, helping them with shipping and compensation contracts. *Chuanhang* also offered a host of related services, such as recruiting crewmembers and arranging for their entry and departure, as well as acting as their guarantor for things like import and export procedures, tax payment, cargo storage and accommodation. Among the *chuanhang*, those engaged in foreign maritime trade were specifically called "*yanghang*" and their business was referred to as "*yangshang*"[2]. The most famous *yanghang* were the Guangdong Shisan Hang (the thirteen *hang* of Guangdong), sometimes referred to as the "*cohong*" (licensed *hang*). This

---

2 *Yanghang* is an abbreviation of *yanghuahang* or *waiyanghang*. The *yanghuahang* were a group of officially sanctioned merchants who handled the overseas trade that was established following the rescission of the ban on maritime activities. In contrast, the *waiyanghang* was a group that handled only Western merchant ships and was newly established from among the *yanghuahang* in 1760.

group was invested with the right of monopoly control over the European and American entities in Guangzhou, and managed not only trade, but all matters related to the Westerners temporarily residing in the city.

In order to handle trade with Japan, a total of eight private merchants from Jiangsu and Zhejiang were appointed in 1726 as *zongshang* (or *shangzong*) to administer and supervise the traders, their merchant ships and their cargo. In the 1740s, trade in copper for government use was contracted out to a group of privileged merchants called "*guanshang*" (official merchants) or "*eshang*" (quota merchants)[3]. These measures were designed to cope with the problem the Qing Empire was facing in procuring copper, used in the minting of copper coins and thus in high demand. Various restrictions on copper exports imposed by Japan had made supplies unstable. This was

**Figure 18: Trading houses in Guangzhou**
Source: Hong Kong Museum of Art.

---

3 *Guanshang* and *eshang* were merchants contracted by the government to procure copper. The *guanshang* borrowed funds from the government, while the *eshang* carried out self-funded trade under official sanction, and no restriction was placed on the sale of the amassed copper.

coupled with an intensifying turf war between one group of merchants based in Jiangsu and Zhejiang and another based in Fujian and Guangdong. To address this problem, the Qing government held the *zongshang* responsible for keeping these merchants under control, and only commissioned *guanshang* or *eshang* to procure copper.

Qing China's trade with Ryukyu was carried out in the port of Fuzhou in Fujian, the designated port for tribute ships from that kingdom. A group of privileged merchants called "Shijia Qiushang" (*liuqiuguan keshang*, local merchants attached to the Ryukyuan visiting house in Fuzhou) acted as mediators in this trade. These local merchants purchased the Chinese goods that the Ryukyuans wanted on their behalf. Similarly, a Xiamen *yanghong* was established in Xiamen, Fujian, in 1720 to carry out South Seas trade. All of these merchant groups consisted of *yahang* of one kind or another.

It should be kept in mind, however, that the term "privileged merchants" does not imply that they enjoyed monopolistic profits. In reality, more than a few of the *hangshang* suffered poor business results or even faced bankruptcy due to considerably harsh competition among the *hangshang*, over-burdensome obligations to various parties or exploitation by government officials. Consequently, many *hangshang* found it extremely difficult to maintain steady growth and earn lucrative profits. Despite their monopoly on a lucrative trade, at some point nearly every member of the well-known Guangdong Shisan Hang fell into bankruptcy or ruin, allowing other middlemen to rise and take their place.

## The East India companies and country traders

Two types of European merchant ships were engaged in maritime trade alongside the Chinese in maritime East Asia. The first was ships owned by the various East India companies of European countries, and the second was those owned by private traders called "country traders". Needless to say, the Dutch East India Company (Vereenigde Oost-Indische Compagnie, or VOC)[4]

---

4 Formally known as the United East India Company, the VOC was established in 1602 through the merger of six trading companies from different parts of the Netherlands. Its base in maritime East Asia was located at Batavia (present-day Jakarta), and it expanded its activities throughout almost the whole region from the Indian Ocean to the East China Sea.

and the English East India Company (EIC)[5] were the most powerful amongst them. Newcomers such as the French, Danish, Swedish and Oostendse East India Companies[6] also joined the competition and sent ships to China in the hope of making profits from the steadily growing tea trade. The VOC was the only company allowed to send ships to Japan by the Tokugawa Shogunate and took advantage of this monopoly, earning large profits by shipping vast amounts of Asian products, rather than European merchandise, to Japan. In contrast, neither Korea nor Ryukyu ever opened diplomatic or trade relations with any European power.

Ships owned by the East India Companies were mostly of a large tonnage, having to sail all the way from their home ports in Europe, pass around the Cape of Good Hope and cross the Indian Ocean. These were sailing ships equipped with keels, but their most important feature was that they were armed with cannons. Each ship was manned by a crew including a captain, senior officers, sailors and apprentice sailors. It also carried officers of the company's trading houses who took care of the company's and colonies' affairs, as well as soldiers, artisans and other passengers. Crew and company members were allowed to conduct private trade deals within fixed quotas. So, aside from performing their official duties, they took advantage of this arrangement by trading for their own benefit, often in excess of their assigned quotas. Passengers occasionally included missionaries working for the Qing court in Beijing. However, due to the anti-Kirishitan laws there, ships bound for Japan were prohibited from carrying missionaries and anything onboard related to Christianity had to be sealed off in footlockers or the cargo-hold before entering the port of Nagasaki.

Unlike these trading companies that functioned as monopolies, country traders were private merchants engaged in intra-regional trade in Asia. They moved back and forth between the Indian Ocean, South China Sea and East China Sea, although they did not travel between their home countries and Asia. Because of the enormous costs involved in owning, renting and operating a seafaring vessel, trading activities performed by country traders were initially carried out by East India Company ships

---

5 The English East India Company (EIC) was a trading company founded by royal charter from Queen Elizabeth I in 1601. It established bases in India and Persia, displacing the Portuguese and competing with the Dutch.
6 The Oostendse Company was officially launched with funding from the Austrian government in the first half of the eighteenth century, but only existed for a short time.

using the quotas allotted to the company ships. In the latter half of the eighteenth century, however, independent ships operated by country traders, who raised the necessary funds through joint investments, became more visible in Asian waters. Especially in the case of England, which had no trading bases in the East or South China Seas, country traders were instrumental in carrying out exchanges between India and China, and often in direct competition with Armenian and Parsi-Zoroastrian merchants[7] living in India. Beginning in the 1780s, ships operated by country traders would crowd into Guangzhou, booming from the tea trade. Once there, they started to undermine the relationship of compartmentalization between the region's early modern states and the monopoly trading companies.

Thus, Chinese and European merchants were instrumental as intermediaries in the flow of people, goods and information in maritime East Asia during the eighteenth century. However, to the extent that they could only be active with the "approval" of the region's states, maritime East Asia remained under the control of these land-based powers. Both Chinese and European merchants were only able to trade vigorously given the consent of the region's land-based authorities. The VOC continued to behave deferentially to the Tokugawa Shogunate in order to continue to benefit from its trade in Japan. England continued to benefit from *hushi* trade (border or frontier trade unaccompanied by diplomatic relations), while it remained silent about diplomatic relations with the Qing Empire; the moment it dispatched the Macartney Embassy[8] to approach the Qing government with a proposal to start negotiating for the establishment of diplomatic ties, it was met by cold refusal. The VOC could behave as an onshore regional power in the South China Sea, but in the East China Sea it had to be content with working within the limits set by the regional powers concerned. This is another clear manifestation of the "inconsistency" or "gap" between the East and South China Seas.

---

7 A group of Zoroastrian adherents who migrated from Iran to India and conducted lively commerce from bases on the west coast of India.
8 The Macartney Embassy was a delegation dispatched by the British government to negotiate changes in the trading system. In 1793 it proceeded directly to Beijing, avoiding Guangzhou, and gained an audience with the Qianlong Emperor at the Rehe Imperial Villa. While Macartney was exempted from the formal rite of kowtowing nine times to the emperor, negotiations for diplomatic relations were firmly refused.

## People and ships connecting countries

Another important cluster of maritime interactions in the eighteenth century involved people who periodically moved by sea between two countries with official diplomatic or quasi-diplomatic relations. The first type of ship that must be mentioned in this diplomatic relations context is the tribute ship.

Among the early modern states under study here, the Ryukyu Kingdom was the one that periodically sent tribute ships to China. Since the latter half of the fourteenth century, the kingdom had been paying tribute to the Ming, but after being invaded in 1609 by the Shimazu family of Satsuma Domain, it officially also became a vassal state of Satsuma and its lords. Thereafter, Ryukyu entered a period of dual subordination to Japan and Ming China. After the Qing rose to power, it made the King of Ryukyu its own vassal by investing him with the new name of King Chūzan, and Ryukyu began periodically to send tributary missions to the Qing Emperor.

During most of the early modern era, Ryukyu dispatched two tributary ships known as *shinkō-sen* biannually, carrying missions of approximately 200 people. However, in each intervening year, it also sent one *sekkō-sen*, a ship embarking for the purpose of bringing back the tribute mission from the Chinese capital and manned by a crew of approximately 100. Ryukyu was thus, in effect, dispatching one tributary ship every year. The emissary duty was called *tabi-yaku* (traveling duty), and officials appointed to perform this duty were called *totō-yakunin* (officials to be dispatched to China). They consisted of diplomatic officials, including the chief delegate, the deputy delegate, interpreters and students sent to study abroad in China, as well as officials in charge of trade and senior crew members. Also aboard each tributary ship was a large number of low-ranking crew members.

Each of these ships entered Fuzhou in Fujian, the designated port of entry for Ryukyuan tribute ships. During the ship's stay in Fuzhou, the *totō-yakunin* would perform their official duties as tributary delegates, which included official trading transactions, and also conduct their own private trade that was allowed within certain specified limits. Through this tributary relationship, products made in Ryukyu and Japan (via Satsuma) were brought to China, while goods procured in China were sent back to Ryukyu, and then through Ryukyu on to Japan. Besides regular tributary ships, the Ryukyu Kingdom frequently sent special envoys to the Qing court. In return, Qing China sent a mission on two ships chartered from private owners in Fujian to Ryukyu on the occasion of the enthronement and investiture of a new king (*sakuhō-shi/okansen*). During these delegations, the Ryukyuan government would purchase large quantities of Chinese goods brought on the delegation's ships. Ryukyuan people called this trade "*hangā*" (valuation) trade, with the word "*hangā*" describing the "valuation" of the purchase price of goods brought in by the delegation.

Additionally, due to its vassal status to both the Tokugawa Shogunate and the Satsuma Domain, the Kingdom of Ryukyu also sent three official ships called "*kai-sen*" each year to Kagoshima, the capital of Satsuma, in order to carry tribute articles and envoys. From Satsuma, licensed *yamato-sen* (private ships based in that domain) made voyages not only to Naha, the main port city of the Ryukyu Kingdom, but also to as far as the Miyako and Ishigaki Islands. In exchange for performing the duty of transporting tributary goods from Ryukyu to Satsuma, these merchant ships were afforded the privilege of doing business in Ryukyu. It was also customary for Ryukyu to send embassies to the Tokugawa Shogunate in Edo, as it did to the Qing court, to celebrate the accession of a new shogun (*keiga-shi* or *gakei-shi*) or to express gratitude for their approval of a new Ryukyuan king (*shaon-shi*). These embassies of congratulation or gratitude were called *Edo-dachi* or *Edo-nobori*, and a total of seventeen such missions were sent to Edo between 1644 and 1850, eight of which occurred during the eighteenth century.

There were also people who traveled between Japan and Korea because of the diplomatic relations that existed between the two countries. Given the fact that Korea communicated with Qing China by land, Busan was its only port open to the outside world, which acted as the gateway for interactions with Japan. After the two Japanese invasions of Korea (1592–1598) led by Toyotomi Hideyoshi, diplomatic relations were reestablished after a series of negotiations between the Tokugawa Shogunate and the Korean Kingdom in the early seventeenth century. It was decided that the Sō family, the domainal lord of Tsushima, would serve as the point of contact on the Japanese side. The first three missions were officially titled "Kaito ken Sakkan-shi" (Kr. Hoedap gyeom Swaehwan-sa), meaning "envoys to respond and repatriate prisoners". They traveled with the duty of delivering an official response to the Japanese sovereign's letter of invitation and to repatriate Korean prisoners taken during Japan's invasions of that country.

## 3.2: Maritime Merchants and "Compartmentalization"

From 1636 onward, the title of "*Chosen Tsushin-shi*" (Kr. Tongsinsa) or "Korean Goodwill Missions" came into use. These diplomatic missions were dispatched to Japan on celebratory occasions such as a new shogun's inauguration or the birth of a shogun's heir. A total of twelve missions had visited Japan by the early nineteenth century, four of which did so during the eighteenth century.

**Figure 19: *Shinkō-sen* ships of Ryukyu**

Source: *Shinkō-sen Zu* (Painting of tributary trading ship), Okinawa Prefectural Museum and Art Museum.

By contrast, the Tokugawa Shogunate never sent missions directly to Korea, although missions were frequently exchanged between that country and the Tsushima Domain. Based on an agreement with Korea, each year Tsushima was allowed to dispatch twenty envoy ships called "*saiken-sen*" (allocated dispatch ships). When it became necessary to send additional ships for specific purposes, higher-ranking envoys called "*sanban-shi*" were dispatched on the orders of the Tokugawa Shogunate. Korea reciprocated by sending missions called "*yakukan-shi*" (Kr. *munwihaeng*, "interpreter embassies") to Tsushima. These were sent far more frequently than the better-known Goodwill Missions, and there were more than fifty such missions during the Tokugawa period.

In Busan, a commercial station and residential district called the "Waegwan" (Jp. Wakan), meaning the "Japan House[9]", was established to accommodate officials and commoners from Tsushima on an ongoing basis. Both officially dispatched ships and other kinds of ships frequently traveled between Busan and Tsushima, and the Tsushima Domain attempted to increase the volume of trade by sending additional ships for various reasons, such as *okomekogi-sen* (rice transport ships)[10]. In the eighteenth century, trading ships accounted for eighty percent of those traveling between Tsushima and Busan. There were so many of these at sea that it was not uncommon for official delegates, such as *sanban-shi*, to cross the western channel of the Tsushima Strait on board these trading ships, and to return home on board Tsushima-based ships that happened to be visiting Busan. Most of these ships were chartered from the commoners who owned them, known as "*isendō*".

As a point of interest, Vietnam was also paying tribute to the Qing Empire, but like Korea it shared terrestrial borders with the Qing and so was obliged to send their tributary missions overland[11]. Thus, Vietnam's

---

9  While the Korean side used the name "Japan" for the country, other than this the term "*wae*", as in *wae-in* (Japanese person), *wae-o* (Japanese language) and *wae-soen* (Japanese ship), was used to refer to things Japanese.

10  The ships that crossed from Tsushima to Busan, in addition to officially dispatched vessels, were trading ships that went under various titles, such as *suimokusen* (fuel and water ships) and *okomekogi-sen*, as well as small, urgent communication ships known as "*hisen*" (flying ships).

11  In Vietnam, the Lê Dynasty declined in the sixteenth century, with the Mạc family usurping the throne. From the seventeenth century onward, the rule of the northern Trịnh lords, who protected the Lê Dynasty Emperor, the central Nguyễn family

tributary relations with the Qing were different from those between the Ryukyu Kingdom and the Qing, or those between Korea and Tsushima. Alternatively, Siamese tributary ships that came from the South China Sea area were assigned to enter at the port of Guangzhou[12].

## Nagasaki, an international trading port city

While Chinese, European and Ryukyuan ships were active in East Asian waters, Japanese traders were absent from the seas in this period because of the Tokugawa Shogunate's ban on overseas travel, with the sole exception of official and authorized ships commuting between Tsushima and Korea, and Ryukyu and Satsuma. In the absence of merchants who would otherwise have conducted trade abroad, the important actors in Japan's international trade consisted of domestic merchants, interpreters and agents who did business with and assisted the Chinese and Dutch merchant ships who visited Japan from abroad. The arena for these Japanese players was Nagasaki, the only port open to Chinese and Dutch ships.

Of Japan's "four gateways", Nagasaki was the only trading port under direct government control, but not all trade and administrative matters were completely carried out by government officials of the higher rank of samurai. In Japan, under the social system imposed by the shogunate, administrative power was monopolized by the samurai class in principle only; in reality, influential commoners from local communities such as merchants and farmers were used in the administration in various ways. This was also the case with maritime trade.

The Nagasaki Bugyō (magistrate) was the chief administrator of the port, but his office was staffed by less than fifty officials from the samurai class. The bulk of municipal administration concerning business and trade was carried out by *jiyakunin* (locally hired government officials), who were

---

rule and the Mạc family rule on the China-Vietnam border existed concurrently, with the Lê family being accredited by the Qing Emperor to invest with the King of Annam.

12 In the seventeenth century, while paying tribute to the Qing Empire, the Ayutthaya Kingdom of Siam (present-day Thailand) also prospered from entering into the Nagasaki trade. Ayutthaya, however, was destroyed in 1767 in a series of attacks by the Burmese (Myanmar) Konbaung Dynasty, and after the short-lived Thonburi Dynasty the current Rattanakosin Kingdom (Chakri Dynasty) came to power in 1782.

commoners. At the beginning of the eighteenth century, the *jiyakunin* machine in Nagasaki was already enormous, employing more than 1,000 people. This staff was in charge of municipal administration under the leadership of the Nagasaki Daikan (governor)[13], six *machi-doshiyori* (town councilors) and eighty-five *machi-otona* (town representatives). The buying and selling of trade goods took place in the Nagasaki Kaisho (trade association)[14], established toward the end of the seventeenth century. Two teams of *otona*, totaling six people, were appointed to take charge of visitors from abroad. One team, called the "*rankata*", managed the Dutch residence and consisted of two elders (Dejima *otona*) in charge of Dutch merchants in the Dutch trading house on Dejima. The other team, the *tōkata*, were the administrators of the Chinese and consisted of four elders (Tō-jin-yashiki *otona*) in charge of Chinese merchants in the Chinese compound. These two *otona* teams exercised jurisdiction over the foreigners and mobilized and supervised groups of lower-ranking *jiyakunin* headed by group leaders known as "*kumigashira*". Dejima, the artificially-built island where the Dutch trading house was located, was treated institutionally as a town and afforded the administrative structure of a township, with both an *otona* and a *kumigashira*. In addition to overseeing trade, the two *otona* teams supervised the members of the Dutch factory on Dejima, the Chinese merchants in the Tō-jin-yashiki and the Japanese people with access to either of the residences, and also maintained the facilities in both compounds.

To deal with Chinese merchants visiting Nagasaki, a system that included a *yado-machi* (lodging town) and a *tsuki-machi* (supporting town) was implemented. A *yado-machi* was a quarter that provided visiting Chinese merchants with accommodation services in Nagasaki and helped them mediate their business deals, while also taking care of related procedures such as the collection of commissions. A *tsuki-machi* supported the various requirements of a *yado-machi*. Beginning in

---

13 Foremost among local officials, the Nagasaki Daikan had a significant impact on Nagasaki area administration, and acted as counsel to the Nagasaki Prefect. He also became the governor of the surrounding imperial demesnes. Passing through Murayama Tōan and Suetsugu Heizō, the position became the hereditary right of the family of Takagi Sakuemon after 1739.

14 A trade management agency established at the end of the seventeenth century, the Nagasaki Kaisho oversaw the finances of the Nagasaki trade and distribution of profits. It had complete control over tribute to the Edo Shogunate and the financial management of Nagasaki.

1666, an arrangement was implemented whereby each town in Nagasaki alternatively served as *yado-machi* and *tsuki-machi*. Although the Chinese residence was built in 1689 and visiting Chinese merchants began to stay there instead of the city, the services of *yado-machi* and *tsuki-machi* survived in the form of the Nagasaki Kaisho. Established around the same time as the Chinese residence, the Nagasaki trade association used *yado-machi* and *tsuki-machi* for their access to the maintenance of ships and cargo handling services.

Translation services were also made available to foreign merchants in the form of *oranda tsūji* (Dutch interpreters) and *tō-tsūji* (Chinese interpreters), who were commoners and officials under the jurisdiction of the magistrate's office. These men were not only interpreters and translators, but also performed a wide range of other functions, including administrative procedures concerning the arrival and departure of ships and related business transactions, the supervision and regulation of foreign merchants during their stay and counseling and advising public authorities on the basis of their professional knowledge of administrative, trade and academic matters. The Dutch were not allowed to employ interpreters of their own, thus merchants at the Dutch trading house often regarded the interpreters as spies or watch-dogs.

Under the social system of the time, the post of interpreter was a hereditary family occupation. To be chosen as *tō-tsūji*, one first had to be a member or descendant of one of the seventy-odd families of resident Chinese (*jūtaku Tō-jin*) who had emigrated from Mainland China to Nagasaki. The position of Dutch interpreter was often assigned to families that had previously served as Portuguese interpreters[15], a clear vestige of the trade links Japan had with Portugal in the sixteenth century. Interpreters in the early eighteenth century were classified into three major ranks: *ō-tsūji* (senior interpreters), *ko-tsūji* (associate interpreters) and *keiko-tsūji* (apprentice interpreters). The first two categories were called "*hon-tsūji*" (qualified interpreter), with the third category acting to support them. They worked under the supervision of the *tsūji metsuke* (director of interpreters), and each had a staff of assistant and student interpreters.

---

15 A vestige of the trade with Portugal since the sixteenth century, communication between the Dutch and the Japanese in the seventeenth century was mainly conducted in Portuguese. It was not until the eighteenth century that communication in and translation to and from Dutch became established.

Even though they held the official government post of *jiyakunin*, the interpreters were still commoners in terms of their social standing, making it possible for government authorities to claim that they conducted private "commercial" activities rather than inter-governmental "diplomatic" relations. Although the international trading city of Nagasaki was under the direct jurisdiction of the shogunate government, it did not directly handle trade and related matters. Instead, they were carried out as business activities at the private level and mediated by the township of Nagasaki.

## Coastal navigation and domestic maritime transportation

Each of the onshore areas surrounding the East China Sea saw the development of methods and technologies for shipbuilding, navigation, transportation, creating contracts and engaging in commerce that were specific to each branch of shipping, be it maritime, coastal or riverine. While there are certainly differences between maritime and riverine transportation, perhaps the greatest divergence lies between ocean-going and coastal shipping due to the phenomena of seasonal winds and Black Currents. These natural occurrences accounted for the difference between maritime and coastal ships regarding the types of ships involved, their size, the composition of their crew and the type of expertise required of each crew member. Additionally, since governments regulated maritime transport far more stringently than river or coastal transport, distinctions came to be made in terms of types of ships, routes, captains and cargo in each country.

The Yellow Sea, which stretches between Mainland China and the Korean Peninsula, teemed with junks engaged in the booming maritime transportation business of the eighteenth century. The primary vessels in this sea, characterized by long stretches of shallow sandbanks, were flat-bottomed shallow draft vessels called "*shachuan*" junks. The largest coastal and inland water transportation terminal was Liujiagang, or Liujia Port in the Jiangnan area, which acted as both the biggest consumer market and the largest industrial base. Located northwest of Shanghai and the outer harbor for Suzhou, through these *shachuan* junks Liujia Port not only connected the Jiangnan area to the Yellow Sea and Bohai Sea, but also linked the region to Beijing via the Grand Canal and a network of inland waterways.

Trade deals took place in various ports between Liaodong to the north and Guangdong to the south involving merchants and seamen from various areas who spoke different languages or dialects, had various way of doing business and used diverse standards for weighing and measuring. In this environment, *yahang* served as mediators and engaged in various matters concerning transactions, financial settlements and taxation. Port cities were also brisk labor markets where unskilled surplus workers could find employment as longshoremen loading and unloading cargo, or as low-ranking crew members hired on a voyage-by-voyage basis. These men were generally viewed by the public as a nuisance due to their lack of skill and steady employment.

On the Korean Peninsula, where the Taebaek Mountain range runs along its eastern edge from north to south, maritime transportation and inland transportation along rivers such as the Han-gang and the Nakdong-gang developed in tandem. From the early years of the Joseon Kingdom, government-administered river and sea networks were established to transport tax grain, tribute and gift items from various parts of the country to Hanseong, the royal capital. Official ships transported most of these goods initially, but private water transport matured over the course of the seventeenth century, and private ships called *Gyeonggang Sa Seon* owned by Gyeonggang merchants in Hanseong began to undertake these shipping operations. Some merchants even started to operate sailboats capable of carrying as much as 1,000 *seok*[16] of grain. Ships owned by local residents were called *jito seon* (local ships).

The growth in private shipping led to the emergence of *seon sang* (shipping merchants) who made a living by shipping goods between markets in various parts of Korea, some of whom began to specialize in the water transportation business. Privately owned ships were usually manned by a crew that included a *seon ju* (ship-owner), *mul ju* (cargo owner), *sa gong* (captain) and *gyeok gun* (sailors). The ways in which these ships were managed and operated varied significantly. In some cases, the ships traded without their owners on board, while in other cases one individual performed the combined roles of ship-owner, cargo owner and captain.

---

16 The weight of one *seok* (unit of volume) in Korea differs depending on the type and condition of the grain. One *seok* is counted as 90 or 120 liters in Korea and Japan, respectively.

A domestic maritime network also developed in Ryukyu, with ships based at the two hub ports of Naha and Tomari sailing to the central and northern parts of the main island of Okinawa and other nearby islands, as well as to distant areas such as the Miyako and Yaeyama Islands. The network was operated primarily by private maritime transporters in Naha and consisted of ship-owners, captains and crew. They operated small- to medium-sized junks called "*māran-sen*", purchasing goods in one place and transporting them to another to sell at a profit. They also earned freight charges by shipping taxes collected in kind, official documents and officials from local areas to Naha. This network was linked both to Mainland China through tributary mission voyages and to the Japanese Archipelago through Satsuma-based private merchant ships called "*yamato-sen*", which moved back and forth between Ryukyu and Satsuma.

In the waters surrounding the Japanese Archipelago, maritime restrictions compelled all the ships and people involved in maritime affairs to work only along the coast. The flip side of these restrictions, however, was that the ban on international voyages made the period an active one for Japanese domestic ventures, prompting widespread developments in various coastal and riverine trade and transportation industries. Though only active in domestic waters, Japanese merchant ships still had a relationship of compartmentalization with the ocean-going ships of Chinese and Dutch merchants and came into contact with them through Japan's "four gateways" to the outside world.

Transportation by water, including both maritime and riverine transportation, was by far the most efficient means of carrying massive cargoes in early modern Japan. Cargo vessels called "*higaki kaisen*" and "*taru kaisen*"[17] were in active service on the shipping route between Osaka and Edo, which served as the major channel for the transportation of goods in Japan at the time. In the latter half of the eighteenth century, *taru kaisen*, known for being faster and having lower freight charges, gained

---

17 *Higaki kaisen* were cargo ships that carried an assortment of different types of freight for a number of consignors. The name "*higaki*" stems from the diamond-shaped grid that was attached to both sides of the ship. In 1730, *taru kaisen*, which were exclusive *sake* transporters, became separate and independent, but later, when the *taru kaisen* came to carry freight other than *sake*, the two types of ships competed with each other.

a competitive edge over *higaki kaisen*. Additionally, cargo ships called "*kitamae-bune*"[18], which sailed between Ezo (present-day Hokkaido) and Osaka, also became active as greater quantities of goods moved from the northern region (in particular, Hokuriku and Hokkaido).

These *kaisen* cargo ships were divided into two groups based on their pattern of operation. Cargo ships carrying goods on commission were called "*chinzumi-sen*" (freight-charging ships), while those directly operated by ship-owners conducting business on their own behalf were called "*kaizumi-sen*"

**Figure 20: *Kitamae-bune* (north-bound ships) congested in Matsumae**
Source: Hokkaido Museum.

18 A generic name for coastal cargo ships that carried goods from Ezo and the Hokuriku (present-day Niigata, Toyama, Ishikawa and Fukui Prefectures) region to Osaka by the western Sea of Japan route. In the north, these ships were known by such names as "*bezaisen*". With a main base on the Sea of Japan coast, many of the ship-owners would engage in trade transactions by also being the cargo consignor.

(ships carrying purchased goods). Ships in the latter category were further divided into two sub-categories depending on who commanded the ship: a *jikinori-sendō* (captain aboard) where a ship-owner went on board, taking full command of the ship and its business dealings himself; or an *oki-sendō* or *yatoi-sendō* (captain hired to manage the ship at sea), where the captain was employed by the ship-owner and charged with the task of navigating the ship and conducting its business. Even on ships under the command of *oki-sendō*, senior crew members were allowed to bring personal cargo on board and to conduct private business deals within certain limits, and the ship-owner allotted some portion of the profits to lower-ranking crew members.

These coastal shipping operations were also in need of services similar to those provided for overseas trade by *yahang* or trading firms, such as the mediation of contracts and transactions between cargo owner and ship-owner, and the creation of arrangements to insure the ship and its cargo against calamities such as shipwreck, theft and wrongdoing. In early modern Japan, these services were provided by *kaisen don'ya* (wholesale-merchants-cum-operators of *kaisen* ships). Especially in Edo and Osaka, wholesale merchants formed guilds, calculated risks and costs jointly and then made use of general averages regarding seafaring. Although their activities were confined to domestic waters, the way in which *kaisen* ships were managed in Japan was very similar to how Chinese and European merchant ships in the East and South China Seas operated.

## Terrestrial powers confronting the seas

During this period, local political powers directly in contact with these traders and voyagers also had to submit to the authority of the central government. The political powers at the local level overlapped with and constituted the bottom layer of the administrative structure of each central state, unlike the period discussed in Part 2. These local powers were submissive to the central state to the extent that they did not threaten to cause upheavals that would, in the manner of the sixteenth century, weaken and disintegrate each country's central government for the sake of local autonomy. Let us consider each state's diplomatic relations and see how local powers on the coast behaved in these situations.

Mainland China, the economic and trading center of East Asia, was under the control of the Manchu-Qing Empire, which had replaced the Ming.

## 3.2: Maritime Merchants and "Compartmentalization"

Having brought most of the area east of the Pamir Mountain Range under its control by the 1750s, the Qing Empire's territory grew to more than twice the size of that of the Ming. In order to govern this enormous and extremely varied area, the Qing government used different types of governance in different localities.

In the former Ming Dynasty's territory, it continued, on the one hand, with the former Ming system by appointing a full hierarchy of local officials, from *zongdu* (governor-general) and *xunfu* (governor) at the top to *zhifu* (prefect) and *zhixian* (county magistrate)[19] at the bottom. Also, at the four *haiguan* (customs houses), it created the new administrative post of *haiguan jiandu* (customs house director), who administered maritime trade and collected taxes on that trade. In addition to these two systems, one for local administration and the other for the administration of maritime trade, two military and police categories were also established. The first, the Eight Banners Garrison (Zhufang Baqi)[20], constituted the core of the Qing Army and stationed its units at major sea ports and at strategic sites nearby. The second, called the Green Standard Army (Luying), was an army established to maintain the public peace and consisted of mostly Han Chinese. Both were assigned to keep watch on land and at sea. Furthermore, in much the same way as the customs houses were established in strategically important ports, officials were dispatched to important industrial areas on special missions not only to procure goods for the imperial and other noble families, but also to collect any information necessary for the governing of their assigned districts. Typical examples of such officials were textile commissioners (*zhizao*), who supervised the manufacture and procurement of silk for official use and were stationed at several locations in the Jiangnan area, such as Jiangning (Nanjing), Suzhou and Hangzhou.

---

19 The *zongdu* and *xunfu* were the highest level of local officials assigned to former Ming Dynasty territory. In general, the governor-general had jurisdiction over two or more provinces while the governor had jurisdiction over one province. The governor-general was also a higher ranked official than governor, but as both were under the direct control of the emperor and not in a hierarchical relationship, they cooperated in governing their territories.

20 Regionally stationed Eight Banners military units were dispatched to garrisons in all Qing regions. In coastal areas they were stationed, for example, at Hanzhou, Fuzhou and Guangzhou, while naval garrisons were also stationed at Zhapu, Fuzhou and Guangzhou.

On the other hand, the Board of Rites (Libu), the office responsible for handling relationships with tributary countries of the central government, traditionally dealt with diplomatic relations. However, the Qing Empire had intensive trade dealings with Japan and with the West outside of the system of tributary relations. Thus both the Board of Revenue (Hubu) in charge of government finance, and the Imperial Household Department (Neiwufu) responsible for the finances of the imperial household, played more important roles than the Board of Rites in handling foreign trade, although officially they did not deal with tributary relations. The Neiwufu was manned by bondservants (*baoyi* or *booi*)[21] from specific banners among the Eight Banners under the direct command of the emperor. Officials who were appointed as customs house directors (*haiguan jiandu*) and commissioners of silk manufacturing were chosen from these bondservants.

One salient feature of the socio-political institutions of the Qing Empire was that the bannermen, people belonging to the Eight Banners, formed the core of the administrative hierarchy. Indeed, more than half of the high-ranking officials of the central and provincial governments, as well as most of the officials administering areas such as Mongolia and Tibet, regions outside the territory of the previous Ming Dynasty, consisted of these bannermen. Moreover, they were mostly Manchu. Thus, of the government entities mentioned above, the units of the Eight Banners Garrison that were stationed in strategically important places along the shore would have been manned by bannermen without exception. The posts of customs house directors were held by officials dispatched by the Neiwufu and the posts of high-ranking provincial officials, such as *zongdu* and *xunfu*, were also mostly held by bannermen. At the central administrative level, too, high-ranking officials were mostly chosen from among members of the royal family or bannermen, and these same people served as the emperor's aides. Thus, the decision-making process

---

21 *Baoyi* or *booi* refers to bannermen (people of one of the Eight Banners) who worked in the household management sector. Many Han Chinese engaged in this work were also incorporated into the Eight Banners framework. Author Cao Xueqin, well-known for his full-length novel *Hongloumeng* (Dream of the Red Chamber), was a descendant of Cao Xi and Cao Yin, who had held the post of Commissioner of Imperial Textiles for many years under the Kangxi Emperor.

regarding maritime matters was largely under Manchu control, a people who at first glance would seem to have had very little experience with the sea. However, it should also be pointed out that approximately half of the high-ranking government posts in the central administration were earmarked for Han Chinese bureaucrats, and middle- to low-ranking bureaucratic posts in the central and local governments in former Ming territory were mostly held by Han Chinese. Therefore, many of the officials who dealt with tributary delegates and trading ships on a first-hand basis were in reality Han Chinese.

It was also common in the Qing Empire for several government offices belonging to different chains of command to have overlapping jurisdictions, so there were often conflicts over authority and duties between or even within offices. This made it impossible for individual government offices to settle matters impartially, since they generally had some stake in the issues at hand. Provincial officials such as governor-general and governor, the customs house directors dispatched with special responsibilities for the administration of trade and commanding officers of the military units stationed along the coast, including *zhufang jianjung* (garrison generals), were all involved in the administration of trade in one way or another. This was ascribable partially to traditions peculiar to the Chinese bureaucracy, but also partially to the peculiar nature of the Qing Empire, where Manchus organized into the Eight Banners, along with the Mongols, were controlling Han Chinese by carefully including and excluding them from certain administrative offices.

It is also important to note that the central government devised its foreign policies by focusing attention primarily on the situation inland rather than on that at sea. Having been continuously in conflict with the Dzungar Empire of Oirat-Mongols on its northwestern frontiers since the 1680s[22], the Qing was typically more interested in the security that stable maritime relations could bring to their coastal borders than in economic profits.

---

22 The Dzungar, who reached their zenith in the mid-seventeenth century, were a western Mongolian nomadic tribe led by a royal family that were not descendants of Chinggis Qan. Until conquered by the Qing Empire in the 1750s, they built a nomadic empire in the central region of the Eurasian continent in coexistence with the Qing and Russia.

Korea's system of governance was also modeled after a similar bureaucratic system. Since the seventeenth century, the highest body of the central government had been the *bibyeonsa* (border defense council), which was established to manage the defense of the state and had taken the place of the former highest body, the *uijeongbu* (state council). The country was divided into eight *do* (provinces), each governed by a *kwanch'alsa* or *kamsa* (provincial governor), who was dispatched from the central government. Each province was then divided into prefectures (*bu*, *mok*, *gun* and *hyeon*). Generally referred to as "*eup*" or "*kol*", these were administered by local officials called "*suryeong*" (district magistrates). Diplomatic relations fell under the jurisdiction of the *yejo*, which was at the central government level and equivalent to the Board of Rites in Chinese dynasties. At the local level, no office specialized in the handling of diplomatic relations, but the Dongraebusa (Dongrae magistrate) in Busan handled day-to-day relations with and conflicts involving Japanese officials and merchants staying in the Waegwan (Japan House). The government office responsible for guarding the Waegwan, supplying it with fuel, maintaining its buildings and carrying cargo on its behalf was called the Busan-jin. A military official known as the Busan-cheomsa was in command of the Busan-jin. Other officials known as "*hunto*" and "*byeolcha*" in turn worked under the Busan-cheomsa or at the Dongraebusa as Japanese-language interpreters and liaison officers with the Waegwan handling day-to-day affairs.

In the Ryukyu Kingdom, the nucleus of the royal government in Shuri, Ryukyu's capital, was a council chamber called the "Hyōjōsho". This council included the King, the Sessei (Prime Minister), the Sanshikan (Council of Three), the Mono Bugyō in charge of finance, supplies and industry and the Mōshikuchihō in charge of foreign affairs, household registration, police and judicial affairs. All affairs of state, from central government policy to pending court cases, were deliberated in the Hyōjōsho. The Mōshikuchihō consisted of four departments: the Sasu no soba, the Board of External Affairs and Education, including foreign diplomacy; the Sōshikuri, the Department of Royal Household Affairs; the Tomari jitō, the Department of Police and Construction; and the Hira no soba, the Department of Judicial Affairs. However, given the enormous implications that external affairs had for Ryukyuan government policy, which pivoted around maintaining dual tributary relations with the Qing and Japan, every office of the royal government was involved in diplomatic affairs to a certain extent.

## Political powers in Japan and maritime transportation

In comparison with these three states, the Tokugawa Shogunate in Japan adopted a political structure called the *"bakuhan* system", which combined the institutions of shogunal rule at the national level and those of lords' rule at the local domainal level. Its base was the master-vassal relationship between the shogunate and *daimyōs*. Consequently, Tokugawa Japan's administrative system for dealing with external relations was radically different from that of the other three countries. More specifically, of the "four gateways" Japan opened to the outside world, the three at Satsuma, Tsushima and Matsumae were administered by the three *daimyōs* with jurisdiction over those areas, i.e. the Shimazu, Sō and Matsumae families. The remaining gateway at Nagasaki, though officially under the direct control of the shogunate government, was supervised by *hatamoto* (bannermen), samurai in the direct service of the shogunate.

Initially, the post of Nagasaki Bugyō (magistrate), the chief administrator of the port, was held by a *daimyō*. However, beginning in the Kan'ei period (1624–1644), the post was reclassified and became one of the *ongoku bugyō*, or an appointment held by *hatamoto* that was under the jurisdiction of *rōjū* (senior counselors). The number of Nagasaki magistrates themselves varied from one period to the next, but basically two persons served in the post, taking turns on an annual basis to serve one year in Edo and one in Nagasaki. The Bugyō was responsible not only for administering matters related to trade, but also for procuring foreign goods for use by the shogun and his government, and for keeping the port in order. He was also required to carry out extensive duties related to the maintenance of public peace and national defense, including collecting information about foreign countries, monitoring the behavior of *daimyōs* in the western part of Japan, commanding security operations in the west of the country and its shorelines and enforcing the ban on Christianity.

In contrast, the shogunate did not put the gateways at Satsuma, Tsushima and Matsumae under its direct control, but permitted the domains to administer them independently. The Tokugawa Shogunate allowed the Shimazu clan, the lord of Satsuma, to exercise control over Ryukyu and to collect tributary goods from it. The shogunate also regarded Ryukyu's tribute trade with Qing China as a trading route that could supplement

Nagasaki's role in procuring Chinese goods, and thus allowed the arrangement to continue under Satsuma's supervision. The Shimazu family, for its part, regarded Ryukyuan trade with Qing China as an important source of income for supplementing the domain's finances. They therefore charged one of the senior retainers with exclusively administering all the affairs related to Ryukyu and dispatched a resident supervisor (*zaiban bugyō*) to Naha, stationing him in a local administrative office called the "*okariya*" so that he could keep watch on the Ryukyu government's handling of tribute trade. Nonetheless, the Ryukyu Kingdom government in Shuri was guaranteed autonomy in domestic and diplomatic policy to some extent.

The Sō family, the lord of Tsushima, was assigned to play an instrumental role in maintaining diplomatic relations between Japan and Korea. The Sō's primary role consisted of inviting Korean Goodwill Missions to Japan, gathering information related to political developments in Mainland China and procuring goods from China and Korea. Because of this arrangement, the Sō family held a unique position of power compared to other *daimyōs*. It was granted the status of a domain with a taxable income of 100,000 *koku* (one *koku* of rice weighs about 150 kilograms), despite the fact that in reality the figure was only approximately 20,000 *koku*. The central government also subsidized the domain and Sō family when it had financial difficulties. The Matsumae family in Hokkaido was also given special treatment; even though it was the only *daimyō* governing a domain with "zero rice production" because its land was unfit for rice cultivation, it was nonetheless granted the status of more than 10,000 *koku*. The exchanges taking place in Hokkaido were different from those occurring at the other gateways in Japan, since the Matsumae were trading with the Ainu in various parts of Ezo and had not yet been united into a state entity. Interactions with such communities took a unique form in the sense that the lord of the Matsumae Domain established relations with communities and their chiefs on a case-by-case basis through trade, tribute and subjugation rituals.

Interpreters were indispensable for the execution of these interactions, as in the case of Nagasaki. In Tsushima, ex-merchants-turned Korean interpreters had been on the scene for some time, but the domainal government tried to train additional interpreters by establishing an interpreter training school in Fuchū (Izuhara) in 1727 according to a proposal put forward by Amenomori Hōshū[23], a Confusion scholar of that domain. Satsuma also had need of *tō-tsūji* (Chinese interpreters) for the administration of Ryukyu and the handling of Chinese trade ships that were often shipwrecked in their domain, and it also trained Korean interpreters under the pretext of preparing for Korean trade vessels that might drift ashore. These interpreters played an active role in handling foreign ships that actually washed ashore and in repatriating their crew, but the very existence of these interpreters is suggestive of the existence of Satsuma's own networks of transportation.

By contrast, Ryukyu, which maintained tributary relationships and an official transportation route with Qing China, sent *kanshō* (government-financed students) and *kangaku* (privately financed students) to Qing China aboard tribute ships to study the Chinese language and other subjects. Thus, unlike Chinese interpreters in Nagasaki, who were in contact with private merchant ships from various parts of China and acquired the Chinese dialects of Nanjing, Fuzhou, Zhangzhou and other localities, interpreters in Ryukyu learned official Mandarin Chinese and other official dialects.

## Relationship between the seas and local political authorities

Of the foregoing political authorities, those in direct contact with the sea included: the customs house director, governor-general and governor in the relevant local areas in the Qing Empire; the Nagasaki Bugyō and the Sō family of the Tsushima domain in Japan; and the Dongraebusa in Korea. Particularly, the customs house director and the Nagasaki Bugyō were specially dispatched from the central government, and shared common significance in that they were oriented to exercise their powers as public authorities with the aim of controlling matters concerning the sea, regardless of their differences in terms of bureaucracy and administrative systems. Due to the shared characteristic of being specially dispatched from the central government, the two offices were also similar in the sense that

---

23 Amenomori Hōshū (1668–1755) was a Confucianist of the Zhu Xi school who studied under Kinoshita Jun'an and who served the Sō family of Tsushima by making significant efforts in the arena of diplomacy with Korea. Among his writings is *Kōrin Teisei*, a book that provides guidelines for diplomacy with Korea

they did not have any military force under their command, despite having been vested with enormous powers to administer trade and monitor trade and emigration. In the case of the Qing Empire, it was not customs houses who guarded the ports, but rather local military units, such as the provincial Eight Banners Garrisons under the command of the garrison general, and the Green Standard Army under the command of the governor-general, governor and provincial military commander (*tidu*). In the case of Japan, the defense of Nagasaki was provided collectively by the *daimyōs*, with the two most important services provided by the Kuroda family of the Fukuoka Domain and the Nabeshima family of the Saga Domain, who took turns every two years to lead the *keigo ban'yaku* (defense service). In the case of an emergency, the Nagasaki Bugyō was mandated to mobilize and command these defense units, an arrangement that proved ineffective in practice. During the Phaeton Incident of 1807, when the British warship *Phaeton* forced her way into the bay to seize Dutch ships, the Japanese side was totally at a loss and could only accede to the warship's demand and ask the ship to leave. Subsequently, Matsudaira Yasuhide, the Nagasaki Bugyō in residence, committed suicide by way of taking responsibility for this failure in leadership.

The policies on transportation and trade adopted by Japan and the Qing Empire had surprisingly similar forms. Both in Nagasaki and in Guangzhou, government authorities avoided direct contact with foreign merchants, maintaining the pretext that foreign trade was carried out by private merchants intermediated by *otona* and *tsūji* (interpreters) in the case of Nagasaki, and by *cohong* in the case of Guangzhou. Certainly, the two governments differed sharply in regard to their attitude toward overseas trade, with the Qing government remaining basically tolerant while the Tokugawa government completely prohibited Japanese from going overseas and severely restricted visits by foreign ships. However, the roles performed by licensed merchant groups, agencies and interpreters in the trading ports of both of the countries, and the characteristics of these roles, were quite similar.

By contrast, in Korea, the Dongraebusa had the Waegwan in his jurisdiction and oversaw diplomatic relations with Japan; however, he was a mere local officer and not a specially dispatched official like the Nagasaki Bugyō in Japan. Still, he was granted greater importance than ordinary *suryong* (district magistrates), both given a relatively high rank and allowed to report directly to the king. This was unique to commissioners of outlying strategic areas, such as the Jeju Moksa (Commissioner of Jeju) and the Uiju Buyun (Magistrate of Uiju).

It should be pointed out that even among these political authorities in direct contact with the sea, the main actors and interests they pursued were not necessarily the same at the national and local levels. Thus, even at a time when central authorities exerted strict control over trading activities, local authorities in the coastal areas, such as *zongdu* and *xunfu* in the case of Qing China or *daimyōs* in the case of Japan, were sometimes engaged in smuggling. The Shimazu family of the Satsuma Domain in particular is known for having conducted smuggling operations on various islands within the domain. It also took advantage of its position to supervise Ryukyu's tribute trade and surpassed the trade with China-via-Ryukyu in amounts far in excess of the permitted limits to such an extent as to exert pressure on the volume of trade handled by Nagasaki in the nineteenth century.

On the whole, the seas of East Asia at the time seem to have been characterized by being both simultaneously open and closed, laissez-faire and regulated. In the sense that these seas were free from any major conflicts or tensions, and that the Chinese and European merchant ships were able to move around them actively, they were quite "open". It should be kept in mind that the regulation of trade in these waters was subject to local political will, and therefore individual players operating under this system of rule were not vested with any guaranteed rights or powers. Compared to the situation of the seas in the preceding era (as described in Part 2), characterized by the intrusion of new players and excessive competition, this era may be characterized by the fact that the "channels" connecting governments and voyagers from the outside world were narrowed but not closed entirely. Rather than directly managing trade, central governments instead completely left it to regional and local contractors.

Only a limited number of maritime merchants and government delegates were able to move through these narrow "channels". At trade ports, the openings in these channels, a hoard of individuals were charged with semi-governmental functions, including *yahang* (middlemen-cum-brokers), *machi doshiyori* (town councilors) and *tsūji* (interpreters). These individuals were afforded the privilege of engaging in trade in exchange for carrying out official duties on behalf of the government, such as collecting taxes and being responsible for the various matters related to a ship's departure, arrival and the accommodation of its crew. In this way, trade and administration were carried out jointly through close collaboration between government officials and privileged commoners. Such a narrowing-down of traffic and of cross-border interactions may be termed "abbreviation" and "concentration". In the next chapter, we will look more closely at how "abbreviation" and "concentration" worked and how the two interacted.

## 3.3: Compression and Concentration of Interactions and Residences

### Shōtoku export restrictions and a trade permit dispute

In Nagasaki in March 1715, Chinese maritime merchants due to sail home were summoned to the Nagasaki Bugyōsho (magistrate's office), where Ōoka Kiyosuke, the Nagasaki Bugyō, informed them about a new trade law called the "Shōtoku Shinrei" (New Edict of the Shōtoku Period) or "Kaihaku Goshi Shinrei" (New Edict on Mutual Trade by Trading Ships). Among the various rules set out in the new law, one provision directly impacting the Chinese merchants was the fixed upper limit on the number of Chinese merchant ships allowed to visit Nagasaki per year, which was to be reduced from eighty to thirty and accounting for ships from different ports of departure. This edict stemmed from the work of Arai Hakuseki (1657–1725)[1], a Confucian scholar and advisor to the sixth and seventh shogun. Since the Qing government had lifted the *haijin* (maritime prohibitions) in 1684, approximately thirty years earlier, the number of Chinese merchant ships sailing to ports in the East China Sea had soared. Nagasaki was no exception. Even though restrictions had been placed on the volume of trade and the number of Chinese ships allowed to visit Nagasaki, outflows of silver and copper, and the smuggling trade carried out by some of the merchant ships denied entry to Nagasaki, still sparked anxiety. Trade permits called *"shinpai"* were also introduced as part of

---

1  Arai Hakuseki was a politician and Confucianist active at the core of the shogunal administration during the rule of Tokugawa Ienobu and Ietsugu. Having studied the Zhu Xi school of Confucianism with Amenomori Hōshū, he promoted the reformist politics of what was known as the *Shōtoku no Chi* (the Rule of Correct Ethics).

the new edict, which were to be issued in the name of Chinese-language interpreters at Nagasaki to a limited number of Chinese merchants. These permits would allow the merchants to trade in Nagasaki, while ships without permits would be denied the opportunity to visit and engage in trade there starting from the following year.

The issuance of the trade permits to a limited number of Chinese merchants caused trouble for the Qing government. Those maritime merchants who had to return home without having obtained the necessary permits to allow them to conduct trade in Nagasaki brought a case against their rivals who had received permits, accusing the latter of "having committed treason against the Qing Dynasty by submitting themselves to Japanese rule, and by receiving documents inscribed with the name of a foreign era" (Jp. *nengō*). Upon receiving the charge, the Qing government authorities were divided on how to deal with it. Boodzai, director of the Zhe Haiguan (Zhe customs house) in Zhejiang, who oversaw the port of departure for trading ships leaving for Japan, thought that Qing China should continue to trade with Japan under the new arrangement without challenging the decision. Oki, director of the Jiang Haiguan (Jiang customs house) in Jiangsu, was concerned that should they make an issue of Japan's new trade licensing system, trade would enter a slump and there would be a corresponding loss in tariff revenue. They were opposed by Duan Zhixi, the *buzhengshi* (provincial financial commissioner), and Yang Zongren, the *anchashi* (provincial judicial commissioner), who took a serious view of the fact that the "trade permits" issued by a foreign country had been accepted by some merchants. It was therefore tentatively decided that Gioroi Mamboo, the Governor-General of Zhejiang and Fujian, and Xu Yuanmeng, the Governor of Zhejiang, a Manchu bannerman, would have a Guangdong-based ship of the maritime merchant Li Taoshi and his party visit Nagasaki the following year (1716). They would sail without a trade permit in exactly the same way as they had previously and see how the Japanese side would react. Upon arrival in Nagasaki, however, Li Taoshi and his party were flatly denied entry and sent on their way in accordance with the new rule. As a result, the case, along with the *shinpai* themselves, was brought to the royal court in Beijing.

The discussion in Beijing became complicated. One proposal insisted that negotiations with Japan be carried out via an official letter demanding that Japan treat certificates issued by the Qing Empire to Qing merchants as equivalent to *shinpai*. Another asserted that the Chinese merchants who had received the trade permits be punished for accepting documents from a foreign government. However, the Kangxi Emperor, after personally examining an actual *shinpai*, rejected both proposals on the grounds that "the document is a simple deed exchanged in private business deals, not an official diplomatic document". He did not see anything wrong with Chinese maritime merchants receiving such permits; therefore, he saw no need to approach the Japanese government with a proposal to start negotiations regarding the issue.

In fact, before this even occurred in Beijing, the *rōjū* (senior counselors) of the shogunate in Japan sought Arai Hakuseki's advice on how the government should behave should a Chinese ship sail to Nagasaki without a *shinpai*. In his report in 1716, Hakuseki advised the counselors as follows: "The trading license is not an official document issued by the Nagasaki Bugyōsho, but rather a private document exchanged between a Chinese-language interpreter and a Chinese trader. It is incomprehensible that the Qing should complain about it". This reply was translated into Chinese and handed over to Li Taoshi and his party before their return to China and was ultimately transmitted to the Qing government. Hakuseki's opinion

**Figure 21: *Shinpai* licence dated April 13, 1734**
Source: Historiographical Institute, the University of Tokyo.

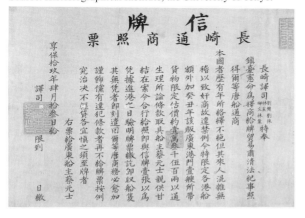

was in perfect agreement with the Kangxi Emperor's judgment, almost as if each had been anticipating the other's intentions.

However, the views of the Kangxi Emperor and Hakuseki were little more than sophistries. Despite Hakuseki's assertion, the new edicts were established in accordance with instructions given by the central government of Japan; these laws were then enforced by the Nagasaki Bugyō, who summoned all the Chinese merchants in Nagasaki in order to explain and promulgate them. The argument that the trade permits were private documents exchanged between Chinese-language interpreters and Chinese maritime merchants is untenable; these interpreters, as explained previously, were *jiyakunin*, who, in their capacity as government officials hired locally from among commoners, worked under the supervision of the Nagasaki Bugyō. Nonetheless, both Hakuseki and the Kangxi Emperor chose to take a pragmatic view of the matter. They prioritized practical and economic interests by attempting in theory to uphold the established policy of each government as much as possible, while in practice averted their eyes from unpleasant developments that ran counter to official policy.

Thus, the question of the validity of the trade permit system was put to rest without developing into either a diplomatic or domestic dispute. The trade permits that had been tentatively put into the Zhe Haiguan's charge were returned to the maritime merchants concerned, who resumed their voyages to Nagasaki in accordance with the new edict. On board one of the first ships that entered the port of Nagasaki in 1717 was Li Taoshi's nephew, Li Yixian, who carried the now-returned trade permit of his uncle. Thereafter, controlled trade based on the issuance of these trade permits became the standard for Japan–Qing trade relations.

## De-politicization of the "sea of politics"

In the areas surrounding the East China Sea in the eighteenth century, regional state powers stood side by side in a strong expression of unity that was unprecedented. Instead of trying to subjugate each other, state authorities adopted a realistic and flexible attitude in line with their individual circumstances, carefully balancing official policy with the practical gains they hoped to achieve. Thus, it is not simply the case that Japan broke away from the tribute system and adopted a "seclusion" policy,

### 3.3: Compression and Concentration of Interactions and Residences 267

just as Qing China rarely invoked its conceptualization as a "Middle Kingdom" that presided over a tribute system. Rather, the Qing didn't attempt to impose a Sinocentric order on others, and flexibly avoided using official diplomatic routes in its foreign relations if at all possible.

Unlike the Ming, which tried in vain to unify all its foreign relations into a tribute system, the Manchu-Qing Empire pursued a policy that was completely the reverse, seeking to reduce and dilute external political relations rather than rebuild or expand them. As described in Part 2, the trend toward downsizing the tribute system began in the sixteenth century, when the combination of it and the maritime prohibition system collapsed. The maritime prohibition system was temporarily restored during the turbulent Ming-Qing transition, but after the Qing managed to defeat its maritime foes in 1684, Chinese merchants rapidly expanded their maritime trading activities and engaged in mutual trade (*hushi*) with foreign merchant ships. Eighteenth-century maritime trade was mostly carried out on a border trade basis in both the East China Sea, surrounded by the early modern states, and the South China Sea, replete with trading ships from Southeast Asia and Europe; tribute trade accounted for only a small share of the total trade in these seas. Neither the East nor South China Seas were defined by the tributary or diplomatic relations that existed between the states, which represented only a small part of the multifaceted relations at play.

When any entity sought to officially negotiate for open diplomatic relations, the Qing government had no choice but to fall back on the time-honored and rigid framework of treating such an approach from the outside world as a tributary relationship and investing the entity with the status of an "external vassal" to China. Not only was the Tokugawa Shogunate unwilling to enter into such a tributary relationship, but the Qing Empire was also eager to avoid, as much as possible, actually realizing such an arrangement. This was exemplified by the fact that Qing China gave tacit approval to Ryukyu's dual subjection to both the Qing and Japan, as well as the fact that it did not require visiting foreign merchant ships to follow tributary formalities.

An important factor underlying this behavior seems to be that, as a Eurasian empire, the Qing Empire itself assumed many different attitudes in dealing with diverse peoples in various areas at different frontiers, one of which was the East China Sea. The Qing Empire assumed a realistic stance that put practical gains first, believing that it would be folly to stubbornly abide by the official stance or formalities in a way that ruined potential trade profits. All that mattered was economic gains and public peace. This view was not only held by the Emperor but was shared by the various bureaucrats belonging to the Eight Banners. As a matter of fact, the provincial officials mentioned earlier who did not see the *shinpai* as an issue were all Manchus or bannermen. In the case of Japan as well, despite the fact that the Nagasaki Bugyō was appointed by the Tokugawa Shogunate and officially in charge of foreign trade, Chinese-language interpreters of the commoner class were used by the Bugyō so that not only trade issues, but also political concerns could be handled within the framework of "private" international interactions.

As the foregoing observations suggest, the conventional understanding that in the eighteenth century the East China Sea operated under the hierarchical order of a tribute system or an investiture system presided over by the Qing Emperor, with Japan as the sole outsider in this framework, is untenable. Certainly, there is no denying that the East China Sea had always been a "sea of politics" where regional political powers vied for control over maritime trade and actors. However, their efforts during this era exceeded all previous endeavors, and these developments may be characterized as the de-politicization of the sea of politics. The governments that surrounded the sea regulated trade and emigration in an unprecedentedly rigorous way, pushing politics and statecraft to the fore. At the same time, they allowed trading activities and international interactions to prosper under the guise of private trading relations without giving rise to political problems, despite their emphasis on politics.

## Various relationship phases among early modern states

Now we are faced with the question of how the region's early modern states forged relationships and came to terms with each other. As state-level regional political powers, the four early modern states may be divided into two groups. One group consisted of the Qing Empire and the Tokugawa Shogunate, each of which denied the existence of any authority or order superior to itself. The other consisted of Korea and Ryukyu, each of which accepted another's authority; yet neither Japan nor the Qing had any intention of staging a confrontation. Nor did the two countries dare to attempt to control Korea and Ryukyu directly, or interfere

## 3.3: Compression and Concentration of Interactions and Residences

with their domestic affairs. Consequently, an effective relationship of compartmentalization was at work among the four powers of the period.

The perception of an ideal form of international order that underlay these relationships was not simply borrowed from a preceding era, but rather formed in the aftermath of the Ming-Qing transition in the mid-seventeenth century, and, as such, was peculiar to the eighteenth century. The radical change in the international order brought about by the fall of the Ming and the Manchu conquest of China sent a shockwave through the various societies in and around the East China Sea. After the Qing managed to largely consolidate its power in the 1680s, contrary to most predictions that it would be unable to overcome its many rivals, it sought to understand the situation in the various areas in and around the East China Sea, including the former territory of Ming China, as well as to explain its present position in relation to the world around it.

Each of the societies that shared knowledge about the Chinese classics tended to adopt a hierarchical view of the world with themselves at the center, derived from the Sinocentric worldview. Each of these societies located itself at the center socio-culturally and, regarding others as inferior in some respect, placed them on the lower rungs of a hierarchical ladder. The most important distinction in this view of civilization separated the "civilized center" from the "barbarian periphery". Following the Ming-Qing transition, this Sinocentric and discriminatory perspective underwent a process both of diversification and relativization. After all, the Manchu, who had previously been deemed "barbarians" from the periphery, were now unquestionably at the "center", thus much discussion unfolded on the question of how to deal with this reversal.

Having taken the helm of an international order, the Qing Emperor told the Han Chinese and China's tributary states that he was sitting at the "center of the world". He justified this claim on the strength of his having protected and practiced Confucianism, and thus accomplished peace on Earth. To the Mongols and Tibetans, on the other hand, he presented himself as an incarnation of Mañjuśrī Bodhisattva (a bodhisattva associated with transcendent wisdom), and as a protector of Tibetan Buddhism[2]. By contrast, the tributary countries of Ryukyu and Korea

---

2 From the seventeenth century, Tibetan Buddhism spread among the Mongols and the Manchu. The Qing Emperor, as Chakravartin (an ideal sovereign who

situated themselves as part of the Sinocentric world order presided over by Qing China. However, it should be noted that members of the Korean intellectual class were displeased about the tributary relationship and privately regarded the Manchus as "barbarians". Within Korea, they also continued to use the era name of "Ming China" even after the Ming had fallen. Meanwhile, the Tokugawa Shogunate in Japan refrained from having any official ties with the Qing Empire in an effort to assert its own authority and to consolidate its independence. The Tokugawa Shogunate even fabricated its own version of the Sinocentric world order[3], in which Japan presided over "foreign countries" such as Ryukyu and Korea; however, this right to lead was not based on Japan's virtue as a protector of a universal authority such as Confucianism, but on the basis of particular virtues such as "military prestige" and the concept that Japan was a "country protected by the gods".

Early modern Ryukyu stood at an intersection between two frameworks of international order. Qing China and Japan, which both maintained master-vassal relationships with Ryukyu, looked upon the island kingdom as an entity that confirmed each state's centrality in the world order. Qing China considered Ryukyu as having been a loyal tributary country since the days of the Ming Dynasty, while Japan regarded it as the "foreign country" that had submitted itself to the military glory of the Tokugawa Shogun. Given this situation, the Ryukyu Kingdom initiated and maintained a kingdom-wide policy of concealing the relationship with Japan from the Qing in fear that the latter would take offense at this dualistic diplomacy.

This policy of concealment was put into effect in the latter half of the seventeenth century in accordance with instructions given by the Shimazu family, the *daimyō* of Satsuma, who were in turn acting on behalf of the

---

promoted the rise of Buddhism) and as an incarnation of Mañjuśrī Bodhisattva, was known as the emperor who ruled in place of Mañjuśrī Bodhisattva.

3 The Japanese worldview of this period, while framing an egocentric order similar to the Sinocentric worldview of the Chinese, established a unique Japanese standard of superiority and interiority known as the "*Nihongata Kaichitsujo*" (Japanese world order). Since this did not seek realization through diplomacy or war and was in force effectively only inside the country (in the sense that it did not refer to the actual international order), it was known as the "imagined Japanese World Order".

Tokugawa Shogunate when it became apprehensive that a conflict with the Qing might erupt over their vassal relationship with Ryukyu. During the eighteenth century, moreover, the royal government of Ryukyu took measures to conceal the Japan–Ryukyu relationship by issuing several regulations on the matter, which were specific and minutely detailed. For example, one reads as follows: "If a Japanese [Satsuma] ship with several Ryukyuan crew members aboard is washed ashore on the land of China, all the Ryukyuans shall dress up as Japanese". In the case of the shipwreck suffered by the Satsuma-based ship mentioned at the outset of Part 3, prior to landing the two Ryukyuan crew members on board cut and arranged their hair in a Japanese style with a topknot. They even went so far as to temporarily adopt Japanese-sounding names, changing "Kinjō" to "Kin'emon" and "Goya" to "Goemon".

This does not mean, however, that the Qing court was oblivious to the Japan–Ryukyu relationship. Despite the sincere efforts of both Ryukyu and Satsuma to conceal their relationship, the Qing Empire was aware from early on that Ryukyu was considered, in the Japanese worldview, to be a vassal of the shogun. Nonetheless, the Qing were determined not to be perturbed, maintaining the image of "Ryukyu as a vassal to the Qing". As long as this façade was intact, the Qing would not reprimand Ryukyu or force Japan into diplomatic negotiations over the issue. Instead, the Qing acted as if unaware of what was happening. Thus, it became an established practice for both the Qing and Japan to quietly condone the status quo, evident in the handling of the question of Ryukyu's vassal status and the issue of the trade permits in Nagasaki. As a result, these governments effectively removed political problems from the East China Sea, a region that would otherwise have likely functioned as a "sea of politics".

Much the same pattern was at work in the relationship between Japan and Korea mediated by Tsushima. The Sō family of Tsushima was a *daimyō* serving as a vassal to the Tokugawa Shogunate, but also functioned as the sole contact for Japan's diplomatic relations with Korea; it also simultaneously maintained its traditional tributary-state-like status in its relationship with Korea as it had done since the medieval era. Because of this relationship, the Korean court regarded the Sō family as one of its tributaries, while the Tsushima Domain circumvented acceptance of the notion that it was a subject of Korea by carefully avoiding the use of expressions or procedures that could be construed as implying a sovereign-subject relationship. Each party interpreted the relationship on their own terms. For example, when Koreans described something as "gifts bestowed on a tributary", Tsushima interpreted this as "taxes exacted from Korea".

The reason why the relationship between Tsushima and Korea remained stable despite the two parties' disparate views was because each found it advantageous to compromise. Tsushima depended economically on trade with Korea, while Korea was interested in maintaining stable relations with Japan. The Tokugawa Shogunate, which backed Tsushima, did not bother to make an issue of the relationship between Tsushima and Korea so long as it found the Sō family useful for maintaining amicable relations between the two countries. In sum, we might conclude that to maintain relationships between Tsushima (and the Tokugawa Shogunate) and Korea, there was a tacit agreement between the two (or three) parties concerned.

## Early modern states' efforts toward compartmentalization

The most crucial issue for the various central governments was the question of sovereign title and era name that was regarded as the index of one's position or status vis-à-vis others in premodern East Asia. Though the question was non-existent in the Qing's relationships with its tributary states of Ryukyu and Korea, this could potentially trigger problems in its relationships with other countries. Given this possibility, Japan avoided official diplomatic relations with the Qing in order to avert precisely such a conflict, and the Qing, for its part, was reluctant to press Japan on the issue. In fact, in handling the incident concerning the trade permits in Nagasaki, the Qing government avoided direct negotiations with the Japanese side. Conversely, Ryukyu, which had to pay tribute to both states, used the Qing era name in documents it submitted to the Qing and the Japanese era name in documents for that country.

Between Japan and Korea, on the other hand, an equitable arrangement was established during the seventeenth century after many complications. The Japanese side would use the Japanese era name, and the Korean side the Chinese Zodiac as well as the Ming era name (before the collapse of that empire). As for the more complicated question of how each country's sovereign should refer to himself in official diplomatic letters, a peculiar practice was established: the Tokugawa Shogun would address himself as "Minamoto no so-and-so of Japan"[4] in the sovereign's messages to the King of Korea, while the latter would address the Shogun by the title of Nihonkoku Taikun (the Tycoon of Japan). This practice continued until the end of the Tokugawa period, aside from a short interval in the 1710s when Arai Hakuseki revived the title of Nihon Kokuō (the King of Japan). Contrary to the authoritative posture each ruler assumed domestically, in

**Figure 22: The Japanese envoy from Tsushima making a bow at a monument in a hall likened to the Korean King in Choryang, Busan**

Source: Part of *Dongnae-busa-jeop-Waesa-do* (Painting of the Magistrate of Dongnae's Reception for Japanese Envoys), National Museum of Korea.

---

4 An unusual form of address that gives the name of the country and family name without indicating the official title, and the designation of the effective ruler of Japan. Used from the fifteenth century onwards, the Tokugawa family were named "Minamoto", referring to themselves as Minamoto (descendant of Genji).

their relations with one another, the central governments adopted a carefully devised practice whereby each would use a favorable way of reckoning the era and carefully balanced the titles and ranks of their respective sovereigns.

Another solution that was often employed was to exchange communications between ministers instead of sovereigns, or even local officials representing the two parties. For example, the Sō family of Tsushima sent letters not to the King of Korea, but to the Yejo (Minister of Rites) who stood on an equal footing. A similar practice was adopted in communications between the Qing Empire and Russia, and negotiations between Japan and the Qing were conducted by the Nagasaki Bugyō and the local administrators of Jiangnan and Fujian through the exchange of letters. When handling inter-governmental problems, each country used a carefully designed scheme to help it avoid, as much as possible, diplomatic contacts at the state level. When unavoidable, these contacts could be made in ways that would not damage the logic of domestic governance that was being used by the other state.

On the other hand, Korea and Ryukyu did not form a direct diplomatic relationship with each other during this period. Under the Chinese world order based on the investiture and tribute relationships, interaction between tributary countries was prohibited in principle as constituting "illicit intercourse". In practice, however, until the early seventeenth century, the Korean and Ryukyuan kings had been dispatching envoys to each other and maintaining official intercourse in Beijing in the name of maintaining *kōrin* (Kr. *kyorin*), or "a friendly relationship between neighboring countries". The reason why such intercourse ceased during this period seems to be due to the consolidation of diplomatic relations by the Qing, which, for example, led to the establishment of the procedure for the repatriation of castaways of each country through the Qing government. However, this consolidation also had the effect of reducing the need for maintaining direct intercourse.

## Qing restrictions on overseas voyages and migration control

The stable maritime order in the eighteenth century described above was established under the determination and power of the early modern states, breaking away from the "freedom" that went hand-in-hand with the chaos of the preceding era. Thus, each government prioritized the preservation of order, which explains why each state took steps to implement strict restrictions on ocean voyages and carefully inspected people entering and leaving the country. Their primary objective was to maintain the public peace by eliminating destabilizing factors deemed harmful to national unification, such as Christianity and autonomous maritime forces. While it is true that during the eighteenth century economic issues such as the control of foreign trade and the prevention of smuggling superseded the question of public peace, it should not be forgotten that at the time of its inception this system of maritime restrictions was aimed primarily at helping to reinforce the Qing's security and creating peace and stability.

Let us first consider the ways in which each country tried to regulate people's entry into and exit from its territory by sea, and their arrival in and departure from its ports. The execution of this task involved controlling the ships, the people on board and the comings and goings of the ships and their complement. With its experience of having fought a protracted war with the Zheng family based in Taiwan, the Qing made it compulsory for all sea-going ships to be registered, to carry several sailing permits issued by local officials when going to sea and to subject themselves at each port to tax collection and a search for contraband.

Large, two-masted vessels were prohibited for a short period after the lifting of the maritime prohibitions in 1684, but this ban was relaxed in tandem with the establishment of regulations on shipbuilding and crew members at the turn of the eighteenth century. Under such regulations, an individual wishing to build a ship had to file applications with the provincial and county offices and then petition the customs house for permission to build a new ship. These applications were to be accompanied by letters of warranty from relatives and neighbors, upon receipt of which a *liaozhao* (permit to purchase shipbuilding materials) would be issued by the officials. Upon the completion of the ship, the would-be ship-owner was required to submit a *baojunbing* (report on the completion of the shipbuilding) and have his ship inspected by the *zhixian* (county magistrate). If the ship passed this inspection, its name and its owner's name would be branded on the ship's body, and a *chuanzhao* or *chuanyin* (certificate of registry) would be issued.

In order for a ship that had been built in this way to set sail, another set of formalities had to be observed. The ship owner was required to file a report with the customs house listing the ship's certificate of registry number and crew members, whose identities would have been checked and confirmed ahead of time, as well as letters of warranty. The owner also had to apply for and obtain as many as four different sailing permits: a *buzhao* issued by the governor, a *sizhao* issued by the provincial financial commissioner, a *xianzhao* issued by the county magistrate and a *tingzhao* issued by the chamber of coastal defense. Then, after receiving these various permits, having the cargo inspected by the coast guard unit stationed at the port and having obtained a certificate of inspection pasted onto the *xianzhao*, the ship would finally be ready to set sail. Entered on the sailing permits were the port(s) of destination and the term of navigation – typically two years in the case of coastal trade and three in the case of offshore trade. The ship was thus prohibited from sailing to ports other than the one(s) specified in the permits and from staying abroad beyond the pre-determined term of navigation.

In order to deal with ships arriving in China from overseas, different ports of entry and entry formalities were specified for different types of ships. Tribute ships from Ryukyu were assigned to enter Fuzhou, Fujian Province, while merchant ships engaged in border trade were allowed to dock at any port under the jurisdiction of the four *haiguan* (customs houses), conducting trade there as long as they followed the expected formalities and paid the specified taxes. Prior to 1757, European ships primarily came to Guangzhou due to factors other than official policy, such as convenience of access, the ease with which one could gather cargo and other conditions applicable to commerce.

However, in 1757 a merchant affiliated with the East India Company called James Flint led a series of British trade voyages to Ningbo in violation of established practice, seeking to expand trade to ports other than Guangzhou. In response to what is now known as the "Flint Incident" or "Flint Affair", in 1757 the Qianlong Emperor issued a well-known decree ordering Guangzhou to become the only port open to commerce with European ships. Furthermore, two years later the *Fangfan Waiyi Guitiao* (Regulation on Foreigners' Activities) was promulgated, which strictly regulated European merchants' freedom of movement and residence in Guangzhou and prohibited foreigners from engaging in maritime ventures aside from border trade and tributary activities. This was the famous regulated trading system that Europeans called the "Canton System", with "Canton" being the European term for Guangdong.

It should be kept in mind, however, that the purpose of this system was simply to confine all European merchant ships arriving in China to

Guangzhou rather than to the doors of Qing China that were "shut" to foreigners. Tribute ships and non-European trade ships continued to visit various other Chinese ports as before, and Chinese maritime merchants were also actively pursuing overseas trade. As a matter of fact, the total amount of trade in Guangzhou rose sharply, more than tripling during the subsequent half century after the 1757 ruling. Although the Qing's trade policy, which was based primarily on a registration and licensing system, undeniably stipulated complicated formalities, it nonetheless allowed enormous latitude on travel and merchants' participation in trade.

## Maritime prohibition systems of Japan, Korea and Ryukyu

In contrast with this latitude, Japan, Korea and Ryukyu strictly restrained the movement of people and goods going in and out of their territories. In particular, the Tokugawa Shogunate of Japan, as discussed previously, put foreign relations under its direct control by implementing what has come to be known as the so-called "seclusion" (*sakoku*) policy in the 1630s. The emphasis of this policy was on the prohibition of overseas travel by Japanese and of their re-entry once they had gone abroad, the outlawing of the practice and teaching of Christianity and a comprehensive enforcement of government-controlled trade. Under this policy, other than ships arriving from Ryukyu and Korea carrying official missions in accordance with diplomatic relations, the only other foreign ships allowed to visit Japan were those belonging to Chinese traders and Dutch vessels. Moreover, a surveillance and warning system was put in place in order to prevent any other foreign ships from approaching Japan.

Chinese and Dutch ships were allowed to enter the port of Nagasaki after undergoing a complicated and strictly implemented procedure that can be roughly summarized as follows. Once *tōmiban* (officials on guard duty) sighted and reported the outline of an approaching ship, a *kenshisen* (inspection official's boat) would set out, commanded by the *kenshi* (official inspector) from the Bugyōsho. They would identify the nationality of the ship by signaling it with cannon-fire and checking the ship's flag against a pictorial index of flags kept by the Bugyōsho. Then the *kenshi*, interpreters and other officials would board the ship and request the presentation of documents, including the list of crew members and passengers and the cargo manifest, before translating and inspecting these documents. Only after passing this strict inspection would the ship be allowed to take up its moorings or its crew to disembark. Furthermore, as each foreign ship entered the port, an intelligence report was compiled and submitted to the Nagasaki Bugyōsho based on information provided by the ship's captain – called either an "*Oranda fūsetsu gaki*" (information submitted by a Dutch captain)[5] or a "*Tōsen fūsetsu gaki*" (information submitted by a Chinese captain)[6].

As for ships within Japan, the large ship confiscation order[7] was issued in the early years of the Tokugawa Shogunate and applied throughout the country by the promulgation of the *Buke Shohatto* (Regulations for Military Houses) in 1635, which banned the building of large vessels of 500 *koku* or more. The primary purpose of this restriction was not the prohibition of overseas travel, but rather to hinder the military potential of *daimyōs*, especially the maritime military power of those in Western Japan. For this reason, the ban was relaxed in 1683 to exempt merchant ships, and ocean-going Chinese-style junk ships that were of a completely different structure from Japanese-style ships had always been exempt from the regulation. Thus, it seems that "seclusion" was enforced not through restrictions on ships per se, but rather by limiting the movements of human beings.

Korea, with bitter memories of having been plagued by the Wokou, also implemented a maritime prohibition policy to maintain public peace along its coast. This policy pivoted around the prohibition of Korean ships from making distant voyages, the forced displacement of island residents and controls and restraints on foreign trade. These restrictions sought to sever contact between armed maritime groups and coastal residents, and to prevent these armed groups from using the islands as bases. What was most

---

5 Reports on overseas information and intelligence were garnered each year from Dutch ships. The Nagasaki Dutch interpreters drew up the reports from interviews with the head of the trading house and sent them to the *rōjū* (senior councilor).

6 Reports on overseas information and intelligence that were gleaned each year from Chinese merchant ships that arrived at Nagasaki. The Nagasaki Chinese interpreters drew up the reports from interviews with or documents from Chinese merchants on the docked ships and sent them to the *rōjū*.

7 A large ship confiscation order was passed down with reference to *daimyōs* in Western Japan in 1609, under which large ships of 500 *koku* or more, irrespective of whether they were military or merchant vessels, were confiscated and banned. However, this was not applied to junk-type ships or ocean-going vessels, which could not be converted into warships.

characteristic about the Korean policy was that the ban on ocean voyages applied not only to private ships but also to military vessels. Consequently, the only Korean ships allowed to set sail beyond the coast were those attached to the diplomatic missions from Busan, the only port open to the outside world, which dispatched ships for the Tsūshinshi (Kr. Tongsinsa; Goodwill Missions) and *yakukanshi* (Kr. *yeokgwansa*; Japanese-language interpreters officially dispatched by Korea to Tsushima).

Ryukyu, surrounded on all sides by the ocean, also adopted this governmental approach of prohibiting its people from traveling abroad and of putting foreign trade under its strict control. With the exception of ships officially dispatched by the Ryukyu Kingdom's government in Shuri to Qing China, such as *shinkō-sen* (tributary ships) and *sekkō-sen* (a ship for welcoming back a tribute voyage to the Qing), vessels were banned from making voyages abroad. The government also regulated intra-regional transport connecting the islands scattered in its territorial waters of the East China Sea. Most of this was implemented by the Mono Bugyō, of the royal office in charge of finance, supplies and industry. A sub-section of the Kyūchihō (Department of Land Control) division was the Funateza, which oversaw the registration of ships, the management of ship fittings, the issuance of sailing permits and the inspection of voyage records. The

**Figure 23: Dutch ship at shore in Nagasaki Bay**

Source: *Tōkan Zu Rankan Zu Emaki* (Scroll Painting of Chinese and Dutch Trading Houses), Nagasaki Museum of History and Culture.

Yōihō (Department of Provisions), also under the jurisdiction of the Mono Bugyō, housed the Yama bugyō (Forest Administrator), which managed the felling of huge trees for use in building ships. Furthermore, the kingdom's government strictly regulated the fishing activities of ordinary people in the hopes of stimulating agricultural production. Thus, despite being surrounded on all sides by the ocean, early modern Ryukyu was by no means a "maritime state" that utilized foreign trade or the fishing industry.

## Reorganizing maritime groups and improving coastal defense

Generally speaking, these land-based early modern states regarded the ocean as something about which they had to remain vigilant. Their most pressing peace and security concern was to dissolve and reorganize the autonomous maritime groups that had run rampant in the past, as well as to prevent the emergence of any new threats.

Over the course of their conquest, the Qing incorporated the armed groups that had surrendered to the Eight Banners into its own military forces. It treated armed maritime groups who surrendered equally and used them in their navy, enabling it to build up its military capability on land and at sea. In the battle with the Taiwan-based Zheng family in the second half of the seventeenth century, the Qing used former Zheng forces in its navy as soon as they had surrendered, putting them on the front-line in assaults on Taiwan. Shi Lang (1621–1696), the admiral who led the ocean-crossing operation to Taiwan against the Zheng forces as the commander of the naval fleet in Fujian, was a native of Jinjiang in Fujian and formerly a general who had served under Zheng Chenggong. However, he had defected to the Qing after internal strife within the Zheng camp.

By contrast, in Japan, the promulgation of the Kaizoku Torishimari-rei (Order for the Prohibition of Pirates) by the Toyotomi regime denied maritime groups the freedom to act independently. Unlike preceding authorities, the Toyotomi and Tokugawa regimes, with their overwhelming military and financial capabilities, managed to contain the "pirates" who had traversed the seas in the past.

The centralizing government of Japan did not opt to incorporate these naval groups into their navy, but instead pursued a policy of integrating them into the shogunal system. The "pirates" were either allowed to continue to exist as naval groups but on a drastically reduced scale, or they were to move onshore and become lords. Thus, the infamous Murakami sea lords of the Seto Inland Sea gave up their independence and became vassals of the Mōri family, an influential *daimyō*. As the Noshima-Murakami family, they served as ship administrators in charge of operating the *gozabune* (ships for the exclusive use of the *daimyōs*) and the ships of the Korean emissaries. The Kuki family[8], which had led the Shima sea lords in Shima (in present-day Mie Prefecture), was forcibly relocated to the inland domain of Settsu-Sanda (in present-day Hyōgo Prefecture). Both the Matsura family in Hirado[9], Nagasaki, and the Kurushima-Murakami family[10] in the Seto Inland Sea had no other option but to move onshore and become *daimyōs*. Thus, the autonomous naval groups that had moved freely among various parts of the coastal waters on the outskirts of the East China Sea in the preceding era were defanged, domesticated and reduced to vehicles for maintaining "compartmentalization" at sea.

In addition to developing a coastal defense system to prevent the emergence of new maritime groups, each government also built up its defense against invasions by enemies from the sea. The Qing reinforced its sea defenses by stationing the Eight Banners Garrison at a newly established naval garrison (*shuishiying*) and by deploying warships at various points along its coasts in order to prevent inflows of people or goods and the rise of destabilizing factors, be they external maritime forces or anti-Qing forces within the country. Various types and quantities of goods were prohibited on merchant and fishing ships, such

---

8  The Kuki family was a band of the *Kumano-suigun* (Kumano navy) based in Shima and Toba that wielded power and influence in the Sengoku period. Acquiescing to Oda Nobunaga and Toyotomi Hideyoshi, they became *daimyō* of the inland domain of Settsu-Sanda and Tanba-Ayabe (in present-day Hyogo and Kyoto Prefectures) after the Battle of Sekigahara.

9  The Matsura family was a warrior group that held territory in the Matsura region of Hizen (present-day Nagasaki Prefecture), becoming prosperous through overseas trade in the sixteenth century. Their path to power and prosperity was stymied by the closure and relocation of the British and Dutch trading factories, but they achieved fame in the cultural sphere through, among others, the Chinshin-style Tea Ceremony and the *Kassiyawa* essays of Matsura Seizan (1760–1841). The *Tōsennozu* (Illustrations of Chinese Ships) were also passed down through the Matsura family of Hirado.

10 The Kurushima-Murakami family, one of the three-island Murakami families, was based on Kurushima Island, Iyo (present-day Ehime Prefecture). Parting company with the Murakami family of Noshima Island, they sided with Oda Nobunaga. After the Battle of Sekigahara they became *daimyō* of the inland domain of Bungo-Mori (in present-day Oita Prefecture).

as firearms, mineral ores like gold, silver, copper, sulfur and potassium nitrate, or food in excess of the crew's rations. These measures were introduced as a precaution against the possibility that these items would end up in the hands of anti-Qing forces at sea or overseas, and thereby supply them with financial resources, military equipment or provisions. The policymakers' primary concern was thus to maintain the peace.

In the case of the maritime prohibition order in the Southern Sea (Nan'yang Haijin Ling), implemented between 1717 and 1727, the primary motive was to aid the war effort against the Dzungars on the northwestern front by removing destabilizing factors in other parts of the Qing Empire. Specifically, the overseas Chinese population had boomed in the South China Sea area, and Zhu Yigui led a rebellion in Taiwan against the central government in 1721[11]. This was a crucial reminder for the Qing, a continental power, to remain attentive to the developments both on land and at sea.

The Tokugawa Shogunate in Japan, as previously noted, took steps to suppress naval groups within the country as potential threats to peace. At the same time, as a means of dealing with foreign ships seeking entry into Japan, the government established a surveillance and warning network and consolidated a system for *daimyōs* in times of emergency. This coastal defense system was established in the 1630s and 1640s during the enactment of the prohibition on Portuguese ships arriving at Japanese ports. The law ordered *daimyōs* to construct guard posts and specified the procedures they should follow to raise the alarm and mobilize defense forces. It also instructed them to adopt and execute a security system in times of peace, and to establish a chain of command for use in an emergency. In dealing with the abundance of Chinese merchant ships in Japan's coastal waters, the Tokugawa Shogunate, in addition to promulgating the Shōtoku Shinrei, constructed a policy to forcibly repel Chinese ships engaged in private trade without *shinpai* (trade permits) by labeling them as "pirates".

Surrounded on all sides by the ocean, Ryukyu was also charged with the task of surveilling foreign ships as part of the Tokugawa Shogunate's foreign policy. A system that virtually mobilized the kingdom's entire

---

11 This was a rebellion that occurred in Taiwan during the Qing era, instigated by Zhu Yigui, a migrant originally from Fujian Province. The rebellion occupied almost all of Taiwan for a time, but was eventually put down by 1723.

government and the entire population from the King down to common people (*hyakushō*)[12] was established in order to cope with any and all foreign ships that might sail to Ryukyu or drift onto its shores. In preparation for the arrival of foreign ships and castaways, reference materials such as *Gojōmoku* (directives concerning the procedures to be followed in the case where a foreign ship arrives or drifts ashore)[13], *Ikokusen Ezu* (drawings of foreign ships) and *Ikokusen Hatajirushi Ezu* (drawings of flags carried by foreign ships) were distributed among residents of *jikata* (countryside) or rural areas. Under the direction of *zaiban* (naval defense officials), who were dispatched from the capital, Shuri, to the countryside on a rotational shift, some of the local officials of the peasant class were organized into *ikoku-hō* (officials in charge of foreigners) and *tōme-ban* (officials on guard duty). If a foreign ship was cast ashore or put in at a port, the news was supposed to be immediately reported to the kingdom's government by relay from one small-sized communication boat called "*hisen*" to another, or by signal fires. Thus, a surveillance and warning system against foreign ships was in place in Ryukyu that was just as comprehensive as that of Japan.

The coastal defense measures adopted by the early modern states did not require each regional power to build its own navy and go to sea. They instead deployed onshore military capability and mounted solid coastal defenses, removing the space for naval groups to secure a foothold on "state" territory. From this perspective, the way the ocean was administered in the eighteenth century was quite different from the modern method of maritime control that emphasizes maintaining control over the sea surface (or territorial waters) through the deployment of an ocean-going navy. The early modern method of maritime control seems to have centered upon restricting the cross-border movement of human beings through a system that included regulating entry into and exit from a country, trade regulation and a coastal defense system.

---

12 *Hyakushō* was the ruled class in the Ryukyu class system. This term refers to the populace in general, including not only peasant farmers but also people engaged in commerce and industry. The ruling or aristocratic class were known as *samurē*, but in contrast to the Japanese samurai, who were warriors, these were civil functionaries.
13 A directive consisting of fifteen clauses that set out the procedures to be followed if a foreign ship arrived or drifted ashore. This was an official notification delivered to the Shuri royal government from Satsuma in 1704, and formed the dominant principle for the handling of ships cast ashore in the Ryukyu Islands until the 1840s.

Furthermore, one feature shared by the coastal defense measures adopted by these states was that instead of being managed by private naval groups, the decision-making process and responsive military capability were virtually monopolized by entities like the Eight Banners in the case of the Qing Empire and by the shogunate and *daimyōs* in the case of Japan. However, these arrangements for coastal defense began to change in the second half of the eighteenth century.

## Foreign settlements and foreign residents

Each government also restricted the behavior and rights of foreign visitors by confining them to designated areas and facilities at the ports of entry assigned to foreign ships. Even though the features of these foreign residential settlements varied depending on the situations peculiar to each, they did share many characteristics. The most noteworthy of these is perhaps the fact that foreigners were segregated as a general rule from the residential quarters of the indigenous population.

## Qing China

The best-known foreign settlement in Qing China was established in Guangzhou specifically for the confinement of Europeans. Called *yiguan* (foreign barbarians' residences) by the Chinese and a "factory" by the British, it was established along the Zhujiang River outside Guangzhou's city wall and was operated in tandem with the Portuguese settlement established at the river's estuary in Macao. At first, it was simply designated as a residential quarter for foreigners, and with few restrictions imposed upon the activities of its residents, foreigners were free to move in and out of the city. However, beginning with the reign of the Yongzheng Emperor, the fifth Qing Emperor (r. 1722–1735), increasingly strict regulations were imposed on the activities of foreigners staying in the factory. These culminated in the promulgation in 1759 of the *Fangfan Wayyi Guitao*, which stipulated that foreigners would only be allowed to stay in the settlement for one trade season at a time; upon the conclusion of the trading season they would have to return to Macao and stay there until the following year. As a general rule, foreigners would not be allowed either to stay in Guangzhou for an extended period, leave the area specified by the government or move freely within the city. While in

Guangzhou, they were allowed to deal only with licensed merchants, and were prohibited from independently employing local residents.

It should be pointed out, however, that there was nothing peculiar about the establishment of a district allocated for the confinement of foreigners at the port designated for foreign ships. This practice occurred at other ports and for other groups, such as in Fuzhou with the establishment of the Rouyuan Station and in a different region of Guangzhou with the Huaiyuan Station. The Rouyuan Station was located outside the gate of the city wall in the southeastern area of Fuzhou and was commonly known as the *Liuqiu guan* (Ryukyuan house), because it was used exclusively by visitors from Ryukyu. Occupying a total area of approximately 5,600 square meters and surrounded by a clay wall, the compound was divided into two areas: the main gate facing the outside world, and the second or inner gate of the inner compound. The space between the main gate and the inner gate was used by the staff of Qing local officials, and it was here that buildings such as

### Figure 24: Ryukyuan house in Fuzhou
Source: *Tobin Kōro Zu* (Sea-lane from Naha to Fuzhou), Okinawa Prefectural Museum and Art Museum.

the gatehouse, manned by *bamenguan* (gatekeepers), and the offices of the *hekou tongshi* (Chinese interpreters) were located. The inner compound was used primarily by visitors from Ryukyu, where there were facilities such as the main hall for clerical work and lodging houses. The area farthest from the inner gate was allocated for enshrining the Chinese goddess of the sea (Cn. Tianhou, Mazu), the Earth deity and the mortuary tablets of Ryukyuans who had died while in China. However, the tombs of these Ryukyuans were located outside of the city wall.

Since the Rouyuan Station was a Qing government establishment, its buildings were completely Chinese architecturally and the station was administered by a Fuzhou provincial government official called *haifang tongzhi* (the sub-prefect of Fuzhou). With Qing gatekeepers scrutinizing anyone entering or leaving the settlement, the Ryukyuans were prohibited from leaving the settlement at night or from staying overnight in other lodgings. During the daytime, however, their behavior was not severely restricted, and they could visit various areas inside and outside the city walls or make day trips to nearby hot-spring resorts and scenic areas. As a general rule, Ryukyuans residing in the compound were limited to members of the official tribute missions dispatched by the Ryukyuan government, whose expenses were paid for by the Qing government as a special favor. The number of Ryukyuans staying in the compound ranged from a little over a dozen to more than 200, depending on the number of Ryukyuan ships in the harbor at any particular point in time. A mission of around twenty members, including chief and deputy delegates, was expected to travel once per year by land to pay tribute to the Qing court in Beijing, while the remaining members of the mission carried out trade and other activities in Fuzhou. Thus, the Rouyuan Station was not only a base for the Ryukyuan tributary mission's activities in Qing China, but also the point of departure and the terminal for the extensive tributary activities that extended from Fuzhou to Beijing.

The Huaiyuan Station in Guangzhou was located at Xiguan, southwest of the city center outside the city wall. It was originally established in the early years of the Ming, but largely fell out of use by the early seventeenth century. However, Huaiyuan Station was reestablished as a compound in 1653 when permission was granted for Siam and the Netherlands to send tributary missions. It was used mainly to accommodate the Siamese tributary missions, and according to early nineteenth century European

3.3: Compression and Concentration of Interactions and Residences    287

records, the gate to the station had "*Xianluoguo Gongguan*" (Siamese tribute envoy's residence) inscribed upon it. A graveyard for deceased Siamese was attached to the station, and there was a Tianhou temple nearby. Aside from high-ranking delegates, the crew from these tributary ships anchored and resided in Huangpu, a port outside Guangzhou.

## Japan

The foreign settlement in Japan specifically established for the confinement of Europeans was the fan-shaped, artificial island of Dejima in Nagasaki. Built by reclaiming land from the sandy coast, the island's original purpose

**Figure 25: Dejima of Nagasaki**
Source: *Oranda Yashiki no Zu* (Picture of the Dutch Trading House), Historiographical Institute, the University of Tokyo.

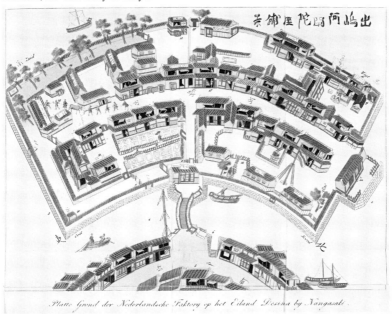

was to accommodate Portuguese merchants. However, following the ban on the Portuguese immediately after its construction, Dejima was instead used to house the Dutch trading post, which was transferred from the port of Hirado (also in present-day Nagasaki Prefecture) in 1641. The man-made island, with a total area of approximately 13,100 square meters, was a single structure on which shogunal administrative facilities and various Dutch facilities and warehouses existed side by side. Surrounded by a fence on top of a stone wall that rose from foundations on the sea bed, the island was connected to the mainland by only a small bridge.

A group of twenty-five wealthy merchants from Nagasaki, Kyoto, Osaka, Sakai, Hakata and other cities, who were collectively known as "Dejima Chōnin" (commoners of Dejima), jointly financed the cost of the construction of the island and its buildings. The VOC employees were not given any right to choose or purchase plots of land or structures on the island but had to be content with their status as tenants paying rent to these merchants. The Dejima Chōnin, in their capacity as landlords of the residences, warehouses and other facilities on the island, were responsible for building maintenance and for controlling the behavior of the residents of the Dutch trading post (*factorij*). The rights and responsibilities of the Dejima Chōnin were treated similarly to *kabu* (trading rights), and so were transferable through either commercial transactions or inheritance.

During the eighteenth century, two Dutch vessels from Batavia (present-day Jakarta, Indonesia) were usually allowed to trade at Nagasaki each year. They generally entered the port of Nagasaki around June or July under the lunar calendar after stopping at the port of Batavia. Around ten VOC personnel stayed on Dejima. In command was the chief or *kapitan*, a term derived from the Portuguese *capitão*, showing that Portuguese influence continued after their expulsion. In his absence, the factory was led by the *feitor* or vice-chief, a term also based on a Portuguese word. Below these positions were a warehouse custodian, a secretary, an assistant to the captain, a doctor and a cook. Even while VOC ships were moored in the harbor, those staying on Dejima never totaled more than a few dozen, with most of the crew members remaining on board the ship. While VOC personnel were forbidden from leaving Dejima, Japanese also had to obtain permission to visit the island and unauthorized entry was strictly prohibited. Even Japanese workers whose services were required on the island, such as craftsmen and manual laborers, had to obtain and present special wooden passes issued by the Dejima Otona called "*monkan*" in order to enter.

In contrast, Chinese maritime merchants were initially allowed to reside freely in the city and were accommodated in various *yado-machi* (lodging towns). Over the course of the seventeenth century however, smuggling between Chinese merchants and Japanese townspeople became a growing issue, and Japanese authorities came to the conclusion that a designated residence might aid in controlling this trend. Thus, they established and confined Chinese merchants in the Tōjin-yashiki (Chinese compound) on the outskirts of the city in 1689. In 1698, a land reclamation project began in front of the compound to build a storage yard for the cargo unloaded from Chinese ships that was connected by a bridge to the Chinese compound. The city undertook the construction of these facilities by borrowing public funds, which it paid back using the rent received from the Chinese merchants for using the yard. After having completely paid off the loan, this rent was added to the town's revenue.

At first, the total area of the Tōjin-yashiki was approximately 26,400 square meters, but in 1760 it was expanded to approximately 31,000 square meters. The compound was heavily guarded, with the entire site encircled by a roofed fence made of clay and tiles and a moat with a bamboo fence built along its outer bank. There were also several sentry stations placed outside the bamboo fence. The inside of the compound was

**Figure 26: Tōjin-yashiki (Chinese compound)**
Source: *Tōkan Zu Rankan Zu Emaki* (Scroll Painting of Chinese and Dutch Trading Houses), Nagasaki Museum of History and Culture.

divided into two spaces by a main gate and a secondary gate. In between the two gates was a public space for the stationing of Japanese officials and for the carrying out of trade, while the space behind the secondary gate constituted the residential quarters of the Chinese.

Unlike Dejima, which was primarily established as part of the effort to expel Christian influences, the Tōjin-yashiki was built with the objective of preventing smuggling and other forms of illicit trade. It was also expected, however, to aid in preventing the import of Christian ideas via Qing China. As a general rule, all Chinese merchants were to stay in the compound during their visits to Nagasaki. Just like the employees of the VOC on Dejima, they were also prohibited from exiting the compound and from bringing Chinese women with them when arriving in Japan. All Japanese persons required a permit to enter the Tōjin-yashiki, and even officials could not step inside the secondary gate without permission. Until the end of the 1730s, the compound was extremely crowded, with the population of Chinese residents peaking somewhere between 1,000 and 2,000. Subsequently, the population stabilized as the number of Chinese ships visiting Nagasaki began to decline.

In Satsuma, the domain through which Ryukyu maintained relations with the Tokugawa Shogunate, there was a facility called the "Kagoshima Ryukyukan" (Ryukyuan visiting station in Kagoshima), which temporarily accommodated official envoys and students who had been dispatched from the kingdom. Originally called the "Ryukyu kariya" or "Ryū-kariya" and located to the southeast of Kagoshima Castle (Tsurumaru Castle), it was relocated to the north of the castle around the end of the seventeenth century, and in 1784 was renamed the "Ryukyukan". At first, it also served as a residence for hostages taken from Ryukyu after Satsuma's invasion of the island kingdom, but around the mid-seventeenth century, it became a trading base that specialized in Chinese goods imported via Ryukyu and sugar. Satsuma Domain sentries kept a close watch to ensure that no unauthorized persons entered or left the compound.

## Korea

Early modern Korea's gateways for foreign relations were basically limited to Uiju in the northwest (Junggang and Chaekmun on the way to Uiju), Gyeongwon and Hoeryeong in the northeast and Busan in the southeast.

*3.3: Compression and Concentration of Interactions and Residences*

Since Korea's diplomatic and economic relations with the Qing Empire were carried out via land, the only potential routes that passed through the sea were those between Japan-via-Tsushima and Korea based in the city of Busan.

**Figure 27: The landscape of Choryang Waegwan (Japan House) in Busan**

Source: *Waegwan-do* (Painting of Japan House), National Museum of Korea.

The facility in Busan for accommodating the Japanese was called the Waegwan (Jp. Wakan; Japan House). Being Japanese did not qualify someone to reside in the Waegwan: only those who received official orders or permits from the Tsushima Domain were accommodated, and no women were permitted entry. After the Japan–Korea rapprochement at the beginning of the seventeenth century, the Waegwan was originally established in Dumopo. Eventually, it became too small and inconvenient to meet Japan's diplomatic needs, and so the facility was relocated in 1678 to a southern suburb of Busan called "Choryang". The new compound had a total area as large as 330,000 square meters, which was ten times the size of the compound in Dumopo, approximately twenty-five times the size of Dejima and nearly sixty times larger than the Rouyuan Station (Ryukyuan house) in Fuzhou. A slight ridge called "Yongdusan" rose at the center of the extensive site, bifurcating the compound into eastern and western halves. Facing the sea on its eastern and southern fronts, the compound was surrounded by a fence approximately two meters in height. A total of six guard stations were placed along the fence, and these were manned by Korean guards.

The guard gate on the east side was typically used for entry into and exit from the Japan House. In between the guard gate and the outer gate were various buildings administered by the Korean authorities, including the guest-house, the reception office for envoys and an interpreters' office, in which official ceremonies and formal banquets were held. Inside the Japanese compound proper, there was the *gaesi dacheong* (Jp. *kaishi daichō*) where trade was carried out, as well as a host of buildings, including residential halls, a Buddhist temple, various stores, a dock and warehouses. The all-male population is estimated to have remained at around 500 people, which was equivalent to approximately one-twentieth of the adult male population of Tsushima at that time.

Residents were permitted to exit the inner compound only for limited purposes, such as to take a stroll near the Waegwan, visit Korean facilities between the guard gate and the outer gate or visit the tombs at the old Dumopo Waegwan. It is therefore possible that the Waegwan was virtually the only point of exchange or contact between Japan and Korea during the eighteenth century. Except for officials involved in its administration, only a very small number of Koreans, such as the privileged Dongrae merchants[14], were allowed to visit the Waegwan. Yet cases of smuggling and adultery between Japanese and Koreans occurred so frequently that in 1709 a new outer gate was built with a stone wall on either side. From the living costs of the residents of the Waegwan to those related to maintaining the compound, including those for building new facilities such as this outer gate, the Waegwan's expenses were generally borne by the Korean government and constituted a heavily strain on its fiscal resources.

Because all the states restricted the entry of foreign women, it is also important to keep in mind that the vast majority of foreigners residing in these foreign settlements were men. Governments were also cautious about contact between foreign men and their own countrywomen. As one might expect, problems or affairs with women were common among such predominantly male societies, but the manner in which the authorities handled these issues varied significantly. In Korea, where societal norms concerning male-female relationships were extremely strict, relationships between Japanese men and Korean women were totally prohibited within the Waegwan. Even *kiisen* (female entertainers) were banned from entering the compound, and a legal principle prescribed that all the parties involved in a case of adultery – the man and woman involved in the affair, as well as any go-between – should be punished by death. Since no such judicial culture existed in Japan, the Tsushima Domain was always thought by Korean authorities to be sluggish and lax in dealing with Japanese men suspected of having committed adultery. This difference in attitude was often the cause of Japan–Korea discord in the eighteenth century. In contrast, in Nagasaki Japanese prostitutes with special permits were authorized to visit the Dutch and Chinese foreign settlements. In Ryukyu, a partial and relaxed ban on relationships between foreign males and indigenous females was at work in theory, but in practice, such relations were virtually unregulated. Qing China did not impose any restrictions on relationships between men and women.

As for the question of mixed-race children born out of such relationships, in Nagasaki there was a common acceptance that the prostitutes who visited

---

14 These were merchants with special trade privileges who had permission to engage in trade with Japan. The core of these merchants was a group known as the "*tojung*". They engaged in transactions by receiving a wooden ID tag from the Dongrae Office for entering and leaving the Waegwan.

Dejima and the Tōjin-yashiki might became pregnant. However, since the Japanese authorities prohibited their fathers from taking the children out of the country, these mixed-race children lived their entire lives as Japanese.

## Castaways and their repatriation system

Regarding the emigration controls and regulations implemented by the early modern states, each government in the East China Sea focused on restricting the movements of people and goods into and out of its own territory more strictly than those into or out of the territory of other countries. Each state also took stringent measures to ban or restrain foreigners from moving into the country and from living freely among its people. The states considered maintaining the public peace in their domain as their most important priority, even in decisions on foreign affairs. As a result, those who left the country willingly would likely never be protected by their government nor even be allowed to return home again. A typical example of this in Japan was the provision of the so-called "seclusion" edict that denied re-entry to any Japanese subject who had left the country. Another example was the decision of the Qing Empire regarding the 1740 Batavia Massacre[15], a pogrom against Han Chinese living in the port of Batavia. On that occasion, the government concluded that the Chinese living in Batavia were no longer subjects of the Qing, and therefore did nothing to protect the remaining Chinese there or to take retaliatory measures.

In contrast, when dealing with castaways who drifted to shore in a foreign country as the result of an unexpected maritime accident, the countries surrounding the East China Sea came to adopt a common practice of rescuing and protecting them instead of regarding them as having "violated the established rule of the state". This eighteenth-century practice of mutual repatriation established among neighboring countries around the East China Sea is quite remarkable.

---

15 The 1740 Batavia Massacre was an incident sparked by a clash between the Dutch and resident Chinese in Batavia, the Dutch base in Java. More than ten thousand Han-Chinese were massacred. The background to the incident was said to have been a deterioration in public order and concerns over a possible uprising due to a rapid increase in the Chinese population.

## 3.3: Compression and Concentration of Interactions and Residences 295

In Qing China, it was customary for local government officials to rescue and protect foreign castaways, receiving instructions from the central government and referring to precedent to accomplish this task. However, there were no uniform guidelines applicable across the country. In 1737, therefore, the Qianlong Emperor issued an edict explicitly making it state policy to "treat all foreign castaways with an attitude of benevolence and compassion, provide them with food and clothing and help them repair their ships and return home". Subsequently, this policy was uniformly instituted throughout China. The guidelines dictated as follows: that the local government office with jurisdiction over the area in which the foreign ship had drifted ashore should provide the castaways with food and clothing and help them repair their ship, all at government expense; that if the cargo and/or ship had been too seriously damaged to be used any longer it might be sold off; that the cargo should be exempted from taxation as a general rule; and that in cases where the castaways were unable to return home on their own due to damage to their ship or other factors, they should be repatriated via a tribute mission from their home country or via a private merchant ship from any third country with which their home country had relations. As for Japanese castaways, an established practice stipulated that they should be temporarily transferred to Zhapu, the base for trade with Japan, where they would be repatriated by putting them aboard a ship bound for Japan. It was thanks to this practice that Denbē and his crew discussed at the beginning of Part 3 were rescued, protected and repatriated. On the other hand, Ryukyuan castaways were transferred to Fuzhou for accommodation in the Rouyuan Station until they were sent home aboard a Ryukyuan official ship visiting Qing China.

In Japan, by contrast, foreign castaways who washed ashore in various parts of the country were first subjected to a strict interrogation process to determine whether they were Christians or not. By convention, those who were discovered to be Christian were immediately arrested and transferred to Nagasaki, while those who were found to be non-Christian were rescued, taken into protective custody, and then also transferred to Nagasaki. Chinese castaways in Japan who proved to be non-Christian were then repatriated to Qing China aboard a Chinese trading ship visiting Nagasaki, while those from Korea and Ryukyu were left to the care of the Sō family or the Shimazu family, the lords of the domains with whom Korea and Ryukyu respectively had diplomatic relations. Generally, the expenses for rescuing and taking care of the foreign castaways were borne locally in the domains where they were cast ashore, and each *daimyō* family had rules of its own that stipulated the procedures for dealing with them. This system of interrogating castaways before repatriating them, most importantly about their faith, was inextricably linked to Japan's coastal defense system.

At the beginning of the early modern era, Ryukyu would transfer foreign castaways rescued in the kingdom to the Satsuma Domain for repatriation. However, after the lifting of the maritime prohibition system in 1684 and the accompanying summons by the Qing Empire to its tribute countries requesting their favor in rescuing and repatriating Qing merchants who might be washed onto their shores, Ryukyu began to repatriate Chinese castaways directly to the Qing. More specifically, a set of directives on the procedures to be followed in dealing with foreign castaways, called "*Gojōmoku*", was issued from Satsuma in 1704, which became the standard for dealing with foreign castaways in Ryukyu. The kingdom's government established a system of rescuing and repatriating foreign castaways by promulgating within the country a set of rules that closely followed the standards set in the *Gojōmoku*.

In Ryukyu as well, castaways were rigorously screened to see whether they were Kirishitan or not, and those who were identified as such were arrested and transferred to Satsuma. Any castaways found to be non-Kirishitan and able to return home on their own were provided with food, water and help in repairing their ships, before being allowed to set sail for their home country. Those unable to return home on their own ships were transferred to Tomari Village (now part of the City of Naha) and then sent home aboard ships bound for Qing China. The expenses for rescuing and taking care of the castaways were borne by the kingdom's government, but any labor was supplied by the localities where they were washed ashore. Even though Ryukyu's system of repatriation differed somewhat from that of Japan, it still treated castaways in compliance with the Tokugawa Shogunate's policy on foreign relations, which centered on the prohibition of Christianity and strict regulations concerning trade.

In Korea, *Waehak yeokgwan* (official Japanese-language interpreters) were stationed in strategic places to deal with castaways from Japan: Busan and Tongyeong (later Geojedo) in Kyongsang-do, and Jwasuyeong, Usuyeoung and Jeju-do in Jeolla-do. When Japanese drifted ashore, these interpreters questioned them about themselves and the circumstances that had led to their shipwreck. They then reported their findings to the central government. In dealing with castaways from Ryukyu, attempts could be made to communicate with them only by means of writing and gesturing, because no interpreters versed in the Ryukyuan language were available in Korea. After this questioning, local officials in each locality managed the rescue and transferral of the castaways after receiving instructions from the central government. Castaways from Japan were transferred to the Waegwan in Busan, while those from Ryukyu were sent to Qing China.

During the eighteenth century, the Qing functioned as a trans-shipment base for persons who had become castaways in the East and South China Seas. Any two countries in the region without direct channels of contact between them, such as Ryukyu and Korea, or Korea and Vietnam, were able to repatriate castaways to each other indirectly through Qing China, which had relations with all of these countries. Furthermore, as is evident from the episode Magotarō described at the outset of Part 3, castaways who had drifted to Southeast Asia from the East China Sea region were sometimes repatriated to their home countries by transferral to Qing China on board Chinese trading ships, or to Japan on board private ships bound for Nagasaki.

On the other hand, there were cases in which traders and their ships used this repatriation system to their own advantage, disguising themselves as castaways and claiming to have suffered a shipwreck before intentionally sailing close to the shore to conduct smuggling operations. Especially in the waters near Kyushu and San'in in Japan, Chinese merchant ships that had not qualified for the annual trade quota appeared frequently under the guise of having drifted or been washed ashore, and official orders to repel these ships were issued from time to time.

To sum up, in the region surrounding the East China Sea in the eighteenth century, freedom of movement was limited to those who were permitted to do so by the public authorities: members of diplomatic envoys, traders and castaways who were being repatriated. At the same time, the places for contact and interaction with "foreigners" were restricted to designated "foreign settlements". The traffic on the sea was stable and brisk, but unlike the state of affairs prevailing in the periods covered in Parts 1 and 2, even international ports, to varying extents, were not hospitable to foreigners' living among the native population, let alone settling in the town permanently. The trans-oceanic worlds of *tōbō* (residential areas of

Tang people – *Tōjin* – spread around the East China Sea) and the Wokou that had once thrived were no longer to be found. A line was clearly drawn to differentiate between the "inside" and the "outside" of groups and territories, and the chances of accidentally coming into contact with foreigners or goods of foreign origin were extremely limited.

This does not mean, however, that trans-oceanic intercourse was blocked. On the contrary, not only in the South China Sea, where restrictions had been lenient, but also in the East China Sea, goods transported by people traversing these waters continued to grow both in volume and diversity. These goods came to be disseminated to various localities and took root in each society. Let us turn to the way developments such as these unfolded.

# 3.4: Trans-Oceanic Movements of Goods and Information

## New-look maritime interactions

In the winter of 1715, the play *Kokusen'ya Kassen* (Battles of Koxinga) by the famous playwright of *jōruri* and *kabuki* Chikamatsu Monzaemon[1] (1653–1724), began its run at the *jōruri* puppet theater Takemoto-za near Ebisubashi Bridge over the Dōtonbori Canal in Osaka. The play follows the adventures of Watōnai, modeled after the historical figure Zheng Chenggong. Born to a Japanese mother and a Han Chinese father, the play dramatizes his fight against the *Dattans* (Tartars), i.e. the Manchus, in an attempt to restore the Ming Dynasty. The play was so successful that it ran for an exceptionally long season of seventeen months.

The fact that this production enjoyed such popularity in Japan in the early eighteenth century reveals another facet to this era in which the majority of Japanese were restricted from engaging in trans-oceanic human interactions. After the period covered in Part 2, when the seas were an arena of competition over influence and territory, came the era of maritime prohibitions, characterized by Japan's so-called "*sakoku*" (seclusion) policy and the Qing's Qian Jie Ling (Great Clearance). During this time, opportunities and places for direct interaction with peoples from across the seas were gradually restricted. Chinese craftsmen no longer participated in major construction projects like Oda Nobunaga's Azuchi Castle or the large Buddha statue at Hōkōji Temple commissioned by Toyotomi

---

1 Chikamatsu Monzaemon was a *jōruri* and *kabuki* playwright active in Kyoto and Osaka. Born into a *samurai* (warrior) family, he threw himself into the world of performing arts, producing many popular plays, including what were then contemporary plays such as *Sonezaki Shinjū* (The Love Suicides at Sonezaki) and historical dramas such as *Kokusen'ya Kassen* (Battles of Coxinga) as the resident playwright of the Takemotoza theater.

Hideyoshi. Nor could British advisors be found in the court of the shogun as they had been under Tokugawa Ieyasu. Manpukuji Temple at Uji, Kyoto, the head temple of the Ōbaku school of Zen Buddhism, had always invited its head priests in succession from China since its first head priest, Ingen Ryūki[2] (Cn. Yinyuan Longqi, 1592–1673) from Fujian, established the practice. However, this custom ceased following the arrival in 1721 of the last Chinese priest, when Li Wei, the governor of Zhejiang, implemented a measure to intensify restrictions on overseas voyages. Even after these restrictions were relaxed in China, Manpukuji Temple's tradition of inviting Chinese head priests was not restored, and Japanese priests subsequently headed the temple.

At the same time, the promulgation of the Shōtoku Shinrei (New Edict of the Shōtoku Period) in 1715, the same year as the first staging of *Kokusen'ya Kassen*, reveals something important: Chinese trade ships were sailing to Nagasaki in such massive numbers that Japan was hemorrhaging silver and copper, and smuggling in Japan's coastal waters was becoming a serious issue. Although restricted and concentrated in terms of agents and locations, the amount of goods and information moving across the seas through the permitted channels continued to increase. In contrast to the preceding chapters, which have focused on the contraction of the routes for transportation and trade in eighteenth-century maritime East Asia, this chapter centers on the goods and information that people transported through these narrowed routes.

## The cargo of a Chinese shipwreck

At dawn on December 4, 1800, a Chinese trading ship was found to have drifted ashore on the coast of Enshūnada (present-day Shizuoka Prefecture). The ship, the *Wansheng-hao*, had left Zhapu for Nagasaki on November 9 with a crew of eighty-five (eighty-six according to one estimate), including its two captains Liu Ranyi and Wang Qingchuan. A storm caught it on the way to Japan and it drifted along the Pacific coast to Enshūnada. Word of the shipwreck was passed from the local residents to the *daimyō*, the local

---

2 Ingen Ryūki, a native of Fuzhou, Fujian Province, was the founder of Japan's Ōbaku school of Zen Buddhism. Arriving in Japan in 1654 after the fall of the Ming Dynasty, he was granted land for a temple by the Shogun Tokugawa Ietsuna and built the Manpukuji Temple in Uji, Kyoto.

governor and on to the shogunate in Edo, and action was taken to recover the cargo and rescue and question the crew.

What sort of cargo was the *Wansheng-hao* carrying to Nagasaki? Luckily, a list of goods written immediately after the rescue has been preserved. According to this list, the cargo consisted mostly of pharmacopeia, textiles such as silk, cotton and wool, white sugar and crystal sugar. The pharmacopeia was the richest in variety, including chocolate vine, licorice, rhubarb[3], betel leaf, cinnamon, smilax rhizomes, *agastache rugosa*, gambir and *magnolia obovata*. All this came to a total weight of as much as about 69.5 tons.

This amount was dwarfed by that of the sugar, which consisted of about 134 tons of white sugar and 3.1 tons of crystal sugar. While the pharmacopeia, textiles and sugar fell under the category of *jōdaka*, or "basic transactions", the cargo also included special goods such as crystals, seals and sculptures that were marked as "high quality goods" (Jp. *jōyō*, Cn. *shangyong*); though small in quantity, these were likely items ordered specially in Nagasaki, made in China and then shipped to Japan. Also included on the cargo list are books, sappanwood (a raw material for making red dyestuff) and ceremonial goods to be dedicated to mausoleums in the Chinese compound in Nagasaki. Most of the cargo was waterlogged, and the majority of the sugar had dissolved entirely. Goods barely recovered from the water were dried in a heavily guarded makeshift stockyard, and then later transferred to Nagasaki along with the crew members.

No record remains of what became of the recovered cargo in Nagasaki, or if it was ever sold. However, according to information obtained by the Dutch about Chinese trade ships that visited Nagasaki around the same time, the main goods these ships purchased to take home were: *sao-dō* (copper ingots); *tawaramono* (goods in straw bags), such as dried sea cucumber, dried abalone and shark's fin; and *shoshiki* (marine products other than *tawaramono*), such as kelp and dried bonito. After stowing sixty tons of *sao-dō*, which was the maximum export quota set for copper per ship, Chinese vessels would purchase a wide variety of other goods for their return voyages depending on the remaining stowage capacity.

---

3 A species of plant in the family Polygonaceae, the rhizome is prized for its efficacy in controlling intestinal disorders, improving the function of the stomach and increasing appetite. Originating from the Gansu and Qinghai region, along with silk and tea it was known as an important item of commerce in Silk Road trade.

Favored items included marine products, shiitake mushrooms, agar (the raw material for making vegetable gelatin), cockscomb (a medicinal flower), *hoelen* (a mushroom used as a raw material in Chinese medicine), soy sauce, *sake*, lacquerware, earthenware, umbrellas and firewood. Obviously, earthenware and firewood served primarily as ballast.

Based on the cargo of these ships, is it possible to discern the noteworthy features of maritime trade in East Asia in the eighteenth century, as well as trace any changes these features were undergoing?

## East and South China Seas in terms of trade routes

The economies of maritime East Asia in the eighteenth century were sustained by the robust trade within and between the regions surrounding the East China Sea, and by the region- and border-crossing trade focused on the South China Sea. The term "region" here connotes a geographical expanse in which a widespread market is viable while maintaining a certain degree of coherence regarding geographical conditions and economic activities such as production, distribution and consumption. In the Japanese Archipelago and the Korean Peninsula, the control exercised by state powers and the development of commercial and distribution activities had the joint effect of making these regions and their markets virtually overlap with those controlled by the two central governments. This led to the creation of self-contained, nationwide markets in these regions. In Qing China, by contrast, due partly to its immense territory, a single market encompassing the entire country did not emerge. Instead, several regional markets, such as those of the North China, Jiangnan, Fujian and Lingnan regions, coexisted. Moreover, the regional market of Fujian and the markets south of it came to have close links with those in various parts of Southeast Asia across the South China Sea.

The maritime routes in the East China Sea reflected the compartmentalization of the early modern states in the area, and so the cross-border transport network was separated from the network for intra-regional transport in each country in such a way that a foreign ship entering Nagasaki, for instance, was prohibited from sailing on to other domestic ports such as Hakata and Osaka. By contrast, the maritime transportation routes in the South China Sea were complex and multilateral, extending from the two major gateways to Qing China – the port of Xiamen in Fujian and the port of Guangzhou-Macao in Guangdong – to the major ports of Southeast Asia.

Due to the trade restrictions and immigration regulations in the various states of the East China Sea during the eighteenth century, the movement of trade goods across borders was also restricted. Although global trade as a whole was on the decline, inter-regional trade along the coastal areas of Mainland China and intra-regional trade within Japan and Korea thrived.

Central to the whole of maritime East Asia both in terms of production and consumption was the regional market of Jiangnan and the neighboring lower reaches of the Yangtze River, which boasted an enormous population and constituted one of the world's largest regional markets at that time. Maritime routes extended from the ports of Jiangnan such as Liuhe-gang, Shanghai, Zhapu and Ningbo to various ports in the north such as Shandong and Tianjin, which served as Beijing's outer harbor. These routes extended to the ports of Liaodong, and, through Wenzhou and other ports of southern Zhejiang, to Fuzhou and Xiamen in Fujian, which were then capable of reaching Chaozhou and Guangzhou in Guangdong to the south. The Zhoushan Archipelago at the mouth of Hangzhou Bay served as the hub for various sea routes in the East China Sea, including not only these southern and northern routes, but also the eastern route that led to Nagasaki. A network of maritime routes also extended southward, from Fuzhou to Ryukyu and from Xiamen and Guangzhou to major ports serving the South China Sea, such as Manila, Ayutthaya and Batavia. Moreover, following the establishment of the "Canton System", Macao, which had functioned as one unit with Guangzhou, emerged as an important base of trade not only for Portugal, but also for the whole of Europe and America.

Until the end of the sixteenth century, the coastal navigation routes along the Japanese Archipelago had been segmented due both to the proliferation of naval groups vying for power and to the constant conflicts among the local *daimyōs*. However, during the seventeenth century, following the emergence of unified central governments, the maritime routes in the Seto Inland Sea began to link up with those in the Sea of Japan, and routes along the Pacific coasts were also established by the end of the century. Thus the entire archipelago, including Ezo-chi (present-day Hokkaido), was closely linked to the country's two production and consumption centers, the Kamigata area (mainly Osaka and Kyoto) and Edo. Although these routes, which connected the various coastal areas of the archipelago, remained closed to the foreign ships that visited the four gateways of Japan, the flow of goods into the gateways was in turn channeled into the regional coastal network that extended along the archipelago.

In contrast, in the South China Sea where control by regional authorities was relatively loose, maritime trade continued to expand throughout the eighteenth century. The tax and tariff revenues of the customs houses at Xiamen and Guangzhou that served the South China Sea increased dramatically throughout the century. Ports in the Jiangnan area, including Shanghai and Zhapu, assumed increasingly important roles as stopover ports, and thus became known as places where merchants might acquire products of Southeast Asian origin without sailing to that region. At Nagasaki, for example, ships owned by the Siamese royal court and operated by Chinese sub-contractors once sailed directly from Ayutthaya to Nagasaki, but they began to disappear from Japanese waters in the early half of the eighteenth century; *oku-bune* (ships from faraway lands) from Southeast Asia took their place by the middle of the century. This shift in supply might have been due to the possibility of procuring products of Southeast Asian origin in the Jiangnan area. Certainly, the comings and goings of ships between Southeast Asia and Nagasaki did not necessarily coincide with the movement of goods between them. Thus, the East and South China Seas may have appeared to be qualitatively different from each other when looked at from a political and institutional perspective, but when viewed in terms of the movement of goods, they were connected and mediated by nodal points such as Guangzhou, Xiamen and Jiangnan.

Another feature of trade in maritime East Asia during this period was that a northern trade route clearly took shape and became closely linked to the trade routes in the East China Sea. Maritime trade over the Sea of Japan remained undeveloped not only due to political constraints, but also because the sea was too rough to be crossed with ease. Thus, trade across this sea was carried out along the route that extended through the inland rivers of Manchuria, such as the Amur River (or Heilongjiang) and the Songhua River, through to Sakhalin Island (Karafuto) and on to Ezo-chi. Trade through this route was called "Santan Trade"[4], with "Santan"

---

4 "Santan" is a term of Ainu origin that refers to the inhabitants of the lower reaches of the Amur River to Sakhalin Island and is the term used to signify the trade between these people and the Ainu on Sakhalin Island and Ezo (Hokkaido). This trade reached its zenith during the roughly one century from the mid-sixteenth century.

referring to one of the indigenous Tungus peoples living in the lower reaches of the Amur River. The most valuable trade items on this route were Chinese embroidered robes called *Ezo-nishiki* (Ezo brocade)[5], which were highly sought after on Japan's mainland. Other goods traded along this northern route were kelp, abalone and sea otter fur, which were shipped all the way to Jiangnan via Nagasaki and Ryukyu. In particular, the northern trade route differed significantly from those in the East China Sea in two ways: no strict control was exercised by local political authorities, and virtually no Chinese merchant ships were involved in the trade.

## Commoditization of goods moving across the sea

Specifically, what sorts of goods were being traded in maritime East Asia in the eighteenth century? Trade records in Nagasaki have been kept in far better shape than in any other location around the East China Sea and can tell us much. Imports from Mainland China to Japan consisted mainly of raw silk in the seventeenth century, but by the mid-eighteenth century the principal import had become finished silk fabric. This was subsequently replaced by pharmacopeia in the latter half of the century. Exports from the Japanese Archipelago to Mainland China were led by silver during the seventeenth century, but in keeping with a decline in its production, copper came to take up an increasingly larger share of the exports. During the eighteenth century, marine products, in particular, *tawaramono* and a large quantity of kelp became the primary exports to China. In other words, trade between Mainland China and Japan during the sixteenth and seventeenth centuries featured raw silk as the main export of China and silver as the primary export of Japan. During the eighteenth century, however, a new pattern emerged, first with finished silk fabric from China and copper from Japan, and then with a combination of pharmacopeia and marine products. This latter pattern was evident in the variety and quantity of pharmacopeia that the ship mentioned above, the *Wansheng-hao*, was carrying when it wrecked off the coast of Enshūnada. In addition to increased imports of pharmacopeia, a phenomenal rise in

---

5 "*Ezo-nishiki*" refers to Chinese-made embroidered robes imported into Japan via Matsumae (in present-day Hokkaido). They were originally official robes bestowed upon chiefs in the lower reaches of the Amur River and the Sakhalin Island region by the Qing Empire, but were brought to Japan as trade goods.

the import of books also occurred in the eighteenth century, paving the way for a flowering of various academic pursuits across Japan from the 1750s onward. Similar developments were observed in trade along the Busan-Tsushima route that connected Japan, Korea and Mainland China, and along the Ryukyu-Fuzhou route that extended from Japan to Ryukyu into Mainland China.

What about the South China Sea? Examining the cargo of merchant ships that moved between Hội An[6] in central Vietnam and Guangdong in the late eighteenth century, exports from Mainland China consisted of artifacts such as accessories, various ceramics, tea and Chinese herbal medicines. Imports into China included a much wider variety of goods, though the primary category consisted of animal and plant products, as well as minerals. Rare and expensive cooking ingredients, such as sea cucumber and swallow's nest, expensive spices and pharmacopeia were also imported by China; however, in terms of tonnage and quantity these were surpassed by inexpensive daily necessities like betel palm and dried fish, and especially by sugar, which was the largest commodity in terms of volume.

Thus, the primary cargo carried by Chinese merchant ships in the South China Sea in the eighteenth century was no longer silver and raw silk, as it had been in the sixteenth and seventeenth centuries. Instead, the cargo of the booming China trade now consisted, to a remarkable extent, of inexpensive daily necessities that might seem to be hardly worth transporting over long distances. A similar change was also taking place quietly and steadily in the East China Sea. For example, the cargo of Ryukyuan tribute ships on their return voyage from Fuzhou in the latter half of the eighteenth century included some pharmacopeia meant for the markets in Mainland Japan, but also large quantities of ordinary daily commodities in general use in Ryukyu, such as winnowing baskets called "*mīzōkī*" and other bamboo farming utensils, tea, oiled-paper umbrellas, iron needles, coarse grass cloth, coarse winter cloth, varnished fans and ceramic ware for daily use. This phenomenon may be termed the "commoditization of trade goods". In the trade undertaken by Western ships as well, the share of both green and

---

6 Hội An was a port town in Central Vietnam that had prospered as a trade port since ancient times. A Japanese quarter and a Dutch East Indies Company (VOC) trading house existed in the town during the first half of the seventeenth century.

black tea in relation to other trade goods had increased significantly by the latter half of the eighteenth century.

Similar changes were taking place along each of the cross-border long-distance maritime trade routes, as ships carried fewer goods of extremely high and universally recognized value or goods traded in huge markets, like the silver and raw silk that used to be traded in massive quantities until the end of the seventeenth century. Instead, shipping became oriented toward a more individualized pattern of trade, wherein each region began to conduct trade in ways more adapted to its locally specific social and economic climate. It seems possible, therefore, to describe the social and economic changes in each region as partially mediated by the sea, in as much as they were the result of certain adaptations to changes in the maritime trade networks.

## Goods and currencies traversing the seas

Setting aside daily commodities, let us now consider goods that served a particular purpose within East Asian society. The shipping and consumption of marine products significantly increased during the eighteenth century. The majority of these were *tawaramono* and kelp, which were transported to Mainland China from Nagasaki or from Satsuma via Ryukyu, as noted above. The expanded trade in marine products between Japan and Qing China was more a matter of convenience than a classic case of supply-and-demand. On the supply side, Japan was seeking to develop new exportable commodities and limit outflows of precious metals; on the demand side, a luxurious "Chinese cuisine" was developing during a period of peace and prosperity under the Qing, which caused a sharp increase in demand for high-quality and expensive ingredients. Areas of the South China Sea exported many of these ingredients to Qing China. In particular, the volume of imported dried shark's fin, sea cucumber and swallow's nest from eastern Indonesia through Sulu and Fujian increased rapidly during the eighteenth century.

The intra-regional trade in marine products also developed significantly during this period, and products such as kelp and dried bonito were widely disseminated to every corner of the Japanese Archipelago through closely interconnected maritime routes. These products even became indispensable to the cuisine of Ryukyu, where they were not locally produced. The flow of these marine products also extended via Nagasaki and Ryukyu all the way to Mainland China. On the other hand, Ezo-chi became the main supply base for these goods. Because the region was under the domainal rule of the Matsumae family, an official production and distribution system called "*basho ukeoi*" (sub-contracted trading post system)[7] was established. Under this system, which was intrinsically tied to the flow of goods across the East China Sea, Ōmi merchants (merchants from present-day Shiga Prefecture) and other mainland traders were sub-contracted to produce and distribute marine products at government trading posts, which were incorporated into an archipelago-wide distribution network. This system exploited the Ainu in various areas, accelerating the process of their impoverishment and depopulation. The rebellion of 1789, the Kunashiri Menashi no Tatakai (Menash-Kunashir Rebellion)[8], was staged by Ainu in the eastern part of Hokkaido island who were forced into such a predicament. The leaders of this uprising were depicted by Kakizaki Hakyō, a samurai artist from the Matsumae Domain, in a series entitled *Ishū Retsuzō* (Sketchbook of Ainu Chiefs).

Another notable international commodity in the eighteenth century as important as marine products from Ezo-chi was sugar, an enormously large quantity of which was loaded aboard the *Wansheng-hao*, the wrecked Chinese merchant ship mentioned earlier. Certainly, sugar had long been traded internationally prior to 1700. However, due to several developments that took place during the seventeenth century, such as improvements in and dissemination of sugar manufacturing technology and the increase in sugar cane production on plantations, sugar became a "global commodity". Sugar

---

7 The *basho ukeoi* was a system whereby trading rights in certain locations in Ezo-chi were sub-contracted to merchants in exchange for payment of a business tax. The *basho* (place) referred to a location covered by the trading rights, but with the expansion in demand for Ezo products these rights were extended to the management of fishing grounds, where Ainu were used as the labor force.

8 Kunashiri Menashi no Tatakai was a large scale incident involving attacks on Japanese people that occurred in 1789 at the Kunashiri Basho (trading post) in south Kunashiri Island and in the Menashi area on the opposite shore. The rebellion ended when Ainu chiefs persuaded the insurgents to surrender. The *Ishū Retsuzō* (Sketchbook of Ainu Chiefs), drawings of twelve Ainu chiefs produced in Matsumae the year following the incident, were done by Kakizaki Hakyō (1764–1826), who was a chief counselor of the Matsumae family.

was a product that appeared in a variety of forms depending on a wide range of conditions, including the agricultural and economic policies pursued by government authorities, the situation regarding maritime transportation and local cuisine. For example, Ryukyu was a producer and exporter of brown sugar, but it also imported white sugar. In the VOC's Nagasaki trade, sugar was used as ballast.

Coins and the materials to mint them also eloquently reveal the state of affairs in maritime East Asia during the eighteenth century. As described in Part 2, silver was the major commodity traded internationally during the seventeenth century. As the eighteenth century wore on, however,

**Figure 28: An Ainu chief, Ikotoi**
Source: *Ishū Retsuzō* (Sketchbook of Ainu Chiefs), Kakizaki Hakyō, Hakodate City Chūō Library.

silver decreased in importance even though that mined in North America continued to flow into East Asia via Manila. It was no longer the primary global currency and commodity that it had been in the sixteenth and seventeenth centuries. Now, regionally-oriented bronze coins were minted in increasingly large quantities. Consequently, copper ingots and bronze coins in significant demand in many countries emerged as Japan's main exports in the latter half of the seventeenth century. Chinese merchants earned huge profits by shipping copper ingots and bronze coins from Japan to China and Southeast Asia, while the VOC did the same mainly from Japan to India. However, as the Tokugawa Shogunate grew apprehensive about the outflow of its copper, it tightened its restrictions on copper exports and the amount of Japanese copper exports decreased sharply after reaching a peak in the early eighteenth century. The Qing government tried to overcome coin shortages by developing copper mines in Yunnan and through other means, but the coin famine (*qian huang*) was not easily solved. In fact, the Japanese bronze coin *Kan'ei Tsūhō* was imported into and circulated widely without any modification in Shanghai and Zhapu in the mid-eighteenth century. It was not until the latter half of the century that the coin famine was brought under control in most parts of China.

## Restructuring and the import substitution process

One thing that merits special attention in discussing the industries of maritime East Asia in the eighteenth century is the development of cash crops. In various parts of the region, this phenomenon was supported by the emergence of a "small farmer society", in which an agricultural household, either a nuclear family or a household with four to seven members (typically, a nuclear family plus grandparents), constituted the basic farming unit.

A "peasant society" emerged during the sixteenth century or thereabouts in Japan and in Korea, and during the eighteenth century in Vietnam. As this form of society became prevalent, farming methods and techniques well-adapted to smaller agricultural endeavors were disseminated through books or by innovative farmers, leading to increased labor productivity in these farms. Surplus labor became available for use in domestic manufacturing and other small side-operations. Moreover, the family or kinship groups in these farms, such as the *ie* (household) system in Japan and the *zongzu* (patrilineal descent groups) among the Han Chinese, were transformed to accommodate various features that accompanied this new type of agro-industry. There was also an increase in the farming of cash crops such as cotton, mulberry (the leaves are used to feed silkworms), tobacco and tea. However, these were not subsidiary crops for earning extra income, but rather the main crop sustaining the family managing the small farm. The distribution networks that had been established in the preceding era proved effective in sustaining the production of specialized crops and dividing labor among different methods of crop cultivation in different areas.

The division of labor in both domestic production and inter-regional trade underwent changes and restructuring over the course of the eighteenth century. Particularly, Fujian and Guangdong became specialized in the production of high-value-added commodities such as sugar and tobacco, with any shortages of rice in the region supplied from hinterland areas such as Taiwan and Guangxi. Since even Taiwan and Guangxi suffered rice shortages from time to time, rice also had to be imported across the South China Sea from Siam and Vietnam. As for the supply of soybeans and soybean cake to the Jiangnan region, Shandong, which used to be the major production base for soybean crops until the early eighteenth century, was replaced during the latter half of the century by Liaodong, where a large number of Han Chinese had settled. Liaodong also emerged as a supply base for cereal grains to various parts of North China. Inland river routes were used to ship some of these goods, but the coastal trade route extending from the East China Sea to the Yellow Sea and the Bohai Sea, which had not been used much during the Ming Dynasty, also played an important role. The development and intensification of inter-regional divisions of labor and the development of distribution networks to sustain this trend went hand-in-hand.

In addition to the development of export items such as marine products, a new development in Japan's international trade that took place during this period was the domestic production and promotion of import-substitution goods. The growth in the export of marine products had the effect of restraining the outflow of copper, but it was still necessary to import some products that were difficult to procure domestically, such as raw silk, sugar and ginseng. Thus, efforts had been made since the mid-seventeenth century to cultivate a number of agricultural crops and develop as many handicrafts as possible domestically.

These efforts led to the promotion of the domestic cultivation and production of raw silk, brown sugar, silk fabric and cotton textiles in the eighteenth century. Local specialties, including the Nishijin silk fabrics of Kyoto and a variety of Japanese sweets produced in many areas of Japan with an abundant supply of sugar, are the result of these efforts. Efforts were made under the leadership of the Shogun Tokugawa Yoshimune to domestically cultivate the expensive medicinal plant ginseng, until then a specialty import from Korea, which proved successful in the 1730s. Sappanwood, a plant used to make red dyestuff that was native to Southeast Asia and extremely difficult to grow in Japan, was substituted by an increase in the domestic production of safflower. The cultivation of safflower spread to various parts of Japan in the eighteenth century. In particular, Dewa Province (present-day Yamagata and Akita Prefectures), advantageously linked by the Sea of Japan and the Mogami River to the major textile production center of Kyoto, became the most successful region to cultivate the import substitute. During the Kyōhō period (1716–1736), the province's share in the domestic production of safflower topped forty percent, and safflower still remains the prefectural flower of Yamagata today. In conclusion, the growth of domestic production as well as the promotion of import-substitution products in Japan and Korea influenced the decreasing volume of international trade that took place in the East China Sea.

In this respect, too, changes in trade in the East China Sea were very different from those in the South China Sea. In the latter, the total amount of trade increased significantly and was not accompanied by any significant efforts to promote domestic production to substitute imported products. Silk, ceramics and other products made in China continued to be exported to various parts of Southeast Asia in large quantities, with the result that the Vietnamese silk and ceramics industries, for example, were edged out of both domestic and international markets. On the whole, an industrial and trading pattern took shape during this era that anticipated intra-Asian trade in the modern era, wherein Southeast Asia served as a base for supplying primary commodities to Mainland China and as a market for purchasing lightweight Chinese crafts.

## Population rise, migration: "Century of ethnic Chinese"

Another significant development that characterized maritime East Asia in the eighteenth century was a population explosion of ethnic Chinese. Both Japan and Korea experienced population growth in the seventeenth century, but their populations had stabilized over the course of the eighteenth century. By contrast, a population explosion occurred in Mainland China between the end of the seventeenth and the end of the eighteenth century, with the population doubling from an estimated 150 million people in the late seventeenth century to 300 million in the late eighteenth. In 1750, the estimated population of Japan stood at thirty million people and Korea at seven million. At this time, 190–220 million of the population in China were Han Chinese. The industrial and agricultural restructurings mentioned in the section above were closely related to these dynamic demographic trends in the various societies surrounding the East China Sea.

The population explosion in Mainland China irreversibly changed that society. The newly increased population expanded into areas that had been rife with hostilities during the Ming-Qing transition and into mountainous regions that had been left undeveloped. In developing these mountainous areas, crops native to South America such as sweet potato and maize proved instrumental because they could be grown on mountain slopes unfit for paddy rice or wheat cultivation. The sweet potato was also introduced into Japan and Korea, where it was cultivated as an emergency crop that played a crucial role in sustaining the population in times of famine.

Some of this increased population left Mainland China altogether, and large numbers of people from Guangdong and Fujian migrated to rural regions in various parts of the South China Sea such as the Mekong Delta and Borneo. Unlike earlier generations of emigrants to the South China Sea area who migrated in pursuit of trade, this new generation moved with the intention of developing farmlands or finding employment. Naturally, emigrants were employed in a wide variety of occupations in their new homes in Southeast Asia: as mine workers in the gold and tin mines, as agricultural workers in sugar and other plantations or as farmer-settlers in the Mekong Delta. Not only did this migratory movement involve the transfer of labor power, it also included the relocation of technologies and expertise.

This migration was facilitated by two factors: 1) the political environment in the South China Sea area was different from that in the East China Sea where immigration was strictly controlled; and 2) these rural areas in the eighteenth century had characteristics quite similar to those of a "frontier". Unlike the East China Sea area where early modern states had established "compartmentalized" relationships, these systems were practically non-existent in the South China Sea region. Emigration abroad was tacitly condoned in the region, and so communities of Han Chinese flourished in various locations during this period, paving the way for the emergence of overseas Chinese communities there in the modern and contemporary eras. By contrast, in the East China Sea area, as noted above, each of the political authorities in power restricted or prohibited the departure of its own people from the country and the entry of foreigners into it. These policies, which seem to have something in common with a modern nation-state's administration of its own population and foreign nationals, may have in some ways influenced the "modern" standards for the countries of the East China Sea.

Thus, the growing emigration of Han Chinese caused a proliferation of Chinatowns in many areas along the coasts of the South China Sea. These overseas ethnic Chinese communities were sustained not by political power, but rather by their own networks built upon regional bonds or blood relations. The lifestyles that ethnic Chinese emigrants adopted in their host countries varied significantly from one locale to the next; some groups preserved the culture of their homeland, such as the worship of Mazu (Jp. Maso, the goddess of the sea), while other groups, notably the Chinese *mestizo* group[9] in the Philippines under Spanish rule, opted to convert to Catholicism and assimilate into the local culture. Some of the Chinatowns, especially those on the coast of the Gulf of Thailand, developed as port cities under the leadership of ethnic Chinese, becoming quasi-autonomous government-

---

9 "Chinese *mestizos*" refers to an interracial person of Chinese and local parentage. They converted to Catholicism and were active as an integral part of local Philippine society. From the eighteenth century onwards, they became an elite social and economic group that rivaled immigrant Chinese.

like entities. The most notable examples of this are Songkla[10] on the Malay Peninsula (in present-day Thailand), which was led by the Wu family, and Hà Tiên[11] (in present-day Vietnam), under the authority of the Mạc family.

The networks and economic influence of Han Chinese extended throughout the periphery of the South China Sea and had a significant impact on the lifestyles of the people of each locality, from food to clothing, shelter and religion. Such lifestyles are thought to have derived primarily from the cultures of ordinary people in the southeastern coastal areas of Mainland China such as Fujian and Guangdong. Thus, this process was not considered "Sinification", a term that evokes concepts such as the dissemination and absorption of Confucianism and its core texts, the *Sishu Wujing* (the Four Books and Five Classics), which did not spread or take hold in most areas around the South China Sea. The sole exception to this was Vietnam, which had traditionally absorbed the high culture of China. In this respect, both Japan and Korea were strikingly different in that they were eager to absorb such intellectual content through the import of books and other means.

## Dissemination of information through print media

A category worthy of special mention among the goods transported by sea during this period was books. Even though the number of persons and the volume of goods that came into and went out of the four early modern states surrounding the East China Sea during the eighteenth century were less than those in the seventeenth century, the flow of information nonetheless increased thanks to the growth in the book trade. Jiangnan and other cities under the rule of the Qing were major sources from which large numbers of

---

10 Songkla is a port city on the east coast of the Malay Peninsula in which Wu Rang, who had traveled from Fujian Province in the mid-eighteenth century, established a power base. As well as prospering from trade, he was appointed chief of his territory by Siam and allowed to regulate tributary states, thus becoming both a political and economic force.
11 Ha Tien was a port city in the south of the Indochina Peninsula in which Mạc Cửu, who had traveled there from Guangdong at the end of the seventeenth century, established a power base. He expanded his forces under the Nguyễn family of Gangnam, which ruled over southern Vietnam and also paid tribute to the Qing Empire.

Chinese books were transported by land and sea to Japan, Korea, Ryukyu and Vietnam.

The most enthusiastic purchasers of Chinese books during this period were the political authorities in Japan, which did not have formal diplomatic relations with the Qing Empire. The Tokugawa Shogunate and local *daimyōs* insatiably collected Chinese books from Chinese merchants who visited Nagasaki and *Tō-tsūji* (the official Chinese interpreters working for the magistrate's office). Perhaps the keenest collector of Chinese books was Tokugawa Yoshimune, the eighth Tokugawa Shogun who succeeded to his post in 1716. He collected Chinese books in a strategic and systematic manner in pursuit of two objectives. The first was to promote the transfer and practical application of technology. In 1720, Yoshimune ordered a relaxation of the ban on the import of foreign books, with the exception of those directly related to Christianity, thereby allowing the import and publication of books on natural science, such as calendar making, astronomy, mathematics and medicine. Yoshimune also manifested a strong interest in things Korean, such as medicinal materials and medical books, and encouraged the acquisition of these items. The flourishing of the sciences in the nineteenth century in Japan can be traced back to the accumulation of knowledge initiated by Yoshimune, along with the simultaneous development of *rangaku* (Dutch studies), which was the study of primarily Dutch texts about the natural sciences and medicine. Supporting these developments was the establishment and propagation of a new scholastic approach, represented best by the *kaozheng* (evidential scholarship)[12] that began in Qing China. This method spurned the pre-existing practice of debating the pros and cons of empirically unverifiable interpretations of classical texts, and instead emphasized the importance of determining the original text in order to read it closely and rigorously.

Yoshimune's second objective in his importation of books was to study the laws and institutions of the Ming and Qing Empires so that he might formulate more effective policies. To facilitate studies on the institutions and laws of the Qing Empire, Yoshimune ordered the importation of a large number of books, including law books and collected regulations, as

---

12 The Qing Dynasty's *kaozheng* was a branch of scholarship that developed in South China during that era, and mainly produced philological studies on the Confucianist classics and historical works. Its characteristics were an emphasis on phonology and geography, and a thorough critique of historical materials.

well as *difangzhi* (local gazetteers). These books were then analyzed and translated by Confucian scholars in his employ, overseen by Ogyū Hokkei[13] (1673–1754), Fukami Gentai (1649–1722) and his son Fukami Arichika (1691–1773)[14]. In addition to undertaking the translation and study of *Dai Qing Huidian* (Collected Statutes of the Great Qing) and other books, they compiled *Shinchō Tanji* (Inquiries about the Qing Empire), a record of interviews with Chinese merchants on the situation in Qing China. Based upon these various texts and analyses, Yoshimune implemented a number of innovative policies: the adoption and promulgation of *Kujikata osadamegaki* (book of rules for public officials); various measures to consolidate and rationalize laws and regulations; the enforcement of a Shokoku Ninzu Shirabe (national census); and the implementation of large-scale river improvement and flood control projects throughout the country by means of the Kuniyaku Fushin-sei (the system of holding *daimyōs* responsible for carrying out civil engineering projects). It is also highly likely that he gained inspiration from the Qing Kangxi Emperor's inspection tours to Jiangnan in reviving the grandiose pageant of the shogun's visit to the Nikkō Tōshōgū Shrine that had not occurred for seventy years.

Yoshimune also had a Confucian scholar, Muro Kyūsō, summarize a book of Confucian maxims entitled *Liuyu Yanyi* (J. *Rikuyu Engi*; Six Courses in Morals)[15] and then compile a textbook on morality based upon this summary entitled *Rikuyu Engi Taii*, disseminating it among the general population. The copy of *Liuyu Yanyi* that was used for this compilation was

---

13 Ogyū Hokkei, a younger brother of Confucian scholar Ogyū Sorai, served as one of the advisers of Tokugawa Yoshimune, entering service as one of the Confucian scholars in Yoshimune's employ. He left significant achievements in the revision of Chinese books and in research on the Qing Empire.
14 The Fukami family was a lineage of Nagasaki Chinese interpreters who arrived from Fujian Province in the early seventeenth century. Fukami Gentai was called to Edo (present-day Tokyo) due to recognition of his scholarly attainments, becoming an official Confucian scholar. His son Fukami Arichika was selected as the head of the Momijiyama Bunko (Maple Leaf Mountain Library), the shogun's library inside Edo Castle.
15 The *Liuyu* were six precepts promulgated in 1397 for the strengthening of the moral life of the masses by the Ming Hongwu Emperor. *Liuyu Yanyi* was a guide to these precepts compiled at the end of the Ming era. Yoshimune received the book as a present from the Shimazu family and had the Zhu Xi school scholar Muro Kyūsō (a fellow student of Arai Hakuseki and Amenomori Hōshū) produce a Japanese translation and summary of the book, which was compiled under the title *Rikuyu Engi Taii* (Summary of the *Rikuyu Engi*).

brought from Fuzhou by the Ryukyuan high-level official and Confucian scholar Tei Junsoku[16] (1663–1734), and later donated to the shogun by Shimazu Yoshitaka of the Satsuma Domain. Interestingly, Yoshitaka's son would later become the "Matsudaira Ōsuminokami", or Shimazu Tsugutoyo, who was mentioned by Denbē, the captain of the wrecked ship based in Satsuma discussed in the first chapters of Part 3. This episode is suggestive of the eagerness with which Yoshimune pursued his policy, while also revealing that not all of the Chinese books that came to Japan from Qing China entered via Nagasaki.

There were also various cases in which important classical books that had virtually disappeared from Qing China were traded back from Japan through Chinese merchants. Bao Tingbo, a famous Huizhou merchant from She County, Anhui Province, compiled information about rare books in a series entitled *Zhibuzuzhai Congshu* (Collection of the Studio of Insufficient Knowledge), featuring two titles that later made their way back to China from Japan. *Guwen Xiaojing Kongziyun* (Ancient Copy of Classics of Filial Piety) and *Lunyu Jijie Yishu* (Collected Explanations and Argumentation of the Analects of Confucius) were purchased in Nagasaki and brought back to Qing China during the 1770s by Wang Peng, a merchant from Zhejiang who often visited the port.

The highlight of this cultural exchange between Qing China and Japan was when the book entitled *Shichikei moshi kobun narabini hoi* (C. *Qi jing Mengzi kao wen bing bu yi*; Commentary and Supplement to the Seven Scriptures and Mencius) was brought to China and issued as part of an enormous collection, the *Siku Quanshu*[17] (Complete Library of the Four Treasuries), published by Qing imperial order. Yamanoi Kanae, a student

---

16 Tei Junsok, a Ryukyuan official, was known as the Leader (*ue-kata*) of Nago or the Saint of Nago. He studied Confucianism in Qing China and worked for Confucianist education and the spread of Confucianism in Ryukyu. He excelled in Chinese calligraphy and Chinese poetry, and corresponded with Japanese and Qing men of letters.
17 An enormous collection of books was compiled by order of the Qianlong Emperor over a ten-year period from 1773, including ancient and contemporary writings. *Siku* (Four Treasuries) refers to the Chinese literary classification of the four treasure houses of *jing* (Confucianism), *shi* (historical texts), *zi* (thought) and *ji* (literature).

of the well-known Confucian Ogyū Sorai (1666–1728), had collated and compiled the seven types of Confucian scriptures by checking them against handwritten copies of books and printed volumes preserved in the Ashikaga Gakkō, Japan's oldest academic institution. The text was then annotated by Ogyū Hokkei (the younger brother of Sorai) after Yamanoi's death. In China, Yamanoi's work was esteemed because of its high scholastic standard and because it contained materials no longer extant in Mainland China. Similarly, annotative studies on *Tanglu Shuyi* (A Commentary on the Tang Code) that were actively undertaken in Japan were sent back to the Qing court in Beijing. It seems possible to say that this cultural transmission, which had primarily been flowing one-way from Mainland China to Japan, finally reached a level of "mutual exchange".

## From copying to adaptation to "traditional culture"

One important feature regarding the introduction of Chinese books into Japan was that *wakoku-bon* (woodblock reprinted editions) of Chinese books were published by private publishing houses in Japan. Large numbers of Chinese books were also brought to Korea and Ryukyu by tribute missions and scholars sent abroad to study in Qing China. For example, the *Liuyu Yanyi* (Six Courses in Morals) that was used by Yoshimune to make a textbook for the general populace was itself a copy of the original edition reprinted in Fuzhou at the request of a Ryukyuan envoy, Tei Junsoku, during his stay there, which he hoped to use to teach the Chinese language, manners and customs in Ryukyu. In the case of Korea also, the *yeonhangsa*[18] (Joseon tributary missions to Beijing) purchased large numbers of Chinese books and Chinese translations of Western books while in Beijing. There were also cases where some of the Korean Tongsinsa (Jp. Tsūshinshi; Goodwill Missions) to Japan brought home quite a number of

---

18  The Joseon tributary missions to Beijing refer to the voyages of envoys to Yanjing (the literary name of Beijing). In addition to regular tributary missions, there were also extraordinary missions dispatched for the purpose of congratulations and condolences. Many people who participated in these missions left travelogues and records of their experiences, these being known as "records of missions to Yanjing" (*Yoenhangrok*).

books on practical knowledge published in Japan, such as the *Wakan Sansai Zue*[19] (Illustrated Sino-Japanese Encyclopedia). In most cases, however, the Chinese books imported into Ryukyu or Korea were read and manually transcribed by a limited number of government officials and scholars, with the result that most of these texts were transmitted as handwritten copies. In contrast, in Japan as early as the seventeenth century, bookstores in Kyoto and elsewhere were already publishing large numbers of *wakoku-bon* (reprinted edition) versions of Chinese books. These reprinted editions were more than simple reproductions of the original copies, and were edited with *kunten* (phonetic guides) for rendering them into Japanese. Books reprinted in such a format covered a wide range of fields, including not only classical Confucian writings and history books but also essays and literary works. Members of the Korean Goodwill Mission to Japan in 1711 are reported to have been surprised to find books originally published in Korea on sale in Japanese bookstores in *wakoku-bon* form; therefore, Japan also seems to have been importing and reprinting Korean books at a ravenous pace.

During the seventeenth century, the dissemination of information through reprinted Chinese books with phonetic guides remained largely confined to intellectuals. However, over the course of the eighteenth century, the effect of these books grew more extensive and intense, reaching Japanese culture and society on many levels. This, however, does not mean that Japan became "Sinified". Rather, both the books and the information contained within went through a process of transcription and adaptation, being reinterpreted and revised to make them better suit the cultural values and systems of Japanese society.

Chinese-style poetry continued to be popular in Japan during the eighteenth century, but this phenomenon was unique to that country. No similar development in contemporary Qing China or Korea occurred, and this particular mode of reception might be regarded as an attempt to integrate Chinese culture at the local level. Moreover, the reception of Chinese culture proceeded alongside the dissemination of "Japanese classical culture". The seventeenth century saw not only the publication

---

19 More precisely known as *Wakan Sansai Zue Ryaku*, this was edited by Terashima Ryōan and published in 1713. Following the style of the Ming era *Sansai Zue* (Cn. *Sancai Tuhui*), it was an illustrated encyclopedia containing explanations of various matters.

of reprinted editions of Chinese books, but also a large number of works either providing phonetic guides for, annotating or commenting on Japanese classics in the fields of history, laws and regulations and literature. These included the *Kojiki* (Record of Ancient Matters), *Genji Monogatari* (The Tale of Genji), *Tsurezuregusa* (Essays in Idleness) and *Taiheiki* (Chronicle of the Great Peace). Subsequently, during the eighteenth century, literary works proliferated that either retold, mimicked or satirized these classics, and it became common to use the contents of these classics as themes for composing haiku and *renga* poems.

Consequently, in towns and villages across Japan, people would place mythical or historical Chinese heroes or heroines alongside their Japanese counterparts, comparing Chinese warlord Cao Cao to Japanese warlord Ashikaga Takauji, Chinese poet Li Bai to Japanese poet Saigyō or Chinese beauty Yang Guifei to Japanese beauty Ono no Komachi. In the *terakoya* (private educational institutions for children of commoners), children recited in unison passages from *Jōei Shikimoku* (Code of Conduct for Samurai) or *Lunyu* (Analects of Confucius). Professional storytellers recounted stories of Zhuge Liang (a famous strategist in Chinese history) and of Kusunoki Masashige (a renowned tactician in Japanese history). This does not mean, however, that people mistook Bai Juyi, a famous poet of ancient China, for a Japanese poet. On the contrary, the distinction between "what is Japanese" and "what is Chinese" was taken as self-evident. Nonetheless, in various parts of Japan during the eighteenth century, "traditional Japanese culture" was in fact a mixture of "Japanese classics" and "Chinese classics", while *wayō* (Japanese style) and *karayō* (Chinese style) were in the process of being created.

## Admiration for and wariness about maritime exchanges

Literary works that incorporated information about foreign countries and memories of interactions with foreigners, like the *Kokusen'ya Kassen* (Battles of Koxinga), enjoyed such popularity in Japan due to the fact that the eighteenth century differed significantly from previous eras, when autonomous local powers actively took part in trans-oceanic interactions. In Japan, where chances for interacting with "foreign countries" were severely limited, people both wanted and were curious about "foreign things". Nagasaki, in its capacity as the point of contact with foreign culture, became a sort of sacred city, especially for intellectuals. Many scholars endeavored to circumvent various restrictions in order to travel there, where they would either try to meet with Chinese people or to communicate with them by means of writing. The desire to communicate with visitors from China was common throughout Japan. For example, a famous intellectual salon in Osaka run by Kimura Kenkadō[20] (1736–1802) overflowed with books and artifacts from abroad. In another example, framed copies of the calligraphy of Cheng Chicheng, a ship-owner and merchant who visited Nagasaki repeatedly and was very famous in Japan for his calligraphy, can be found in many areas of Kyushu and elsewhere in Japan.

The arrival of a diplomatic envoy was perhaps the golden chance to interact with foreigners, and drew the attention of non-governmental scholars, intellectuals and ordinary people alike. Wherever they stayed on their way to Edo, members of Korean Goodwill Missions or Ryukyuan missions were asked by intellectuals of the area to recite Chinese poems or write calligraphy. The procession of a diplomatic mission drew a huge crowd of people, who would watch the foreigners with a great deal of curiosity. In particular, the visits by the 1748 and 1764 Korean Goodwill Missions were received with great excitement, and a mixture of true and false information about the envoys was published in both Kamigata (the Kyoto-Osaka area) and Edo shortly after the missions landed in Kyushu. In many places along the routes traveled by the Korean Goodwill Missions, the Ryukyuan missions and the *hofreis* (Jp. *Edo sanpu*) of the VOC, the processions came to be imitated or reproduced as *Tō-jin odori* (foreign dancing) or *Tō-jin shibai* (foreign theatrical performance) at local festivals or other festivities. Thus the foreign processions became part of the "traditional culture" of the areas concerned.

The situations in Qing China and Korea were different in this regard. In the Qing Empire, Christian missionaries served at the imperial court in Beijing, and a number of European merchants resided in Guangzhou and

---

20 Kimura Kenkadō, an intellectual of Osaka who was an earnest scholar and skilled writer, was also engaged in the brewing industry and collected valuable objects of art and curios. He fraternized with men of letters and prominent figures nationwide, one of whom was Matsura Seizan of Hirado.

Macao[21]. The Qing itself, governed by the Manchu, consisted of a diverse variety of ethnic groups, and Han society in the former territory of the Ming Dynasty was far from monolithic. Christian missionaries who had infiltrated Jiangnan and Sichuan to propagate their religion were able to travel within the country without arousing too much suspicion. This was in stark contrast to the situation in Japan, where the Italian missionary Giovanni Battista Sidotti[22] (1668–1714) tried to infiltrate that country via Manila in 1708. Contrary to his belief that he had managed to disguise

**Figure 29: Foreigners' images in pre-modern Japan**

Source: *Shōtokudo Chosen Tsuushinshi Gyōresu Zumaki* (Scroll Painting of Joseon Missions to Japan in the Shōtoku Period), Osaka Museum of History.

21 The Qing emperors initially tolerated Christianity, but banned missionary work in the eighteenth century. Missionaries continued to work, however, as academic and arts and crafts counselors in the imperial court. They were not subject to constant strict surveillance while in the regions as they were in Japan.
22 In 1708, Giovanni Battista Sidotti, an Italian-born missionary, attempted to propagate Christianity in Japan, but was captured and subsequently died in prison. Arai Hakusei interrogated him in Edo and wrote *Sairan Igen* (Various Sights and Strange Words) and *Seiyō Kibun* (Accounts of the West) based on what he heard from Sidotti.

himself as a Japanese, he was immediately discovered to be a foreigner and captured. Furthermore, although it was customary for foreign tribute missions to travel to Beijing, they did not attract much public attention, contrary to their reception in Japan. Objects of far greater public interest were the inspection tours to Jiangnan[23], which the Kangxi and Qianlong Emperors made frequently.

In Korea, there were cases where Koreans and Japanese working closely together in the Waegwan while handling trade and other matters became close friends. However, once they stepped outside the compound, Japanese were the target of hatred and were often pelted with stones by ordinary people. Consequently, the dispatch of a Korean Goodwill Mission to Japan, which was viewed as very important news in that country, received no public attention in Korea.

Only when the members of a society can consciously distinguish themselves from other societies, and when they can access symbols for representing "others", does the presence of foreigners arouse such an array of reactions spanning from adoration to antagonism. In the period under consideration during the firmly established relationship of compartmentalization, there were limited chances for individuals of different countries to come into direct contact with each other. Foreigners came to be understood on a progressively abstract basis and in an increasingly stereotypical fashion. For instance, not only clothes but also hairstyles came to be perceived as important criteria for distinguishing among people from other countries, and a scene in *Kokusen'ya Kassen* finds the protagonist Watōnai forcing the surrendered Dattans to change their hairstyle from that of the Manchu *queue* to one similar to a Japanese topknot. In this way, members of each of the early modern states surrounding the East China Sea regarded hairstyles and clothes as the markers through which they could differentiate themselves from foreigners. This explains why the two Ryukyuans aboard the Satsuma-based ship under the command of the sea captain Denbē cut their hair and wore a Japanese-style topknot to conceal their true identities.

---

23 The Qing emperors frequently embarked on inspection tours of Mongolia and Manchuria as well as South China and other regions. Starting from 1684, the Kangxi and Qianlong Emperors each conducted six visits to South China, the economic and cultural center of that country, to emphasize the state of universal peace of their reigns.

The tendency to emphasize certain aspects of foreigners' appearances was particularly extreme in Japan, which was likely due to the severely reduced opportunities for direct contact with foreigners there. This occurred not only in relation to Westerners, but also to Chinese and Koreans from neighboring countries, and was based on preconceived notions like "Chinese and other foreigners should be hairy and have thick sideburns". Ideas such as this continued to grow stronger and become more deep-rooted, and associating the term "*ketō*" (hairy foreigner) with all foreigners became common as the eighteenth century wore on. This practice of encoding "foreign countries" and of evoking them through certain symbols can be regarded as a product of the major shift in international interactions that took place during the eighteenth century. Exchange no longer occurred in the form of direct person-to-person interactions, but instead through the indirect absorption of foreign knowledge through such things as books and drawings.

## Localization and modernization of the Sea Goddess cult

Some characteristic features of maritime interactions during this period can be gleaned from the way the safety of maritime navigation was prayed for and how the manner of this prayer changed over time. The Chinese goddess of the sea, Mazu (Jp. Maso), also called Tianhou (Jp. Tenkō) or Tianfei (Jp. Tenpi), came to be worshipped in all of the places visited by ships based in Mainland China. In Ryukyu, the Tenpi Temple was the place to pray for safe travel to Fuzhou in China. In the South China Sea, many Mazu statues were enshrined throughout Chinese communities. In Nagasaki as well, Maso-dō (Mazu Halls) were erected in Tō-dera (Chinese temple) compounds that had been founded by Chinese maritime merchants, as well as in the Tōjin-yashiki (Chinese compound). Upon entering Nagasaki, Chinese ships would temporarily deposit the Mazu statues on board in these halls. The *bosa-age* processions for carrying the Mazu statue to a Mazu Hall immediately after a ship's arrival became one of Nagasaki's exotic attractions in the eighteenth century.

In Satsuma (present-day Kagoshima Prefecture), Kyushu and Hitachi in the northern Kantō region, Japanese fishermen and sailors also enshrined Mazu. In Satsuma Mazu was incarnated as Nouma Gongen Shrine and enshrined at the top of Mt. Noma, which was visible from the sea. The history of Nouma Gongen is recorded in the *Nouma-san Hiki* (inscription on the monument of Mt. Noma) compiled in 1706 by Fukami Gentai, which is an adaptation of a Chinese book, *Tianhou Xian Sheng Lu* (Records of the Manifest Sacred Deeds of Tianhou). The story tells that the dead body of Mazu, who drowned herself in the sea in a fit of remorse for having failed to rescue her elder brother, washed ashore at the foot of Mt. Noma. As for the Mazu enshrined in Hitachi (present-day Ibaraki Prefecture), legend claims that the faith was introduced by the Zen monk Tōkō Shin'etsu (Xin Yue), who emigrated from Ming China and was invited to Mito toward the end of the seventeenth century by the *daimyō* there, Tokugawa Mitsukuni (1628–1701). In this area, Mazu or Tenpi was believed to be none other than the legendary Lady Otohime of the Ryūgū (Palace of the Dragon King). Tenpi Maso Gongen-sha Shrines were erected on top of small hills at the mouths of the two main ports of the area, Nakaminato and Isohara, and these shrines acted as lighthouses at night. Belief in Mazu spread north of Hitachi by sea, with shrines dedicated to Tenpi being erected in Shichigahama, facing the Bay of Sendai, and in Ōma on the Shimokita Peninsula at the northern tip of Japan's mainland. The erection of these shrines reflects a faith practice that localized belief in Mazu, a deity that originated in Mainland China.

Not only was Mazu localized, but she also became part of the pantheon of gods native to Japan in safeguarding and upholding traditional maritime culture. Shipbuilding rites such as the sealing of a coin into a ship's body as the *funadama* (spirit of a ship) had been practiced in Japan since ancient times, but during the eighteenth century the deification of *funadama* as the guardian deity of a ship came to be widely practiced. In addition, holding a New Year's feast in front of this deity aboard a ship as a rite of contract between the ship-owner and the crew, including the captain, also became an established custom. In some cases, indigenous Japanese gods such as Sumiyoshi Ōkami and Sarutahiko Ōkami were identified as the gods of a ship's spirit, but often Mazu was chosen as this deity in deference to the widely shared view of sailors who believed that a ship's guardian god must be female.

In contrast, in the eighteenth century there was a growing awareness of the differences between "inside" and "outside" groups and ideas, which affected belief in Mazu by the early nineteenth century. When the naturalist Sugae Masumi[24] (1754–1829) visited Ōma in 1793, he

---

24 Sugae Masumi was a well-traveled scholar of classical Japanese literature. From 1783 for more than forty years, he traveled extensively in Japan's northeast region, leaving a large number of travelogues and records of his journeys.

stated that "Tenpi, enshrined here, and Sarutahiko, an indigenous god of Japan, are the same insofar as their sanctity is concerned". But in the early nineteenth century, Ono Takakiyo (1747–1829), a scholar of Japanese classical literature, wrote in his collection of essays "*hyakusō ro*" that "The *funadama-shin* [the god of a ship's spirit] ought to be the Sumiyoshi Sanjin [the three gods of Sumiyoshi], who guarded the ship of Jingū Kōgō [the Empress-Consort Jingu] at the time of her invasion and conquest of Korea, and therefore the vulgar belief that identifies Tenpi as this god should be rejected". Tokugawa Nariaki[25] (1800–1860), who succeeded the lord of the Mito Domain in 1829, condemned the festivals celebrating Tenpi in Nakaminato and elsewhere as vulgar. He confiscated the Tenpi idols and instated Ototachibana-hime, the wife of the legendary Prince Yamatotakeru, as the deity of the shrines once dedicated to Tenpi. Moreover, around the time of the Meiji Restoration, the Nouma Gongen Shrine in Satsuma was transformed into the Noma Shrine and dedicated to Ninigi no Mikoto (the god sent by Amaterasu to pacify Japan), while the Tenpi Gongen Shrine in Ōma was abolished altogether. Thus, against a backdrop of growing nationalism, Mazu began to disappear, replaced by various gods featured in the *Nihonshoki*, an eighth century Japanese text. This replacement constituted one facet of the conflict between "traditional culture", which had been formed from diverse sources and origins and through maritime exchanges, and a modernization movement intent on reorganizing that culture into one that was standardized and had a single value system.

In Mainland China, by contrast, under mounting external pressure from Western powers, Mazu took on greater importance as a national guardian. The 1870 edition of *Tianhou Shengmu Shengji Tuzhi* (The Pictorial Annals of the Traces of the Heavenly Empress and Holy Mother), compiled at the court of the Tongzhi Emperor[26], the tenth Qing Emperor, was enlarged to feature a number of miracles that had taken place from the days of the Song

---

25  Tokugawa Nariaki was head of the Mito Tokugawa family, one of the three branches of the Tokugawa house. He was the biological father of the last shogun, Yoshinobu.
26  The Tongzhi Emperor, whose name was Aisin Gioro Dzaišun (Zaichun), was the tenth Qing emperor, reigning from 1862 to 1874. He came to the throne at a very young age under the guardianship of his birth mother, the Empress Dowager Cixi. During his reign, there was a lull in the reform of the Qing Dynasty, but the emperor had no real power and died while still young.

Dynasty to the present reign and were ascribed to Mazu. Each of the state-of-the-art warships of the Beiyang Fleet, built in Britain and Germany in the latter half of the 1880s, featured a magnificent shrine on the bridge with a monumental inscription to "the Holy Mother", Mazu.

## Seas as "boundaries": Towards an era of "divided seas"

Throughout the eighteenth century, the perception of seas as "boundaries" continued to be shaped in parallel with the notion of "foreign countries". These were developments that occurred not in the East and South China Seas, but instead in the northern seas.

At the beginning of the eighteenth century, Korea drastically changed its coastal defense policy, switching from the existing practice of forcibly evacuating all island residents to a new policy of establishing coastal defense garrisons on the islands. This change in official policy was prompted first by the Qing removal of the maritime prohibition policy, after which fishing boats and pirate ships from Mainland China proliferated in the Yellow Sea. Other factors in this policy change were the population growth and commercial activities that resulted from the general peace and prosperity of the late seventeenth and early eighteenth centuries, which caused emigration to and development of nearby islands. Given these changes, the new policy, instead of making the islands totally uninhabitable and thus removing destabilizing factors, chose to acknowledge the rights of merchants and fishermen to visit and live on them. It aimed to administer the islands and their inhabitants proactively by placing them under the supervision of the coastal garrisons. This policy shift would eventually give rise to territorial issues with Japan over the islands known as "Takeshima" and "Utsuryōtō" (Kr. Ulleungdo)[27].

---

27 These were the territorial issues regarding the two islands northwest of the Oki Islands. In the seventeenth century, present-day Takeshima (Kr. Dokdo) Island was known as Matsushima Island, and Utsuryōtō (Kr. Ulleungdo) Island was known as Takeshima Island. When contact with Korean fishing people occurred at Utsuryōtō Island, the Japanese banned crossings to that island by Japanese people. Present-day Takeshima Island was not recognized as Korean territory, and was formally incorporated into Japanese territory in 1905. It was occupied by the Republic of Korea after the Second World War, however, resulting in a territorial dispute.

Further to the north in the Sea of Okhotsk, Russians had appeared as a major player and introduced a new practice in the latter half of the eighteenth century of declaring their "territorial jurisdiction" by erecting a monument when they first landed on each island. This practice did not cause much of a problem in the East China Sea region, where the relationship of compartmentalization was firmly established. In the northern part of East Asia, however, given the existing perception of borders as consisting not of lines but rather of expanses or sweeps, this Russian practice made the question of "territorial jurisdiction" an international issue.

Against this background several Japanese explorers, including Mogami Tokunai[28] (1755–1836), Kondō Jūzō[29] (1771–1829) and Mamiya Rinzō[30] (1775–1844), began to explore areas north of Japan in the late eighteenth century with the approval of their government. Their achievements were not simply the results of each man's personal ambition to be an explorer. As each blank in Japan's territorial map was filled in by their accomplishments, a line of demarcation and place names were written into the map that differentiated Japan's territory from that of other countries. Thus, each specific portion of sea and each island was classified as belonging to one country or another.

An incident symbolic of these developments took place in 1798, when Kondō Jūzō and Mogami Tokunai, vassals of the Tokugawa Shogunate, were exploring Iturup Island in the Kuril Islands at the behest of the government. There they erected a banner pole that read "*Dainippon Etorofu*" (Etorofu (Iturup) of Great Japan). This moment might be marked

---

28 Mogami Tokunai was a retainer of the shogun. He studied astronomy, navigation and surveying techniques under Honda Toshiaki in Edo. From 1785, he explored the area of Ezo (Hokkaido), the Chishima Islands (the Kuril Islands) and Karafuto under orders from the shogunate.

29 Kondō Jūzō, born in Edo, was a retainer of the shogun. In 1798, he became the official director of Matsumae in Ezo and explored the area of the Chishima Islands.

30 Mamiya Rinzō was a retainer of the shogun and the author of the books *Tōdatsu Chihō Kikō* (Travelogue of the Lower Reaches of the Amur River) and *Kita Ezo Zusetsu* (Illustrated Account of North Ezo). He studied surveying techniques under Ino Tadataka and was engaged in the surveying of Ezo. In 1808, he explored Karafuto with Matsuda Denjūrō, confirming that it was an island and giving his name to the Mamiya Strait. The following year, he crossed over to the continent, meeting Qing bannermen bureaucrats at Deren in the lower reaches of the Amur River (present-day Heilongjiang River).

as pivotal in the transformation from the early modern era, when the seas in East Asia were characterized by relationships of "compartmentalization", to the modern era, when clear lines representing national borders would be drawn across them. These seas would then become "divided seas", where neighboring countries would come into conflict over the question of how and where to demarcate lines of sovereignty.

# Bibliography

The English titles of books and articles published in non-English languages were translated by the editors of this book and are included in parentheses next to their original titles for the convenience of readers. In many cases formal English titles do not exist for these works.

## Prologue

### Cited Sources
Tei, Junsoku, *Shinan Kōgi* (Broad Interpretation of Navigation Guide). Cambridge: Harvard Yenching Library.
Xu, Yang, *Chong Xiu Nanhai Putuo Shan Zhi*. Tokyo: Naikaku Bunko.

### Japanese Bibliography
Adachi, Hiroyuki, 1998. *Nihon no Fune: Wasen Hen* (Ships in Japan: Japanese-Style Ships). Tokyo: Museum of Maritime Science.
Iwao, Seiichi, 1985. *Shuinsen Bōekishi no Kenkyū* (Study of the History of the Red-Seal Ship Trade: New Edition). Tokyo: Yoshikawa Kōbunkan.
Yamagata, Kinya, 2004. *Rekishi no Umi o Hashiru: Chūgoku Zōsen Gijutsu no Kōseki* (Sail on the Sea of History: The Trail of the Shipbuilding Technology of China). Tokyo: Nō-San-Gyo Son Bunka Kyōkai.

## Part 1

### Cited Sources
Ibn Battuta, 1994. *The Travels of Ibn Baṭṭūṭa, A.D. 1325–1354, Vol. IV*, trans. and annotated by H. A. R. Gibb; trans. completed with annotations by C. F. Beckingham. London: Hakluyt Society.
Kitabatake, Chikafusa, 1980. *A Chronicle of Gods and Sovereigns: Jinnō Shōtōki of Kitabatake Chikafusa*, trans. H. Paul Varley. New York: Columbia University Press.
Ōba, Kōji (ed.), 2008. *Chūsei Toshi Hakata wo Horu* (Excavating the Medieval City of Hakata). Fukuoka: Kaichōsha.

Polo, Marco, 1994. *The Travels of Marco Polo*. Translated into English from the text of L. F. Benedetto by Aldo Ricci; with an introduction and index by E. Denison Ross. Reprint by Asian Educational Service (New Delhi). First published in London by Routledge & Kegan Paul, 1931.

## *Japanese Bibliography*

Aida, Nirō, 1972. *Chūsei no Sekisho* (Barriers in the Middle Ages: Reissued and Enlarged Edition). Tokyo: Arimine Shoten.

Arano, Yasunori (ed.), 1992–1993. *Ajia no Naka no Nihonshi* (Japanese History in the Context of Asia), vols. 1–6. Tokyo: The University of Tokyo Press.

Degawa, Tetsurō (ed.), 2001. *Ajia Tōgeishi* (History of Asian Ceramics). Kyoto: Shōwadō.

Enomoto, Wataru, 2006. "Shoki Nichi-Gen Bōeki to Jin-teki Kōryū" (Japan-China trade and human interaction in the early Yuan period). In *Chōkō Ryūiki no Sōdai: Shakai Keizaishi no Kanten kara* (The Yangtze River Basin during the Song Period: From a Socio-economic Perspective). Tokyo: Kyūko Shoin.

Enomoto, Wataru, 2007. *Higashi Ajia Kai'iki to Nitchū Kōryū: 9-14 Seiki* (East Asian Maritime Region and Japan-China Relations from the Ninth to Fourteenth Century). Tokyo: Yoshikawa Kōbunkan.

Enomoto, Wataru, 2010. *Sōryo to Kaishōtachi no Higashi Shina Kai* (East China Sea of Buddhist Priests and Sea Merchants). Tokyo: Kōdansha.

Fujita, Akiyoshi, 1997. "Ranshūzan no Ran to Higashi Ajia no Kai'iki Sekai: 14 Seiki no Shūzan Guntō to Kōrai-Nihon" ("The revolt of Ranshū Island" and the East Asian maritime world in the fourteenth century). *Rekishigaku Kenkyū* (Historical Science), 698.

Fujita, Toyohachi, 1932. *Tōzai Kōshōshi no Kenkyū: Nankai-hen* (An Investigation of the History of East and West Relations: Part of the Southern Sea). Tokyo: Oka Shoin.

Fukami, Sumio, 2004. "Gendai no Marakka Kaikyō: Tsūro ka Kyoten ka" (Passage or emporium? The Malacca Straits during the Yuan period). *Southeast Asia: History and Culture*, 33.

Fukami, Sumio, 2006. "Tambralinga no Hatten to 13 Seiki Tōnan Ajia no Commercial Boom" (The rise of Tambralinga and the Southeast Asian commercial boom in the thirteenth century). *Kokusai Bunka Ronshū* (Intercultural Studies), 32, Research Institute of St. Andrew's University.

Ikehata, Setsuho (ed.), 2001. *Tōnan Ajia Kodai Kokka no Seiritsu to Tenkai* (The Formation and Development of Ancient States in Southeast Asia). Iwanami Kōza: Tōnan Ajia-shi, vol. 2. Tokyo: Iwanami Shoten.

Ikeuchi, Hiroshi, 1931. *Genkō no Shin Kenkyū* (A New Study on the Mongol Invasions). Tokyo: The Oriental Library.

Kawazoe, Shōji, 1987. "Kamakura Chūki no Taigai Kankei to Hakata" (Foreign relations in the middle Kamakura period and Hakata). *Kyūshū Shigaku*, 88–90.

Kawazoe, Shōji, 1988. "Kamakura Shoki no Taigai Kankei to Hakata" (Foreign relations in the early Kamakura period and Hakata). In Yanai Kenji (ed.), *Sakoku Nihon to Kokusai Kōryū* (Japan in the Sakoku and its International Exchange). Tokyo: Yoshikawa Kōbunkan.

Kawazoe, Shōji, 1993. "Kamakura Makki no Taigai Kankei to Hakata" (Foreign relations in the late Kamakura period and Hakata). In Ōsumi Kazuo (ed.), *Kamakura Jidai Bunka Denpa no Kenkyū* (Study on Cultural Diffusion in the Kamakura Period). Tokyo: Yoshikawa Kōbunkan.
Kim Mungyeong, Heon Haengja and Satō Haruhiko (eds), 2002. *Rō-Kitsu-Dai: Chōsen Chūsei no Chūgokugo Kaiwa Tokuhon* (A Textbook of Colloquial Chinese in Medieval Korea). Tokyo: Heibonsha.
Kimiya, Yasuhiko, 1955. *Nikka Bunka Kōryūshi* (History of the Cultural Exchange between Japan and China). Tokyo: Fuzanbō.
Kinoshita, Naoko (ed.), 2009. *13-14 Seiki no Ryukyu to Fukken* (Ryukyu and Fujian in the Thirteenth and Fourteenth Centuries). Report for the Ministry of Education, Culture, Sports, Science and Technology Grants-in-Aid for Scientific Research (2005–2008).
Kitamura, Hideto, 1979. "Kōrai Jidai no Sōsō-sei ni tsuite" (The port storehouse system for grain tax transportation in the Goryeo period). In *Chōsen Rekishi Ronshū: Hatada Takashi Sensei Koki Kinen* (Commemoration for the Seventy Years of Age Memorial of Prof. Hatada Takashi), vol. 1. Tokyo: Ryūkei Shosha.
Kuwabara, Jitsuzō, 1989. *Ho Jukō no Jiseki* (Deeds of Pu Shogeng). Tokyo: Heibonsha.
Maeda, Motoshige, 1978. "Kanesawa Bunko Komonjo ni Mieru Nichi-Gen Kōtsū Shiryō: Shōmyōji Sō Shun'nyobō no Totō wo megutte" (Historical sources for the exchange between Japan and Yuan China from the collection of ancient documents of Kanesawa Bunko: On the travel to China of Buddhist priest of the Shōmyōji Temple, Shun'nyobo). *Kanesawa Bunko Kenkyū*, 249–250.
Masuya, Tomoko, 2009. *Sugu Wakaru Isuramu no Bijutsu: Kenchiku, Shahon Geijutsu, Kōgei* (A Plain Introduction to Islamic Art: Architecture, Manuscript Arts and Crafts). Tokyo: Tokyo Bijutsu.
Miya, Noriko, 2010. "Tanksūq nāmah no 'Mo-chue' wo Tazunete: Mongoru Jidai no Shomotsu no Tabi" (Search for the original text of 'Mo-chue' of Tanksūq Nāmah: Travel of books during the Mongol period). In Kubota Jumpei (ed.), *Eurasia Chūōiki no Rekishi Kōzu: 13-15 Seiki no Tōzai* (The Historical Composition of Central Eurasia: The East and the West in the Thirteenth to Fifteenth Century). Kyoto: Research Institute for Humanity and Nature.
Momoki, Shirō (ed.), 2008. *Kai'iki Ajia-shi Kenkyū Nyūmon* (An Introduction to Maritime Asian History). Tokyo: Iwanami Shoten.
Mori, Katsumi, 2008–2010. *Shin Mori Katsumi Chosakushū* (Works of Mori Katsumi: New Edition), vols. 1–3. Tokyo: Bensei Shuppan.
Morihira, Masahiko, 2011. *Mongoru Teikoku no Haken to Chōsen Hantō* (The Hegemony of the Mongol Empire and the Korean Peninsula). Sekai-shi Libretto, vol. 99. Tokyo: Yamakawa Shuppansha.
Morihira, Masahiko, 2013. "Kōrai ni okeru Gen no Jamči: Rūto no Hitei wo Chūshin ni" (The Mongolian post system, Jamči in the Goryeo Dynasty: Focusing on routes). In Morihira Masahiko, *Mongoru Hakenka no Kōrai: Teikoku Chitsujo to Ōkoku no Taiō* (Goryeo under the Hegemony of the Mongol

Empire: The Imperial Order and Handling by the Kingdom). Nagoya: The University of Nagoya Press.

Moriyasu, Takao, 2010. "Nihon ni Genzon suru Mani-kyō Kaiga no Hakken to sono Rekishiteki Haikei" (The discovery of Manichaean paintings in Japan and their historical background). *Nairiku Ajia-shi Kenkyū* (Inner Asian Studies), 25.

Mukai, Masaki, 2007. "Ho Jukō Gunji Shūdan to Mongoru Kaijō Seiryoku no Taitō" (The role of Pu Shogeng's private militia in the emergence of Mongol maritime power). *Tōyō Gakuhō* (Reports of the Oriental Society), 89(3).

Mukai, Masaki, 2008. "Kubiraichō Shoki Nankai Shōyu no Jitsuzō: Senshū ni okeru Gunji Kōeki Shūdan to Connection" (Another aspect of the legation to the southern seas during the early part of Khubilai's reign: Military and trade groups and their connections). *Tōhō Gak* (Eastern Studies), 116.

Mukai, Masaki, 2009. "Mongoru Chika Fukken Enkaibu no Musurimu Kanjinsō" (Muslim officials in the Fujian coastal region during the Yuan period). *Arabu Isuramu Kenkyū* (Journal of Arabic and Islamic Studies), 7.

Mukai, Masaki, 2009. "Genchō Shoki no Nankai Bōeki to Kōshō: Mangutai no Shihaku Gyōsei Kanyo to sono Haikei" (Nanhai trade and mobile secretariat during the early Yuan period: On the background of Mangutai's influence over maritime trade administration). *Machikaneyama Ronsō* (*History*), 43.

Murai, Shōsuke, 1988. *Ajia no Nakano Chūsei Nihon* (Medieval Japan in the Context of Asia). Tokyo: Azekura Shobō.

Murai, Shōsuke, 2005. *Chūsei no Kokka to Zaichi Shakai* (Medieval States and the Local Society). Tokyo: Azekura Shobō.

Murakami, Masatsugu, 1993. *Mongoru Teikoku-shi Kenkyū* (Study of the History of the Mongol Empire). Tokyo: Kazama Shobō.

Nakajima Gakushō, 2013. "Genchō no Nihon Ensei Kantai to Kyū Nansō Suigun" (Organization of the expedition fleet of the Mongol invasion to Japan and its relationship with the Southern Song naval fleet). In Nakajima Gakushō and Itō Kōji (eds), *Ningbo to Hakata* (Ningbo and Hakata). Tokyo: Kyūko Shoin.

Nam, Ki-Hak, 1996. *Mōko Shūrai to Kamakura Bakufu* (Mongol Invasions and the Kamakura Shogunate). Kyoto: Rinsen Shoten.

Okada, Hidehiro, 2010. *Mongoru Teikoku kara Daishin Teikoku e* (From the Mongol Empire to the Great Qing Empire). Tokyo: Fujiwara Shoten.

Ōta, Kōki, 1997. *Mōko Shūrai: Sono Gunji-shi-teki Kenkyū* (Mongol Invasions: A Study of Military History). Tokyo: Kinseisha.

Otagi, Matsuo, 1987. *Chūgoku Shakai Bunka-shi* (Sociocultural History of China), Otagi Matsuo Tōyōshigaku Ronshū, vol. 2. Tokyo: San-ichi Shobō.

Ozaki, Kikuko, 2007. "Gendai no Nichiyōruisho *Kyoka Hitsuyō Jirui* ni mieru Hui-hui Shokuhin" (Islamic foods in *The Guide to Running a Household*, a Book of household items in Yuan China). *Tōyō Gakuhō* (Reports of the Oriental Society), 88(3).

Saeki, Kōji, 2003. *Mongoru Shūrai no Shōgeki* (The Impact of Mongol Invasions). Nihon no Chūsei, vol. 9. Tokyo: Chūō Kōron Shinsha.

Saeki, Kōji, 2009. "Chinzei Tandai, Chinzei Kanrei to Higashi Ajia" (The Chinzei Tandai, the Chinzei Kanrei and East Asia). In Higashi Ajia Chiikikan Kōryū Kenkyūkai (ed.), *Karafune Ōrai: Nihon wo Sodateta Hito, Fune, Machi, Kokoro* (The Traffic of Chinese Ships: People, Ships, Cities and the Heart that Fostered Japan). Fukuoka: Chūgoku Shoten.

Sasaki, Ginya, 1994. *Nihon Chūsei no Ryūtsū to Taigai Kankei* (The Distribution System and Foreign Relations in Medieval Japan). Tokyo: Yoshikawa Kōbunkan.

Shiba, Yoshinobu, 1968. *Sōdai Shōgyōshi Kenkyū* (Commerce and Society in Song China). Tokyo: Kazama Shobō.

Shiba, Yoshinobu, 2006. "Gōshu, Gōshi, Kōshi: Junk-Shōsen no Keiei wo megutte" (Gaoshou, Gaosi and Gongsi: On the management of Chinese junk commercial ships). In Morikawa Tetsuo and Saeki Kōji (eds), *Nairikuken / Kai'ikiken Kōryū Network to Isuramu* (The Inland and Maritime Network of International Exchange and Islam), the 21st Century COE Program of the Kyushu University (Humanities): *East Asia and Japan: Interaction and Transformation*.

Shinjō, Tsunezō, 1994. *Chūsei Suiun-shi no Kenkyū* (Study of the History of Water Transportation in Medieval Japan). Tokyo: Hanawa Shobō.

Sugiyama, Masaaki, 1995. *Kubirai no Chōsen* (Challenge of Qubilai Qa'an). Tokyo: Asahi Shimbunsha.

Sukawa, Hidenori, 1997. "Kōrai Kōki ni okeru Shōgyō Seisaku no Tenkai: Taigai Kankei wo Chūshin ni" (The development of the commercial policy during the late Koryo period: With a focus on foreign trade relations). *Chōsen Bunka Kenkyū* (Korean Culture), 4.

Uematsu, Tadashi, 2004. "Gen-dai no Kaiun Bankofu to Kaiun Seika" (The maritime tumens and the marine aristocratic families during the Yuan period). *Kyoto Joshi Daigaku Daigakuin Bungaku Kenkyūka Kenkyū Kiyō* (*Shigaku*), 3.

Yajima, Hikoichi, 1993. *Umi ga Tsukuru Bunmei: Indo-yō Kai'iki Sekai no Rekishi* (Civilization Created by the Sea: History of the Indian Ocean World). Tokyo: Asahi Shimbunsha.

Yajima, Hikoichi, 2006. *Kai'iki kara Mita Rekishi: Indo-yō to Chichūkai wo Musubu Kōryūshi* (History Seen from the Sea: Historical Relations between the Indian Ocean and the Mediterranean). Nagoya: The University of Nagoya Press.

Yamauchi, Shinji, 2002. "Nissō Bōeki no Tenkai" (The development of the trade between Japan and Song China). In Katō Tomoyasu (ed.), *Sekkan Seiji to Ōchō Bunka*: Nihon no Jidaishi, vol. 6. Tokyo: Yoshikawa Kōbunkan.

Yamauchi, Shinji, 2003. *Nara-Heian-ki no Nihon to Ajia* (Japan in the Nara and Heian Periods and Asia). Tokyo: Yoshikawa Kōbunkan.

Yamauchi, Shinji, 2009. *Nissō Bōeki to Iō no Michi* (Japan-Song China Trade and the "Sulfur Road"). Nihon-shi Libretto, vol. 75. Tokyo: Yamakawa Shuppansha.

Yokkaichi, Yasuhiro, 2000. "Genchō Kyūtei ni okeru Kōeki to Teishin Shūdan" (Trade in the court of Yuan China and the group of courtiers). *Bulletin of the Graduate Division of Literature of Waseda University*, 45(4).

Yokkaichi, Yasuhiro, 2002. "Genchō no Chūbai Hōka: Sono Igi oyobi Nankai Kōeki Orutoku tono Kakawari ni tsuite" (Zhong-mai Bao-huo in the Yuan period: On its meaning and relationship with the Nanhai trade and ortuγ merchants). *Nairiku Ajiashi Kekyū* (Inner Asian Studies), 17.

Yokkaichi, Yasuhiro, 2006. "Genchō Atsudatsu Seisaku ni miru Kōeki Katsudō to Shūkyō Katsudō no Shosō: Fu Gentenshō Atsudatsu Kankei Jōbun Yakuchū" (Aspects of trade and religions under the Yuan Dynasty from the perspective of ortuγ merchants policy, with the appendix: The interpretations and notes of articles of Yuan-dian-zhang related to ortuγ policy, part 1). In the 21st Century COE Program of the Kyushu University (Humanities) (ed.), *East Asia and Japan: Interaction and Transformation*, vol. 3.

Yokkaichi, Yasuhiro, 2006. "Genchō Nankai Kōeki Keiei Kō: Monjo Gyōsei to Senka no Nagare kara" (The Yuan government's control and management of the Nanhai trade: From the aspect of formal documents and flow of trading capital). *The Tōyōshi Ronshū* (Oriental Studies), Kyushu University, 34.

Yokkaichi, Yasuhiro (ed.), 2008. *Mono kara mita Kai'iki Ajia-shi: Mongoru-Sō-Gen Jidai no Ajia to Nihon no Kōryū* (History of the Maritime Asian Sphere Viewed from the Distribution of Goods: The Relationship between Japan and Asia in the Mongol Empire and the Song-Yuan Periods). Fukuoka: Kyushu University Press.

Wada, Hisanori, 1959. "Tōnan Ajia ni okeru Shoki Kakyō Shakai 960-1279" (The Chinese Colonies in Southeast Asia in the Song Period, 960–1279). *Tōyō Gakuhō* (Reports of the Oriental Society), 42(1).

Wajima, Yoshio, 1965. *Chūsei no Jugaku* (Confucianism in Medieval Japan). Tokyo: Yoshikawa Kōbunkan.

## Chinese Bibliography

Chen Gaohua, 2005. *Yuandai Yanjiu Xinlun* (A New Study of the History of Yuan China). Shanghai: Shehui Kexueyuan Chubanshe.

Chen Gaohua and Wu Tai, 1981. *Song Yuan Shiqi de Haiwai Maoyi* (Foreign Trade in the Song and Yuan Periods). Tianjin Renmin Chubanshe.

Gao Rongsheng, 1983. "Yuandai Haiyun Shixi" (An essay on the marine transportation of the Yuan period). In *Yuanshi Ji Beifang Minzushi Yanjiu Jikan* (Collection of Treatises on the History of Yuan China and the Northern Peoples), 7.

Gao Rongsheng, 1998. *Yuandai Haiwai Maoyi Yanjiu* (Study of Foreign Trade in the Yuan Period). Sichuan Renmin Chubanshe.

Wang Saishi, 2005. *Shandong Yanhai Kaifashi* (History of the Development of the Coastal Area of Shandong). Qilu Shushe.

## Korean Bibliography

Dongbuga Yeoksa Jaedan and Han-Il Munhwa Gyoryu Gigeum (eds), 2009. *Monggol-ui Goryeo, Ilbon Chimgong-gwa Han-Il Gwangye* (Mongol Invasions to Goreyo and to Japan, and the Relationship between Korea and Japan). Seoul: Gyeongin Munhwasa.

Dongbuga Yeoksa Jaedan and Gyeongbuk Daehakgyo Hanjung Gyoryu Yeonguwon (eds), 2011. *13-14 Segi Goryeo-Monggol Gwangye Tamgu* (Studies on Goryeo-Mongol Relations in the 13th–14th Centuries). Seoul: Dongbuga Yeoksa Jaedan (The Northeast Asian History Foundation).

Guksa Pyeonchan Wiwonhoe (ed.), 1994–1996. *Hanguksa* (History of Korea), vols. 19–21. Gwacheon: Guksa Pyeonchan Wiwonhoe (National Institute of Korean History).

Kim Ilu, 2000. *Goryeo-sidae Tamnasa Yeongu* (Study of Tamna (Jejudo Island) during the Goryeo Period). Seoul: Sinseowon.

Lee Kang-hahn, 2008. "Won, Ilbon-gan Gyoyeokseon-ui Goryeo Bangmun Yangsang Geomto" (Review of Yuan-Japan merchant ships visiting Goryeo). *Haeyang Munhwajae* (Maritime Cultural Heritage), vol. 1.

Yun Yonghyeok, 2000. *Goryeo Sambyeolcho-ui Dae-mong Hangjaeng* (The Resistance of Sambyeolcho of Goryeo against the Mongols). Seoul: Iljisa.

# Part 2

### Cited Sources
Blair, Emma Helen, and James A. Robertson (eds), 1903–1909. *The Philippine Islands, 1493–1803*. Cleveland: A. H. Clark.
Bocarro, Antonio, 1635. *Livro das Plantas de Todas as Fortalezas, Cidades e Povoações do Estado da India Oriental*. Biblioteca Pública de Évora.
Bronson, Bennet, 1977. "Exchange at Upstream and Downstream Ends". In Karl L. Hutterer (ed.), *Economic Exchange and Social Interaction in Southeast Asia*. Ann Arbor: Center for South and Southeast Asian Studies, University of Michigan.
Carletti, Francesco (trans. Herbert Weinstock), 1964. *My Voyage around the World*. New York: Pantheon Books.
Pires, Thomé (Armando Cortesão trans. and ed.), 1944. *The Suma Oriental of Tomé Pires and the Book of Francisco Rodrigues*. London: Hakluyt Society.

### Japanese Bibliography
Amino, Tetsuya, 2008. *Inca to Spain Teikoku no Kōsaku* (The Intersection between the Inca and the Spanish Empire). Kōbō no Sekaishi, vol. 12. Tokyo: Kōdansha.
Aoki, Yasuyuki, 2000. *Nanbei Potosi Ginzan* (Potosi Silver Mine in South America). Tokyo: Chūō Kōron Shinsha.
Arakawa, Hirokazu, 1971. *Namban Shitsugei* (Namban Lacquer Art). Tokyo: Bijutsu Shuppansha.
Araki, Kazunori, 2007. *Chūsei Tsushima Sōshi Ryōgoku to Chōsen* (The Domain of the Sō Family in Medieval Tsushima and Korea). Tokyo: Yamakawa Shuppansha.
Arima, Seiho, 1962. *Kahō no Kigen to sono Denryū* (The Origin of Fire Guns and Their Diffusion). Tokyo: Yoshikawa Kōbunkan.
Banno, Masataka, 1973. *Kindai Chūgoku Seiji Gaikō-shi: Vasco da Gama kara Goshi Undō made* (The Political and Diplomatic History of Modern China: From Vasco da Gama to the May Fourth Movement). Tokyo: The University of Tokyo Press.
Cheng, Liang-Sheng, 1985. *Min-Nichi Kankei-shi no Kenkyū* (Study of the Relationship between Ming China and Japan). Tokyo: Yūzankaku Shuppan.
Dana, Masayuki, 1991. "Ko-Ryukyu no Kumemura" (Kume Village of ancient Ryukyu). *Shin Ryukyu-shi: Ko-Ryukyu-hen* (New History of Ryukyu: Part of Ancient Ryukyu). Naha: Ryukyu Shimpōsha.
Danjō, Hiroshi, 1997. "Minsho no Kaikin to Chōkō: Minchō Sensei Shihai no Rikai ni yosete" (Maritime exclusion and tribute in the early Ming period: On the comprehension of the autocracy of the Ming Dynasty). In Mori Masao (ed.), *Min-Shin Jidai-shi no Kihon Mondai* (Fundamental Questions of the History of the Ming and Qing Periods). Tokyo: Kyūko Shoin.
Danjō, Hiroshi, 2004. "Mindai Kaikin Gainen no Seiritsu to Sono Haikei: Ikinkakai kara Gekaitsūban e" (The formation and background of the concept of maritime exclusion: From a prohibition on voyages in foreign waters to a prohibition on voyages for trading with foreigners". *Tōyōshi Kenkyū* (The Journal of Oriental Research), 63(2).

Danjō, Hiroshi, 2005. "Mindai Kaikin no Jitsuzō: Kaikin-Chōkō System no Sōsetsu to Sono Tenkai" (The real image of the maritime exclusion of the Ming Dynasty: Creation and development of the maritime exclusion and tributary system). In Rekishigaku Kenkyūkai (ed.), *Minatomachi to Kai'iki Sekai* (Port Cities and the Maritime World). Tokyo: Aoki Shoten.

Ejima, Hisao, 1999. *Mindai Shinsho no Joshinshi Kenkyū* (Study of the History of the Jurchen in the Ming and the Early Qing Periods). Fukuoka: Chūgoku Shoten.

Enoki, Kazuo, 1984. *Shōnin Carletti* (Merchant Carletti). Tokyo: Daitō Shuppansha.

Flynn, Dennis, 2010. *Global-ka to Gin* (Globalization and Silver), Akita Shigeru and Nishimura Takeshi (eds). Tokyo: Yamakawa Shuppansha.

Fujiki, Hisashi, 1985. *Toyotomi Heiwarei to Sengoku Shakai* (The Peace Ordinance of Toyotomi and the Society of the Sengoku Period). Tokyo: The University of Tokyo Press.

Fujiki, Hisashi, 2005. *Zōhyōtachi no Senjō* (The Battlefields of Common Soldiers: New Edition). Tokyo: Asahi Shimbunnsha.

Fujimoto, Yukio, 1993. "Insatsu Bunka no Hikakushi" (Comparative history of printing culture). In Arano Yasunori (ed.), *Ajia no Nakano Nihonshi: Bunka to Gijutsu*, vol. 6. Tokyo: The University of Tokyo Press.

Fukase, Kōichirō, 2007. "16-17 Seiki ni okeru Ryukyu, Minami Kyūshū to Kaishō" (Sea merchants in the maritime region of Ryukyu and the southern Kyūshū in the 16th and 17th centuries). *Shikan*, 157.

Gōda, Masafumi, 2006. *Magellan: Sekai Bunkatsu o Taigenshita Kōkaisha* (Magellan, the Navigator Who Embodied the Division of the World). Kyoto: Kyoto University Press.

Hagiwara, Jumpei, 1980. *Mindai Mōkoshi Kenkyū* (Study of the Mongols during the Ming Dynasty). Kyoto: Dōhōsha Shuppan.

Haino, Akio, 1985. *Nihon no Bijutsu: Shikkō, Kinsei-hen* (Japanese Art: Lacquerware, Part of the Early Modern Period), vol. 231. Tokyo: Shibundō.

Hamashita, Takeshi, 1997. *Chōkō System to Kindai Ajia* (The Tributary System and Modern Asia). Tokyo: Iwanami Shoten.

Hashimoto, Yū, 1998. "Erizeni-rei to Rettō Naigai no Senka Ryūtsū" (The exclusion of bad money and the currency circulation inside and outside of Japan). *Shutsudo Senka* (Excavated Coins), 9.

Hashimoto, Yū, 2002. "Ken-Min-Sen no Haken Keiki" (The opportunity of dispatching envoy ships to Ming China". *Nihonshi Kenkyu* (Journal of Japanese History), 479.

Hashimoto, Yū, 2005. *Chūsei Nihon no Kokusai Kōryū: Higashi Ajia Tsūkōken to Gishi Mondai* (The International Relationship of Medieval Japan: The East Asian Trade Area and the Problem of Imposter Envoys). Tokyo: Yoshikawa Kōbunkan.

Hidaka, Kaori, 2008. *Ikoku no Hyōshō: Kinsei Yushutsu Shikki no Sōzōryoku* (Image of a Foreign Country: The Creativity of Lacquerware Exported from Japan in the Early Modern Period). Tokyo: Brücke.

Hidaka, Kaori, 2008. "Ikoku e Okurareta Shikki: Tenshō Shōnen Shisetsu no Miyagemono" (Lacquerware sent to foreign countries: The Tensho Mission to Europe and their gifts". *Bulletin of the National Museum of Japanese History*, 140.

Hirosue, Masashi, 2004. *Tōnan Ajia no Kōshi Sekai: Chiiki Shakai no Keisei to Sekai Chitsujo* (The World of the Port Polities of Southeast Asia: The Formation of Local Societies and the World Order). Tokyo: Iwanami Shoten.
Hora, Tomio, 1991. *Teppō: Denrai to Sono Eikyō* (The Arrival of Guns to Japan and Its Influence). Kyoto: Shibunkaku Shuppan.
Igawa, Kenji, 2007. *Daikōkai Jidai no Higashi Ajia: Nichiō Tsūkō no Rekishiteki Zentei* (East Asia in the Age of Exploration: Historical Premise for the Diplomatic Relationship between Japan and Europe). Tokyo: Yoshikawa Kōbunkan.
Ikehata, Setsuho (ed.), 1999. *Tōnan Ajia-shi vol.2: Tōshobu* (History of Southeast Asia II: Insular Regions). Shinpan Sekai Kakkokushi, vol. 6. Tokyo: Yamakawa Shuppansha.
Ikuta, Shigeru, 1998. *Daikōkai Jidai to Molucca Shotō: Portugal, Spain, Ternate Ōkoku to Chōji Bōeki* (The Age of Exploration and the Moluccas: Portugal, Spain, the Ternate Kingdom and the Clove Trade). Tokyo: Chūō Kōronsha.
Inokuma, Kaneki, 2006. "Kanzō Daikōkai Jidai no Kōgeihin ni kansuru Shōkō" (A brief analysis on the crafts of the Age of Exploration from the collection of the Kyushu National Museum). *Tōfū Seisei* (The Bulletin of Kyushu National Museum), 2.
Inoue, Susumu, 2002. *Chūgoku Shuppan Bunkashi* (History of the Publishing Culture in China). Nagoya: The University of Nagoya Press.
Ishihara, Michihiro, 1964. *Wakō* (The Wokou). Tokyo: Yoshikawa Kōbunkan.
Ishizawa, Yoshiaki, and Shigeru Ikuta, 1998. *Tōnan Ajia no Dentō to Hatten* (The Tradition and the Development of Southeast Asia). Sekai no Rekishi, vol. 13. Tokyo: Chūō Kōronsha.
Itō, Kōji, 2002. *Chūsei Nihon no Gaikō to Zenshū* (Diplomacy of Medieval Japan and Zen Buddhism). Tokyo: Yoshikawa Kōbunkan.
Itō, Kōji, 2002. "Chūsei Kōki Gaikōshisetsu no Tabi to Tera" (The journies of diplomatic envoys and temples in the late Middle Ages). In Nakao Takashi (ed.), *Chūsei no Jiin Taisei to Shakai* (The Temple Systems and Society in the Middle Ages). Tokyo: Yoshikawa Kōbunkan.
Iwai, Shigeki, 1996. "16-17 Seiki no Chūgoku Henkyō Shakai" (Society in the frontier regions of China in the sixteenth and seventeenth centuries). In Ono Kazuko (ed.), *Min-matsu Shin-sho no Shakai to Bunka* (Society and Culture of China in the Late Ming and Early Qing Periods). Kyoto: Institute for Humanities Research, Kyoto University.
Iwai, Shigeki, 2004. "16 Seiki Chūgoku ni okeru Kōeki-Chitsujo no Mosaku" (Search for the order of trade in sixteenth-century China). In Shigeki Iwai (ed.), *Chūgoku Kinsei-Shakai no Chitsujo-Keisei* (The Formation of Order in Modern Chinese Society). Kyoto: Institute for Humanities Research, Kyoto University.
Iwai, Shigeki, 2005. "Min-dai Chūgoku no Reisei Haken Shugi to Higashi Ajia no Chitsujo" (The hegemony of the Li-system in Ming China and the order of East Asia). *Tōyō Bunka* (Oriental Culture), 85.
Iwai, Shigeki, 2009. "Teikoku to Goshi" (The empire and trade). In Kagotani Naoto and Wakimura Kohei (eds), *Teikoku to Ajia Network – Chōki no 19-Seiki* (The Empire and the Asian Network: The Long Nineteenth Century). Kyoto: Sekai Shisōsha.

Iwao, Seiichi, 1966. *Nanyō Nihon-machi no Kenkyū* (Study on Japan Towns in the South Seas). Tokyo: Iwanami Shoten.
Kage, Toshio, 2006. *Sengoku Daimyō no Gaikō to Toshi, Ryūtsū* (The Diplomacy of Daimyōs, Cities and the Distribution System in the Sengoku Period). Kyoto: Shibunkaku Shuppan.
Kage, Toshio (ed.), 2008. *Sengoku Daimyō Ōtomo-shi to Bungo Funai* (The Warlord Ōtomo and Bungo Funai). Tokyo: Kōshi Shoin.
Kage, Toshio, 2011. *Ajian Sengoku Daimyō Ōtomo-shi no Kenkyū* (A Study on Asian Warlords, the Ōtomo Family). Tokyo: Yoshikawa Kōbunkan.
Kamiya, Nobuyuki, 1990. *Bakuhan-sei Kokka no Ryukyu Shihai* (The State under the Baku-han System and the Rule of Ryukyu). Tokyo: Azekura Shobō.
Kanaya, Masato, 1998. *Kaizoku-tachi no Chūsei* (The Medieval Ages of Pirates). Tokyo: Yoshikawa Kōbunkan.
Kankoku Toshokan-gaku Kenkyūkai (ed.), 1978. *Kankoku Ko-Insatsu-shi* (History of Old Printing in Korea). Kyoto: Dōhōsha.
Katsumata, Shizuo, 1996. *Sengoku Jidai Ron* (Treatise on the Sengoku Period). Tokyo: Iwanami Shoten.
Kawase, Kazuma, 1967. *Ko-Katsuji-ban no Kenkyū* (A Study on Old Movable-Type Printing), New Edition. Tokyo: Antiquarian Booksellers Association of Japan.
Kishida, Hiroshi, 2001. *Daimyō Ryōgoku no Keizai-Kōzō* (The Economic Structure of Daimyōs' Territory). Tokyo: Iwanami Shoten.
Kishimoto, Mio, 1997. *Shin-dai Chūgoku no Bukka to Keizai-Hendō* (Prices and Economic Changes in Qing China). Tokyo: Kenbun Shuppan.
Kishimoto, Mio, 1998. *Higashi-Ajia no 'Kinsei'* (The Early Modern Period of East Asia). Sekai-shi Libretto, vol. 13. Tokyo: Yamakawa Shuppansha.
Kishimoto, Mio, 1998. "Higashi-Ajia, Tōnan -Ajia Dentō-Shakai no Keisei" (The formation of the traditional society of East and Southeast Asia). In Kishimoto Mio (ed.), *Higashi-Asia, Tōnan-Asia Dentō-Shakai no Keisei* (The Formation of the Traditional Society of East and Southeast Asia). Iwanami Kōza: Sekai Rekishi, vol. 13. Tokyo: Iwanami Shoten.
Kishimoto, Mio, and Hiroshi Miyajima (eds), 1998. *Min Shin to Richō no Jidai* (Periods of Ming, Qing and Lee Korea). Sekai no Rekishi, vol. 12. Tokyo: Chūō Kōronsha.
Kitajima, Manji, 1995. *Toyotomi Hideyoshi no Chōsen Shinryaku* (Toyotomi Hideyoshi's Invasions of Korea). Tokyo: Yoshikawa Kōbunkan.
Kitō, Hiroshi, 2000. *Jinkō kara Yomu Nihon no Rekishi* (History of Japan Seen from Its Population). Tokyo: Kōdansha.
Kobata, Atsushi, 1942. *Nihon Kahei Ryūtsū-shi* (History of the Currency Circulation of Japan: Revised and Enlarged Edition). Tokyo: Tōkō Shoin.
Kobata, Atsushi, 1976. *Kin Gin Bōeki-shi no Kenkyū* (Study of the History of the Gold and Silver Trade). Tokyo: Hōsei University Press.
Kobata, Atsushi, 1941. *Chūsei Nisshi Tsūkō Bōeki-shi no Kenkyū* (Study of the History of the Diplomacy and Trade between Japan and China in the Middle Ages). Tokyo: Tōkō Shoin.
Kobayashi, Hiromitsu, 1995. *Chūgoku no Hanga* (Art Prints of China), Collection of World Art, vol. 4. Tokyo: Tōshindō.
Kuba, Takashi, 2010. *Higashi-Ajia no Heiki Kakumei: 16 Seiki Chūgoku ni Watatta Nihon no Teppō* (The Revolution of Weapons in East Asia: Japanese

Arquebuses Transmitted to China in the Sixteenth Century). Tokyo: Yoshikawa Kōbunkan.
Kudamatsu, Kazunori, 2004. *Ise-Onshi to Danna: Ise-Shinkō no Kaitakusha-tachi* (The Onshis of Ise and Masters: Pioneers of Ise Worship). Tokyo: Kōbundo.
Kuroda, Akinobu, 2003. *Kahei System no Sekaishi: <Hi-Taishō-sei> o Yomu* (The World History of the Monetary System: Reading the "Asymmetry"). Tokyo: Iwanami Shoten.
Li, Xian-Zang, 1961. "Kasei Nenkan ni okeru Sekkō no Shishō oyobi Hakushu Ōchoku Kōsekikō, I & II" (Research on the private traders along the Chekiang coast during the Chiaching (sixteenth century) period and on the history of Captain Wan Zhi, I & II). *Shigaku*, 34(1) & 34(2).
Maehira, Fusaaki, 2004. "16-17 Seiki ni okeru Ryukyu-Kai'iki to Bakuhansei-Shihai" (Maritime region of Ryukyu and shogunate domination in the sixteenth and seventeenth centuries). *Nihonshi Kenkyu* (Journal of Japanese History), 500.
Miki, Seiichiro, 1969. "Chōsen-no-eki ni okeru Suigun-Hensei ni tsuite" (The naval organization in the Korean expedition of the Toyotomi regime). In *Nagoya Daigaku Bungakubu 20 Shūnen Kinen Ronshū*. Nagoya: School of Letters, Nagoya University.
Miyajima, Hiroshi, 1994. "Higashi-Ajia Shōnō-Shakai no Keisei" (The formation of the East Asian Society of Small Farmers). In Mizoguchi Yūzō (ed.), *Chōki Shakai Hendō: Ajia kara Kangaeru* (Long-Term Social Change: Thinking from Asia), vol. 6. Tokyo: The University of Tokyo Press.
Momoki, Shirō, 1996. *Rekishi Sekai toshite no Tōnan-Ajia* (Southeast Asia as a Historical Region). Sekai-shi Libretto, vol. 12. Tokyo: Yamakawa Shuppansha.
Momoki, Shirō (ed.), 2008. *Kai'iki Ajia-shi Kenkyū Nyūmon* (An Introduction to Maritime Asian History). Tokyo: Iwanami Shoten.
Morigami, Osamu, and Tadao Yamaguchi, 1990. "Keichō-chokuhan *Chōgonka Biwa-kō* ni tsuite, I– Keichō-chokuhan no Shokuji-Kumitate-Gihō o Chūshin toshite" (On the Keicho Imperial Editions of *The Song of Everlasting Regret* and *The Biwa Song*: First part. Focusing on the typesetting technology of the Keicho Imperial Edition). *Biblia: Bulletin of Tenri Central Library*, 95.
Morigami, Osamu, 1991. "Keichō-chokuhan *Chōgonka Biwa-kō* ni tsuite (II) – Waga Ko-Katsujiban to Kumitateshiki-Kumihan Gihō no Denrai" (On the Keicho Imperial Editions of *The Song of Everlasting Regret* and *The Biwa Song*: Second part. Old Japanese printing and the arrival of the new method of typesetting-kumitateshiki). *Biblia: Bulletin of Tenri Central Library*, 97.
Murai, Shōsuke, 1993. *Chūsei Wajin-Den* (Records of Wa People in the Middle Ages). Tokyo: Iwanami Shoten.
Murai, Shōsuke, 1997. *Umi kara Mita Sengoku-Nihon: Rettō-shi kara Sekais-shi e* (Japan in the Sengoku Period Seen from the Sea: From the History of Islands to the History of the World). Tokyo: Chikuma Shobō.
Murai, Shōsuke, 2010. "Wakō towa Dareka" (Who were the Wokou?). *Tōhō Gaku* (Eastern Studies), 119.
Nagahara, Keiji, 1992. *Nairan to Minshū no Seiki* (The Century of the Civil War and of the Common People). Taikei Nihon no Rekishi, vol. 6. Tokyo: Shōgakukan.

Nagasawa, Kikuya, 1976. *Zukai Wa-Kan Insatsu-shi* (Illustrated History of Printing in Japan and China). Tokyo: Kyūko Shoin.

Nakajima, Gakushō, 2004. "16-17 Seiki no Higashi-Ajia-Kai'iki to Kajin-Chishikisō no Idō – Minami-Kyūshū no Min-jin Ishi wo megutte" (East Asian sea area and the migration of Chinese intellectuals in the sixteenth and seventeenth centuries: Focusing on a doctor from Ming China who lived in the southern part of Kyushu. *Shigaku Zasshi* (Journal of the Historical Society), 113(12).

Nakajima, Gakushō, 2005. "Portugal-jin no Nihon Hatsu-Raikō to Higashi-Ajia-Kai'iki Kōeki" (The first voyage of the Portuguese to Japan and East Asian maritime trade). *Shien*, 142.

Nakajima, Gakushō, 2007. "16 Seiki-matsu no Fujian – Philippine – Kyūshū Bōeki (The development of Fujian-Philippine-Kyushu maritime trade in the late sixteenth century). *Shien*, 144.

Nakajima, Gakushō, 2009. "Portugal-jin Nihon-Hatsu-Raikō Sairon" (Re-examination of the first arrival of the Portuguese in Japan). *Shien*, 146.

Nakajima, Gakushō, 2009. "16 Seiki-matsu no Kyūshū – Tōnan-Ajia Bōeki – Katō Kiyomasa no Luzon-Bōeki wo megutte" (Maritime trade between Kyushu and Southeast Asia during the sixteenth century: The case of Kato Kiyomasa's Luzon trade). *Shigaku Zasshi* (Journal of the Historical Society), 118(8).

Nakajima, Gakushō, 2011. "Jyūtō kara Furankijyū e – 14-16 Seiki no Higashi-Ajia Kai'iki to Kaki" (From hand-gun to swivel gun: Firearms in the sea areas of East Asia from the fourteenth to sixteenth century). *Shien*, 148.

Nakajima, Gakushō, 2011. "14-16 Seiki, Higashi-Ajia Bōeki-Chitsujo no Henyō to Saihen – Chōkō-Taisei kara 1570 nen System he" (Transformation and reorganization of the international trade order in East Asia from the fourteenth to sixteenth centuries: From the tributary system to the "1570 System"). *Shakai Keizai Shigaku* (Socio-economic History), 76(4).

Nikaidō, Yoshihiro, 2007. "Kaijin, Garanjin toshite no Shōhōshichirō-Daigenshuri" (Shoho Shichiro Daigen Shuri, as a god of the sea and a temple guardian god). *Hakusan Chugoku Gaku* (Journal of Chinese Studies of Hakusan), 13.

Oka, Mihoko, 2010. *Shōnin to Senkyōshi: Namban-bōeki no Sekai* (Merchants and Missionaries: The World of the Namban Trade). Tokyo: University of Tokyo Press.

Okada, Jō, 1973. *Namban-Kōgei* (Namban Crafts), *Japanese Art*, 85. Tokyo: Shibundō.

Okamoto, Hiromichi, 2010. *Ryukyu-Ōkoku Kaijō-Kōshō-shi Kenkyū* (Research on the History of Maritime Interaction of the Ryukyu Kingdom). Ginowan: Yōju Shorin.

Okamoto, Takashi, 2007. "Chōkō to Goshi to Kaikan" (Tribute, trade and the maritime customs system in sixteenth to nineteenth century China). *Shirin*, 90(5).

Okamoto, Yoshitomo, 1974. *Kaiteizōho: 16 Seiki Nichi-Ō Kōtsūshi no Kenkyū* (Study of the History of Interaction between Japan and Europe in the Sixteenth Century: Revised and Enlarged Edition). Tokyo: Hara Shobō.

Ōki, Yasushi, 2004. *Min-matsu Kōnan no Shuppan-Bunka* (The Publishing Culture of the Jiangnan Region in the Late Ming Period). Tokyo: Kenbun Shuppan.

Ono, Kazuko, 1996. *Minki Tōsha Kō: Tōrin-tō to Fukusha* (The Dong-Lin Movement and Restoration Society in the Late Ming). Kyoto: Dōhōsha Shuppan.

Osa, Setsuko, 1987. *Chūsei Nitchō-Kankei to Tsushima* (The Medieval Japan-Korea Relationship and Tsushima). Tokyo: Yoshikawa Kōbunkan.
Osa, Setsuko, 2002. *Chūsei Kokkyō Kai'iki no Wa to Chōsen* (Japan and Korea in the Sea Frontiers during the Middle Ages). Tokyo: Yoshikawa Kōbunkan.
Ōta, Yukio, 2011. "15-16 Seiki no Higashi Ajia Keizai to Kahei Ryūtsū" (The economy and the currency circulation in East Asia in the fifteenth to sixteenth century). *Atarashii Rekishigaku no Tameni* (For a New Historical Science), 279.
Rokutanda, Yutaka, 2013. "15-16 Seiki Chōsen no Suizoku: Sono Kisoteki Kōsatsu" (Some basic considerations on Korean pirates in the fifteenth and sixteenth centuries). In Morihira Masahiko (ed.), *Chū-Kinsei no Chōsen Hantō to Kai'iki Kōryū* (The Korean Peninsula and the Cultural Interaction in the Maritime Region during the Middle Ages and the Early Modern Period). Tokyo: Kyūko Shoin.
Saeki, Kōji, 1997. "16 Seiki ni okeru Kōki Wakō no Katsudō to Tsushima Sō-shi" (The activities of later Wokou and the Sō family of Tsushima in the sixteenth century). In Nakamura Tadashi (ed.), *Sakoku to Kokusai Kankei* (Seclusion Policy of Japan and International Relationships). Tokyo: Yoshikawa Kōbunkan.
Saeki, Kōji, 2008. *Tsushima to Kaikyō no Chūseishi* (History of Medieval Tsushima and Its Straits). Nihon-shi Libretto, vol. 77. Tokyo: Yamakawa Shuppansha.
Saeki, Kōji, 2008. "Hakata Shōnin Kamiya Jutei no Jitsuzō" (The real image of Kamiya Jutei, merchant of Hakata). In Kyushu Shigaku Kenkyūkai (ed.), *Kyōkai kara Mita Uchi to Soto* (Inside and Outside Viewed from the Border). Tokyo: Iwata Shoin.
Sakamoto, Mitsuru, and Motoo Yoshimura, 1974. *Nihon no Bijutsu: Namban Bijutsu* (Namban Art), vol. 34. Tokyo: Shōgakukan.
Sakuma, Shigeo, 1992. *Nichi-Min Kankei-shi no Kenkyū* (Study of the History of the Relationship between Japan and Ming China). Tokyo: Yoshikawa Kōbunkan.
Sakurai, Eiji, 1996. *Nihon Chūsei no Keizai Kōzō* (The Economic Structure of Medieval Japan). Tokyo: Iwanami Shoten.
Sakurai, Yumio, 2006. *Zen-Kindai no Tōnan Asia* (Southeast Asia in the Premodern Period). Tokyo: The Society for the Promotion of the Open University of Japan.
Seki, Shūichi, 2002. *Chūsei Nitchō Kai'iki-shi no Kenkyū* (Study of the Maritime History between Japan and Korea in the Middle Ages). Tokyo: Yoshikawa Kōbunkan.
Sugaya, Nariko, 2001. "Spain-ryō Philippines no Seiritsu" (The formation of the Spanish Philippines). In Ishii Yoneo (ed.), *Tōnan Ajia Kinsei no Seiritsu* (The Formation of Early Modern Southeast Asia). Iwanami Kōza: Tōnan Ajia-shi, vol. 3. Tokyo: Iwanami Shoten.
Suntory Museum of Art (ed.), 2007. *BIOMBO: Byōbu Nihon no Bi-ten* (BIOMBO: Japanese Heritage as Legend of Gold). Tokyo: Nikkei.
Suzuki, Tsuneyuki, 1998. "Tōnan-Ajia no Kōshi Kokka" (Port polities of Southeast Asia). In Kishimoto Mio (ed.), *Higashi-Ajia, Tōnan-Ajia Dentō-Shakai no Keisei* (The Formation of the Traditional Society of East and Southeast Asia). Iwanami Kōza: Sekai Rekishi, vol. 13. Tokyo: Iwanami Shoten.
Takahashi, Kimiaki, 1989. "16 Seiki no Chōsen, Tsushima, Higashi-Ajia Kai'iki" (Korea, Tsushima and maritime East Asia in the sixteenth century). In Katō

Eiichi (ed.), *Bakuhansei Kokka to Iiki, Ikoku* (The State under the Bakuhan System and Overseas, Foreign States). Tokyo: Azekura Shobō.
Takara, Kurayoshi, 1993. *Ryukyu-Ōkoku* (The Kingdom of Ryukyu). Tokyo: Iwanami Shoten.
Takeno, Yōko, 1979. *Han Bōeki-shi no Kenkyū* (Study of the Trade by Japanese Feudal Lords). Tokyo: Minerva Shobō.
Tamanaga, Mitsuhiro, and Yoshihiro Sakamoto, 2009. *Ōtomo Sōrin no Sengoku-Toshi: Bungo Funai* (Bungo Funai: Sengoku City of the Ōtomo Sōrin). Tokyo: Shinsensha.
Tanaka, Takeo, 1997. *Higashi Ajia Tsūkōken to Kokusai Ninshiki* (The East Asia Trade Zone and Its International Perception). Tokyo: Yoshikawa Kōbunkan.
Tanaka, Takeo, 2012. *Wakō: Umi no Rekishi* (The Wokou: History of the Sea). Tokyo: Kōdansha.
Tenri Central Library (ed.), 1973. *Kirishitanban no Kenkyū* (Study on the Kirishitan Ban). Tenri: Tenri Central Library.
Tsien, Tsuen-Hsuin, 2007. *Chūgoku no Kami to Insatsu no Bunkashi* (Cultural History of Paper and Printing in China). Tokyo: Hōsei University Press.
Tsuno, Tomoaki, 2012. *Chōsokabe-shi no Kenkyū* (Study of the Chōsokabe Clan). Tokyo: Yoshikawa Kōbunkan.
Udagawa, Takehisa, 1993. *Higashi Ajia Heiki Kōryūshi no Kenkyū* (Study of the History of the Diffusion of Weapons in East Asia). Tokyo: Yoshikawa Kōbunkan.
Udagawa, Takehisa, 2002. *Sengoku Suigun no Kōbō* (The Rise and Fall of the Pirates in the Sengoku Period). Tokyo: Heibonsha.
Ueda, Makoto, 2002. *Tora ga Kataru Chūgokushi: Ecological History no Kanōsei* (History of China from the Perspective of the Tiger: The Possibility of an Ecological History). Tokyo: Yamakawa Shuppansha.
Ueda, Makoto, 2005. *Umi to Teikoku: Ming Shin Jidai* (Seas and the Empire: Ming and Qing Periods). Chūgoku no Rekishi, vol. 9. Tokyo: Kōdansha.
Uezato, Takashi, 2005. "Ko-Ryukyu Naha no 'Wajin' Kyoryūchi to Kan-Shinakai Sekai" (The Japanese settlement in Naha, the Ryukyus and the maritime world of the China Sea). *Shigaku Zasshi* (Journal of the Historical Society), 114(7).
Wada, Hironori, 1958. "Min-dai no Teppō Denrai to Osuman Teikoku: *Jingi-fu* to *Saiiki Tochi Jinbutsu Ryaku*" (The arrival of guns to Ming China and the Ottoman Empire: *Treatise on Extraordinary Weapons* (*Shen-Qi Pu*) and *Summary of the Land and People of Western Regions*). *Shigaku*, 31(1–4).
Yamauchi, Yuzuru, 1997. *Kaizoku to Kai'iki – Setouchi no Sengoku-shi* (Pirates and Sea Areas: History of the Sengoku Period in Setouchi). Tokyo: Heibonsha.
Yamauchi, Yuzuru, 1998. *Chūsei Setouchi Kai'iki-shi no Kenkyū* (Study of the History of the Medieval Seto Inland Sea Region). Tokyo: Hōsei University Press.
Yamazaki, Takeshi, 2010. "Hakushu Ōchoku Kōzai-kō no.I – *Kaikōgi* to sono Shūhen" (A critical inquiry into the life of Captain Wang Zhi, part I: The essay on the pirates and its background). *Tōhō Gakuhō* (Journal of Oriental Studies), 85.
Yamazaki, Takeshi, 2003. "Junbu Shu-Gan no Mita Umi – Min-dai Kasei-nenkan no Enkai Eisho to 'Dai-Wakou' Zenya no Hitobito" (The people of the seacoast under the government of the Ming Dynasty, as seen from the viewpoint of the Commissioner, Zhu Wan). *Tōyōshi Kenkyū* (The Journal of Oriental Research), 62(1).

Yamazaki, Takeshi, 2007. "Kōkai no Zoku kara Soshō no Kou e – Aru 'Kasei Wakou Zenshi' ni Yosete" (From water-side bandits to "Japanese pirates": Another pre-history of the Jiajing Wokou). *Tōhō Gakuhō* (Journal of Oriental Studies), 81.

Yamazaki, Takeshi, 2007. "Chōkō to Kaikin no Ronri to Genjitsu – Min-dai Chūki no 'Kansai' Sō Sokei wo Daizai to shite" (The logic and reality of the tributary system and maritime exclusion: Focusing on "treacherous" Song Su-Qing in middle Ming China). In Fuma Susumu (ed.), *Chūgoku Higashi-Ajia Gaikō Kōryū-shi no Kenkyū* (Study of the History of the Diplomacy and Relationship between China and East Asia). Kyoto: Kyoto University Press.

Yamazaki, Tsuyoshi, 2001. *Umi o Watatta Nihon-Shikki, 1: 16-17 Seiki* (Lacquerware Exported from Japan, First Part: Sixteenth and Seventeenth Centuries), *Japanese Art*, 426. Tokyo: Shibundō.

Yonetani, Hitoshi, 2002. "Toyotomi-Seikenki ni okeru Kaizoku no Hikiwatashi to Nitchō Kankei" (The extradition of the pirates and the Japan-Korea relationship under the Toyotomi government). *Nippon Rekishi* (Japanese History), 650.

Yonetani, Hitoshi, 2003. "Kōki Wakō kara Chōsen Shinryaku e" (From the later Wokou to the Japanese invasions of Korea). In Ike Susumu (ed.), *Tenka-Tōitsu to Chōsen-Shinryaku* (The Unification of Japan and the Japanese Invasions of Korea). Nihon no Jidai-shi, 13. Tokyo: Yoshikawa Kōbunkan.

Yuba, Tadanori, 2008. *Seika no Michi: Chūgoku Tōjiki ga Kataru Tōzai-Kōryū* (The Road of the Blue and White Porcelain: The Exchange between the East and the West Seen from Chinese Ceramics). Tokyo: NHK Publishing.

## *Chinese Bibliography*

Chao, Zhongchen, 2005. *Mingdai Haijin yu Haiwai Maoyi* (Maritime Exclusion and Foreign Trade in Ming China). Renmin Chubanshe.

Cheng, Wing-sheung, 2004. *Laizi Haiyang de Tiaozhan: Mingdai haimao zhengce yanbian yanjiu* (The Challenge from the Sea: Study of the Transition of Maritime Trade Policies of Ming China). Daoxiang Chubanshe.

Chiu, Hsuan-yu, 1995. *Mingdiguo yu Nanhai Zhufanguo Guanxi Yanbian* (The Change in the Relationship between the Ming Empire and South Sea Countries). Lantai Chubanshe.

Huang, Yi-long, 1996. "Hongyipao yu Ming Qing Zhanzheng" (Dutch cannons and the war in Ming and Qing China). *Qinghua Xuebao* (The Tsing Hua Journal), 26(1).

Li, Jinming, 1990. *Mingdai Haiwai Maoyishi* (The History of Foreign Trade in Ming China). Zhongguo Shehui Kexue Chubanshe.

Li, Qingxin, 2007. *Mingdai Haiwai Maoyi Zhidu* (The System of Foreign Trade in Ming China). Shehui Kexue Chubanshe.

Liu, Xu, 2004. *Zhongguo Gudai Huoyao Huoqishi* (A History of Gunpowder and Firearms in Ancient China). Daxiang Chubanshe.

Li, Yunquan, 2004. *Chaogong Zhidu Shilun: Zhongguo Gudai Duiwai Guanxi Tizhi Yanjiu* (Treatise on the History of the Tributary System: Study of the Foreign Relationship in Ancient China). Xinhua Chubanshe.

Wan, Ming, 2000. *Zhongguo Rongru Shijie de Bulü*: *Ming yu Qing Qianqi de Haiwai Zhengce Bijiao Yanjiu* (China in World History: Comparative Research on

Foreign Policy in the Ming and Early Qing Periods). Shehui Kexue Wenxian Chubanshe.
Wan, Ming, 2001. *Zhong Pu Zaoqi Guanxishi* (History of the Early Relationship between China and Portugal). Shehui Kexue Wenxian Chubanshe.
Wang, Zhaochun, 1991. *Zhongguo Huoqishi* (History of Firearms in China). Junshi Kexue Chubanshe.

## *European and American Bibliography*

Abu Lughod, Janet L., 1991. *Before European Hegemony: The World System A.D. 1250–1350.* London: Oxford University Press.
Atwell, William S., 1998. "Ming China and the Emerging World Economy, c. 1470–1650". In *Cambridge History of China*, vol. 8. Cambridge: Cambridge University Press.
Atwell, William S., 2002. "Time, Money, and the Weather: Ming China and the 'Great Depression" of the Mid-Fifteenth Century'. *The Journal of Asian Studies*, 61(1).
Boxer, Charles R., 1959. *The Great Ship from Amacon: Annals of Macao and Old Japan Trade, 1555–1640*. Lisbon: Centro de Estudos Historicos Ultramarinos.
Fairbank, John King (ed.), 1968. *The Chinese World Order: Traditional China's Foreign Relations.* Cambridge: Harvard University Press.
Febvre, Lucien, and Henri-Jean Martin, 1957. *L'apparition du Livre*. Paris: Albin Michel.
Gil, Juan, 2007. *Hidalgos y Samurais: España y Japón en los siglos XVI y XVII.* Madrid: Alianza Editorial.
Impey, Oliver, and Christiaan Jörg, 2005. *Japanese Export Lacquer 1580–1850*. Amsterdam: Hotei Publishing.
Morga, Antonio de, 2015. *History of the Philippine Islands* (*Sucesos de las Islas Filipinas*). Create Space Independent Publishing Platform.
Needam, Joseph, 1986. *Science and Civilization in China, vol. 5, Chemistry and Chemical Technology, Pt. 7: Military Technology; The Gunpowder Epic*. Cambridge: Cambridge University Press.
Ptak, Roderich (ed.), 2003. *China, the Portuguese, and the Nangyang: Oceans and Routes, Regions and Trade (c. 1000-1600)*. Aldershot: Ashgate Publishing Limited.
Reid, Anthony, 1988 and 1993. *Southeast Asia in the Age of Commerce, 1450-1680*, vols. 1–2. New Haven: Yale University Press.
Sousa, Lucio de, 2010. *Early European Presence in China, Japan, the Philippines and South-East Asia 1550-1590: The Life of Bartolomeo Landeiro*. Macao: Macao Foundation.
Souza, George Bryan, 1986. *The Survival of Empire: Portuguese Trade and Society in China and the South China Sea 1630-1754*. Cambridge: Cambridge University Press.
Von Glahn, Richard, 1996. *Fountain of Fortune: Money and Monetary Policy in China, 1000-1700*. Berkeley: University of California Press.
Wallerstein, Immanuel, 1974. *The Modern World-System, vol. 1: Capitalist Agriculture and the Origins of the European World-Economy in the Sixteenth Century*. New York: Academic Press.

# Part 3

## *Japanese Bibliography*

Adachi, Hiroyuki, 1995. *Iyō no Fune – Yōshiki-Sen Dōnyū to Sakoku-Taisei* (Extraordinary Ships: Introduction of Western-Style Ships and the National Seclusion Policy). Tokyo: Heibonsha.

Akamine, Mamoru, 2004. *Ryukyu Ōkoku – Higashi Ajia no Cornerstone* (The Kingdom of Ryukyu: A Cornerstone of East Asia). Tokyo: Kōdansha.

Arano, Yasunori, 1988. *Kinsei Nihon to Higashi Ajia* (Early Modern Japan and East Asia). Tokyo: University of Tokyo Press.

Arano, Yasunori (ed.), 2003. *Edo Bakufu to Higashi Ajia* (The Edo Shogunate and East Asia). Nihon no Jidai-shi, vol. 14. Tokyo: Yoshikawa Kōbunkan.

Arano, Yasunori, Masatoshi Ishii and Shōsuke Murai (eds), 2010. *Kinsei-teki Sekai no Seijuku* (The Maturation of Early Modern Society). Nihon no Taigai-Kankei, vol. 6. Tokyo: Yoshikawa Kōbunkan.

Chōsen-shi Kenkyūkai (ed.), 2011. *Chōsen-shi Kenkyū Nyūmon* (Introduction to the Study of Korean History). Nagoya: The University of Nagoya Press.

Enoki, Kazuo (ed.), 1971. *Seiō-Bummei to Higashi Ajia* (West European Civilization and East Asia). Tōzai-Bummei no Kōryū, vol. 5. Tokyo: Heibonsha.

Fujita, Akiyoshi, 2006. "Nihon Kinsei ni okeru Ko-Maso-zō to Funadama-shin no Shinkō" (Old statues of the goddess Maso and the worship of the god Funadama in early modern Japan). In Huang Zi-Jin (ed.), *Jinxiandai Riben Shehuide Tuibian* (Social Transformation of Contemporary Japan). Taipei: Research Institute for the Humanities and Social Sciences.

Fujita, Satoru (ed.), 2000. *17 Seiki no Nihon to Higashi Ajia* (Japan and East Asia in the Seventeenth Century). Tokyo: Yamakawa Shuppansha.

Fuma, Susumu, 2008. "1609 nen, Nihon no Ryukyu Heigō-ikō ni okeru Chūgoku, Chōsen no Tai-Ryukyu Gaikō: Higashi Ajia 4 Koku ni okeru Sakuhō, Tsūshin soshite Tozetsu" (The policy of China and Korea towards Ryukyu after the annexation of Ryukyu by Japan in 1609: Tribute, communication and the rupture of relations between four countries of East Asia). *Bulletin of the Society for Korean Historical Science*, 46.

Fuma, Susumu (ed.), 1999. *Zōtei Shi Ryukyu-roku Kaidai oyobi Kenkyū* (Explanatory Notes and Research of the Report of a Mission to Ryukyu: New and Revised Edition). Ginowan: Yōju Shorin.

Fuma, Susumu (ed.), 2007. *Chūgoku Higashi Ajia Gaikō Kōryū-shi no Kenkyū* (Study of the History of the Diplomacy and Relationship between China and East Asia). Kyoto: Kyoto University Press.

Ha, Ubong (ed.), 2011. *Chōsen to Ryukyu: Rekishi no Shin'en o Saguru* (Korea and Ryukyu: Exploring the Abyss of History), trans. supervised by Akamine Mamoru. Ginowan: Yōju Shorin.

Hamashita, Takeshi (ed.), 1999. *Higashi-Ajia-Sekai no Chi'iki Network* (Regional Networks in the East Asian World). Kokusai Kōryū, vol. 3. Tokyo: Yamakawa Shuppansha.

Haneda, Masashi, 2007. *Higashi-Indo-Gaisha to Ajia no Umi* (East India Company and Asian Seas). Kōbō no Sekai-shi, vol. 15. Tokyo: Kōdansha.

Haruna, Akira, 1995. "Hyōryū-min Sōkan Seido no Keisei ni tsuite" (Creation of the extradition system for castaways). *Kaijishi Kenkyu* (Journal of the Japan Society for Nautical Research), 52.

Haruna, Akira, 1996. "Kōshi Saho Oboegaki" (A memorandum for Zhapu, port city). *Chofu Nihon Bunka* (Japanese Culture of Chofu), 6.

Haudrère, Philippe, 2006. *France Higashi Indo-Gaisya to Pondicherry* (Original title: *La Compagnie française des Indes orientales et Pondicherry*), ed. and trans. by Haneda Masashi, and trans. by Ōmine Mari. Tokyo: Yamakawa Shuppansha.

Hirakawa, Arata, 2008. *Kaikoku eno Michi* (Way for the Opening of Japan). Zenshū Nihon no Rekishi, vol. 12. Tokyo: Shōgakukan.

Hokkaidō Tōhoku-shi Kenkyūkai (ed.), 1996. *Menashi no Sekai* (World of Menashi). Sapporo: Hokkaido Shuppan Kikaku Center.

Ikeda, Akira (ed.), 1968. *Nihon Shomin Seikatsu Shiryō Syūsei* (The Collection of Historical Sources for the Life of Ordinary People in Japan), vol. 5. Tokyo: San-ichi Shobō.

Ikehata, Setsuho (ed.), 1999. *Tōnan Ajia-shi vol.2: Tōshobu* (History of Southeast Asia II: Insular Regions). Shinpan Sekai Kakkokushi, vol. 6. Tokyo: Yamakawa Shuppansha.

Ikeuchi, Satoshi, 2006. *Taikun Gaikō to 'Bui' : Kinsei Nihon no Kokusai Chitsujyo to Chōsen-kan* (Tycoon Diplomacy and the "Bui": International Order and the View of Japan towards Korea in the Early Modern Period). Nagoya: The University of Nagoya Press.

Ishii, Kendō (ed.), 1927. *Ikoku Hyōryū Kitanshū* (Collection of Marvelous Stories of Castaways in Foreign Lands). Tokyo: Fukunaga Shoten.

Iwai, Shigeki, 2009. "Teikoku to Goshi: 16-18 Seiki Higashi Ajia no Tūkō" (The empire and trade: Commerce and diplomacy of East Asia from the sixteenth to eighteenth century). In Kagotani Naoto and Wakimura Kōhei (eds), *Teikoku to Ajia Network: Chōki no 19 Seiki* (The Empire and the Asian Network: The Long Nineteenth Century). Kyoto: Sekai Shisōsha.

Iwai, Shigeki, 2010. "Chōkō to Goshi" (Tribute and trade). *Higashi Ajia Sekai no Kindai*. Iwanami Kōza: Higashi Ajia Kin-Gendai Tsū-shi, vol. 1. Tokyo: Iwanami Shoten.

Iwashita, Tetsunori, and Fusaaki Maehira (eds), 1997. *Kinsei Nihon no Kaigai Jōhō* (Overseas Information in Early Modern Japan). Tokyo: Iwata Shoin.

Kaitokudō Kinenkai (ed.), 2008. *Sekaishi o Kakinaosu, Nihonshi o Kakinaosu: Handai-Shigaku no Chōsen* (Rewriting World History, Rewriting Japanese History: Challenge of the Historical Study of Osaka University). Osaka: Izumi Shoin.

Kamiya, Nobuyuki, 2003. *Ryukyu to Nihon, Chūgoku* (Ryukyu, Japan and China), Nihon-shi Libretto, vol. 43. Tokyo: Yamakawa Shuppansha.

Katagiri, Kazuo, 2000. *Dejima: Ibunka Kōryū no Butai* (Dejima, a Stage of Cultural Exchange). Tokyo: Shūeisha.

Katō, Eiichi, Manji Kitajima and Katsumi Fukaya (eds), 1989. *Bakuhansei Kokka to I'iki,Ikoku* (The State under the Baku-han System and Marginal Areas, Foreign States). Tokyo: Azekura Shobō.

Kato, Yūzō (ed.), 2008. *Higashi Ajia Naikai Sekai no Koryū-shi: Shūen Chi'iki ni okeru Shakai Seido no Keisei* (History of Exchanges inside the Inland Sea World of East Asia: Formation of Social Systems in Marginal Areas). Kyoto: Jinbun Shoin.

Kawakatsu, Heita (ed.), 2000. *'Sakoku' o Hiraku* (Clarifying the National Seclusion Policy). Tokyo: Dōbunkan.

Kikuchi, Isao, 1994. *Ainu Minzoku to Nihonjin: Higashi Ajia no Naka no Ezochi* (The Ainu and the Japanese: Ezo in the Context of East Asia). Tokyo: Asahi Shimbunsha.

Kikuchi, Isao (ed.), 2003. *Ezogashima to Hoppō Sekai* (Ezo Island and the Northern World), Nihon no Jidai-shi, vol. 19. Tokyo: Yoshikawa Kōbunkan.

Kikuchi, Isao, and Fusaaki Maehira (eds), 2006. *Rettō-shi no Kita to Minami* (The North and the South of the History of Japanese Islands), Kinsei Chi'iki-shi Forum (Forum of Early Modern Regional History), vol. 1. Tokyo: Yoshikawa Kōbunkan.

Kishimoto, Mio, 1997. *Shin-dai Chūgoku no Bukka to Keizai Hendō* (Prices and Economic Changes in Qing China). Tokyo: Kenbun Shuppan.

Kishimoto, Mio, 1998. *Higashi Ajia no 'Kinsei'* (The Early Modern Period of East Asia), Sekai-shi Libretto, vol. 13. Tokyo: Yamakawa Shuppansha.

Kishimoto, Mio, 1998. "Higashi-Ajia, Tōnan-Ajia Dentō-Shakai no Keisei" (The formation of the traditional society of East and Southeast Asia). In Kishimoto Mio (ed.), *Higashi-Ajia, Tōnan-Ajia Dentō-Shakai no Keisei* (The Formation of the Traditional Society of East and Southeast Asia), Iwanami Kōza: Sekai Rekishi, vol. 13. Tokyo: Iwanami Shoten.

Kishimoto, Mio and Hiroshi Miyajima, 1998. *Min Shin to Richō no Jidai* (The Periods of Ming and Qing China and Lee Korea), Sekai no Rekishi, vol. 12. Tokyo: Chūō Kōronsha.

Liu, Shiuh-Feng, 1993. "17–18 Seiki no Chūgoku to Higashi Ajia: Shin-chō no Kaigai Bōeki Seisaku o Chūshin ni" (China and East Asia in the seventeenth and eighteenth centuries: Focusing on the foreign trade policy of the Qing Dynasty). In Mizoguchi Yūzō (ed.), *Chi'iki System: Ajia kara Kangaeru*, vol. 2. Tokyo: The University of Tokyo Press.

Matsui, Yōko, 2009. "Nagasaki Dejima to Ikoku Josei: 'Gaikoku Fujin no Nyūkoku Kinshi' Saikō" (Dejima at Nagasaki and foreign women: The "ban" on foreign women entering Japan: A reexamination). *Shigaku Zasshi: Journal of the Historical Society*, 118(2).

Matsukata, Fuyuko, 2010. *Oranda Fūsetsu-gaki* (News and Reports from the Netherlands). Tokyo: Chūō Kōronshinsha.

Matsuo, Shinichi, 2010. *Edo Bakufu no Taigai Seisaku to Engan Keibi* (Foreign Policy and the Coast Guards of the Edo Shogunate). Tokyo: Azekura Shobō.

Matsuura, Akira, 2002. *Shin-dai Kaigai Bōeki-shi no Kenkyū* (Study of the Foreign Trade History of Qing China). Kyoto: Hōyū Shoten.

Matsuura, Akira, 2003. *Chūgoku no Kaishō to Kaizoku* (Sea Merchants and Pirates of China), Sekai-shi Libretto, vol. 63. Tokyo: Yamakawa Shuppansha.

Matsuura, Akira, 2003. *Shin-dai Chūgoku Ryukyu Bōeki-shi no Kenkyū* (Study of the History of Qing-Ryukyu Trade). Ginowan: Yōju Shorin.

Matsuura, Akira, 2007. *Edo Jidai Tōsen ni yoru Nitchū Bunka Kōryū* (Cultural Exchange between Japan and China by Chinese Ships during the Edo Period). Kyoto: Shibunkaku Shuppan.
Mizubayashi, Takeshi, 1987. *Hōken-sei no Saihen to Nihon-teki Shakai no Kakuritsu* (The Reformation of the Feudal System and the Establishment of Japanese-Style Society), Nihon Tsūshi, vol. 2. Tokyo: Yamakawa Shuppansha.
Momoki, Shirō (eds), 2008. *Kai'iki Ajia-shi Kenkyū Nyūmon* (An Introduction to Maritime Asian History). Tokyo: Iwanami Shoten.
Murao, Susumu, 1999. "Kaien Eki" (Huaiyuan-Yi Station). *Chūgoku Bunka Kenkyū*, 16.
Murao, Susumu, 2007. "Kenryū Kibō: Toshi Kōshū to Macao ga Tsukuru Henkyō" (The twenty-fourth year of Qianlong (1759): The border formed by Canton and Aomen (Macao)). *Tōyōshi Kenkyū* (The Journal of Oriental Research), 65(4).
Nagamori, Mitsunobu, 2010. "Chōsen Kinsei Hyōryū-min to Higashi Ajia Kai'iki" (Korean castaways and maritime East Asia in the early modern period). In *Higashi Ajia no Kai'iki to Nihon no Dentō Bunka no Keisei – Nimpō o Shōten to suru Gakusai-teki Sōsei* (Cross-Cultural Maritime Exchange in East Asia and the Formation of Japanese Traditional Culture: Interdisciplinary Creation Focusing on Ningbo), vol. 6, Report for the Ministry of Education, Culture, Sports, Science and Technology Grants-in-Aid for Scientific Research (2005–2009).
Nagazumi, Yōko (ed.), 1999. *Sakoku o Minaosu* (Re-examining the National Seclucion Policy of Japan), Kokusai Kōryū, vol. 1. Tokyo: Yamakawa Shuppansha.
Nakagawa, Tadateru, 1966. *Shinzoku Kibun* (Record of the Customs of Qing China), ed. by Bochun Sun and Muramatsu Kazuya. Tokyo: Heibonsha.
Nemuro Symposium Jikkō Iinkai (ed.), 1990. *37 Hon no Inaws – Kansei Ainu no Hōki 200 nen* (37 Inaws: 200th Anniversary of the Kansei Ainu Uprising). Sapporo: Hokkaido Shuppan Kikaku Center.
Nishizato, Kikō, 1997. "Chū-Ryū Kōryū-shi ni okeru Dotsūji to Gakō (Kyūshō)" (Tutonghsi and Yahang (Qiushang) in the history of international relations between China and Ryukyu). *Bulletin of College of Education, University of the Ryukyus*, 50.
Ōba, Osamu, 1997. *Kanseki Yunyū no Bunka-shi: Shōtoku Taishi kara Yoshimune he* (Cultural History of the Import of Chinese Books: From Prince Shotoku to Tokugawa Yoshimune). Tokyo: Kenbun Shuppan.
Ōba, Osamu, 1999. *Tokugawa Yoshimune to Kōkitei: Sakoku-ka de no Nitchū Kōryū* (Tokugawa Yoshimune and the Kangxi Emperor: The Relationship between Japan and China under the Seclusion Policy of Japan). Tokyo: Taishūkan Shoten.
Ōba, Osamu, 2001. *Hyōryū-sen Monogatari: Edo Jidai no Nitchū Kōryū* (Story of Drifting Ships: The Relationship between Japan and China during the Edo Period). Tokyo: Iwanami Shoten.
Ogata Isamu (eds), 1994–2009. *Rekishi-gaku Jiten* (Dictionary of Historical Science), vols. 1–15 and supplementary volume. Tokyo: Kōbundo.
Okada, Hidehiro (ed.), 2009. *Shin-chō towa Nani ka* (What was the Qing Dynasty?), *Kan-Bessatsu*, vol. 16. Tokyo: Fujiwara Shoten.
Okamoto, Takashi, 1999. *Kindai Chūgoku to Kaikan* (Modern China and Maritime Customs). Nagoya: The University of Nagoya Press.

Okinawa-ken (ed.), 2005. *Okinawa-kenshi Kakuron-hen Dai 4 Kan: Kinsei* (History of Okinawa Prefecture, Part of Essays IV, The Early Modern Period). Naha: Okinawa-ken Kyōikuchō.
Rekishigaku Kenkyūkai (ed.), 2005–2006. *Minato-machi no Sekai-shi* (World History of Port Cities), vols. 1–3. Tokyo: Aoki Shoten.
Sakurai, Yumio (ed.), 2001. *Tōnan Ajia Kinsei Kokka-gun no Tenkai* (The Development of Early Modern States in Southeast Asia), Iwanami Koza: Tōnan Ajia-shi, vol. 4. Tokyo: Iwanami Shoten.
Sasaki, Shirō, 1996. *Hoppō kara Kita Kōeki-Min: Kinu to Kegawa to Santan-jin* (Traders from the North: Silk, Fur and Santan People). Tokyo: NHK Publishing.
Sasaki, Shirō, and Yūzō Katō (eds), 2011. *Higashi Ajia no Minzoku-teki Sekai: Kyōkai-Chi'iki ni okeru Tabunka-teki Jōkyō to Sōgo Ninshiki* (The Ethnic World of East Asia: The Multicultural Situation and Mutual Perception in Boundary Areas). Tokyo: Yushisha.
Sugiyama, Kiyohiko, 2008. "Dai Shin Teikoku no Shihai Kōzō to Hakki-sei: Manju Ōchō to shite no Kokusei Shiron" (The structure of Qing imperial rule as seen from the Eight Banner System: A tentative study of its constitution as a Manchu Dynasty). *Chūgoku Shigaku* (Chinese History), 18.
Tashiro, Kazui, 1981. *Kinsei Nitchō Tsūkō Bōeki-shi no Kenkyū* (Study of the History of the Relationship and Trade between Japan and Korea in the Early Modern Period). Tokyo: Sōbunsha.
Tashiro, Kazui, 2007. *Nitchō Kōeki to Tsushima-han* (Japan-Korea Trade and the Tsushima Domain). Tokyo: Sōbunsha.
Tashiro, Kazui, 2011. *Shin Wakan: Sakoku-Jidai no Nihonjin-machi* (Waegwan, New Edition: Japanese Towns during the National Seclusion Period). Tokyo: Yumani Shobo.
Terada, Takanobu, 1966. "Shin-chō no Kaikan Gyōsei ni tsuite" (On the administration of Qing Dynasty maritime customs). *Shirin*, 49(2).
Toby, Ronald, 2008. *'Sakoku' to Iu Gaikō* (Foreign Diplomacy Called "Sakoku"), Zenshū Nihon no Rekishi, vol. 9. Tokyo: Shōgakukan.
Tomiyama, Kazuyuki, 2004. *Ryukyu Ōkoku no Gaikō to Ōken* (The Diplomacy and Royal Authority of the Ryukyu Kingdom). Tokyo: Yoshikawa Kōbunkan.
Tomiyama, Kazuyuki (ed.), 2003. *Okinawa/Ryukyu-shi no Sekai* (World of the History of Okinawa and Ryukyu), Nihon no Jidai-shi, vol. 18. Tokyo: Yoshikawa Kōbunkan.
Tsuruta, Kei, 2006. *Tsushima kara Mita Nitchō Kankei* (The Japan-Korea Relationship Seen from Tsushima), Nihon-shi Libretto, vol. 41. Tokyo: Yamakawa Shuppansha.
Ueda, Makoto, 2005. *Umi to Teikoku: Min Shin Jidai* (Seas and the Empire: Ming and Qing Periods), Chūgoku no Rekishi, vol. 9. Tokyo: Kōdansha.
Yamamoto, Hirofumi, 1995. *Sakoku to Kaikin no Jidai* (The Age of National Seclusion and Maritime Exclusion). Tokyo: Azekura Shobō.
Yamawaki, Teijirō, 1964. *Nagasaki no Tōjin Bōeki* (Trade by Chinese Merchants at Nagasaki). Tokyo: Yoshikawa Kōbunkan.
Yanagisawa, Akira, 1999. "Kōki 56 Nen no Nanyō Kaikin no Haikei: Shin-chō ni okeru Chūgoku Sekai to Hi-Chūgoku Sekai no Mondai ni yosete" (The background

of an edict to control overseas trade and emigration in 1717: A preliminary study on interaction between the Chinese and non-Chinese world in the Qing Empire). *Shirin*, 140.

Yonetani, Hitoshi, 1995. "Kinsei Nitchō Kankei ni okeru Tsushima-Hanshu no Jōhyōbun ni tsuite" (Letters of the Lord of Tsushima to the Korean King in the context of the Japan-Korea relationship in the early modern period). *Chōsen Gakuhō* (Journal of the Academic Association of Koreanology in Japan), 154.

Watanabe, Miki, 1999–2000. "Shin-dai Chūgoku ni okeru Hyōryū-min no Shochi to Ryukyu" (The treatment of castaways in Qing China and Ryukyu 1–2). *Nantō Shigaku*, 54–55.

Watanabe, Miki, 2005. "Shin ni taisuru Ryū-Nichi Kankei no Impei to Hyōchaku Mondai" (Concealing Ryukyu-Japanese relations from Qing China and the problem of castaways). *Shigaku Zasshi* (Journal of the Historical Society), 114(11).

Watanabe, Miki, 2006. "Chū-Nichi no Shihai Ronri to Kinsei Ryukyu: 'Chūgokujin, Chōsenjin, Ikokujin' Hyōchaku no Shochi o Megutte" (Early modern Ryukyu between China and Japan: Repatriating castaways from China, Korea and "unidentified places"). *Rekishigaku Kenkyū* (The Journal of Historical Studies), 810.

## *Chinese Bibliography*

Liu, Shiuh-feng, 1993. "Qingdai de Zhapugang yu Zhong Ri Maoyi" (Port of Zhapu and China-Japan trade in the Qing period). In Chang Pin-tsun and Liu Shih-chi (eds), *Zhongguo Haiyang Fazhanshi Lunwenji* (Collection of Treatises of the History of the Maritime Development of China), vol. 5. Zhongyang Yanjiuyuan Zhongshan Renwen Shehui Kexue Yanjiusuo.

Liu, Shiuh-feng, 2005. "Qingzhengfu dui Chuyang Chuanzhi de Guanli Zhengce (1684–1842)" (The management policy of ships for international voyages by the Qing government (1684–1842)). In Liu Shiuh-feng (ed.), *Zhongguo Haiyang Fazhanshi Lunwenji* (Collection of Treatises of the History of the Maritime Development of China), vol. 9. Zhongyang Yanjiuyuan Renwen Shehui Kexue Yanjiusuo.

## *Korean Bibliography*

Ha, Ubong (ed.), 1999. *Joseon-gwa Yugu*. Seoul: Areuke.

U Insu, 2007. "Joseon Hugi Haegeum Jeongchaek-ui Naeyong-gwa Seonggyeok" (The contents and characteristics of the maritime exclusion in the late Joseon period). In Yi Mungi (ed.), *Han, Jung, Il-ui, Haeyang Insik-gwa Haegeum* (Perceptions of the Sea and Embargoes of Korea, China and Japan). Seoul: Dongbuga Yeoksa Jaedan.

# Historical Geography Index

## Political power / regime

Burma (present-day Myanmar)
  Taungoo Kingdom  137, 180
Brunei  77, 170

Cambodia  65, 77, 80, 90, 96, 130, 151, 210
China and North Asia
  regimes that succeeded the Mongol Empire  58, 136, 167
  Later Jin Dynasty  218
  Ming Dynasty  59, 151, 188, 192–193, 199–202, 204, 206, 209, 286
  Mongol Empire  18, 47, 50–51, 83, 97–98
  Qing Empire/Dynasty  14, 19, 167, 182, 192, 202, 218, 252–255, 259–260, 263, 268–269, 274, 277, 279, 282, 284, 293, 296–297, 302, 310, 316, 319, 323–324, 328
  Southern Song  47, 93, 96, 117
  Yuan Dynasty (the Great Yuan)  17–18, 47, 54–58, 68–72, 74, 81, 85, 87, 89, 98, 193

European nations
  Britain  150, 229
  France  229
  Portugal  123, 135–137, 146–148, 159, 176, 190, 195, 200, 247
  Russia  220, 255, 274
  Spain  136, 159, 163, 176, 183–184
  The Netherlands  150, 184, 238, 286

India
  the Pandyan Dynasty  90, 96
  the Tughlaq Dynasty  50

Japanese Archipelago
  Ashikaga (Muromachi) Shogunate (warrior government)  74, 84, 128, 131

imperial court (aristocratic government)  58, 62–63, 70, 73, 93, 99, 193
Kamakura Shogunate (warrior government)  47, 57–58, 62–63, 70, 73, 93, 97, 101, 115
*Nanbokuchō jidai* (Northern and Southern Courts period)  18, 47, 63, 100, 115, 127, 129
Tokugawa (Edo) Shogunate (warrior government)  19, 191, 215, 218, 239–240, 242, 244–245, 248, 257, 259–260, 270, 272, 277–278, 282, 284, 296, 310, 316, 329
Toyotomi regime  137, 145, 181–182, 192, 200, 208, 210, 280
Warring States period  134, 147, 191, 210, 232, 281
Java
  Majapahit Kingdom  66, 97, 130
  Singhasari Kingdom  66, 97

Korean Peninsula
  Goryeo Dynasty  4, 18, 47, 64, 70, 74, 84, 90, 97, 104–105, 127
  Joseon (Yi) Dynasty  111, 128, 131, 144, 207–209, 219, 221, 249, 256, 319

Malacca
  San-Fo-Chi  65
  Sultanate of Malacca  130, 135, 146, 171

Ryukyu Islands
  Chūzan Kingdom  5, 129, 241
  Ryukyu Kingdom  128, 146, 152, 174, 219, 221, 241, 256, 258, 279

Siam (present-day Thailand)
  Ayutthaya Kingdom  130, 137, 245

Sulu Islands
  Sulu Kingdom  234, 307
Sumatra Island
  Ache  147
  Samudera and Pasai  65

Vietnam
  Champa (present-day South-Central Vietnam)  57, 65, 70, 77, 90, 96, 112, 151
  Lê Dynasty  100, 129, 134, 244
  Mạc Dynasty  129, 135, 244, 315
  Trần Dynasty  57, 64, 96, 100, 127

West Asia
  Ilkhanate of Persia  83
  Ottoman Empire  159

## Geographical names

Aru  90

Brunei  77, 170
Busan  242, 244, 256, 273, 279, 290–292, 306

Calicut  86
Canton  see Guangdong

Daidu (present-day Beijing)  62
Dazaifu  69, 73, 77

Edo  218, 250, 252, 257, 303, 329
Ezo (present-day Hokkaido)  39, 64, 219, 251, 258, 303–305, 308, 329

Fujian  26, 49, 59, 61, 67, 86, 132, 135, 142, 152, 170, 173, 187, 200, 280, 300, 302–303, 307, 311, 313, 315
Funai in Bungo Province (in present-day Oita Prefecture)  185–187, 192, 209–210
Fuzhou  26, 128, 241, 253, 276, 285–286, 292, 295, 300, 303, 306, 325

Gaegyeong (present-day Gaeseong)  17, 70, 74, 78
Gimhae (Gimju)  70, 75, 91
Goa  136, 148, 151, 171, 177–178, 183, 190, 197, 203
Gotō Islands  25, 140, 146, 156, 206

Granada  164–165
Guangdong/Canton  61, 67, 140, 153, 161, 165, 200, 234, 249, 303, 306, 311, 313, 315
Guangzhou  16, 27, 72, 75–77, 80, 128, 136, 153, 168, 174, 192, 237, 240, 253, 260, 276–277, 284–286, 303–304, 322
Gujarat  86, 172, 198

Ha Tien  315
Haicheng, the port of  166, 168, 174
Hakata  17, 25, 69, 73–75, 77–79, 84, 101–103, 180, 288
Hangzhou  17, 25, 54, 80, 139, 176, 253
Happo (present-day Changwon)  94
Hirado (present-day Nagasaki Prefecture)  151, 156, 189, 288
Hizen (present-day Nagasaki Prefecture)  76, 147, 156, 191, 281
Hoi An  27, 306
Hormuz  136, 147

Iwami (silver mine)  158, 178

Java  57, 64–66, 70, 90, 97, 100, 114, 130, 134–135, 146–147, 160, 170, 294
Jeju-do  26, 296
Jiangnan  26, 234, 248, 253, 303–305, 311, 315, 317, 323

# Historical Geography Index

Kamakura  62, 83, 110
Kampei  90
Kūlam Malay  77, 86, 90, 96
Kyoto  32, 62–63, 78, 83, 133, 151, 180, 190, 281, 288, 303, 312, 320
Kyushu  18, 69, 101, 151, 172–173, 185, 188, 190, 194, 206, 210, 325

Langbaiao (Lampacau) (present-day Nanshuizhen, Zhuhai City)  152
Liampo (name used by the Portuguese for Ningbo)  150
Liujia, the port of (in Taicang)  86, 248

Ma'bar  86
Malabar  86
Malacca (My. Melaka)  27, 65, 123, 126, 130, 136, 146–148, 160, 171, 190
Malacca, the Strait of  27, 60, 65, 86, 146–147
Maluku (Molucca) Islands  66, 130, 135–136, 163
Manchuria  218, 304, 324
Matsumae (in present-day Hokkaido)  251, 305, 308
Mindanao Island  170, 223

Nagapattinam (on the Coromandel Coast of India)  77
Nagasaki  20, 38, 123, 126, 147, 168, 171, 173, 175, 180, 192, 194, 245, 258–260, 263, 271–272, 277–278, 281, 287–288, 293, 295, 302, 305, 316, 321, 325
Naha  125, 143, 146, 250, 258, 285, 296
Nanjing  127, 130, 253
Ningbo  17, 26, 125, 128, 139, 150, 152, 206, 234, 276, 303

Osaka  32, 39, 250–252, 288, 303

Peureulak  90
Phatthalung (Southern Thailand)  77
Phnom Penh  27
Pusan  25

Qingyuan (present-day Ningbo)  56, 72, 75–77, 80, 94, 96, 101
Quanzhou  26, 34, 42, 49, 52, 55, 75–77, 80, 95, 128

Ryukyu Islands  59, 64, 88

Saint John  see Shangchuan
Sakai  174, 180, 201, 288
Sampo (Three Port Towns, a collective term for the three ports of Naeipo, Busanpo and Yeompo)  25, 125
São João  see Shangchuan
Satsuma (present-day Kagoshima Prefecture)  76, 190, 241, 250, 259–270, 283, 290, 296, 325
Shangchuan (São João, Saint John)  151, 152
Shanghai  26, 234, 248, 303–304, 310
Shimonoseki  25
Shuangyu, the port of  135, 150–152, 154, 165, 200
Songjiang  80, 132, 141, 176
Songkla  315
Sulawesi  148, 234
Sulu  170, 223, 307
Sumatra  65–66, 80, 147, 160, 170
Suzhou  132, 176, 248, 253

Taizhou  17
Tambralinga  65, 90, 96
Tanegashima  154, 200, 210
the Philippines  27, 125, 147, 163, 171, 181, 314
Tsushima  18, 25, 75, 93, 131, 143, 159, 207, 242, 244, 258, 271–272, 279, 291, 306

Wuyu  152

Xiamen/Amoy  182, 234, 302–304
Xian  65, 326

Yeseong  70, 74–75
Yesung Port  17

Zhapu  141, 234, 253, 295, 303–304, 310

Zhejiang  17, 59, 61, 68, 80, 88, 110, 116, 132, 142, 152, 159, 188, 193, 234, 264
Zhigu (present-day Tianjin)  75, 86
Zhoushan Islands  25, 88, 135, 139, 188, 303

## Port polities

Aceh  147
Ayutthaya  27, 65, 130, 180, 303

Banten  147
Batavia (present-day Jakarta)  21, 27, 238, 288, 294, 303

Lambri (Lamuri)  65

Macao  27, 124, 126, 149, 152–153, 165, 168, 171, 173–175, 191–192, 204, 210, 284, 303, 323

Makassar  148
Manila  27, 124, 126, 149, 163, 166, 168, 170, 172, 174, 176, 184, 191, 303, 310, 323
Melayu  65

Samudera and Pasai  65

## Rivers and deltas

Amur River  24, 220, 304–305, 329

Chang Jiang River  26, 303
Chao Phraya Delta  130

Mekong Delta  313

Red River Delta  57, 64, 133

Yangtze Delta  132, 140–141, 152, 179
Yangtze River  86, 122, 132, 179, 303

# Name Index

Almeida, Luís de  191
Arai, Hakuseki  263, 273, 317
Ashikaga family, the Ashikaga
　　Shoguns  70, 73–74, 115, 132, 156

Ban Bu  92–93

Carletti, Francesco  123, 125, 184
Cheng, Chicheng  322
Chikamatsu, Monzaemon  299
Cook, James  229

Dongyan, Jingri  56

Eisai  78
Eison  63
En'ni  78
Enchin  4, 17
En'nin  4, 17

Fan, Wenhu  94, 98
Fróis, Luís  195, 208–210
Fujiwara, Seika  170
Fukami, Arichika  317
Fukami, Gentai  317, 326

Go-Daigo (Tennō)  115, 118
Gutenberg, Johannes  203

Hayashi, Razan  170
Hōjō family (regents of the Kamakura
　　Shogunate)  56, 62–63, 68, 76,
　　83–84, 93, 97
Hong Taiji  182, 218–219
Hongwu (Ming Emperor)  18, 127, 317
Hosokawa family  131, 152
Hu Zongxian  141, 156–157

Ibn Battuta  50–54, 80–81, 86
Ingen Ryūki (Cn. Yinyuan Longqi)  300

Jang, Bogo  66
Jiang, Zhou  156, 206, 210
Jungjong (Joseon King) / Yi Yeok  144

Kamiya, Jutei  158
Kangxi (Qing Emperor) / Aisin Gioro
　　Hiowanyei  43, 220, 229–230, 254,
　　265, 317, 324
Kimura, Kenkadō  322
Kanesawa family  83–84
Kondō, Jūzō  329
Kanō-school  194, 197, 205
Kanō Eitoku  194–195

La Pérouse, Jean-François de  229
Li, Wei  300
Li, Zicheng  219

Mamiya, Rinzō  329
Matsumae family  257–258, 308
Matsura family  151, 281
Mogami, Tokunai  329
Mōri family  143, 158, 281
Möngke  83, 89
Murakami families (Noshima,
　　Kurushima and Innoshima)
　　142–143, 280–281
Muro, Kyūsō  317
Mutō family  73, 92–93

Nurhaci (Qing Emperor)  167, 182, 202,
　　218

Oda, Nobunaga  180, 194–195, 218, 281
Ogyū, Hokkei  317, 319
Ogyū, Sorai  317, 319
Ōmura family  191
Ōmura Sumitada  147, 175
Ōtomo family  156, 185, 210
Ōtomo Sōrin  156, 207, 209–210

Ōuchi family  131, 151–152, 156, 158, 210

Pérez Dasmariñas, Gomez  163
Pinto, Fernão Mendes  151
Pires, Tomé  123
Polo, Marco  48–49, 51, 86
Pu Shougeng  83, 95, 97, 103

Qianlong (Qing Emperor) / Aisin Gioro Hung-li  230, 240, 276, 295, 318, 324
Qubilai Qa'an  18, 48, 83, 95

Raden Wijaya  97
Ricci, Matteo  192, 204
Ryūzan, Tokken  56

Sahwadong  146, 151
Seongjong (Joseon King) / Yi Hyeol  144, 207
Sha, Kokumei (Cn. Xie Gouming)  17
Shihāb al-Dīn  96
Shimazu family  152, 210, 219, 241, 257, 270, 295, 317
Shunjō  118
Sidotti, Giovanni Battista  323
Sin, Sukju  207
Sō family of Tsushima  131, 156, 208, 219, 242, 257–259, 271–272, 274, 295
Soγatu  95–97
Sugae, Masumi  326

Tanegashima family  152
Tei, Junsoku  28, 318–319
Tokugawa family, the Tokugawa Shoguns  229, 273
Tokugawa Hidetada  218
Tokugawa Iemitsu  218, 229

Tokugawa Ienari  230
Tokugawa Ieyasu  201, 218, 300
Tokugawa Nariaki  327
Tokugawa Tsunayoshi  229
Tokugawa Yoshimune  213, 312, 316–317, 319
Tōkō Shin'etsu (Xin Yue)  326
Tongzhi (Qing Emperor) / Aisin Gioro Dzaišun  327
Toyotomi, Hideyoshi (the Toyotomi regime)  111, 146, 175, 180, 195, 204, 209, 218, 281, 299

Valignano, Alessandro  194, 196, 203

Wang, Zhi  139, 154–157, 206

Xavier, Francis  151–152, 186, 190, 209
Xijian, Zitan  68
Xue, Jun  206, 208

Yi, Sunsin  145
Yigmiš  96
Yishan, Yining  56, 68
Yongle (Ming Emperor)  8–9, 128
Yongzheng (Qing Emperor) / Aisin Gioro Injen  284
Yōsai see Eisai
Yu, Dayou  155

Zheng, Chenggong  19–20, 182, 220, 280, 299
Zheng, He  34, 86, 125, 128, 130, 146, 188
Zheng, Ruozeng  156, 206
Zheng, Shun'gong  206–207, 210
Zheng, Zhilong  20, 182
Zhu, Wan  154
Zhu, Yigui  282

# Subject Index

## Maritime regions *see also* Historical Geography Index

East China Sea 17–18, 22, 25, 27, 30, 59, 75, 77, 100–106, 125–126, 136–137, 150, 209, 216–217, 226–229, 231, 233, 240, 263, 266–269, 271, 279, 281, 294, 297–298, 302–306, 308, 311–315, 329

Java Sea 27, 135, 146

Sea of Japan 22, 24–25, 38–39, 229, 251, 303–304, 312

Sea of Okhotsk 22–23, 329

South China Sea 16–17, 20, 26–27, 58–59, 66–67, 77, 80, 95–97, 104, 126, 135–137, 225–227, 234, 236, 240, 267, 282, 298, 302–304, 306–307, 311, 313–315, 325

Yellow Sea 19–20, 22, 25, 59, 248, 311, 328

## Conception of the world and consciousness

anti-Mongol consciousness 98
Ptolemaic geographical conceptions 49

**Japan**

a belief in the land of the gods 99, 270
a worldview with three realms (*sangoku*) 196

Japanese World Order 270

**Korea**

*Jewang-ungi* (Songs of Emperors and Kings) 99

myth of Dangun (the legendary founder and god-king of Gojoseon) 99

*Samguk-yusa* (Memorabilia of the Three Kingdoms) 99

**China**

reversal of the Sinocentric worldview 269

Sinocentric view of the world, *Hua-Yi zhi bian* 267, 269–270

## Perceptions of the times and maritime regions

1570 system 166, 169, 178

Age of Commerce 126, 136–137, 176, 182

Age of Exploration 124
Age of Reclamation 133
Age of Silver 178
Age of the Wokou 135, 137, 139, 141, 165

*359*

maritime peace  217, 221

Pax Mongolica  50–51, 58

Sea of Competition  180

sea of politics  19, 268
   de-politicization of the "sea of politics"  266
seas as boundaries  328

## Ships and shipbuilding

*baochuan* (treasure ships)  34
*bezaisen* (Japanese cargo ships)  38–39, 251

caravel  148, 149
carrack/*nau*/*carraca*  148–149

galleon  149, 184
galliot  150

*jiandichuan* (sharp-bottomed ships)  32, 35

junks  33–36, 38, 233–234, 278

*niaochuan* (bird ships)  33, 233

*omoki zukuri* (Japanese technique for ship fortification)  38

*shachuan* (sand ships)  32, 35, 142, 248

*tanaita zukuri* (Japanese shipbuilding technique)  36, 38

## Trade

Chinese junks trading with Japan  234

Eastern and Western routes for Chinese merchants (in the 1570 system)  168–170

fortification of trading ports  147

illict/smuggling trade  75, 82, 126, 134–136, 142, 150–154, 158, 165–168, 170, 173, 261, 263, 289–290, 293, 297, 300
Indian Ocean trade  176
inner Asian caravan trade  176
intermediary trade via Ryukyu  126, 129, 131, 150, 166

*kango* (Cn. *kanhe*, tally) trade  151

Nanhai trade (trade in the South China Sea and Indian Ocean)  54, 67, 72

public trade  54

*Santan* Trade (trade with the people living along the Amur River)  304
seaborne trade  65, 109, 124, 166, 221, 225
*shuinsen* (red-seal ships) trade  5–6, 36–37, 172, 218
South Seas trade  234–236, 238
Spainish trade in Asia  171
spice trade  66, 97, 136, 147

three ways of Portuguese trade in Asia  170–171
trans-Pacific trade  166, 171

*zhufan* type trade (trade by settler-merchants with overseas trading hubs)  102

# Trade and diplomatic policies

*bai jian* / *cheng yang* (presenting tribute to authorities at court) 82
*basho ukeoi* (sub-contracted trading post system) 306, 308
*benguandi* (hometown of registration) 72

emporium 130, 147

factory (trading post) 123, 147, 246, 284, 288

*gongping* (*gongju* or *gongyan* – official exit permit) 72
*guanben chuan* (imperially financed overseas trade system) 73, 81

*haijin* (maritime prohibition policy) 8–9, 19, 59, 127, 220, 231, 263
*hushi* (mutual trade) 134, 160, 166, 240, 267

*mashi* (horse markets) 136, 167

*shizhen* (market towns) 132, 141

*yitiao bianfa* (single whip tax reforms) 178

## Japan

### Kamakura period
edict to expel newly arrived foreigners 102

### Momoyama period
Nagasaki under direct jurisdiction 175, 180

### Edo period
maritime prohibition policy 277
  large ship confiscation order 278

Nagasaki as a trading port city 245–248
  interpreter as a hereditary family occupation 247

*jiyakunin* (locally hired government officials) 245–246, 248, 266
*jūtaku Tō-jin* (resident Chinese emigrated from mainland China to Nagasaki) 247
*machi-doshiyori* (town councilors) 246
*machi-otona* (town representatives) 246
Nagasaki Bugyō (magistrate) 37, 245, 257, 259–260, 266, 268, 274
Nagasaki Bugyōsho (magistrate's office) 263, 278
Nagasaki Daikan (governor) 37, 246
Nagasaki Kaisho (trade association) 246–247
*oranda tsūji* (Dutch interpreters) 247
Portuguese interpreters 247
*tō-tsūji* (Chinese interpreters) 247, 259, 316
  under the direct jurisdiction 218, 248, 257
*yado-machi* (lodging town) and *tsuki-machi* (supporting town) system 246, 289

seclusion policy 38, 277, 299
  four gateways 218, 245, 250, 257, 304
    Matsumae 219, 257
    Nagasaki 218, 245, 257
    Satsuma 219, 257
    Tsushima 219, 257
*shinpai* (trade permits) 263, 265, 268, 282
Shōtoku Shinrei (New Edict of the Shōtoku Period) or Kaihaku Goshi Shinrei (New Edict on Mutual Trade by Trading Ships) 263–266, 282, 300

## Ryukyu

dual subordination to Japan and Ming/Qing China 241–242, 267, 270–272 maritime prohibition policy 279–280

relations with Japan 242
relations with Qing China 241–242
   *hangā* (valuation) trade 242
   *totō-yakunin* (officials to be dispatched to China) 241

### Korea

**Joseon Korea**
diplomatic relations between Korea and Japan 271–274

evicting island residents 278, 328

Hoedap Gyeom (Jp. Kaito ken Sakkanshi / envoys to respond and repatriate prisoners) 242

Joseon Tongsinsa (Jp. Chosen Tsūshinshi / Korean Goodwill Missions) 243–244, 279, 319

*kyorin* (a friendly relationship between neighboring countries) 274

maritime prohibition policy 278–279

*saiken-sen* (allocated dispatch ships) 244
*sanban-shi* 244

*munwihaeng/yeokgwansa* (Jp. *yukukanshi* – interpreter embassies) 244, 279

### China

**Yuan Period**
ban on Japanese ships 103

invasion of Japan 89–95
  Goryeo Korea 91
  Japan 90, 93–94
invasion of Java 97
invasion of the South Seas 95–97

**Ming Period**
*kongdao* policy (evicting island residents) 19

Longqing Peace Agreement 167

principle of "no trade without tribute" 128, 166

relaxed tributary trade-maritime prohibition system 135, 165–166

tributary trade-maritime prohibition system 19, 124, 127, 130–131, 134, 136–137, 162
  coexistence of tributary, mutual and voyaging trade 166–167
  maritime prohibition 136, 155
  non-tributary mutual trade 134, 161–162, 165

tributary system 128–129, 165–166
  tributary trade 128

*wangshi* (voyaging trade) 166
*wenyin* (sailing permit) 166

**Qing Period**
Canton System 276, 303

de-politicization 271–272

maritime restriction policy 274, 277
  *Fangfan Waiyi Guitiao* (Regulation on Foreigners' Activities) 276

trade outside of tributary relations 254
tributary relations 245

# Subject Index

## Government officials / administration / defense force for maritime regions

*baoyi* or *booi* (bondservants) 254
*Baqi* (Eight Banners) 219, 253
*bibyeonsa* (Border Defense Council) 256
bureaucratic system 119, 129, 256
Busan-jin 256

*capitão-mor* (captain-major) 148, 153, 171
Chinzei Tandai (Shogunal Deputy in Kyushu) 70, 73, 101
Circuit Superintendant for Gyeongsangdo 93
coastal defense system 283–284
   in Qing China 280–282
   in Ryukyu 282
   in Tokugawa Japan 280–282

Dongraebusa (Dongrae magistrate) 256, 260

Gyeongsangdo Provincial Commissioner of Inspection 94
Goryeo military government 91–92, 97

Haidaofushi (Coastal Defense Circuit Vice Commander) 155
*haiguan* (customs house) 220, 253–254, 276
*haiguan jiandu* (customs house directors) 254–255

*ikoku keigo banyaku* (guard duty against foreign invasion) 101

Joseon navy 144–146

Kyushu Tandai / Chinzei Kanrei (Regional Governor of Kyushu) 70

Luying (Green Standard Army) 253, 260

maritime prohibition order in the Southern Sea (Nan'yang Haijin Ling) 282

privatization of Ming China's coastal defense 153–154

Rokuhara Tandai (Kyoto Shogunal Deputy) 84

Sambyeolcho (Three Patrols) 92–93
*shibosi* (maritime trade supervisorate) 17, 54, 69, 72–73, 75, 82–83, 101, 127–128, 161
*syahbandar* (port managers) 172

textile commissioners (*zhizao*) 253

Viceroy of Goa 148

*xingquanfusi* (branch of supervising money bureau) 54, 69, 82
*xingsheng* (branch secretariats) 54, 69
*xunfu* (governor) 253

*Zhifu* (Prefect) 155
*Zhufang Baqi* (Eight Banners Garrison) 253–254, 260, 281
*zongdu* (governor-general) 253

## Agents of maritime trade

Armenian merchants 240

British traders 232

Chinese maritime merchants 52–53, 59–60, 66–67, 77, 101, 126, 140, 151, 168, 170, 231–232

*chuanhu* (ship-owners)  66, 142, 168, 233, 236, 250–251
commercial and religious networks  52–53, 67–68, 80–81 *see also* Deities and religion
*caidong* (consigners remaining in China)  233

Dongrae merchants  293
*dougang/gangshou* (head merchants)  5, 66, 102, 168
Dutch traders  232

Fujian maritime merchants  167

*gōshi* (head merchants)  83

Han Chinese maritime merchants  17
Huizhou merchants (Xin'an merchants)  132, 318

Japanese maritime merchants  172

*keshang/sanshang* (guest merchants)  168, 238

maritime merchants of diverse origins  59, 168, 171–172

Muslim maritime merchants  16–17, 52, 67, 77, 80

operation of Chinese junks  233–234
*orang kaya* (merchant elite)  171, 174

Parsi-Zoroastrian merchants  240
Portuguese maritime merchants  19, 126, 140, 148, 151–152, 168, 171, 197
*pushing* (government-certified brokers)  168, 268

sea merchants from Zhangzhou and Quanzhou  168
seagoing merchants (*hangshang* or *chuhai*)  233, 238
Shanxi merchants  132
shipmasters (Cn. *chuanzhu* or *bozhu*, Pt. *capitão*)  168, 233
Silla maritime merchants  66
Spanish maritime merchants  19, 171

*xiangshen* (local gentry)  153
*Xinluo shanke* (merchants from Silla)  17

## Merchant organizations

*chuanhang* (mediated interactions between consigners and ship-owners)  236
country traders  238–239

East India companies of European countries  238
 Danish East India Company  239
 Dutch East India Company (*Vereenigde Oost-Indische Compagnie,* or VOC)  21, 238–240, 288, 290, 306, 310, 322
 English East India Company (EIC)  238–239
 French East India Companies  239

 Oostendse Company  239
 Swedish East India Companies  239
*eshang* (quota for privileged merchants to procure copper)  237

*gangyun* (contracting out shipping duties)  82
Guangdong Shisan Hang (the thirteen *hang* of Guangdong)  236, 238
*guangya* (*yahang* in the service of government offices)  236
*guanshang* (official privileged merchants to procure copper)  237

Hanseatic League  10

*kaisen don'ya* (wholesale merchants-cum-operators of *kaisen* ships) 252

*ortuy* (mercantile association sponsored by the Yuan Dynasty) 54, 69, 81, 85, 96, 109

Shijia Qiushang (*liuqiuguan keshang*, local merchants attached to the Ryukyuan visiting house in Fuzhou) 238

*sihuo jiadai* (private shipping enterprises) 82

Xiamen *yanghong* 238

*Xinluo shanke* (merchants from Silla) 17

*yahang* (middlemen-cum-brokers) 236, 238–249, 252, 261

*yanghang* (a group of officially sanctioned merchants who handled overseas trade; an abbreviation of *yanghuahang* or *waiyanghang*) 236

*zongshang* (or s*hangzong*, administrator and supervisor of traders) 237–238

## Ethnic groups

Ainu 219, 258, 304, 308–309

barbarians 16, 186, 196–197, 269 *see also* Sinocentric view of the world, **Conception of the world and consciousness**

Buginese 234

Chinese *mestizo* group 314

*fanke* (barbarian guests) 16

Han Chinese 14, 17, 20, 135, 161, 220, 224, 253–255, 269, 294, 311, 313–315

*huaren* (ethnic Chinese, or person(s) of Chinese descent) 14

Jurchens 13, 19, 144, 167, 179, 201–202, 218

Manchus 19, 219, 224, 255, 269–270, 299, 323

Mongols 13, 17, 80, 135, 165, 179, 255, 269

Oirats 59, 255

Portuguese 135, 152, 154, 191–192, 194–195, 197, 199–200, 208, 247, 282, 284, 288

Semu people 80

Sogdians 12

Uigurs 55, 68–69, 80, 82

*Xintangren* (New Chinese, literally new Tang people) 80

## Foreigners' settlements

*Bosituan* (accommodation of Persian traders) 17, 77

Chinese (Tang) Quarter of Hakata Port (Hakata-tsu Tōbō) 77
Choryang (Japanese compound in Busan) 273, 291–292

Dejima/Deshima, Nagasaki 246, 287–289

*fanfang* (foreigner ward) 16, 77
foreigners' settlements 172, 174

guesthouse 70, 78, 92, 292

Huaiyuan Station, *Xianluoguo Gongguan* (Siamese tribute envoy's residence) 286–287

Intramuros 174

Kagoshima Ryukyukan (Ryukyuan visiting station in Kagoshima) 290

Parian (the Chinese settlement in Manila) 174
proliferation of Chinatowns 314

relationships between foreign males and indigenous females 293
Rouyuan Station, *Liuqiu guan* (Ryukyuan house) 285–286, 292, 295

Tōjin-machi (Chinese settlements, Chinatown) 175, 185
Tōjin-yashiki (Chinese compound) 289–290, 294, 325

Waegwan (Jp. Wakan, Japan House) 25, 244, 256, 292–293, 297

*Xinluo-fang* (quarter for traders from Silla) 17

*yiguan* (foreign barbarians' residences, British factory) 284–285

## Weather

**ocean currents**
Kuroshio Current (Black Tide) 30–31, 144, 248

Tsushima Current 31–32

**winds**
monsoons 10, 49

prevailing westerlies 27–28, 30–31

trade winds 10
typhoons 29–30, 99

## Deities and religion

Avalokiteśvara (Cn. Guanyin, Jp. Kannon) 187

Christian missionaries 20, 202, 210, 239, 322–323
commercial activities of religious organizations 82

Dragon King 187–188

Ise-Shinto 191

Kirishitan (Christian) *daimyō* 147, 191, 194
Kubrawī Ṣufi orders 81

Manichaeism 116
Mazu (Jp. Maso) 42–43, 86, 187–188, 325, 327–328
　localized belief in Mazu 325–326
　Mazu replaced along with modernization 326–327
mosques 80

prevalence of Islam 81, 130, 146, 223

Rinzai Zen 56, 68, 78

saint Khidr 81
Shaykh Abū Isḥāq of Kāzarūn 53, 81
Shichirō Gongen 189
Society of Jesus 147, 151, 175, 186, 190–192, 194–195, 202–204, 208–210
Spanish mendicant orders 190

Theravada Buddhism 100
Tianfei (Queen of Heaven) 43, 86, 188, 325
Tianhou (Empress of Heaven) 43, 325

voyage-protecting deities 41–42

Zen and Ritsu schools of Buddhism 114
Zen and Ritsu monks 117–118

## Conflicts and uprisings

Batavia Massacre (1740) 294

Flint Incident 276

Huang Chao Rebellion 67

Japanese invasions of Korea 111, 137, 145, 181, 184, 204, 210, 242

*kami-zokusen* 143
Kunashiri Menashi no Tatakai (Menash-Kunashir Rebellion) 308

Mongol invasions of Japan 57, 70, 75, 92, 94

Nigatsu Sōdō (Second Month Disturbance) 93
Ningbo Incident 131

Ōnin War 131

Phaeton Incident 260
pirates 18, 63, 82, 105, 136, 140–144, 146, 148, 153, 155, 158, 188, 190, 206, 280, 282
"punish foreign countries" plan 101, 105

Rebellion of Zhu Yigui 282
Red Turban Rebellion 98

Revolt of the Three Feudatories 220
riots by "*woshang*" 103

*sujeok* (water bandits, Korean pirates) 144

Takeshima (Kr. Dokdo) Island
　territorial dispute 328
　territorial jurisdiction 329

Three Ports Uprising 132
Tumu Incident 131

Wokou 135, 140, 141
　early Wokou 18, 75, 94, 105, 131
　later Wokou 18, 36, 118, 200, 207
Wokou incidents in Ryukyu 143
Wokou invasion of Sonjukdo 146
*wozei* (Japanese robbers) 141

## Technology

arquebus 200, 202, 210

circulation and diffusion of firearms technology 199–200, 202

European firearms 137, 200

*folangji-pao* (Frankish cannon) 148, 199–201, 210

*haifuki* (a method of silver extraction) 158

*joun* (water transportation system) 64

magnetic compasses 41

Ottoman Turkish musket 202

transfer and application of technology 316

## Movement of goods and culture

*Azuchijō zu byōbu*, Azuchi Castle screens 194

blue-and-white porcelain 110–111, 113, 116, 186, 193–194
books 118, 301, 306, 315–316, 318–319 *see also* **Books and print culture**
bronze coins 159, 310

celadon wares 110–111
ceramics 110–111, 164, 183, 186–187, 192–194, 199, 306, 312
Champa Rice (Cn. *zhancheng mi*, Jp. *daitō mai*) 112, 133
Chinese style dishes (*karayō no zen*) 115

cloves 147, 160
cobalt 113, 193
*colegio* (seminary) 186
commoditization of trade goods 305–306
cookbooks and domestic encyclopedias 113
copper 159, 237, 263, 282, 300–301, 305, 310–311
copper coins from China (known as *toraisen*) 63, 73, 109–110, 177, 237
cotton
　cotton fabric/cloth 132–133, 163–165, 170, 176–178, 183, 301, 312
　cotton yarn 132, 160
counterfeit coins 159, 177

dark-glazed bowls (known as *tenmoku* in Japanese) 110

folding screens 149, 152, 187, 194–196, 199
 *Namban byōbu* 149, 196, 197

grains 311

imperial gifts 128
Indo-Portuguese style 197–198
Islamic miniature paintings 113, 116

Jingdezhen ware 110, 113, 116, 185, 193

*kraak* ware (*fuyōde*) 193

marine products 301, 305, 307–308, 311
medicine 113, 116, 316
mother-of-pearl 197–199

Namban lacquerware 187, 197–199
new culinary culture 113–115, 120
Ningbo Buddhist paintings 115, 117
nutmeg 147, 160

pepper 148, 160, 170, 176
pharmacopeia 301, 305–306
porcelain 111, 176–178, 183
processed food 177

*qinghua* (blue flowers) 186

saltpeter 160, 177, 199–200

silk
 raw silk 111, 126, 132, 159, 164, 170, 172, 176–178, 183, 305–307, 311–312
 silk fabric/textiles 111, 126, 132, 159, 163–164, 170, 176–178, 183, 301, 305, 312
silver 110, 178–179, 183, 282, 309
 Japanese silver 124, 126, 151, 157–158, 166–167, 170, 177–178, 206, 209, 217, 263, 300, 305
 New World silver 125–126, 164, 166, 170–171, 178
silver ingots, *süke* (axe) in Mongolian, *bālish* (pillow) in Persian 108–109
sugar 115, 177, 290, 301, 306, 308, 311–313
 as a "global commodity" 198, 308
sulfur 114, 177, 282
Swatow ware (Jp. *gosude*) 193

tea-drinking custom 110, 115
timber 114
tributary goods 128, 151, 242, 257

unifying Confucianism and Zen Buddhism 118

war materiel 177, 179

Zhangzhou (ware) 152, 185, 193
*zheqing* (cobalt) 193
Zhu Xi Neo-Confucianism 170, 259, 263, 317

## Books and print culture

age of old typeset editions 204–205

books with *kunten* (phonetic guides) 320

Chinese books traded back from Japan 318

*Chuogeng Lu* (Records Compiled After Returning from the Farm) 98
commercial publishing 203
culture of copying manuscripts 203

*Dai Qing Huidian* (Collected Statutes of the Great Qing) 317

*Dijian tushuo* (The Emperor's Mirror, Illustrated and Discussed, Jp. *Teikan zusetsu*) 204–205

Five Mountains editions (*Gozan-ban*) 118

*Jin'nō Shōtō-ki* (A Chronicle of Gods and Sovereigns) 100

*kaozheng* (evidential scholarship of the Qing Dynasty) 316
Kirishitan editions (*Kirishitan-ban*) 194, 204

*Liuyu Yanyi* (Jp. *Rikuyu Engi*, Six Courses in Morals) 317, 319

*Rikuyu Engi Taii* (Summary of Six Courses in Morals) 317

*Shinchō Tanji* (Inquiries about the Qing Empire) 317
*Siku Quanshu* (Complete Library of the Four Treasuries) 318

*Wakan Sansai Zue* (Illustrated Sino-Japanese Encyclopedia) 320
*wakoku-bon* (wood-block reprinted editions) of Chinese books 319–320

## Information on other maritime regions

| | |
|---|---|
| *Haedong chegukki* (Record of Countries to the East) 144, 207 | *Riben Yijian* (A Mirror on Japan) 207 |
| *Historia de Japam* (History of Japan) 195, 208–209 | *Ryukyu tushuo* (Illustrated Guide to Ryukyu) 206 |
| *Riben kaolue* (Summarized Studies of Japan) 206, 208 | *Vocabulário da Língua do Japão* (Jp. *Nippo Jisho*) (the first Japanese-Portuguese Dictionary) 208 |
| *Riben tuzuan* (Atlas of Japan) 156, 206 | |

## Coastal navigation and domestic maritime transportation

| | |
|---|---|
| in Goryeo Korea 64 | *higaki kaisen* (cargo ships) 39, 250 |
| in Joseon Korea 249 | *kitamae-bune* (northgoing cargo ships) 39, 251 |
| in Kamakura Japan 62–64 | *taru kaisen* (originally cargo ships carrying *sake*) 39 |
| in Qing China 248–249 | in Yuan China 62 |
| in Ryukyu 250 | |
|   *maran-sen* 250 | |
| in Tokugawa Japan 250–252 | |
|   general averages regarding seafaring 252 | |

## Rescuing and repatriating foreign castaways

in Joseon Korea  296–297
in Qing China  294–295
in Ryukyu  296
in the South China Sea  225

in Tokugawa Japan  295–296

mutual repatriation in the East China Sea  216–217

## Symbols for representing "others"

in Joseon Korea  324
in Qing China  322–324
in Tokugawa Japan  321–322

clothes and hairstyles  324

interest towards foreigners
  *Tō-jin odori* (foreign dancing)  322

*Tō-jin shibai* (foreign theatrical performance)  322

*queue*  224

stereotyped image of Japanese males  207

## Shrines and temples

Engakuji Temple  56

Hakozakigu Shrine  6

Ise Jingū Shrine  191

Jōtenji Temple  77–78, 102, 158

Kenchōji Temple  76

Myōrakuji Temple  102

Shōfukuji Temple  77–78, 102, 158
Shōmyōji Temple  84

Tenryūji Temple  74, 103
Tōfukuji Temple  6, 74, 78

## Society

*akutō* (evil bands)  63, 135

ban on wearing Chinese clothes  164

*daimyōs* (warlords, feudal lords)  133–134, 156, 172
Danjia (Tankas)  161
development of paddy fields  112, 132–133
*dianhu* (tenant farmers)  141

gap between rich and poor  157

*kenmon* (influential families and powerful institutions)  78

*mestizos*  171, 314
monetary economy  109–110, 177

paying taxes with copper coins  109
peasant communities  133, 310

*pojagin* (abalone harvesters)  145
population explosion in Mainland China  313

*qian huang* (coin famine)  310
Qing Emperors' inspection tours to Jiangnan  317, 324

*shamin* (boat people)  142
*shidafu* (scholar-officials)  2, 98, 192

*shōen* (private estates)  62
Sinified  315, 320

tax grain  68, 82, 86, 249

warrior families  62–63, 83, 93

*zhongmai baohuo* (procurement of treasure for the royal court of the Yuan Dynasty)  82